OUTSTANDING PRAISE FOR

Banishing Bureaucracy

"If you want to reinvent your government, you need this book."
—Kurt L. Shmoke, Democratic Mayor of Baltimore

"The strategies in this book provide a useful methodology for creating fundamental change at all levels of government."
—Rudolph W. Giuliani, Republican Mayor of New York

"*Banishing Bureaucracy* not only focuses on a topic of deep interest to all businesspeople but breaks away from the anti-government rhetoric of some politicians and business groups to offer practical and sensible solutions."
—*Soundview Executive Book Summaries*

"Every precept of reinventing is richly illustrated from the real-life battles of actual people in state, local, and national governments. The book focuses on strategies and steps that were used to reinvent government under some very rough circumstances. . . . Of profound interest to those seeking good ideas and better government."
—*Government Technology*

"Like *Reinventing Government*, this volume will fuel the debate over government reform. Essential for specialists in public administration, government officials, and informed lay readers."
—*Library Journal*

DAVID OSBORNE is the managing partner of the Public Strategies Group in St. Paul, Minnesota, which does research and consulting on economic development. He has served as an adviser to Vice President Al Gore, providing intellectual guidance to his National Performance Review and authoring its 1993 report; as a consultant to America's public sector managers at every level; and as a counselor to leaders worldwide. His column,"What Works," appears monthly in the *Washington Post* Sunday magazine.

PETER PLASTRIK has served as chief deputy of the Michigan Department of Commerce and president of the Michigan Strategic Fund under Governor Jim Blanchard. Today he serves as a consultant to numerous public organizations and foundations.

BANISHING BUREAUCRACY

DAVID OSBORNE
and PETER PLASTRIK

BANISHING BUREAUCRACY

THE FIVE STRATEGIES FOR REINVENTING GOVERNMENT

A PLUME BOOK

PLUME
Published by the Penguin Group
Penguin Putnam Inc., 375 Hudson Street, New York, New York 10014, U.S.A.
Penguin Books Ltd, 27 Wrights Lane, London W8 5TZ, England
Penguin Books Australia Ltd, Ringwood, Victoria, Australia
Penguin Books Canada Ltd, 10 Alcorn Avenue, Toronto, Ontario, Canada M4V 3B2
Penguin Books (N.Z.) Ltd, 182–190 Wairau Road, Auckland 10, New Zealand

Penguin Books Ltd, Registered Offices: Harmondsworth, Middlesex, England

Published by Plume, an imprint of Dutton NAL, a member of Penguin Putnam Inc.
This is an authorized reprint of a hardcover edition published by Addison-Wesley Publishing
Company. For information address Addison-Wesley Publishing Company, Reading, MA 01867.

First Plume Printing, May, 1998
10 9 8 7 6 5 4 3 2 1

Many of the designations used by manufacturers and sellers to distinguish their products are
claimed as trademarks. Where those designations appear in this book and if publisher was aware of
a trademark claim, the designations have been printed in initial capital letters.

The excerpts from D. Osborne/T. Gaebler, *Reinventing Government* © 1992 by David Osborne and
Ted Gaebler are reprinted by permission of Addison Wesley Longman, Inc.

The excerpts from W. Bridges, *Managing Transitions: Making the Most of Change* © 1991 by
William Bridges and Associates, Inc., are reprinted by permission of Addison Wesley Longman, Inc.

 REGISTERED TRADEMARK—MARCA REGISTRADA

LIBRARY OF CONGRESS CATALOGING-IN-PUBLICATION DATA
Osborne, David (David E.)
    Banishing bureaucracy : the five strategies for reinventing
government / David Osborne and Peter Plastrik.
        p.   cm.
    Originally published: Reading, Mass. : Addison Wesley Pub. Co., 1997.
    Includes bibliographical references and index.
    ISBN 0-452-27392-7
    1. Administrative agencies—United States.   2. Bureaucracy—United
States.   3. Government productivity—United States.   4. Customer
relations—United States.   5. Entrepreneurship—United States.
I. Plastrik, Peter.   II. Title.
JK421.O72   1998
351.3'0973—dc21   97–49894
                                                              CIP

Original hardcover design by Diane Levy
Printed in the United States of America

BOOKS ARE AVAILABLE AT QUANTITY DISCOUNTS WHEN USED TO PROMOTE PRODUCTS OR SERVICES.
FOR INFORMATION PLEASE WRITE TO PREMIUM MARKETING DIVISION, PENGUIN PUTNAM INC.,
375 HUDSON STREET, NEW YORK, NY 10014.

For my children,
Nick, Emily, Molly, and Anne,
with a lifetime of love

—D.O.

For Deb, David, Steven, and my mother.

—P.P.

CONTENTS

Acknowledgments   xi

Introduction: Uphill Battle, USA   1

PART I: FINDING YOUR LEVERAGE

1 The Five C's: Changing Government's DNA   21

2 Levels of the Game: Targeting the Strategies   49

3 Gut Check: What It Takes to Use the Strategies   67

PART II: THE FIVE STRATEGIES

4 The Core Strategy: Creating Clarity of Purpose   75

5 The Consequences Strategy: Creating Consequences
for Performance   115

6 The Customer Strategy: Putting the Customer in the
Driver's Seat   157

7 The Control Strategy: Shifting Control Away from
the Top and Center   203

8 The Culture Strategy: Creating an Entrepreneurial
Culture   241

PART III: USING THE STRATEGIES

9 Aligning the Strategies   301

10 The Courage to Reinvent   320

Appendix A: The Principles of Reinventing Government   347

Appendix B: Resources for Reinventors   350

Notes   359

Index   383

ACKNOWLEDGMENTS

It took a village to write this book—a virtual village of thousands of far-flung reinventors who shared with us their knowledge and experiences and gave us their support. We interviewed them, e-mailed them, listened to their presentations, and read their articles, memos, and private papers. They took us on tours of their organizations, invited us in to staff meetings, even asked us to critique their efforts. What always came through was their magnificent spirit, the joy of innovators who undertake important work. We are grateful to every one of these extraordinary pioneers.

Many friends and colleagues played a special role in easing this book through the birth canal all authors must traverse. They urged us to take on the task, led us to many of the reinventors and stories that taught us important lessons, and helped us develop many of our key concepts.

Babak Armajani, Peter Hutchinson, Connie Nelson, and our other colleagues at the Public Strategies Group were a constant source of inspiration, ideas, experience, and support. John Cleveland and Joann Neuroth at On Purpose Associates stood with us almost daily, offering the pointed but gentle critique that only the best of friends and partners can get away with. Both organizations provided financial support that helped us stay focused on our work. Our colleagues at the Alliance for Redesigning Government and the National Academy of Public Administration helped connect us to their growing network of reinventors and resources across the nation.

To these and other veteran reinventors we turned repeatedly for advice and information. For this we owe particular thanks also to Jeremy Cowper, Bill Creech, Jim Flanagan, Don Forbes, Craig Holt, David Jones, John Kamensky, Tom Lewcock, Michael Marsh, Mike Masterson, Karl Mettke, Martin Raff, Bob Stone, and Peter Wilkinson.

Many of these colleagues commented extensively on an outline of the book and drafts of chapters. For this fundamental guidance we owe great thanks also to Jonathan Boston, Lorraine Chang, Joel Getzendanner, Lou Glazer, Larry Grant, Tharon Greene, Neal Johnson, Ted Kolderie, Cheryl Lange, Butch Marita, Mike Monteith, Joe Nathan, Laurie Ohmann, Bob O'Leary, Bob O'Neill, Doug Ross, John Scully, Ted Staton, Skip Stitt, Janet Topolsky, and Steve Weiss.

Many people went beyond the call of duty in other ways. Ted Gaebler continued to share with us his wealth of experience and knowledge. Ian Ball and Fran MacDonald helped plan and coordinate a weeklong trip to New Zealand. Diana Goldsworthy, Catherine Stratton, Michael Clarke, Doug Forbes, and Keith Fernett did the same in the United Kingdom. Duncan Wyse and Barbara Roberts helped us plan our research in Oregon.

Janet Topolsky, Bob O'Leary, Mike Monteith, and Meriwether Jones opened their homes to us. Larry Payne and Jim Jordan shared with us their two-day inspection tour through the Mark Twain National Forest. Rob Smith and Peter Matwijiw helped immensely in shipping us information from the U.K.

We are especially grateful to Ruth Sheets, without whose hard work and good humor we would not have met our deadlines. Ruth, Andrew List, Sally LaCross, and Julie Price typed numerous interview transcripts; they came to admire the reinventors they met on tape.

As always, our literary agent Kristine Dahl guided us gently and skillfully through the murky financial waters of the publishing industry. And our editor, William Patrick, proved once again his genius. His light editing touch endears him to us, of course. But his unerring judgment about the essence of our book—what to keep in and what to leave out—was crucial; it saved us more than once from losing focus.

Pat Jalbert and Beth Burleigh Fuller, production editors at Addison-Wesley, shepherded us across the production finish line with enormous skill, patience, and grace.

Lastly, we thank our families. They put up with it all: the trips we took away from home, the long hours we spent writing, the uncertainties of the whole process, and the particular strains of the final year. Their patience and love sustained us. They are the heart of our village.

—*David Osborne and Peter Plastrik*
October 1996
Essex, Massachusetts
East Lansing, Michigan

INTRODUCTION:
UPHILL BATTLE, USA

Every year they cut us. We've taken creativity as far as we can. The guy responsible for building repairs also has responsibility for parks and lots of other things. He's got so many hats; how many more can he wear?

—Department head

You've got the go-getters, who are about 25 percent, and the do-nothings, who are about 25 percent, and the ones in the middle, who do what they have to do—the regular workers. Nothing happens to the do-nothings. It's just part of the system.

—Employee

The union is to blame for a lot that has happened here, because we fought management all the way, up until about '90, '91, when we realized we're all in the same boat. We saw what happened if management didn't do its job— the burden fell on the workers. So we want people out if they're not doing their jobs.

—Local union president

Call it Uphill Battle, USA. It is a midsize American city with an economy in transition. Its traditional economic base has been declining for 15 years, while a new base in high technology and tourism slowly replaces it. For over a decade, the city has taken a financial beating. First a statewide property-tax initiative put a lid on revenues. Then the state legislature passed an education reform bill that forced the city to shift revenues to the schools. Finally, the recession of the early 1990s hit too hard and stayed too long.

The result: a decade of budget cuts that sliced through the fat, through the muscle, and into the bone. Employees talk of the early 1990s as a time of deep troubles. Their unions went four years without contracts. The mayor and city council closed fire stations and laid off employees. Management centralized every function it could— supplies, maintenance, building repairs—and then slashed their budgets. "It's got so that people won't recommend anything, because money is so tight," says one employee. "It stifles everything."

In short, Uphill Battle is typical of many places where public officials decide they want to reinvent: it is desperate.

Several years ago a newly elected mayor read *Reinventing Government* and got excited by the vision it painted. He immediately assigned the book to all his department heads and held management seminars on it. But no one was sure just how or where to start. Meanwhile, more immediate crises demanded his attention: a bond rating near junk status; a major infrastructure problem; a desperate need to attract more jobs.

For two years the mayor made remarkable progress. He balanced the books, got the bond rating back up, pushed through a controversial solution to the infrastructure problem, and worked hard on economic development. In the process he took his lumps, but public perceptions improved, finances began to stabilize, and employee morale began to recover—particularly after he negotiated new contracts with the city's unions.

Still, the mayor had not found a way to improve the performance of his frontline agencies. He had no money to invest. He had no time. And he had no spare management capacity. His department heads were running as fast as they could just to stay in the same place.

Finally he went to the business community and asked for help. He convinced three major companies to pitch in and hire a consulting firm to help the city develop a change strategy. This is how we came to know Uphill Battle.

Our consulting team interviewed several dozen employees, managers, elected officials, and citizens. As is usually the case, we could have been in any public organization under duress—a school district, a county, a state or province, or a national agency. The problems were all too familiar.

Productivity in Uphill Battle was low, and most employees didn't seem to care. "It could be so much higher, and happily higher," one manager told us. "So much of it is an attitude thing, particularly of the old timers: 'I'm going to look out for me, my benefits, my pension, my turf, and that's it, and I'm not going to extend myself for anyone else.' "

Employee attitudes were reinforced by the working conditions: shabby offices, deteriorating facilities, and old equipment. When things got bad enough and something new was needed, the centralized purchasing operation picked the cheapest product. When the fire department needed new radios, for instance, no one asked the employees which kind to buy. "So now when the radios break, people just say, 'Friggin' chief and his radios,' " one employee told us. "Pretty soon people quit thinking on the job; they just figure someone else makes all the decisions."

To managers it was the red tape that was most frustrating. Purchasing was a nightmare. Paying a bill could take 90 days. "It's the toughest place I've ever worked, with all the red tape and roadblocks that are set up to stop progress," said one department head. "The auditor's mindset is, 'Keep the systems as tight as is humanly possible, so we don't incur any abuse.' "

Another described the problem in more graphic terms:

In this environment, if something is bought and there isn't a purchase order in place, the auditor will take that error to a public flogging before the city council. There was one manager who bought a sink for $60 out of his own pocket, in an emergency, and at a big savings to the city. When he asked for reimbursement they publicly flogged him over it. I said to myself, "What a terrible thing to do, when that's exactly the kind of behavior you want from people."

In many departments, middle management was weak. "Seniority has reigned on promotions," explained a union official. "Not quality or qualifications, but seniority. It's not the rules, it's habit. It's easier for management to do it that way." Managers "don't fire people, and nobody ever gets demoted, even if they can't run the equipment."

To make matters worse, there was a history of favoritism: if you knew the right people, you got better treatment. Some employees

seemed to get away with anything. When employees were found falsi-
fying time records, no one was disciplined or fired. Every employee in
town knew that one unit padded its overtime, but no one did anything
about it. Like most elected officials, the mayor "has difficulty confront-
ing people and telling them they have to go," said one manager. "He
has trouble firing people—especially his friends."

The result was an organization with no accountability, in the eyes of
most employees. "From the bottom to the top, people have to be held
accountable for their actions," one employee almost pleaded.

*If you destroy a vehicle, you should be reprimanded—across the
board. It happens to some, not others. Managers should be the
same: account for how you spent the money. Explain the overtime.
Explain why you're mowing grass in cemeteries in October to use
up money. Somebody needs to be in charge of everything, so
people are accountable. And there need to be consequences: if the
guy at the bottom is not working, he should be gone.*

Yet there were hopeful signs. The new union contract had lifted
morale. The city had always had enormous community spirit. The
schools were making significant progress. Some of the other managers
and employees, after repeated seminars on reinventing government and
total quality management, were eager to begin implementing new
ideas. Finances were getting a little better. And the city's most important union was desperate to help management improve performance
and reach financial stability, because its members had suffered so many
layoffs in the early 1990s. "We used to fight management as a union,"
said one official.

*Now we go and say, "This guy is abusing sick leave, what are you
going to do about it?" We've got it down from 18 days average
three years ago to single digits. We have a good core of union
officers that do want to work with the mayor. We really need good
managers, and the union will back them.*

There was clearly some low-hanging fruit, some opportunities for
quick victories. Cutting the red tape in purchasing and accounts pay-
able would do wonders for morale, and one major department was ripe
for a labor-management partnership. But there were also some daunt-

ing obstacles. The civil service system was not only archaic, it was embedded in state law. And most department heads, overburdened already, wondered where they could possibly find the time for a change initiative.

More important, however, was a deep-seated feeling that Uphill Battle didn't have what it took to reinvent. When we asked about performance measurement or customer surveys or competition between internal service units, managers and employees alike sounded wistful: That would be nice, but "our problems are so much more basic than that." Said one top manager:

> *This system is not sophisticated enough yet. We're provincial. You need well-trained technocrats who are highly professional and paid quite well to do that. That's not [Uphill Battle].*

Managers were frustrated, in other words, but they also felt powerless. A sense of hopelessness pervaded the organization.

Uphill Battle's leaders were grappling with some of the classic issues reinventors face. They were struggling to get a purchase, to find a strategy that could actually make a difference. Where should they start? How could they create enough urgency to get people to embrace change? How could they get some leverage? How could they make sure they started a process of change that built on itself—that gained momentum rather than lost it?

Some governments are further along the reinvention path than Uphill Battle, and they ask different questions: How can we speed up the process of change? How can we get more employee buy-in? How can we make sure every organization and employee feels compelled to improve?

Even battle-scarred veterans of reinvention have questions: We've changed the incentives, we've changed the structure, we've changed the administrative systems—but how do we change the *culture*? And how can we institutionalize reinvention? How can we make sure the organization doesn't slip back into old ways when we leave?

This is the world reinventors inhabit, a world of many unknowns. There are no easy answers in a city like Uphill Battle. Leaders must struggle to get traction on very slippery terrain, often with very few resources other than their own wits. Like the pioneers, they must find pathways through the wilderness, discover water holes, and pick out mountain passes. But they have one advantage those pioneers did not have: they have access to maps.

Reinventing Government drew a rough map of the new world of twenty-first-century governance. This book begins to put routes on that map, to make it easier for reinventors to follow the pioneers and stake their own claims. In this book you will learn the strategies that have worked for the pioneers of reinvention—not only in the United States but in Canada, the United Kingdom, Australia, and New Zealand. You will not only see the dramatic results they have produced, you will learn *how* they did it—and some of the lessons they learned along the way.

THE PIONEERS' PROGRESS

In Indianapolis, for example, Mayor Steve Goldsmith created urgency by forcing his departments to compete with the private sector. He put more than 27 services out to competitive bid, with public agencies bidding against private businesses. In the process, he saved more than $100 million over seven years and trimmed his nonpublic-safety staff by more than 40 percent—while maintaining service levels, forcing agencies to improve, and keeping peace with the unions.

In Hampton, Virginia, a city of 130,000 that was losing population, losing businesses, and struggling with debt, City Manager Bob O'Neill and Mayor James Eason began by developing a new vision and selling it to the community and the employees. They redefined the mission of city government, from providing services to brokering the community's resources. Then they aligned city operations with that new mission, using performance contracts with managers and a concerted campaign to change the culture and values of the organization—the habits, hearts, and minds of employees. Over the next ten years downtown development surged, property taxes fell, debt payments were cut in half, citizen satisfaction with city government reached 90 percent on annual surveys, and the city earned a reputation as the leading public innovator in Virginia.

In Minnesota, a group of civic and business activists convinced the governor and legislature that the best way to improve schools was to take away district monopolies, give parents their choice of public schools, and force the districts to compete for both enrollment and dollars. Within a few years, districts were scrambling to attract students by improving their programs. They doubled the number of advanced-placement courses offered by high schools and almost tripled the number of "alternative" public schools in the state. Public approval of school choice rose from 35 to 86 percent.

In the U.S. Forest Service, reinvention began with a "pilot test" in three national forests and a research station. Headquarters gave managers flexibility to spend their budgets as they saw fit, waived regulations that stood in their way, and encouraged them to push decision making down to frontline employees. In two years, productivity in the four sites soared 18 percent. Seizing on this victory, the eastern region headquarters eliminated many of its own bureaucratic controls and gradually trimmed its staff by a third. As performance climbed throughout the region, regional office overhead fell to nearly half that of the nation's other regions.

In Australia, reinventors minimized managers' frustration with red tape by carving 13 business enterprises out of the mammoth Department of Administrative Services, taking away their monopolies, and making them earn their income by selling services to other government agencies, in competition with private companies. In five years these enterprises shrunk their staffs by 32 percent, turned a $100 million annual loss into a $46.7 million annual profit, and increased their productivity by 5.6 percent a year. (We are using Australian dollars, which were worth about 75 American cents at the time.)

In Great Britain, Prime Minister Margaret Thatcher sold £20 billion (roughly $30 billion) worth of public activities—with more than 600,000 employees—to private owners. She then broke the massive departments that remained into more than 100 semiautonomous agencies, giving them enormous flexibility in return for rigorous performance contracts. Her successor, John Major, forced most government organizations to publish customer service standards and "market test" many functions, letting private companies bid against public units for work. While trimming its staff by a third, the British civil service dramatically improved its performance.

In New Zealand, the Labor Party and a cadre of top civil servants were even more radical. They scrapped nearly all civil service rules, reshaped the core public sector into dozens of small departments operating under performance budgets, and sold more than $8.2 billion in publicly owned industries (about $5 billion in U.S. dollars). They converted other public industries into state-owned enterprises (SOEs), free to operate as businesses. In their first five years, the SOEs increased their revenues by 15 percent, quadrupled profits, and cut their workforces in half.

We will look in detail at these and other efforts in the pages that follow. They have many labels: "reinvention," "redesign," "public sector reform," "the new public management." But whatever the label, a process of profound public sector restructuring is sweeping the developed world. In March 1996, the 24-member Organization for Economic Cooperation and Development (OECO) held its first ministerial-level meeting on public management. Alice Rivlin, then director of the U.S. Office of Management and Budget, chaired the meeting. In her OECO summary report, she explained that most of the 24 governments were facing the same fundamental pressures for change, including a global economy, dissatisfied citizens, and fiscal crisis. "Equally startling to me and, I suspect, to many of my colleagues," she added, "countries are responding in remarkably similar ways." She then ticked off a list that read like the table of contents of this book:

a. *decentralisation of authority within governmental units and devolution of responsibilities to lower levels of government . . .*

b. *a re-examination of what government should both do and pay for, what it should pay for but not do, and what it should neither do nor pay for;*

c. *downsizing the public service and the privatisation and corporatisation of activities;*

d. *consideration of more cost-effective ways of delivering services, such as contracting out, market mechanisms, and user charges;*

e. *customer orientation, including explicit quality standards for public services;*

f. *benchmarking and measuring performance; and*

g. *reforms designed to simplify regulation and reduce its costs.*

As we approach the twenty-first century, reinvention is like an adolescent striving for adulthood: full of energy and enthusiasm; fueled by ideals; stumbling often but learning in leaps and bounds. It was born almost two decades ago at the margins of public life, with the American tax revolt that began in 1978 and the British election of Margaret Thatcher in 1979. It spread throughout the 1980s, with the election of Labor Party governments in Australia and New Zealand in 1983 and 1984 and the development of Thatcher's "Next Steps" agencies in 1988.

With the exception of New Zealand, this process unfolded rather quietly, far from the public eye. In the U.S., four events converged to thrust it into the spotlight: the recession of the early 1990s; a painful fiscal crisis at every level of government; the publication of *Reinventing Government*; and the election of a president who promised to reinvent government. Mayors and city managers from Philadelphia to Seattle and Milwaukee to Portland, Oregon, joined the parade. By 1995, for example, New York, Boston, Philadelphia, Chicago, Milwaukee, Charlotte, Dallas, Indianapolis, Phoenix, and Portland, Oregon, were all measuring performance and using that information to improve their management.

States such as Florida, Oregon, Texas, Ohio, North Carolina, Iowa, Utah, Minnesota, and Wisconsin also made significant strides. By mid-decade, 39 states reported quality initiatives, 29 indicated at least some efforts to measure performance, 28 said they were seeking customer feedback, more than 30 were simplifying their personnel systems, 10 were experimenting with eliminating budget line-items, and 10 were testing competitive public-versus-private bidding for service delivery. Meanwhile hundreds of counties embraced reinvention. In 1993, the Clinton administration weighed in with Vice President Al Gore's National Performance Review.

Not all these initiatives have succeeded, of course. But for all the setbacks—and there have been plenty—American progress since 1990 has been remarkable. The debate about public sector reform is light-years ahead of where it stood even five years ago. And with their parliamentary systems, some of our overseas allies—particularly the British, New Zealanders, and Australians—have put American efforts to shame.

Make no mistake, reinvention is still a work in progress in all these countries. Most reinventors are still operating without a road map, making it up as they go along. *Reinventing Government* offered some clues about how to proceed. Some readers used its ten principles to assess their own governments and develop change agendas.

But *Reinventing Government* was not designed to help readers figure out how to proceed. It described the characteristics of entrepreneurial governments—how they act and what they do—but it did not discuss how to create them. It did not lay out the strategies by which bureaucratic systems and organizations could be transformed into entrepreneurial systems and organizations.

This book does. A few of the principles of *Reinventing Government*, such as "customer-driven government," also define key strategies you can use to leverage transformation. But not all do. *Reinventing Government* was primarily *descriptive*, while this book is *prescriptive*. It provides practical know-how you can apply, whether you are a politician, a public servant, or a citizen.

Reinventing public institutions is Herculean work. To succeed, you must find levers that can move mountains. You must find strategies that set off chain reactions in your organization or system, dominoes that will set all others falling. In a phrase, you must *be strategic*. This book lays out the five strategies that have proven most effective—and describes how the world's most successful reinventors have used them.

WHAT REINVENTION IS NOT

Before we move on to the strategies, we should revisit what we mean by "reinvention." *Reinventing Government* laid out a clear definition, but one price of popular success has been a loss of clarity. Like "reengineering," the term "reinventing government" has been used so often by so many people to describe so many agendas that it has lost its meaning.

To make our definition clear, let us start by explaining what reinvention is *not*.

Reinventing government is not about change in the political system: campaign finance reform, legislative or parliamentary reform, term limits, and the like. In the United States, political reform is critical if we are to achieve significant policy and governance reform—but it is not what we mean by reinvention.

We do not mean reorganization, either. Reinvention is not about moving boxes on an organizational chart. As we will explain in chapter 1, it is about restructuring public organizations and systems by changing their purposes, their incentives, their accountability, their distribution of power, and their cultures. As one does this, it sometimes makes sense to alter the organizational chart. But if you start with the chart, you will exhaust yourself in turf wars long before you change anything important.

Nor is reinvention about cutting waste, fraud, and abuse. It is not about efficiency reviews that generate a list of onetime changes to save money; it is about creating public organizations that *constantly* look for ways to become more efficient. It is not about weeding the garden; it is about creating a regimen that keeps the garden free of weeds.

Perhaps most important, reinventing government is not synonymous with downsizing government. Some public organizations would be more effective with smaller budgets and staffs, others would not. We have never met a soul—liberal, conservative, or moderate—who thought we could improve our schools by cutting their budgets and laying off teachers. Part of reinventing government is finding, for any particular organization, the size that maximizes performance. But just as form should follow function, size should follow strategy. If we simply lop off 30 percent of most public organizations, we have done nothing to change their nature or improve their performance. Downsizing is like removing grains from a pile of sand: afterward, it's still a pile of sand. Reinvention is like mixing the sand with carbon or magnesium and blasting it with intense heat: afterward, it is pure silicon.

Nor is reinvention synonymous with privatization. Asset sales, contracting out, and other tools that fall under the heading of privatization are part of the reinventor's tool kit. But as *Reinventing Government* argued, it is competition and customer choice that force improvement, not simply private ownership. Shifting from a public monopoly to a private monopoly seldom leads to a happy ending.

Reinventing government is also not a stand-in for simply making government more efficient. Part of the goal is efficiency, but more important is *effectiveness.* What is the point of making an organization or system more efficient, if it is completely ineffective? Citizens in the industrial democracies are not clamoring only for cheaper government, they are clamoring for government that works. They want more productivity, but they also want more value—as the British say, they want "value for money." Ask yourself: Do you want cheaper schools, or better schools? Cheaper police forces, or lower crime rates? Cheaper training programs, or better jobs?

Finally, reinvention is not simply a synonym for total quality management or business process reengineering. These are both tools that can help a reinventor succeed, if used in strategic ways. But they are not *sufficient.* We have enormous respect for W. Edwards Deming, Peter Drucker, Tom Peters, Michael Hammer, Rosabeth Moss Kanter, and other private sector management experts. But if the goal is transformation, business management tools are not enough.

There are many differences between business and government. Making change within public organizations requires far more political effort, for example, because public organizations live in a political sea, while businesses live in a market economy. But the most profound difference is that private organizations exist within larger systems, or markets, that are generally fairly functional. Most private, for-profit organizations have clear missions, know how to measure their bottom-line performance, face competition, experience very real consequences for their performance, and are accountable to their customers. So business management literature focuses primarily on changing *the organization*, not the system within which it exists. Management theorists leave the latter field to economists.

In government, most organizations exist within fairly dysfunctional systems. Many organizations have multiple (sometimes conflicting) missions; few face direct competition; few experience consequences for their performance; few have clear bottom lines (few even measure their performance); and very few are accountable to their customers. These system realities create the incentives and conditions that drive organizations to act in a bureaucratic fashion. Until they are changed, it is difficult to build entrepreneurial organizations. Hence the most important strategic levers in the public sector lie within the larger system, not within the organization. Civic entrepreneurs must change these larger systems—education systems, welfare systems, regulatory systems, federal-state-local systems, budget systems, personnel systems, and the like. Here business management theory is of little help.

Consider an analogy. Imagine a discussion of how to improve the performance of a state enterprise in the Soviet Union, back when it still existed. Imagine that we told you the solution was to bring in new management, do strategic planning, adopt mission and vision statements, change the organizational chart, and bring in organization development consultants to change the culture of the workforce. Your response, more than likely, would have been, "Nonsense!" You would have pointed out that Soviet enterprises faced no competition, had captive customers, were controlled from above by central planners, and had no incentives to improve. Until those realities were changed, you would have argued, all the efforts in the world to improve management practices would yield marginal improvement, at best. And you would have been right.

We would make the same argument about our own public bureaucracies. The bureaucratic state operates much as the Soviet economy did. Until we reinvent the *systems* within which public organizations work, improvement will be marginal.

The Five Myths of Public Sector Reform

Our colleague Babak Armajani, CEO of the Public Strategies Group and the Reinventing Government Network, describes five myths about making government work.

1. The Liberal Myth is that government can be improved by spending more and doing more. In reality, pouring more money into a dysfunctional system does not yield significantly better results.

2. The Conservative Myth is that government can be improved by spending less and doing less. In reality, withdrawing funds from a dysfunctional system may save the taxpayers money, but it will not improve government performance.

3. The Business Myth is that government can be improved by running it like a business. In reality, while business metaphors and management techniques are often helpful, there are critical differences between public and private sector realities.

4. The Employee Myth is that public employees could perform just fine if they had enough money. (See the Liberal Myth.) In reality, we have to change the way resources are used if we want the results to change.

5. The People Myth is that government can be improved by hiring better people. In reality, the problem is not the people; it is the systems in which they are trapped.

SO WHAT IS REINVENTION?

By "reinvention," we mean *the fundamental transformation of public systems and organizations to create dramatic increases in their effectiveness, efficiency, adaptability, and capacity to innovate. This trans-*

formation is accomplished by changing their purpose, incentives, accountability, power structure, and culture.

Reinvention is about replacing bureaucratic systems with entrepreneurial systems. It is about creating public organizations and systems that habitually innovate, that continually improve their quality, without having to be pushed from outside. It is about creating a public sector that has a built-in drive to improve—what some call a "self-renewing system."

It is not enough for your local school and police force to get better at what they do this year; you want them to *keep* getting better. To do that, they need "adaptive capacity," the capacity to address new issues as they arise. The same is true for agencies that protect the environment or distribute social security benefits—indeed, for every aspect of government. Worrying about improving government's short-term productivity and results is important. But focusing solely on efficiency and effectiveness is like learning how to fight the last war. After you know how to do that, you find out that the next war is quite different—and that you're not prepared for it.

Reinvention, in other words, gets government ready for challenges we cannot yet anticipate. It not only improves effectiveness today, it creates organizations capable of improving their effectiveness tomorrow, when their environments change.

This requires a fundamental transformation of our industrial era public systems. There are many ways to portray this transformation. Some writers have described the goal with phrases such as "high-performing organizations," "quality organizations," "learning organizations," "intelligent organizations," and "self-renewing organizations." We often use the phrase "entrepreneurial government" to convey what we mean. But all of these phrases seek to communicate the same basic message.

Reinventing Government described ten principles around which such systems and organizations are structured. Appendix A lists them and briefly defines each one.

Reinvention creates public systems that act very differently from the bureaucracies we have come to know and loathe. It creates organizations that show up in ratings with the best customer service in the business—as the Social Security Administration did in 1995 for its telephone service. It creates organizations that put their services where their customers can most easily use them—as several state motor

---

The Meaning of "Entrepreneurial Government"

"The phrase *entrepreneurial government* ... may surprise many readers, who think of entrepreneurs solely as business men and women. But the true meaning of the word *entrepreneur* is far broader. It was coined by the French economist J. B. Say, around the year 1800. "The entrepreneur," Say wrote, "shifts economic resources out of an area of lower and into an area of higher productivity and greater yield." An entrepreneur, in other words, uses resources in new ways to maximize productivity and effectiveness.

Say's definition applies equally to the private sector, to the public sector, and to the voluntary, or third, sector. Dynamic school superintendents and principals use resources in new ways to maximize productivity and effectiveness. Innovative airport managers do the same. Welfare commissioners, labor secretaries, commerce department staffers—all can shift resources into areas of higher productivity and yield. When we talk about public entrepreneurs, we mean people who do precisely this. When we talk about the entrepreneurial model, we mean public sector institutions that *habitually* act this way—that constantly use their resources in new ways to heighten both their efficiency and their effectiveness."

—From *Reinventing Government*, p. xix.

---

vehicle agencies did by opening offices in malls and retail stores. It creates inner-city public schools that send 210 of 248 graduates to four-year colleges and an additional 31 to two-year colleges, as East Harlem's Manhattan Center for Science and Math has. And it creates organizations the private sector uses as benchmarks of excellence because they provide the best service in the business, like the Air Combat Command's pharmacy at MacDill Air Force Base in Tampa, Florida.

We are convinced that the appearance of these entrepreneurial organizations in the late twentieth century is no accident. We believe that it represents an inevitable historical shift from one paradigm to another. It is a shift as profound as that which took place at the beginning of the century, when we built the bureaucratic public institutions we are busy reinventing today.

During the nineteenth century, the industrializing democracies had far smaller governments with far less ambitious goals. As Gary Sturgess points out in his essay "The Decline and Fall of the Industrial State," in the nineteenth century the British still used a private navy in times of war. Canals and railroads were private, and there were more than 1,000 private turnpike trusts. The postal service, ports, and even lighthouses all began as private services. Some public offices, including seats in Parliament, were private—they could be bought, sold, leased, and mortgaged. Even the early fleets that took convicts to Sturgess's Australia were owned by private contractors.

By the end of the century, the old paradigm—of small central governments with limited authority—was breaking down, because it was incapable of dealing with the new realities emerging in the industrial democracies. Factories were sprouting up; cities were growing at breakneck speed; whole new industries were being born. With these new realities came new needs: for mass transit systems and roads and bridges, for massive new sewer and water systems, for universal education systems. Our old model of government could not meet these needs, so we invented a new model. We invented bureaucracy.

We copied our model from the military and the new mass production industries that had sprung up. Max Weber, the great German sociologist, summed up the principles by which these new bureaucracies were structured:

- They were centralized and hierarchical: "The professional bureaucrat . . . is only a single cog in an ever-moving mechanism which prescribes to him an essentially fixed route of march."
- They were ordered by rules: "that is, by laws or administrative regulations" which were "more or less stable, more or less exhaustive."
- They were standardized and impersonal, offering the same treatment or service to everyone.
- They used administrative processes—i.e., their own staffs rather than contractors or market mechanisms—to achieve their goals.
- They chose their staffs on the basis of examinations, not subjective criteria.

To top it off, most public bureaucracies were monopolies. And to combat the fraud and abuse so rampant in the urban political machines of the era, we wrapped them up in endless rules, red tape, and internal controls.

The resulting bureaucracies have been described as systems designed by a genius to be run by idiots. That may be a little harsh, but it contains a kernel of truth. In the soul of the bureaucratic machine there lurks a control freak. Employees are cogs in a highly regulated machine. Their work is broken down into different functions and described in great detail. Managers do the thinking; workers do the tasks they are assigned. Detailed rules and procedures specify behaviors. Inspectors check for compliance.

This model served us well in its day. As long as the tasks were relatively simple and straightforward and the environment stable, it worked. But for the last 20 years it has been coming apart. In a world of rapid change, technological revolution, global economic competition, demassified markets, an educated workforce, demanding customers, and severe fiscal constraints, centralized, top-down monopolies are simply too slow, too unresponsive, and too incapable of change or innovation.

Five years ago, when *Reinventing Government* was published, this conclusion was still hotly debated. Today it is hard to find any thoughtful observer who does not agree that traditional public bureaucracies must change. The average citizen certainly understands, at a gut level. In survey after survey, citizens bemoan the failures of government. Researchers who conducted a massive survey in Canada expressed the new reality particularly well:

> *General attitudes to government have deteriorated. Most Canadians are cynical and hostile to government. There is a widespread belief that governments are self-serving, inefficient and ineffectual. The strength of these responses would suggest an underlying rage but for the fact that these negative sentiments have been evident for too long a period of time to characterize them as rage. Perhaps deep resentment and frustration would be better descriptors of the current public mood.*

Most politicians understand this. They know that bureaucracy isn't working; they just don't know what to replace it with. And many of those who work in government know it, too, because they live in the belly of the beast. No one knows better how nightmarishly frustrating bureaucracy can be than those trapped inside it.

This book is for those who want to end the nightmare, whether they are public employees or elected officials, members of citizens groups or business organizations. If you want to help your city save $100 million, as Indianapolis has; if you want to double the effectiveness of your organization, as the Tactical Air Command did; if you want to double the productivity of your services, as the Phoenix Department of Public Works did; if you need to do more with half the staff, as New Zealand's state-owned enterprises did; or if you simply want your public systems and organizations to embrace continual improvement and innovation—we hope this book will help you find the way.

-I-

FINDING YOUR LEVERAGE

– 1 –

THE FIVE C'S: CHANGING GOVERNMENT'S DNA

MARGARET THATCHER:
DISCOVERING THE POWER OF STRATEGY

By 1986, Margaret Thatcher was frustrated with her inability to move the British bureaucracy. For seven years, she had administered dose after dose of tough medicine: downsizing, privatization, efficiency audits, war with the unions. But she had failed to change the behavior of her civil service.

Thatcher and her Conservative Party had come to power in the winter of 1979, pledging to revive Great Britain's slumping economy by reducing the size of government, cutting spending, and slashing taxes. Gross domestic product (GDP) was in free fall. Inflation, at 10 percent, was accelerating. Public revenues were stagnating, public spending was rising, and public services were eroding. Government consumed 44 percent of GDP. It owned huge portions of the economy: coal mines, the oil industry, the gas and electrical industries, auto companies, an airline, an aerospace firm, and dozens of other nationalized industries. (By comparison, government in the United States consumed about 35 percent of GDP at the time.)

Thatcher's instinct had been to slash away. At her first cabinet meeting, she announced a hiring freeze and a 3 percent cut in the civil service; several months later she imposed an additional 5 percent cut. On her fourth day in office, she asked Sir Derek Rayner, who ran the well-known retail firm Marks & Spencer, to lead a crusade against waste and inefficiency. Rayner recruited six aides and launched a classic exercise favored by politicians determined to root out waste: efficiency audits of targeted programs and processes. Designed to streamline operations and eliminate waste, they became known as "efficiency scrutinies."

Under the watchful eye of Rayner's Efficiency Unit, government departments conducted 223 scrutinies in the first three years. They led to the elimination of 12,000 positions and recurrent annual savings of £180 million. (A pound was worth $1.50 to $2.32, depending on the year.) They were effective in making specific changes, but, as leaders of the Efficiency Unit readily admitted when we talked with them, they did not lead organizations to pursue continuous improvement. They helped weed the garden, patch by patch, but they did not develop a regimen that kept the garden weed-free.

Thatcher also took on the public sector unions, pushing through reforms that outlawed secondary pickets, restricted union shops, and encouraged secret ballots in union elections. In 1981 she stared down the civil service unions when they struck for five months. And in 1984 and 1985, she defeated the powerful mine workers union, which struck to keep the government from closing coal pits that were losing money.

But Thatcher's big weapon was privatization. In her 11 years, the government sold more than 40 major state-owned enterprises— including British Petroleum, Britoil, Jaguar, British Telecommunications, British Steel, British Airways, and Rolls-Royce—plus many smaller enterprises and more than 1.25 million public housing units. By 1987 these sales were pulling in £5 billion a year, helping Thatcher balance her last four budgets. (By 1994, the cumulative total was $75 billion.) "By the time I left office," she later boasted, "the state-owned sector of industry had been reduced by some 60 percent. . . . Over six hundred thousand jobs had passed from the public to the private sector."

Thatcher also clamped a spending lid on local government, most of whose revenues came from the national level. In 1980 she required "compulsory competitive tendering"—competitive bidding between public and private providers—for all local building and highway construction. Two years later she established an independent Audit Commission, to oversee auditing of local governments and pressure them to increase their efficiency. And in 1984 she imposed limits on local tax rates.

These reforms not only forced local governments to change the way they did business, they helped shrink the size of government. During Thatcher's reign public employment fell from 30 to 24 percent of the workforce, dropping to its 1961 level, and government spending fell from 44 to 40.5 percent of GDP. Privatization not only reduced the size of government, it freed companies like British Airways to transform themselves into world leaders. But in the core civil service—the non-enterprise, non-health-care departments where 600,000 civil servants still labored—performance changed very little.

In short, jamming the bureaucracy was not getting the prime minister where she wanted to go. When she privatized an enterprise or cut a budget or launched an efficiency scrutiny, nothing changed in other departments. No other dominoes fell. She needed a strategy beyond privatization and efficiency scrutinies.

The Next Steps: Uncoupling Steering and Rowing

When Thatcher and her colleagues entered office, they held most public employees in contempt. They threw around slogans like "Deprivilege the Civil Service." But as Thatcher worked with administrators who impressed her, her attitude changed. "She found herself confronted with civil servants who were entrepreneurial," says Michael Clarke, head of the University of Birmingham's School of Public Policy. "She encouraged and promoted a range of those people—she had an eye for 'can do' civil servants." In fact, Thatcher triggered a revolt in her own party in 1985 by raising salaries for top civil servants by as much as 50 percent.

Thatcher also began to learn more about the systemic problems behind government's waste and inefficiency. In 1982, the Efficiency Unit and one of her ministers, Michael Heseltine, convinced her to launch a new management initiative. Upon taking office, Heseltine had discovered that his department had no adequate financial management system, so he had set about creating one. He and his civil servants had built a system that set objectives for each unit, defined their budgets, and measured both their spending and progress toward objectives.

Thatcher, Rayner, and the Treasury Department took the idea government-wide. Their Financial Management Initiative required departments to set performance objectives for all managers: what they expected to achieve, by when, and at what cost. It broke departmental budgets down and made each unit responsible for managing its own funds. It required new management information systems that could give managers reliable data on the costs of their activities. All this was held together by a "top management system," through which departments prepared annual statements summarizing the performance and plans of their units. Ministers, top management, and unit managers would review these and agree on action plans.

Thatcher invested considerable sums in the computer systems necessary to run the Financial Management Initiative. The government built up more than 1,800 performance objectives, most of them focused on cost and efficiency. But the impact of the new system was disappointing; it had little effect on the behavior of the civil service. It created valuable information, but it did not change the fundamental dynamics of government organizations. In 1986 Thatcher asked Rayner's successor, Sir Robin Ibbs, to assess the initiative and recommend the next steps.

By now the Efficiency Unit had six years of experience under its belt. Its members—drawn from both business and government—had learned a great deal about the realities of management in the public sector. They had long since lost interest in knee-jerk solutions.

In the previous 150 years, prime ministers had commissioned many blue-ribbon inquiries into the problems of public management. But not one had asked the bureaucrats what they thought. The Efficiency Unit did just that. Over three months, its members interviewed hundreds of civil servants, as well as businesspeople and experts on public management.

They found—indeed, they no doubt already knew—that the time-honored British system of public administration made good management almost impossible. Senior civil servants were not trained for management and did not care about management. The elite members of the civil service advised ministers on the great policy issues of the day. They did not stoop to get their hands dirty with implementation, and they looked down on managers—who did—as second-class civil servants. They took their marching orders from elected ministers, who were consumed by politics and policy. Like cabinet secretaries in any large nation, few ministers even saw management as their job. As Rayner once put it, "leadership has too often in the past fallen into the hands of those who know nothing of management and despise those who do."

Managers were so far down the civil service pecking order that they had little real control over what they were supposed to manage. Power was centralized at the top of the departments and in the Treasury Department, which combined the powers of a central office of management and budget, a central personnel office, and an American-style Treasury Department.

The results of the system were predictable. The Efficiency Unit report described a shortage of good managers; little top-level focus on the delivery of public services; a budget and finance system focused more on controlling spending than on making it effective; and few external pressures on government managers and organizations to improve performance.

In addition, the Efficiency Unit pointed out, the civil service was "too big and diverse to manage as a single entity." "Recruitment, dismissal, choice of staff, promotion, pay, hours of work, accommodation, grading, organization of work, the use of IT [information technology] equipment are all outside the control of most civil service managers at all levels," it said. The civil service rule book was "structured to fit everything in general and nothing in particular." Managers viewed the personnel system as a huge constraint on good management—but a constraint that was impossible to change.

In sum, the Efficiency Unit concluded, the civil servants were not the problem; the systems were. Ibbs had not intended to recommend radical reform, but it was clear that the systems and structure of the bureaucracy would have to change if effective management were to become a priority.

The unit's 1988 report, "Improving Management in Government: The Next Steps," argued that to solve the management problem, the government would have to separate service-delivery and compliance functions from the policy-focused departments that housed them—to separate steering from rowing. Second, it would have to give service-delivery and compliance agencies much more flexibility and autonomy. And third, it would have to hold those agencies accountable for results, through performance contracts.

The Efficiency Unit proposed, in other words, an arm's-length performance contract between departments and their agencies, in which departments traded the freedom agencies needed to manage effectively for the performance standards ministers needed to hold them accountable. Ibbs and his staff envisioned a civil service with a small core at the center supporting ministers, doing policy work, and managing departments, while the bulk of civil servants worked in relatively independent agencies.

Now in her ninth year as prime minister, Margaret Thatcher stepped up to the challenge. She accepted all of the unit's recommendations—including its urging that an "extremely" senior official be appointed project manager and given "unequivocal personal responsibility for achieving the change." She appointed Peter Kemp, a senior Treasury official who had come into the civil service from the private sector and was known as a maverick, to oversee the Next Steps program. Kemp staffed his team with bright, young, high-level civil servants on loan from their departments. They fleshed out the Next Steps proposals, developing a process that would:

- separate departments' service-delivery and compliance functions into discrete chunks, each one called an "executive agency";
- give those agencies much more control over their budgets, personnel systems, and other management practices;
- use a competitive public-private sector search—a radical break with civil service practice—to find chief executives for executive agencies;
- require chief executives to develop three-to-five-year corporate plans and one-year business plans;
- negotiate a three-year "framework document" between each agency and its departmental minister, specifying the results it would achieve and the flexibilities with which it would operate;
- pay chief executives whatever it took to get the talent needed, including performance bonuses of up to 20 percent of their salaries;
- deny chief executives the civil service's normal lifetime tenure; and
- require them to reapply for their jobs every three years.

Kemp quickly signaled the importance of Next Steps and captured the imaginations of reformers by announcing that his target was to move 75 percent of the civil service into executive agencies. The

Treasury asked all departments to review their functions and decide upon one of five options for each: abolition, sale, contracting out, conversion to executive-agency status, or preservation with no change. Once a functional area within a department had been nominated for agency status, it was referred to a project executive team, whose members included representatives from the department, Kemp's staff, and the Treasury. They negotiated framework documents outlining the flexibilities granted the agency and the outputs expected. The Treasury acted as a gatekeeper, refusing to approve agency status until it was satisfied that true performance accountability was in place.

Kemp and his Next Steps team hit the ground running. Deliberately starting with organizations that were ready for agency status, they created eight agencies in the first year, 1988–1989. By early 1991 they had established 51 agencies, a pace that surprised most observers. By mid-1992 half the civil service worked in executive agencies, and by late 1996 the process was all but complete: nearly 75 percent of the civil service worked in 126 agencies. (The 75 percent figure includes 50 executive offices within two large departments, Inland Revenue and Customs and Excise, that operate along Next Steps lines but are not technically described as executive agencies.)

Finding the Leverage Points

There are many lessons to be learned from the British experience. It shows, for example, that reinvention requires collaboration between elected officials and civil servants—between what we call the political and institutional sectors. There were many things the civil servants would never have done on their own, and there were an equal number of things the politicians would never have seen on their own. Both sides had their blind spots.

More important for this book, however, is the lesson the British learned about strategy. Margaret Thatcher could not succeed on instinct alone. Her first attempts to reform the civil service bureaucracy—staff cuts and efficiency scrutinies—were inadequate. They did not create a domino effect, forcing everything else to change. In a word, they were not *strategic*. It was not until her Efficiency Unit developed strategies capable of creating that domino effect that she began to make headway.

By strategy, we do not mean detailed plans. There is no recipe you can follow to reinvent government, no step-by-step progression you must adhere to. Many writers and consultants discuss organizational change in terms of "stages" that they put into a neat, linear order. But the process is not linear, and it is certainly not orderly. Things rarely go as planned; reinventors must constantly adjust their approaches in response to the resistance and opportunities they encounter.

By strategy, we mean the use of key leverage points to make fundamental changes that ripple throughout government, changing everything else. Reinvention is large-scale combat. It requires intense, prolonged struggle in the political arena, in the institutions of government, and in the community and society. Given the enormity of the task and the resistance that must be overcome, the reinventors' challenge—whether in the U.K., the U.S., or elsewhere—is to leverage small resources into big changes. Being strategic means using the levers available to you to change the underlying dynamics in a system, in a way that changes everyone's behavior.

The word "strategy" originated in a military context: the Greek *strategos* means "general." Good generals begin by developing strategies: not operational plans, but basic approaches capable of altering the balance of forces in the field. When the U.S. chose to force Iraq out of Kuwait in 1991, its generals decided their leverage was twofold: massive bombardment to blind and debilitate the enemy, then quick, stealthy movement of divisions to create a pincer-like ground attack. These two strategies set the stage for day-to-day operational tactics, which guided the use of tools such as jets and tanks.

Margaret Thatcher and her advisors did something similar. They located their government's key leverage points and used them to change the balance of forces—to alter the basic dynamics within the public sector. The Next Steps process changed three leverage points: it uncoupled rowing organizations from steering organizations, so each could focus on its primary mission; it gave rowing organizations control over most of their own decisions, so they could make the changes necessary to improve their operations; and it created consequences for their performance, so they would have incentives to improve.

These new dynamics unleashed tremendous changes within many agencies. The basic tasks of writing the framework document, corporate plan, and business plan quickly forced into the open many of the problems that had to be dealt with. They forced agencies to define their missions, objectives, and performance targets. "Before Next Steps," explains Treasury official Mark Perfect, "the Department of Transport could say convincingly that it was far too complicated to define outputs for all of what it did. The agencies can't say that."

Agencies improved at varying speeds—some rapidly, some slowly. But overall, they managed to hit 75 percent of their performance targets in the early years. They have gradually raised many of these targets, but by 1995 they were hitting 83 percent. To improve their performance, agencies have used almost every tool in the reinventor's kit: contracting out, public versus private competition, accrual accounting, performance bonuses, group bonuses, total quality management, customer surveys, business process reengineering, internal markets, marketing to new customers, credit card payments, "one-stop" offices, and on and on.

The Vehicle Inspectorate, the first agency created under Next Steps, quickly opened offices on Saturdays and Sundays, for example. It introduced a series of new services, contracted out some old ones, removed a layer of management, and established group performance bonuses keyed to overall efficiency increases. In its first three years it reported operating cost efficiency increases of 4.5, 4.1, and 3.6 percent—triggering bonuses of up to £213 per employee. (Operating costs in the U.K. are known as "running costs"; they include all payroll, overhead, rent, and other operating expenses, but not direct program costs such as benefits paid to customers.)

The Information Technology Services Agency in the Department of Social Security set up customer account managers for all its customers, developed service agreements spelling out what it would deliver at what price, launched annual customer surveys, and contracted with private firms to supply virtually all of its information technology services. In its first five years it reported running-cost efficiency increases of 5.5, 4.5, 16.2, 30, and 17.4 percent.

The Employment Service, one of the largest executive agencies, began measuring performance and publishing comparative data about each of its nine regions, to force improvement. Later it pushed the comparisons down to the local office level; each now displays its performance record and the records of up to six neighboring offices. At the same time, Chief Executive Michael Fogden gave his regions great flexibility. Many have cut waiting times dramatically. Most have changed the look and layout of their offices, putting in carpeting, bringing in plants, having employees wear name tags, and getting rid of glass barriers. The entire agency has eliminated a layer of management and restructured its personnel system, including pay, grading, and recruitment. Fogden has instituted regular customer surveys, customer panels, and customer service standards. The surveys show general improvement, while other indicators show a 40 percent increase in job placements with no new resources, gradual improvements in the accuracy of benefit payments, and 2 percent annual increases in running-cost efficiency.

Some departments were reluctant to give the agencies the freedom they needed to maximize performance, according to a 1994 review of the agency process. This created a tug-of-war between departments and agencies. But the agencies' record of achievement gradually convinced the Treasury Department to give them enormous flexibility on budget and personnel matters, which resolved their most pressing problems. Once convinced that agencies would not overspend their budgets, Treasury gave them (and all government departments) control over their own budgets, pay structures, bargaining, and personnel grading systems for all but the most senior civil servants. It consolidated a stack of thick volumes into one book of essential personnel rules.

Treasury also allowed agencies to carry over any unspent funds into the next year. The trade-off was a four-year spending freeze on running costs, requiring agencies to generate any pay increases or inflation adjustments out of their own savings—their "efficiency dividend." In 1994–1995, the 80-plus agencies in existence decreased their running costs by an average of 4.7 percent. The fiscal squeeze contributed to a 15 percent reduction in the size of the civil service between 1988 and 1996.

Overall, Next Steps is widely viewed as a resounding success. In November 1994, Parliament's Treasury and Civil Service Committee called it "the single most successful Civil Service reform programme of recent decades." The unions have not opposed it, and as early as 1991 the Labor Party announced it would keep Next Steps in place if it won power.

Market Testing: Increasing the Consequences for Performance

While pleased with the initial improvements the Next Steps agencies offered, Thatcher and her advisors wanted more. They had watched privatization produce sudden, quantum leaps in productivity. Their initial experiments with competitive contracting, at both the national and local levels, had also yielded large savings. They wanted to inject the sense of urgency created by privatization and competition into the agencies—an urgency far greater than they could achieve with performance contracts and bonuses. They decided they needed a new strategy.

The result was a white paper called "Competing for Quality." Actually published in 1991, after John Major succeeded Thatcher as prime minister, it announced a series of decisions to inject more competition into public service delivery. First, it required that agencies be reviewed every time their framework documents expired. Every three years (now every five years), departments put agencies on trial for their lives. Using what they call a "prior options review," they examine each agency's function and performance to see if the entire agency or pieces of it should be abolished or sold. If they decide to keep an agency alive, the department tells it how much of its work it must competitively bid—a process called "market testing." The agency can ask for private sector bids only, or it can let its units bid against private companies for the work.

The white paper actually covered all government activities, not just executive agencies. It ordered local governments to competitively bid (public versus private) many white-collar services. (In 1988 Thatcher had required them to competitively bid more blue-collar services.) It required departments to bring in private sector help in analyzing the most promising areas for privatization and contracting, and it gave them an incentive to privatize by allowing them to keep any savings achieved. It offered no job guarantees to civil servants, effectively ending their job-for-life tenure. It did, however, promise that if agencies lost work, "every effort will be made to deploy staff elsewhere within the department. The contractor will be encouraged to re-employ staff."

Within the first five years, prior options reviews resulted in decisions to privatize more than a dozen executive agencies. In September 1995, the government reported that it had also conducted hundreds of market tests, covering £2.6 billion of services (about $4.3 billion) and resulting in annual savings of more than £500 million (about $815 million).

The pressure of competition has driven rapid change inside public organizations. Where public and private providers have competed head-to-head, public providers have won twice as many contracts (although the private sector has won larger contracts, on average). Regardless of who wins, savings are averaging 21 percent.

The Citizen's Charter:
Making the Customer Powerful

Even their advocates admit that while Next Steps and market testing created internal management improvements and heightened efficiency, they did much less to improve effectiveness—the *quality* of public services. These strategies pushed agencies to improve their performance *in the eyes of the government,* and the Conservative government was obsessed with efficiency. But the public cared about far more than efficiency. Citizens wanted public services to be effective: they wanted the subways and commuter trains to run on time, the mail to arrive in one day, and their children to receive a quality education.

To force agencies to look beyond efficiency—to produce quality services for their customers—the government needed a new strategy. It needed to make agencies directly accountable to their customers. The answer was John Major's favorite reform, the Citizen's Charter.

Major was the rare Conservative leader who had grown up working-class, experiencing firsthand the shoddy quality of public services. As one aide put it, he knew too well the attitude of many local councils toward citizens: "We know what you want, and this is what you're going to get, and you're going to like it."

Major launched his new strategy in July 1991. It was a typical political initiative, rushed out by a politician intent on making a point with the electorate before the next election, which was a year away. Diana Goldsworthy, a Next Steps team member who became deputy director of the Citizen's Charter unit, tells the story:

> *The Charter was launched precisely at the point when managers needed to do something about the question of quality. As we set these agencies up, they started talking about "customers" and "customer service." To start with we used the words very loosely. Then people began to say, "Well, what is in it for the customer? What gets better? What are we actually saying about quality of service?"*
>
> *When we looked at that question, we found we had no language to describe quality, no currency. What's more, we didn't have a*

sponsor for quality. Who was it that was saying, "You can't launch this agency unless the service gets better"? There was nobody saying that. In fact, I've still got some overheads from a seminar that we invited a consultant to do with us, to tackle this question of quality. Quite literally, as we were finishing the seminar, we got this note from them saying, "The prime minister has decided he wishes to launch a public service initiative called Citizen's Charter." We all said, "What does this mean?" And they said, "You work it out." Almost literally, we said, "Right, let's go. Now we've got political will as well as managerial need."

The basic approach they developed was elegant. All public organizations—national and local—would establish customer service standards, created with input from customers, and promise to meet them. (For example, "90 percent of trains should arrive within 10 minutes of the scheduled time," or "When you telephone a Jobcentre your call should be answered within 30 seconds.") They would be encouraged to offer redress if they failed to meet their standards— British Rail would offer discounts on commuter passes, for instance. They would set up systems to deal with customer complaints. And the government would require audits and inspections and publish comparative performance tables on local services, schools, and health services. If a public organization succeeded in meeting nine charter criteria— including customer choice, service quality standards, independent validation of performance, and continuous improvement in both quality and customer satisfaction—it could apply to use the "Charter Mark," a new symbol of public sector quality. But every three years it had to reapply, and to win again it had to demonstrate continued improvement.

Despite its conceptual elegance, Major's initiative got off to a horrible start. He announced it with great fanfare, but the white paper had no actual charters in it—only examples of what charters might say. When agencies and departments began to publish charters, most were long on general promises—"We will deliver prompt and courteous service"—but short on specific commitments, and shorter still on redress. They had no *teeth.*

With a name like "the Citizen's Charter," people also expected a Magna Carta, a document giving certain rights to the public. When the media discovered it was more about waiting times and how quickly public servants would answer the phone, there was a great feeling of disappointment. As one reformer put it, "You promised us a revolution, and we got a hotline?"

Because the Charter was so closely identified with the prime minister, the press and politicians paid close attention—and did not hesitate to express their cynicism. The Labor Party took every opportunity to ridicule the idea.

It took several years to overcome the initial black eye. But by 1995, the media were beginning to treat the charter idea with grudging respect. It had led, after all, to comparative performance tables on public schools, hospitals, and local services, which were so popular they consumed pages in the newspapers every time they were published. There were 40 national charters—some of which had been rewritten at least once to strengthen them—and hundreds of charters published by local authorities, hospitals, general practice medical groups, police departments, and schools.

Some organizations had used their service standards to drive very visible improvements in service.

- The National Health Service had lowered waiting times that had once been as long as two hours to a maximum of 30 minutes. It had also cut waiting times for elective surgery. In March 1990, for instance, more than 200,000 patients had been waiting more than a year for hospital admission; by March 1995 the number was down to 32,000.

- British Rail had improved service on many lines. On one heavily used commuter line in the London area, known as the "Misery Line," it raised the percentage of trains arriving within ten minutes of their scheduled time from 78 percent in 1991 to 88 percent by the end of 1994. In 1993–1994, British Rail had to pay £4.7 million in compensation to passengers and £2.4 million in discounts to season ticket holders (excluding strike compensation); in 1994–1995 BR got the numbers down to £3.5 million and £0.2 million.

- The Passport Office had lowered the time it took to get a passport from up to 95 days to a maximum of 15 working days.

By early 1996, the London Underground (the subway system) had met its standards and revised them upward three times. More than

Excerpts from the Patient's Charter

■ "When you go to an outpatient clinic you can expect to be given a specific appointment time and be seen within 30 minutes of that time."

■ "If you call an emergency ambulance, you can expect it to arrive within 14 minutes in an urban area, or 19 minutes in a rural area."

■ "If you go to an accident and emergency department you can expect to be seen immediately and have your need for treatment assessed." If you are admitted, you will be given a bed within two hours.

Excerpts from the Passenger's Charter

■ "If you are delayed for more than an hour on any leg of your rail journey, we will normally offer vouchers to the value of 20 percent or more of the price paid for that journey."

■ "If, over the last year, your train service didn't meet its punctuality or reliability targets, British Rail will offer you a discount when you renew your season ticket." [Typical punctuality and reliability targets: that 90 percent of trains should arrive within 10 minutes of the scheduled time and that 99 percent of scheduled trains should run.]

■ "If on average over the previous 12 months *either* punctuality has been more than three percentage points below target *or* reliability has been more than one percentage point below target we will give a discount of 5 percent."

■ "If both punctuality and reliability were below those thresholds, we will give a discount of 10 percent."

■ "Our standard for ticket office service is that you should not have to wait more than five minutes at any time. Outside the busy periods we aim to serve you within three minutes."

■ As the railways are privatized, the new railway companies will have to produce their own charters. Compensation payments will be at least as good as those in British Rail's current charter.

400 public organizations had won the right to display the Charter Mark. But the Charter was still only beginning to tap its potential. Like the competition spurred by market testing, the Citizen's Charter will never stop pushing public organizations to improve. "This is the thing that I think is so interesting about the Charter," says Diana Goldsworthy:

> *Imagine getting a politician to sign up to do something which invites the public to raise their expectations and never be satisfied. Because you're never going to be able to turn around and say, "We've done it." The public will always want better service.*

WHAT A DIFFERENCE A STRATEGY MAKES

Margaret Thatcher did not start out with a full-blown strategy to reinvent government. She came into office determined to make it smaller, privatize many functions, and force the bureaucrats to be more efficient. But unlike her counterpart in the U.S., Ronald Reagan, she learned from the failure of her "jam the bureaucrats" approach. She also had more time in office, and in her third term, she began to apply a consistent philosophy of extending choice and competition to public services and decentralizing authority so providers had the flexibility to respond to their customers' needs.

Thatcher had a team of advisors she trusted, who came to understand the real problems that lay behind public sector performance. In her ninth year in office they articulated a set of systemic changes that applied her philosophy to core government functions. It took them a long time to get there, and they made many mistakes along the way. There are still internal consistencies in some of their strategies. They embraced decentralization, for instance, while using top-down orders to dictate how local governments work—a practice that sowed cynicism at the local level and created the potential for political backlash. Still, they managed to find and use a series of key levers:

- privatization of functions better performed by businesses operating in competitive markets;
- uncoupling steering and rowing;
- performance contracts;

- decentralization of authority to units responsible for work;
- public-private competition; and
- accountability to customers through choice, customer service standards, and customer redress.

In our research, we have found these same levers used again and again: in the U.S., in the U.K., in Australia, in New Zealand, and in Canada. We have found them at all levels: national, state, provincial, and local. Why? Because these are the levers that change the framework within which organizations and people work. "It is usually not possible to command large organizations to make painful changes in long-settled routines," explains Ted Kolderie, one of the reformers who brought public school choice to America. "It is possible, however, to redesign the institutional arrangement in which they operate, so that they come to perceive these changes as necessary and desirable, in their own interest."

Business professors Michael Beer, Russell Eisenstat, and Bert Spector made the same point in a 1990 *Harvard Business Review* article titled "Why Change Programs Don't Produce Change":

> *Most change programs don't work because they are guided by a theory of change that is fundamentally flawed. According to this model, change is like a conversion experience. Once people "get religion," changes in their behavior will surely follow. . . . In fact, individual behavior is powerfully shaped by the organizational roles people play. The most effective way to change behavior, therefore, is to put people into a new organizational context, which imposes new roles, responsibilities and relationships on them.*

Dan Loritz, one of Kolderie's co-conspirators for public school choice in Minnesota, uses an agricultural analogy. "A farmer goes out and spends a lot of time making sure that the fields are just right, gets all of the weeds out, plants the corn with great care, puts enough herbicides on it to make sure that there aren't any weeds, and hopes that there's enough water," he says. "And if everything is right, the corn grows all by itself."

Reinventors should think like farmers, Loritz argues. If they create the right conditions, the results will follow.

Rewriting the Genetic Code

To extend the agricultural metaphor, think of public systems as organisms: complex, adaptive systems that live, grow, change over time, and die. Organisms are shaped by their DNA: the coded instructions that determine who and what they are. DNA provides the most basic, most powerful instructions for developing an entity's enduring capacities and behaviors. Change an organism's DNA and new capacities and behaviors emerge; change enough of the DNA and a different kind of organism evolves. Usually organisms change very slowly, as their DNA randomly mutates and some of these mutations make them more successful in their environments.

The same is true for public systems: normally they evolve very slowly. Bureaucratic public systems were designed to be stable. But we have reached a point in history where this stability is counterproductive. In today's fast-changing, globally competitive information age, systems that cannot change are doomed to failure. They are like the dinosaurs, which could not evolve fast enough to survive when their environment changed.

In this situation, the solution is genetic engineering: change the system's DNA. Our research tells us that the most fundamental pieces of public sector DNA are those we have discussed in our story of British reinvention—a system's purpose, its incentives, its accountability systems, its power structure—and one other we have not yet discussed, its culture. Successful reinventors have all stumbled across the same basic insights: that underneath the complexity of government systems there are a few fundamental levers that make public institutions work the way they do; that these levers were set long ago to create bureaucratic patterns of thinking and behavior; and that changing the levers—rewriting the genetic code—triggers change that cascades throughout the system.

There are many ways to categorize these fundamental levers of change. We have grouped them into five basic strategies, each of which includes several distinct approaches and many tools. For each lever, we have designated a strategy. And to help people remember the strategies, we have given each one a label that begins with the letter *C*.

The Five C's

Lever	Strategy	Approaches
Purpose	Core Strategy	Clarity of Purpose Clarity of Role Clarity of Direction
Incentives	Consequences Strategy	Managed Competition Enterprise Management Performance Management
Accountability	Customer Strategy	Customer Choice Competitive Choice Customer Quality Assurance
Power	Control Strategy	Organizational Empowerment Employee Empowerment Community Empowerment
Culture	Culture Strategy	Breaking Habits Touching Hearts Winning Minds

The Core Strategy

The first critical piece of DNA determines the *purpose* of public systems and organizations. If an organization is unclear about its purpose—or has been given multiple and conflicting purposes—it cannot achieve high performance. As Yogi Berra is reputed to have said, "If you don't know where you're going, then any road will take you someplace else."

We call the strategy that clarifies purpose the *core* strategy, because it deals with the core function of government: the steering function. While the other four strategies focus more on improving rowing, the core strategy is primarily about improving steering. It eliminates functions that no longer serve a valid public purpose or that can be better done by the private sector or another level of government. It uncouples steering from rowing (and service from compliance), so each organization can focus on one purpose. And it improves government's ability to steer by creating new mechanisms to define goals and strategies. (For more, see chapter 4.)

In the U.K. for example, Margaret Thatcher's first effective strategy was privatization of functions that were better left to the private sector. The Next Steps initiative then uncoupled steering and rowing, helping departments focus on policy and direction and agencies focus on service delivery or compliance.

The Consequences Strategy

The second key piece of DNA determines the *incentives* built into public systems. Bureaucratic DNA gives employees powerful incentives to follow the rules and keep their heads down. Innovation can only bring trouble; the status quo brings steady rewards. Employees are paid the same regardless of the results they produce. And most organizations are monopolies—or near-monopolies—that are insulated from their failures. Unlike private firms, they do not lose revenues or go out of business if the competition does a better job.

Reinventors rewrite the genetic code to change these incentives, by creating *consequences* for performance. When appropriate, they put public organizations into the marketplace and make them dependent on their customers for their revenues. When that is not appropriate, they use contracting to create competition between public and private organizations (or public and public organizations), as the British did through market testing and compulsory competitive tendering. When neither is appropriate, they simply measure performance and create consequences (both positive and negative), as the British did with their Next Steps agencies. Markets and competition create much stronger incentives and therefore greater performance improvements, but not all public activities can be put into competitive markets or competitive bidding. (For more, see chapter 5.)

The Customer Strategy

The next fundamental piece of system DNA focuses primarily on *accountability*: specifically, to whom are the organizations accountable? (To be precise, all five strategies touch on the issue of account-ability. The core strategy defines *what* an organization is accountable for; the consequences strategy determines *how* it will be held account-able; the control strategy affects *who* will be accountable; and the culture strategy helps employees internalize their accountability. But by making organizations accountable to their customers, the customer strategy deals most powerfully with the issue of accountability.)

Most public entities are accountable to elected officials, who create them, determine their functions, and fund them. Because these officials are under constant pressure to respond to the demands of interest groups, they often care more about where public resources are spent than about the results they purchase.

In response to widespread abuses by politicians, bureaucratic reformers long ago established a professional civil service to insulate the management of departments from political influence. Managers and employees gradually became accountable for following the rules of the civil service. Hence managers are held most tightly accountable for following these rules and for spending their funds as appropriated by elected officials. Rarely is anyone held accountable for the results.

The *customer* strategy breaks this pattern by shifting some of the accountability to customers. It gives customers choices of service delivery organizations and sets customer service standards those organizations must meet. In the U.K., Major's Citizen's Charter put the customer strategy into play.

Creating accountability to the customer increases the pressure on public organizations to improve their results, not just to manage their resources. It creates information—customer satisfaction with specific government services and results—that is difficult for elected officials, public managers, and employees to ignore. And it gives public organi-zations the right target to shoot at: increased customer satisfaction.

This does not mean that public organizations are no longer account-able to their elected representatives; it means they often have dual accountability. As we explain in chapter 6, this works best when elected officials align these dual accountabilities by stating their goals in terms of customer satisfaction and holding organizations accountable for meeting customers' needs.

Nor does the customer strategy suggest that the role of customer supplants that of citizen, as some critics argue. Both roles are impor-tant. Citizens vote, influencing the policies set by their representatives.

Public organizations then implement those policies. But in bureaucratic systems, citizens have no practical way to hold those organizations accountable for their performance—or even to give them feedback on their performance. The customer strategy puts them in the feedback loop.

The Control Strategy

The fourth critical chunk of DNA determines where decision-making *power* lies. In bureaucratic systems, most of the power remains near the top of the hierarchy. In democracies, power first flows from citizens to elected officials; then from elected officials to central "staff" agencies such as budget and personnel offices; finally from those central control agencies down to agency ("line") managers. Typically, elected officials keep as much power as possible in their own hands, and the central control agencies guard their power even more jealously. Line managers find their options limited and their flexibility constrained by detailed budget instructions, personnel rules, procurement systems, auditing practices, and the like. Their employees have almost *no power* to make decisions. As a result, government organizations respond to new orders rather than to changing situations or customers' needs.

The control strategy pushes significant decision-making power down through the hierarchy, and at times out to the community. It shifts the form of control used from detailed rules and hierarchical commands to shared missions and systems that create accountability for performance. It empowers organizations by loosening the grip of the central control agencies—as the U.K.'s Treasury Department did in response to the success of the Next Steps agencies. It empowers employees by pushing authority to make decisions, respond to customers, and solve problems down to those with frontline knowledge—as some executive agencies have. Some reinventors use a third approach: they shift control from public organizations to the community, empowering community members and organizations to solve their own problems and run their own institutions. Margaret Thatcher did this when she sold 1.25 million public housing units to tenants and gave control over schools to community-based governing bodies. (For more, see chapter 7.)

The Culture Strategy

Finally, the last critical piece of DNA determines the *culture* of public organizations: the values, norms, attitudes, and expectations of employees. Culture is shaped powerfully by the rest of the DNA: by an organization's purpose, its incentives, its accountability system, and its power structure. Change these and the culture will change. But culture does not always change just as its leaders would wish it to. At times it will harden into resistance and resentment. Often it will change too slowly to satisfy customers and policy makers. Hence we have found that virtually every organization that has used the other four C's has eventually decided it needed a deliberate campaign to rewrite the genetic code that shaped its culture. We have not discussed these efforts in the U.K., but we found them in every organization we visited.

Bureaucratic systems use detailed specifications—functional units, procedural rules, and job descriptions—to mold what employees do. They make initiative risky. As employees become habituated to these conditions, they become carriers of the culture. They become reactive, dependent, fearful of taking too much initiative themselves. In this way, bureaucratic DNA creates cultures of fear, blame, and defensiveness.

Reinventors use three approaches to reshape the culture; they mold the organization's habits, hearts, and minds. They develop new habits by giving people new experiences—new kinds of work and interactions with new people. They reinforce these new behaviors by helping people shift their emotional commitments: their hopes, fears, and dreams. And they support this new emotional covenant by building a shared vision of the future, a new mental model of where the organization is going and how it will get there. (For more, see chapter 8.)

Increasing Your Leverage

Most reinventors start with just one or two strategies in mind. Inevitably, they discover the need for another, then another, until they are using all five. Why? Because using only one or two strategies does not give them enough leverage. Any one strategy is to reinvention as rain is to farmers: indispensable but not sufficient. Farmers also need seeds, rich soil, adequate fertilizer, and sunshine. If all five of these elements are aligned with one another, the crops grow.

One way to put multiple strategies into play is to use what we call "metatools." They are like MIRVs—missiles that deploy multiple warheads. For example, the Next Steps initiative combined the core, control, and consequences strategies. School choice systems in which money follows the child combine customer and consequences. Total quality management and business process reengineering deploy elements of the customer, control, and often culture strategies. (For more on metatools, see chapter 9.)

Indeed, you will find that the five strategies often overlap. Some tools, like customer councils or performance management systems, implement only one strategy. But just as many involve multiple strategies. It is only natural, for example, to combine the uncoupling of steering and rowing (core) with a performance contract (consequences) and more flexibility for rowing organizations (control)—as the British did. (We have dubbed this metatool, which we will discuss further in chapter 4, a "flexible performance framework.") Similarly, it is only natural to combine customer service standards (customer) with rewards and penalties for organizations that succeed or fail to meet those standards (consequences).

It is so natural to combine two or three strategies in one tool, in fact, that the boundaries between strategies can get very blurry. We have separated the strategies to give you a clear conceptual framework you can use to think through possible strategies, approaches, and tools. In our experience, reinventors have found a clear map of the basic levers immensely helpful. It makes them aware of all their options and helps them fill in their blind spots. In practice, however, multiple strategies are often joined at the hip—as they must be to yield maximum power.

But Will the Five C's Work Here?

Some of you may be saying to yourselves, "This all sounds logical, but it will never work here. My city (or county, or province, or country) is different." Your government may not be *ready* to reinvent, but when it is, rest assured, these strategies will apply. They work in small cities and large nations, in parliamentary systems and presidential systems, in strong mayor cities and council-manager cities. Purpose, incentives, accountability, power, and culture are the fundamental DNA of every public system we have examined.

The appropriate *tactics* differ in different political systems. In a Westminster parliamentary system like that of the British, Australians, New Zealanders, and Canadians, the party (or coalition of parties) with a majority in Parliament also leads the executive branch. In American terms, it is as if only one house of Congress really matters, its majority leader is president, and its leadership forms the cabinet. Therefore parliamentary systems avoid the squabbles between the executive and legislative branches that so often paralyze American governments. Ministers can decide on a course of action and make it happen— quickly.

This has an enormous impact on the tactics reinventors choose, how fast they go, and how much they take on. It means they must spend less time organizing political support for their reforms than their American counterparts. And it means they tend to start in different places than Americans do: they can often go straight at large-scale systemic reform, using the powerful but controversial core and consequences strategies. American reinventors, in contrast, often start with the "softer" strategies of control and culture to avoid political disputes.

Similarly, the council-manager form of local government creates more separation between elected officials and managers than the strong mayor form. This makes it easier for elected officials to focus on policy and let managers handle administration. Nonpartisan elections and rational political climates also make it easier to reinvent, because political distrust and warfare between parties interferes less. In nonpartisan, council-manager environments, local governments tend to go straight at reinvention, changing basic systems and using all the strategies—much like their counterparts in parliamentary governments. In highly partisan, strong-mayor cities, reinventors more often try to stay out of the political limelight, using the less controversial strategies of control and culture and reinventing at a slower pace.

Different kinds of organizations require different approaches as well. There are four basic types of public organizations: policy, regulatory, service, and compliance. Service organizations deliver services. Policy organizations make policy decisions. Regulatory organizations set rules, and compliance organizations enforce them. (There is a fine line between these last two, and many organizations perform both functions. But as we will argue in chapter 4, it is usually best to separate them.) Regulatory organizations are actually a subset of policy organizations, because their job is to steer society by setting the rules, while compliance organizations row the boats. As some put it, service organizations deliver services, while compliance organizations deliver obligations.

These distinctions are important, because reinventors who work at the organization level must apply the five strategies differently in different types of organizations. This can be tricky, since many organizations perform a mix of functions. Often they combine policy and service functions, or regulatory and compliance functions. Many service organizations, from schools to public housing developments, must also win compliance with standards of behavior. Police departments are compliance organizations, but they perform services as well: guiding traffic around construction sites; performing crowd control at concerts; running youth sports programs. Many social benefit agencies, such as employment services and welfare offices, deliver services,

A Typology of Government Organizations

Organization Type	Example
Policy	Planning Office; School Board
Regulatory	Federal Communications Commission Securities and Exchange Commission
Service Delivery	
External Customers	Public Works Department School District
Internal Customers	Data Processing Office Maintenance Department
Compliance	
External Compliers	Police Department; Occupational Safety and Health Administration
Internal Compliers	Auditors; Inspectors General

write regulations, and enforce compliance with their rules. Tax collection agencies are in the compliance business, but they typically offer services such as information hot lines. And many policy advice organizations are actually service rather than policy organizations, because they provide services to policy makers, rather than making policy decisions themselves.

To make matters more complex, many organizations of one kind have units of another within them. Environmental regulatory and compliance agencies have personnel offices that provide services within them. Service organizations house compliance organizations, such as auditors' offices, within them. Finally, while most public organizations serve "external customers," such as the general public or a particular community, others serve "internal customers"—other government units.

The five strategies play out quite differently in policy and compliance organizations than they do in service organizations. In compliance agencies, for instance, the customer strategy is more complex. These agencies' primary customers are the public at large, represented by elected executives and legislators. But "compliers"—taxpayers, drivers, polluters—are also important. Then there are noncompliers: people and organizations that break the law, don't pay the taxes they owe, or ignore environmental regulations. Compliance organizations have to pay attention to all three categories.

Similarly, the control strategy plays out differently in compliance organizations. Because some compliance organizations, such as the police and courts, are normally required to treat every complier the same—or at least to treat similar classes of compliers equally—there are limits to how much flexibility they can allow their employees.

We will address these issues more fully as we discuss each of the strategies and approaches. For now, suffice it to say that reinvention applies to all types of organizations. Some people in regulatory and compliance organizations argue that reinvention is only about policy and service delivery, but this is at best an excuse for inaction.

None of these differences changes the basic levers that create fundamental change. In all public organizations and systems, the difference between isolated innovations and coherent reinvention is spelled s-t-r-a-t-e-g-y. If you want a qualitatively different kind of public system or organization, you must rewrite the genetic code. You can generate a series of innovations without using the five C's, but you cannot create a continuously improving, self-renewing system. Consider this the first rule of reinvention: *No new DNA, no transformation.*

– 2 –

LEVELS OF THE GAME: TARGETING THE STRATEGIES

Government is big, complex, and messy. It employs millions of people and spends trillions of dollars every year. It is heavily layered, with thousands of overlapping political jurisdictions and public institutions. It is a churning nexus of politicians, public servants, and citizens, who compete, conspire, and collaborate in endlessly re-forming combinations.

If you want to change performance in this complex system, we have argued, you need leverage. The first way to increase your leverage is to use the five strategies. The second is to aim them at the best possible target.

You can unleash the five strategies at any of five levels within a public system: its governing system, its administrative systems, its organizations, its work processes, or its people. The higher the level, the higher the leverage.

In the United Kingdom, Margaret Thatcher and John Major targeted the highest level, the basic systems within which public organizations work: the central government system of departments and agencies, the National Health Service, the local government system, and the education system. (For the latter, see pp. 174–175.) We call these "governing systems." Change the way these systems work—by creating autonomous agencies on performance contracts, for instance—and you force every organization within them to change.

Thatcher's and Major's reforms forced *thousands* of public organizations to reexamine their performance, their relations with their customers—the very way they worked. Next Steps alone rippled into the administrative systems, forcing radical change in budget and personnel rules; into organizations, where managers became responsible for delivering contractually specified outputs; into work processes, which had to be redesigned to meet output targets; and into people, who had to change their habits, hearts, and minds.

The rules by which governing systems operate are aggregated into what people call "administrative systems," "operating systems," or "management systems." The best known are the budget and finance system, the personnel system, the procurement system, and the auditing system. These administrative systems are the means by which the governing system controls its member (or "line") organizations. They tell each organization how it can spend its money, who it can hire, how much it can pay them, and how it can manage them. It is no exaggeration to say that the administrative systems create the straitjacket known as bureaucracy.

For reinventors, there is enormous leverage here as well, for changes in administrative systems ripple outward, changing everything they touch. Indeed, one cannot change a governing system without changing its administrative systems. If the British wanted their Next Steps agencies to work, for instance, they had to change their budget and personnel systems.

The Hierarchy of Leverage

Level	Examples
Governing System	National, State, Provincial, or City Government, Education System, Health Care System, Welfare System
Administrative System	Budget & Finance, Personnel, Procurement, Auditing, Planning
Organization	Municipal Department of Public Works, U.K. Employment Service
Work Processes	Benefit Processing, Permit Processing, Fire Fighting, Complaint Handling
People	Manager, Supervisor, Road Crew, Police Officer

Most managers cannot change the governing system within which they work, nor its administrative systems. This is one of the differences between public organizations and businesses we mentioned in the introduction. Unless they are part of large conglomerates, businesses are not subsets of "governing systems." Therefore, most business organizations control their own administrative systems. In government this is rare. Special authorities and quasi-public organizations often have this luxury, and top managers in cities and counties can change administrative systems, if the elected officials buy in. But most public organizations are nested within much larger governing systems that dictate their administrative systems.

Managers can use the five C's to change their own organizations, however—the next level down the hierarchy of power. They can instill more accountability to customers in their organization, clarify their missions, create consequences for performance, push decision making down to frontline employees, and change the culture. Sometimes they can even get waivers from the administrative systems, allowing their agencies more freedom and creating different incentives. Working at the organization level obviously has less leverage than systems change, because it affects only one organization at a time. But it has more leverage than the next two levels: processes and people.

Thanks to the sudden popularity of total quality management (TQM) and business process reengineering (BPR), people in government are now focusing significant attention on the way work is organized—the processes organizations use to carry out their tasks. These work processes can be changed through continuous small improvements, using TQM, through radical redesign, using BPR, or through other redesign methods. But whatever the method, process improvement will force less reinvention than changes at the systems, administrative systems, or organization levels. Private sector reengineering advocates argue that changing a process will *force* change in organizations and administrative systems. They are correct, in theory. When the Regional Veterans Administration Office in New York City reengineered its work processes, for example, it discovered this. "We started with the work flow and ended up saying that everything has to change," says Regional Director Joe Thompson. "If you don't change the way you compensate and measure performance, if you just try to change work flow, you'll fall short."

Unfortunately, as we have said, in the public sector these administrative systems are often out of the organization's reach. So reengineering a process, as much as it may help quality and productivity, rarely leverages change in administrative systems.

Finally, the least leverage comes from changing the people in an organization. The basic problem with government today is not its people, but its DNA. We will never fix our governments just by getting "better" people, because good people cannot make bad systems work unless they change those systems. Many of the most learned people we know in government work for New York City or the U.S. federal government—two of the worst performing governments we know. In contrast, when we visit places like Hampton, Virginia, Phoenix, Arizona, and Sunnyvale, California, we find people with fewer fancy degrees and less impressive credentials, working in good systems, achieving extraordinary results.

Businesspeople who enter government soon discover this reality. "I imagined this huge resistance by civil servants," says Michelle Hunt, who in 1993 left her management position with Herman Miller, a major furniture manufacturer, to run the U.S. Federal Quality Institute.

I imagined the media depiction of civil servants, and it was all wrong. I thought I was going to come here and I was going to see a bunch of people that didn't want to change, because they were fat and lazy. I thought it was going to be a bunch of cynics who were going to say to me, "Get out of my face." I found the reverse.

I know the vice president says it's about good people caught in bad systems. I think it's worse than that. I think there's institutional slavery and they want to get out. You almost see tears in their eyes, there's so much passion about wanting to get out.

People in government *do* have to change their ideas, attitudes, beliefs, and behavior. That is why organizations need culture strategies. But changes at the people level have less *leverage* than changes at higher levels. Changing peoples' habits, hearts, and minds is retail work; it happens one by one. Rarely does it force changes at other levels. We have occasionally seen powerful change agents, including *Reinventing Government* coauthor Ted Gaebler, leverage culture change back up through the system. But it is very difficult. In contrast, changing governing systems, administrative systems, and organizations forces *many* people to change.

To reinvent your government, you will ultimately have to use the five C's at all five levels. If you change your systems, organizations, and people but leave the work processes alone, or change your systems, organizations, and processes but not the way your people work, think, and feel, you will sentence your organization to ongoing conflict. To reach your destination, you must bring all five levels into alignment.

This is one reason you will need both politicians and public servants to succeed. Few public servants have the power to change governing and administrative systems, but few politicians have the knowledge or familiarity needed to change organizations, processes, and people. To make sure your changes will become permanent, you will even need buy-in from a third key sector: the public. If you try to change governing systems without securing public buy-in, you may find that the next time power changes hands, the new administration throws your changes right out the window.

What you choose to work on, of course, depends not only on where the most leverage lies, but on where you sit. If you are an elected official or a citizen, you will probably push for change at the system level. If you are a manager, however, you may not have the authority to change the system or its administrative systems. So you will work at the organization, process, and people levels. This is where the rubber meets the road, after all. Systems may have more leverage, but systems change only makes a difference if it forces *organizations* to change.

One of the most dramatic reinvention stories we have ever seen was led by managers. They transformed a public organization larger than most Fortune 500 companies. In the process, they used all five reinvention strategies. They proved that managers do not have to wait for the politicians—they don't have to wait for permission before they reinvent. They showed how managers can win exemptions from the most onerous of the system's rules. More important, they demonstrated how managers can use their success to leverage change back up through the higher levels.

REINVENTION AT THE ORGANIZATION LEVEL: THE TACTICAL AIR COMMAND

Readers may recall the Tactical Air Command (TAC) from *Reinventing Government*. In 1991 it won a place of honor in American history with its stunning display of air power in Operation Desert Storm. Television viewers around the world watched its devastating impact up close. For 43 days, in a desert war halfway around the globe, TAC maintained 95 percent of its aircraft as "mission capable"—better than it was expected to do during practice at home. Flying against 15,000 surface-to-air missiles and more than 6,000 antiaircraft guns, it lost only 13 fighters—an average of one shot down every 3,200 combat sorties. While it rained destruction on the enemy, TAC's fighter forces suffered only three deaths.

TAC had not always been so effective. In the late 1970s, only 58 percent of its planes were mission capable on any given day; its pilots were getting only 60 percent of the training time they needed; and seven planes were crashing for every 100,000 hours flown. It got so bad that in 1978 the Air Force chief of staff called in an organization doctor: General W. L. (Bill) Creech.

Creech had a history of turning around floundering Air Force organizations. In three previous commands, he had come to understand the service's basic problem: overcentralized systems were strangling people in red tape. Because so much control rested with central organizations, no one owned the job of producing results.

Creech's initial cure was the control strategy. He wanted people committed to achieving TAC's goals, not to following its rules. He wanted decisions in the hands of people who fixed and flew the planes. So he started to build, in his words, "small teams that integrated different functions, with leadership right at the front line." And he started tearing down the system of centralized, top-down controls.

The key was breaking apart "functional silos"—the pilots in one unit, the mechanics in others, the support staff in others—and building cross-functional teams that were responsible for achieving specific goals. Under the old regime, different mechanics were even in different silos—the electricians in one, the hydraulic specialists in another, the aircraft mechanics in a third. That "required lots of telephone coordination, paperwork, and going to and fro," Creech explains. So he tore down the functional walls, put all flightline maintenance people into teams, cross-trained them, and assigned each team to a squadron. Creech also took the aircraft out of the central pool and gave them to the squadrons. Each squadron—now made up of pilots *and* mechanics—owned 24 planes.

"Each squadron had its own set of goals," says Creech. "Each did its own scheduling, which had been done centrally before. Each made its own decisions and charted its own course." One crew chief—his or her name emblazoned on the plane's nose—was responsible for making each airplane fly.

Creech did this with every specialty he could. He broke up the centralized supply operation, where it took 243 entries on 13 forms, involving 22 people and 16 man hours, to get one part into an F-15. He moved aircraft parts and supply specialists directly to the flightline. Now the supply specialists felt personally responsible for having the part on hand when the mechanics needed it. This cut paperwork by 65 percent and reduced the average time between the order of a part and its delivery from 3.5 hours to *eight minutes*. As Creech later wrote, "The theme was *Fix it now, fix it fast, and fix it right*."

Creech asked frontline teams to eliminate at least half the internal regulations in their areas—and TAC's employees loved it. Then TAC began giving each team information on the costs of its activities. Their "new cost-awareness, alongside their newfound authority over their part of the total system, triggered a stream of value-oriented recommendations on practices to change or abandon," Creech writes. He estimates that one change suggested by a young engine technician—to leave the titanium "turkey feathers" off the engine tailpipe of F-15s—saved $70 million.

Creech understood one of the basic rules of the control strategy: don't eliminate one control system without creating a new one to take its place. As he removed centralized, bureaucratic controls, he replaced them with performance goals and measures, the organization's new guiding hands. He understood that without some form of control, every team might head off in its own direction. TAC distributed the performance data to all employees. That way the squadrons not only knew what they were supposed to accomplish, they knew how well they were doing.

When teams compared their performance with one another's, Creech says, it motivated them to do better.

Accountability for poor performance now was easy to track. It was equally easy to single out those who deserved recognition for stellar performance—both individuals and groups. . . . The peer pressure began working in positive not negative directions, and the multidiscipline teams produced far more effective interaction

*and integration. . . . Where problems did emerge, it was far easier
to find them, and to get them fixed efficiently and rapidly. There
was then no need for the all points bulletins (broad-based
harangues) that were a staple of the centralized approach.*

TAC's personnel system did not allow performance bonuses, so
when it was time to introduce consequences, Creech relied mostly on
psychology. Taking advantage of the natural pride found in teams, he
encouraged competition between squadrons and bases. TAC also began
giving out trophies and holding annual awards banquets to honor the
best squadrons. And Creech rewarded every squadron that achieved its
monthly goals with a three-day weekend.

He also tried the culture strategy, initiating a program for automotive
repair units called "Proud Look," which featured spotless facilities and
special work uniforms for the mechanics. Quality and productivity
soared. So he did the same in all TAC workplaces, launching a campaign to root out physical eyesores and to bring everything up to quality
standards. Fresh coats of paint, immaculate facilities, and special uniforms became commonplace.

By 1983, TAC's productivity had increased 80 percent. Reenlistment
rates had soared. The crash rate was one-third what it had been in 1978.
(According to Creech, this saved more than 100 lives and $1.6 billion
in aircraft during his six years.) Four out of five aircraft that needed
repair were fixed in the same day, compared to one out of five in 1978.
The result: TAC was now capable of generating more than double the
number of attack sorties it had been in 1978.

TAC did this without significant infusions of money or people. And
according to a 1984 analysis TAC commissioned, new aircraft played
only a small role. Most of the improvement was due to Creech's
management changes.

Creating a Culture of Continuous Improvement

One of the problems all reinventors face is leadership succession. In
most examples of successful reinvention we have studied, it has taken a
decade to achieve significant, lasting transformation. (TAC was the
fastest turnaround we have seen; Creech did it in five years.) When the
leaders who are driving reinvention leave before the process is complete, they put everything they have done at risk. If the new leaders do

not understand or buy into the basic reinvention strategies at work, progress often comes to a screeching halt.

Creech managed this problem by personally grooming his successors. He taught a class in leadership philosophy for senior officers, and he picked out those with potential and began moving them into important commands. When he left, he lobbied for them: his next three successors were all his protégés. As a result, the changes Creech made stayed firmly in place. By the late 1980s, the mission capable rate was up to 88 percent, savings from the reduced crash rate amounted to $4.6 billion, and reenlistment rates for first-term employees were up from 25 percent in 1980 to 64 percent.

John Michael Loh, a four-star general and 30-year TAC veteran, took command of TAC in March 1991, a few weeks after the end of the Gulf War. Yet as his officers were still returning from the Gulf, he told them to get ready for big changes. And to emphasize his view, he tore up TAC's mission statement. It might be good enough for one of the best performing government organizations in the world, but it was a barrier to the kind of "continuously renewing" organization Loh wanted TAC to become.

Loh saw that TAC's environment was changing drastically. The Cold War had ended and the U.S. had entered an era of regional threats that might erupt unpredictably. TAC would have to perform numerous functions: combat, peacekeeping, counterterrorism, and drug enforcement. Meanwhile, bases were closing around the world. Becoming a smaller, home-based force meant new problems moving equipment and supplies.

TAC had adapted well to the challenges of Desert Storm. But in the future, it would have to adapt again and again—often quickly and without warning, sometimes to more than one challenge at a time. Loh felt that TAC was not ready for this new, more chaotic world.

Loh chose not to abandon Creech's foundation, but to build on it. TAC would stay decentralized and team-based, and it would keep measuring results and rewarding success. But Loh developed a new culture strategy and a new focus on continuous improvement of work processes. He built both around the metatool of total quality management (TQM). Creech had worked primarily at the organization and process levels—decentralizing control, revamping the structure, and creating consequences. Inheriting a healthy organization, Loh concentrated instead on processes and people.

Loh's vision of quality started with the idea that every TAC employee was part of work processes that had customers. TAC had external customers—the Air Force commanders, the Joint Chiefs of Staff, the president, and Congress. But it also had internal customers, such as a mechanic waiting for a part from the supply line. The needs of these varied customers would define quality standards for the organization.

Using the methodology of TQM, employees would constantly improve processes they used. They would do this in a standardized, highly disciplined way, using scientific methods to identify and analyze problems, test hypothetical solutions, and then apply solutions that worked. Around these methods Loh would build a culture of continuous improvement.

Loh's first task was to make sure that TAC employees bought into his vision. He launched a massive effort to change the hearts and minds of 150,000 people. It began with TAC's mission statement—a beacon that signaled the organization's purpose and values to its employees.

The existing mission statement—"to fly and fight"—didn't fit TAC's new environment. It expressed a purpose that was much too narrow, and it signaled that the organization valued its pilots above its other employees. "We had two standards, two classes of citizens," Loh explains. "If you were on the flying side of our business, you were okay. If you were on the other side, you weren't expected to create, be innovative."

Instead, Loh wanted a mission statement that described a post–Cold War purpose for TAC, valued every employee equally, and committed the organization to continuous improvement. He pulled his top officers together to craft a new mission statement.

The task was complicated by the fact that on June 1, 1992, the Air Force merged TAC with the Strategic Air Command (SAC), to form the Air Combat Command (ACC). The new organization housed two hostile entities. "The SAC guys"—who came from the world of bombers and ICBMs—"looked at me as though I was diphtheria," says Loh. So he took officers from both sides on a three-day retreat.

Together, the nearly 90 top managers hammered out a mission statement for the new ACC. Then Loh told them to take the draft back to their bases and squadrons to check it out with their people. The statement that emerged broadened the fly-and-fight mission, making logistics and maintenance people as important as anyone else. The new mission: "Delivering rapid, decisive air power—Anytime, anywhere." The statement also committed the ACC to "strive for a culture of continuous improvement."

Loh distributed the mission statement far and wide. Then he began building the organization's capacity to practice continuous improvement. To educate all ACC employees, he created a Quality School, built quality into the curriculum of the Airman Leadership School, and launched a Right Start training program to orient new personnel to the quality focus and methods.

Next he sent a cadre of more than 300 Quality School graduates out to advise each of the ACC's bases and squadrons and train other employees. They taught squadrons the same seven-step improvement process. As the training took hold, it led to a rash of improvements. A team in Utah cut by 33 percent the time it took to rearm, refuel, and reservice fighters. A team in Tacoma, Washington, cut by 63 percent the time it took to identify aircraft flying in their area. The ACC's pharmacies, which fill 4.5 million prescriptions a year, reduced their waiting times. (When Walmart wanted to benchmark against the best, it chose the ACC pharmacy at MacDill Air Force Base.) The entire organization shortened the time it took to pay travel vouchers: 95 percent of the time, it now takes less than ten minutes.

To keep the bottom line plainly in view, the ACC updated and expanded the measurement system Creech had built. By 1995 it included more than 150 measures—for all ACC squadrons, not just those with airplanes. "We are a unit of 567 organizations," Loh explains:

> Each one of those 567 squadrons I have out there is an operating unit that has its own resources, its own authority, responsibility, and accountability. Each one of them operates pretty much as an autonomous whole. But they operate under our standards. I hold them accountable for performance. I set performance standards, and I get a lot of input. How they are achieving those standards at the local level is their business. I don't tell them how to do it.

But Loh still felt he had not done enough to reach the ACC's 150,000 people. He wanted to deepen the control strategy: to empower every individual. To do that, he needed to upgrade their skills, to the point where they could function without supervisors, managing their own work. So he created the Bright Flag program, which beefed up individual training and established performance measures for every job, so employees could judge their work.

Finally, Loh decided he needed a way to measure whether people's habits, hearts, and minds were changing. He wanted to know how his employees felt about the organization—and he wanted his managers to know.

The tool he chose was an annual employee survey. Beginning in 1991, every May tens of thousands of employees have voluntarily responded to a 15-minute, 50-item questionnaire, designed to measure changes in the ACC's culture. The results showed significant improvement from 1991 through 1993 in job satisfaction, communication, teamwork and cooperation, support for and understanding of ACC quality principles, freedom to work with a minimum of supervision, and other key indicators. Employees indicated strong agreement (about 5.7 on a 1–7 scale) with statements such as "I know my unit's mission" and "I know how my work contributes to my unit's mission accomplishment."

In 1993 the command began to close bases and cut staffing by 20 percent, a disruptive process. Indicators in all survey areas except leadership (confidence and trust in the leadership's ability to carry out its responsibilities) leveled off or declined slightly. Still, they stayed significantly above 1991 levels.

Overall, the surveys suggest that even with downsizing and restructuring, employees feel good about the organization. "People have had every reason to gripe and complain and bitch about their workplace, their environment, and everything," says Loh. "And yet, the results are just about the opposite. This reinforces my notion that the way to go through significant change is by the adoption of quality principles."

Culture change "is a lot of subtle things, some very gradual," says Jeanie Spence, who joined TAC back when General Creech ran it. She points to one simple example: the fact that participants in top command meetings hand in written feedback at the end of each meeting.

That would have been unheard of in the old culture. . . . Imagine, some of these colonels sitting in the room telling General Loh that he was dominating the meeting, that he was not letting people express their views. . . . General Creech was very progressive, but that was not a part of the Creech culture.

LEVERAGING THE SYSTEM

Generals Creech and Loh proved how much leverage one can generate at the organization, process, and people levels. They also illustrated one of the skills a master reinventor brings to the task: the ability to carve out changes at the level above his or her own.

"You can be a principal catalyst for change—whatever your particular level might be," says Creech. He made sure to keep his direct superior informed on what he was doing, he explains.

> But I also operated on the principle that I had full latitude and empowerment to do anything that made sense to me—so long as it was not specifically ruled out by a regulation. When I ran into any regulation (or policy) that created a partial roadblock, I worked hard to be relieved of it. And in every case I succeeded. If other ways didn't work, I got permission to conduct a special "test."
>
> I've found top leaders much more likely to approve a "test" than they are to grant a priori approval for one part of the organization to be a completely different duckling.

At one point, Creech made sure that Bob Stone, then assistant secretary of defense for installations, and his deputy, Doug Farbrother, visited Langley Air Force Base, TAC headquarters. Stone and Farbrother credit those visits with completely changing their management paradigms. They became the leading crusaders for decentralization and deregulation within the Department of Defense, and Creech helped them launch a "test" called the Model Installations Program. It gave 40 base commanders tremendous freedom to manage the way they saw fit, encouraging them to ask for waivers when regulations got in their way. After two years of success, Deputy Secretary of Defense William Howard Taft IV issued a memorandum applying the Model Installation approach to every defense installation. (See *Reinventing Government*, pp. 8–11 and 132–135.) While Creech went on to author a marvelous management book, *The Five Pillars of TQM*, Stone went on to become director of Vice President Gore's reinventing government initiative, the National Performance Review. Within his first two months on the job, he took Gore to Langley Air Force Base to see a reinvented organization for himself.

Creech's experience proves how much an organizational leader can do to carve out flexibilities from the system in which he works. As Creech says, it is often just a matter of guts:

At an impromptu get-together of wing commanders, several in the group I was sitting with were complaining about their lack of leadership latitude. I said I didn't feel that way at all—that I had all the maneuvering room needed—and I asked them to give me some examples. So they told me about things they perceived they couldn't do. I was doing all those things. . . . My point is, a lot of the barriers to change are to be found in the minds of those who could carry it out, if only they would.

General Loh had the same attitude. Federal managers complain bitterly about the inspectors general, for example. Part of the auditing system, each IG's office has hundreds of auditors and inspectors—many of them former law enforcement people—who comb through the organization looking for wrongdoing. Created by Congress in the late 1970s, they are a legacy of the Watergate era. Unfortunately, they operate as an enormous barrier to innovation, because when reinventors try new things they often have to bend a few rules. The IGs typically slap their wrists, regardless of how petty the infraction or how silly the rule. When Vice President Gore held town meetings about reinvention in each department in 1993, he heard more bitter complaints about the IGs than about any other problem.

Departmental managers have no authority over their inspectors general. But Loh didn't let that stop him. He convinced the ACC inspector general to take on a new role: to help squadrons learn from one another by teaching best practices. When IG teams visit squadrons, they measure compliance required by law—for example, compliance with environmental laws, nuclear safety regulations, and flight safety requirements. But they now also share information about what other squadrons are doing well and help squadrons learn how to assess their own processes. Slowly the ACC has begun turning its old auditing system into part of a new learning system.

Recode Before You Reorganize

We trained hard, but every time we were beginning to form up into teams, we would be reorganized. I was to learn later in life that we tend to meet any new situation by reorganizing . . . and a wonderful method it can be for creating the illusion of progress while producing inefficiency and demoralization.
—Petronius, A.D. 66

The TAC/ACC story also illustrates the relationship between what we call strategy and organizational structure. Many public leaders instinctively reorganize when they want to improve performance. They reshuffle the organizational boxes—consolidating agencies and functions, eliminating duplication, and streamlining the organizational chart. The newspapers duly report that the public's leaders are making big changes, but improved performance rarely follows.

Why? Because organizational structure is not a fundamental lever of change. Structure is dictated by the organizational DNA of purpose, incentives, accountability, power, and culture—not the other way around. When the genetic code is set to create stable bureaucracies, bureaucratic structures gradually evolve to fit the underlying DNA. Changing those structures without changing the DNA is foolhardy. It is like asking a right-handed person to pitch left-handed: the DNA keeps signaling that the right hand works better.

The Canadians copied the British Next Steps initiative by turning about 15 organizations into special operating agencies (SOAs), for instance. But they failed to change the SOAs' accountability, incentives, or power in any fundamental way. The result: their performance didn't change much. The DNA kept signaling the need for bureaucratic behavior. Frustrated by the halfhearted reform, SOA managers argued that they needed the sweeping flexibilities granted Next Steps agencies. One civil servant told Canadian academic Donald Savoie, "SOA no longer stands for Special Operating Agencies; it stands for Screwed Once Again."

We are not saying that structure is unimportant. It is *very* important. Bureaucratic structures are a huge barrier to reinventing government. At some point in the process of change it becomes imperative to change the structure. To make change last, reinventors must embed the new DNA in the organizational structure, just as they must embed it in the administrative systems, the work processes, and the people. But structural change is useful only *in tandem with* strategies to change the DNA. As management sage Peter Drucker says, structure is important, but "structure has to follow strategy."

Yet the "reorg" remains enormously popular with officials who want to create the impression of change, because it is much easier to reorganize than to recode. The TAC/ACC story shows how to accommodate this impulse. In any reorganization, *change the DNA first*. When Creech took apart the centralized functional silos of maintenance, supply, purchasing, and scheduling, he moved these functions into frontline teams working directly for their primary customers, the pilots. He empowered these teams to make their own decisions. And he measured and compared their performance. He used the control, consequences, and customer strategies. This is how restructuring should be done: it should create a new structure that flows logically from the new DNA.

Select Strategies Before You Select Tools

Finally, the TAC/ACC story illustrates the proper relationship between strategies and tools. Let us first be clear about our definitions. By strategies, we mean change efforts that rewrite the genetic code. By tools, we mean readily available practices that can be applied to implement those strategies. Making public organizations more accountable to their customers and empowering their employees to make decisions are strategies. Total quality management and business process reengineering are two tools—among many—that help implement those strategies.

A Tool Kit for Reinventors

In Part II we will briefly describe more than 90 tools reinventors use to implement the five strategies. Unfortunately, we did not have room in this book to provide details about how to use each tool, the pitfalls you may encounter, and other lessons learned by reinventors. However, our next book will be a full-scale handbook for reinventors, detailing the use of these tools as well as other important implementation steps. For more on what will be in the handbook, see Resources for Reinventors, p. 350.

Many reinventors begin by reaching for off-the-shelf tools, whether TQM or performance measurement or customer surveys. Often, they use these tools without connecting them to strategies capable of changing the basic DNA. They treat the tools as *add-ons* to a bureaucratic system. They create quality improvement teams, for example, without fundamentally decentralizing the organizational power structure. This is not only ineffective, it breeds cynicism. When TQM is used this way, employees are trained to use complicated analytic and process improvement tools, put into teams, and set to work fixing minor processes. But decisions about more important issues are still made upstairs—despite the fact that the employees know best how to fix them.

As a result, "Employees soon write 'TQM' . . . off as but one more in the long chain of crusades, all of which involved a new set of bugles and bangles," says Creech.

> They can't be fooled by new slogans and innovative ways to hold meetings. They're either organized small, with real authority, or they're not. They're either given a greater voice, or they're not. They either receive a share of any added success they produce, or they don't. No group in America is better at sorting out the difference between mouth and movement than the frontline employees. They've had lots of experience.

At TAC, Creech says, process improvement teams and quality tools helped, but only when the organization pushed authority down to frontline teams and created "new incentives to get every employee committed to eliminating defects at the source" did quality and productivity improve dramatically. "Centralism was strangling incentive as well as precluding ownership, so trying to graft somewhat better techniques onto that system would have availed us little."

In the absence of strategies, then, the effect of any tool is greatly weakened. Using tools without changing the DNA is like casting valuable seeds on barren ground. It is like trying to build a house by starting to hammer boards together, without a blueprint that tells you how the rooms are laid out or where the bearing walls will be. It can keep you busy, but it won't put a roof over your head.

Work Up and Down the System

If you don't believe it is possible to change your organization, you will find no shortage of good reasons why it cannot be done. "The politicians won't let us." "There's just too much bureaucracy." "We don't have enough power." But if the ACC example shows anything, it shows that excuses are just that: excuses. You *can* change your organization without the politicians. You *can* transform the world's largest, most bureaucratic organizations. You *can* leverage your power back up through the system, using your example to convince the level above you to reinvent.

Lessons for Managers from TAC/ACC

1. Don't wait for permission to reinvent.
2. Apply the five C's to your organizations, processes, and people.
3. Leverage change in the levels above your organization.
4. Fight for exemptions from administrative system rules.
5. Make sure your successors are reinventors.
6. Reinvent before you reorganize: structure follows strategy.
7. Use tools to reinvent only if they are embedded in strategies.

If you want to be successful, in fact, you must work both up and down your system. In the ACC, Generals Creech and Loh did this. In the U.K., high-level civil servants helped the politicians redesign the nation's governing systems and administrative systems, then sometimes shifted jobs to move the revolution through a specific organization, its work processes, and its people. When a determined handful of citizens and politicians brought public school choice to Minnesota, a process we will describe in chapter 6, they could not have succeeded without the help of key civil servants in the state Education Department and at the University of Minnesota.

Regardless of where you sit, in other words, you can generate leverage. Hence our second rule for reinventors: *The game has five levels; change as many as you can reach.*

– 3 –

GUT CHECK: WHAT IT TAKES
TO USE THE STRATEGIES

*Nothing so undermines organizational change as the failure to think through
who will have to let go of what when change occurs.*
—William Bridges, *Managing Transitions:
Making the Most of Change*

Reinvention is a long, hard slog. It requires leadership, skill, dedication, and perseverance. But even more, it requires everyone—politicians, managers, employees, and citizens—to change their behavior.

Perhaps the toughest challenge is that of letting go. To implement the core strategy, for example, elected officials must relinquish direct control over management. They must be content to steer, and let others row—as the ministers in Great Britain did when they set up an arm's-length, contractual relationship with their agencies. Legislators need to think of themselves as the board of directors of the enterprise, not as the management. This can be very difficult when things go wrong—as the British discovered when the executive agency that ran the prisons experienced a rash of jailbreaks.

This does not mean that elected officials should let managers do whatever they please. Steering is serious business. It means setting a direction, defining the purpose, goals, and performance standards of organizations, and holding them accountable for meeting those objectives. Politicians will never loosen the reins of accountability. But if they want high performance, they will need to shift from accountability

for following rules and spending according to instructions to accountability for delivering results to customers.

This means politicians must learn to live with managers taking
actions they do not like, as long as the managers are acting ethically
and are producing the desired results. But it does not mean politicians
must give up control. It means they must trade control over *inputs* for
control over *outputs*. Alan Fiander, at the National Audit Office in the
U.K., observes that Next Steps has given elected officials much more
real control than they had previously. "In the past, politicians had
direct relationships only with the permanent secretary [the top civil
servant in a department] and his coterie of senior people. They found it
difficult to see what was actually going on in an operating sense within
their ministries, because there weren't the reporting functions and the
separation that now exists." Today, each agency has clear performance
measures, and chief executives report to ministers, so ministers can
hold them directly accountable. But ministers cannot micromanage the
agencies. They can fire the chief executive, as the home secretary did
after the series of jailbreaks in 1995. But they cannot manage for him.

To implement the customer strategy, politicians and managers must
let some of the accountability shift to the customers. They must make
the overall objectives of the organization clear, but within those
bounds, they must let the customers define what quality service means.
The good news for elected officials is that customers who have choices
are much tougher on provider organizations than politicians can ever
be. When politicians define the overall policy goals, empower customers, and then get out of the way, accountability for performance is
enormously strengthened.

The customer strategy requires managers and employees to shift
their focus from pleasing their superiors up the chain of command to
pleasing their customers. This can be difficult, when customers want
something the managers and employees don't value. When parents
want schools that integrate computers fully into the learning system,
many teachers will feel they cannot make the adjustment. Elected
school board members may be unwilling to shift funds from paying
teachers to buying computers. But in a competitive, customer-driven
system, all providers must learn to listen to their customers and
respond—or the customers will abandon them for their competitors.

The consequences strategy requires something far more difficult. It
requires elected officials to let public organizations shrink and die.

When a government embraces competitive bidding, for instance, some existing public organizations must inevitably be closed down. Long before that happens, their members and their unions begin visiting the newspapers and elected officials to plead for protection—just as the auto companies did when the Japanese took away market share. In their view, the new contracting system is not there to help taxpayers and customers, it is there to hurt public employees. Politicians should soften the blow, as we argue in chapter 5, by helping those whose jobs disappear find other jobs. But they should not give in, because government is there to serve the citizens, not the service providers.

The consequences strategy also requires that we reward our public employees and organizations for work well done and penalize them for work that is inferior. It requires rewards that elected officials have traditionally been uncomfortable offering their "public servants": bonuses and higher salaries for excellent performers. It also requires consequences that those public servants have traditionally been uncomfortable accepting: the chance that if their organization cannot perform, it might lose its place to a competitor, for example. These are not easy realities to impose in a political environment. But there is no industry in which we consistently get high performance without incentives that reward it.

The control strategy requires that we break the one-size-fits-all mold and control-from-the-center model we have embraced for 100 years. It requires that we let public agencies be managed not according to the central rule book, but according to what it takes to fulfill their missions. It requires that we let our centralized budget and personnel systems go the way of history.

When governments embrace community empowerment—the third control-strategy approach—the challenge is even greater. Elected officials must cede power over the use of resources to their constituents. They can usually handle this—*until* the constituents begin using the money in ways that undermine their political base. At that point, war often breaks out. For their part, public servants must learn to simply get out of the way. In our experience, this is the most unnatural thing one can ask public managers to do. They have spent their adult lives in a system that assumes that the central role of government is to provide services or to enforce compliance. They think of these roles as the be-all and end-all of government. Even when they embrace reinvention, it never occurs to them that the best solution might at times be to get government out of the service business. Yet this is often what community empowerment requires.

Finally, the culture strategy may demand the toughest change, for it is a change that only the public can make. It is difficult—not impossible, but difficult—to create an entrepreneurial, customer-focused, results-oriented culture in a society that looks down on public employees as lazy, selfish bureaucrats. If we want such organizations, we must begin to treat our public employees with respect. This will require enormous changes on the part of our politicians, our media, and our citizens. But there was a time when public service was seen as an honorable profession, and there is no reason it cannot be seen that way again. The truth is that most public employees are hardworking, dedicated individuals. As we have said many times before, most of them are good people trapped in bad systems. If we can change those systems and prove that government can produce excellence, perhaps even the media will be willing to give up their favorite scapegoats and honor quality when they see it.

W e say all this here, rather than waiting for the chapters that follow, to communicate a fundamental truth about the five strategies: they require key interests to let go of things they hold very dear. Reinvention requires more than knowledge and technique. It requires courage. The mayor and his employees in Uphill Battle, USA, needed help finding the strategies and tools that would work for them, but more important, they needed the courage to use them. If "politics ain't beanbag" and "the revolution is not a tea party," reinvention is not simply a matter of sweet reason.

Sometimes, people let go because they have no choice. In Great Britain, the Conservative Party imposed its will on civil servants, local governments, and school systems. But it is hard to get enough power to consistently impose one's will—particularly in the American political system. A second option is to offer people something of equal or greater value in return, when asking them to give up something important. People will not let go of power simply because it is the right thing to do. Self-interest does not disappear because we are talking about making government work better for its citizens.

At the heart of reinvention, in other words, lie a series of "deals." Politicians accept less control over day-to-day affairs in return for some degree of control over results. They give up some of their power to direct resources in return for more satisfied constituents. Employees accept the loss of guaranteed jobs in return for the opportunity to earn more through gainsharing and the opportunity to control their work environments, enrich their work lives, and upgrade their skills. Managers accept the loss of their responsibilities for managing service delivery in return for other, equally challenging roles: helping to steer, leading change, measuring performance, or coaching employees or communities. And perhaps the public and its elected representatives will let go of their favorite whipping boy—the bureaucracy—in return for public institutions that work better and cost less.

In sum, reinvention is the art of the deal. This is our third rule for reinventors: *When you want people to let go, give them something in return.*

– II –

THE FIVE STRATEGIES

– 4 –

THE CORE STRATEGY:
CREATING CLARITY
OF PURPOSE

THE BIG BANG DOWN UNDER

In late 1987 the government of New Zealand began auctioning off its publicly owned businesses. In just two and a half years it sold banking, finance, insurance, oil, film, printing, hotel, steel, shipping, and telecommunications operations, as well as Air New Zealand. The sales generated more than $8.2 billion in New Zealand dollars (about $5 billion in U.S. dollars). The government also put its coal and forestry businesses on the block and prepared its railroad system for privatization.

This was not a case of conservative politicians ending public ownership, as in the United Kingdom. In New Zealand, the sell-off was initiated by the Left. The Labor Party, long an exuberant champion of public ownership and aggressive government intervention in the economy, was beginning its fourth year in power. From the beginning, it had been forced to abandon its long-held philosophy and develop a new one on the fly.

When it won the 1984 elections, the Labor Party had been out of power for all but six of the previous 34 years. Then fortune smiled, quite unexpectedly. Prime Minister Robert Muldoon of the National Party called a surprise election for Parliament, hoping to catch his Labor opponents napping. He did—but voters turned overwhelmingly to Labor anyway. They had good cause: the economy was in rough shape.

In 1950, New Zealanders enjoyed the third-highest per capita income on the globe. Since then, this island nation of 3.4 million had experienced one of the slowest annual rates of productivity growth in the industrialized world. Real wages had stagnated since 1960. In 1973, a combination of the international oil shock and the United Kingdom's entry into the European Economic Community—which created serious competition in New Zealand's major export market—brought economic growth to a temporary halt. Unemployment, virtually zero in the 1960s and early 1970s, climbed to 5.4 percent by 1983, a major cause for alarm among people long accustomed to full employment. By 1984, New Zealand was twenty-first in per capita income.

Both major parties in New Zealand had long been committed to active intervention in the nation's economic affairs. The government owned a huge portion of the economy. Extensive public subsidies, high tariffs, and import controls protected New Zealand businesses. Markets were heavily regulated. In addition, New Zealand had developed an extensive social safety net. Public pensions dated from 1898; health care, housing, and college education were heavily subsidized.

As the economy worsened, National Party leaders had increased spending rapidly, particularly for social services and large economic-development projects. They had tried to restrain other spending with a series of across-the-board cuts, but had failed. By 1984, the national budget exceeded 40 percent of gross domestic product (GDP) and the government was borrowing heavily. This helped drive inflation—which averaged 12 percent between 1970 and 1984—to 15 percent by 1982. Interest payments on the debt ballooned to nearly 20 percent of government spending. In desperation, National Party leaders played their last card: in 1982 they froze wages, prices, and interest rates.

Labor's new ministers took office with no plan for changing these trends and little time to develop one. Within days of the election, the country almost defaulted on its foreign debts. The Reserve Bank had to suspend foreign-exchange transactions, while the Labor government devalued the currency by 20 percent.

Meanwhile, senior officials in the powerful Treasury Department, which managed fiscal policy (budgets and financial management) as well as economic and regulatory policy, were feverishly updating a set of recommendations the Muldoon government had ignored. Within weeks of the election, they handed their report, called "Economic Management," to the incoming ministers. It advocated far-reaching economic deregulation to end government's direct control over large parts of the economy. And it proposed to streamline, break up, and radically reform the nation's public bureaucracies.

The Treasury's advice struck at the heart of the Labor Party's philosophy. For most of the twentieth century, Labor had championed the expansion of the national government. Now it was being told that the only way out was to dismantle the system it had helped build.

Roger Douglas, Labor's new finance minister, pushed hard for the new direction. A combative third-generation Labor politician, Douglas was first elected to Parliament in 1970. He had routinely supported both government intervention in the economy and the expansion of the state. But by 1984, he says, he "had decided that governments didn't have to run so many things. Their role was to design an environment that positively encouraged the people they represented to go out and run things."

Necessity became the mother of reinvention: Douglas and his colleagues embraced the Treasury recommendations. It was a pragmatic decision, says Graham Scott, then a senior Treasury economist who had helped prepare the report. "[Labor] found themselves in the middle of a crisis. Everything else had been tried. There was only one way left to go." Still, Scott recalls, the decision was a surprise: "Suddenly, I was working for people who were saying yes instead of no."

Labor initiated shock therapy. They focused first on the domestic economy, ending decades of public subsidies and regulations and revamping social programs. They lowered tariffs that protected industries, removed wage and price controls, lowered the tax rate, and broadened the tax base. By 1988, they had cut the top individual tax rate (which kicked in at only 2.5 times the average income) from 66 to 33 percent and the corporate rate from 45 to 33 percent, while adding a 12.5 percent tax on consumption. In addition, they:

- deregulated several major industries, including finance, transportation, and energy;
- ended most public subsidies to agriculture and industry;
- eliminated controls on most foreign investment;
- ended all subsidies written into the tax code;
- instituted a means test for government pensions; and

■ provided low-income people with funds to spend on either private or public housing, rather than placing them in state-owned housing.

Then they trained their sights on the bureaucracy.

Big Bang Day

By 1984, New Zealand's government owned and operated 12.5 percent of the nation's economy, including some of the nation's largest banks, its largest automobile insurer, the largest farm-mortgage lender, the entire telecommunications industry, all wholesale electricity distribution, all the ports, the rail system, the only national airline, a national shipping line, more than half the commercial forest land, the only two television channels, most of the coal industry, and a major hotel chain.

Some of these businesses "operated under the direct control of ministers," explains Douglas:

> If those enterprises failed to deliver what the public wanted, then anyone could write to the minister, seeking political assistance—to get a telephone, for example. What could be more open or more democratic? People wrote to MPs in their thousands, for help to get telephones. They also believed that the system gave them better control over the prices charged by State-owned enterprises. Interest groups offended by suggested price increases could lobby the minister successfully to prevent or defer the increase. . . .
>
> Every year, Cabinet sat down solemnly and decided how much money to vote to government businesses. They approved or vetoed all capital expenditure. Their ability to match prices to their own political priorities was very convenient. If unemployment became a problem in a particular part of the country, ministers could absorb those people into the State workforce.

These publicly owned businesses performed a conflicting mix of business, regulatory, and social roles. For example, the state coal agency owned most of the nation's coal mines. But it also regulated coal mining, and in that role it was responsible for licensing its private competitors.

Overall, government-run businesses suffered from poor management, low productivity, and poor investment decisions. The Post

Office, which handled telecommunications, had a two-year supply of dial telephones that nobody wanted. The average wait to have a telephone installed was six to eight weeks. The coal business had lost money for 20 of the past 22 years. The organization managing government property was paying bills on facilities it could not even identify. The bureaucracy's attitude, says then-minister Richard Prebble, was, "There's no mistake that money can't fix."

In the previous two decades, the government had invested $5 billion in these business activities, but the net return on that investment had been zero.

Douglas pressed his colleagues to turn government agencies that produced goods and services with commercial value into public corporations, known in New Zealand as state-owned enterprises (SOEs). This immediately triggered hot disputes within Labor's ranks, as well as resistance from public sector unions and the bureaucracy's managers. After Douglas won Cabinet approval of a massive corporatization initiative, department managers stonewalled the effort. "Every conceivable attempt was made to delay, sidetrack, relitigate and reinterpret the thrust of the principles, and turn the government's nose in some other direction," Douglas complained.

Douglas called in Graham Scott, who was by now Treasury secretary, and a few other allies. "He said, 'Look, I want this problem fixed and fixed quickly,' " says Scott. "He set up meetings with a handful of us that he thought agreed with the policy, and asked, 'How are we going to get this fixed?' "

After many late-night sessions, the breakthrough came in a hallway conversation. Scott, Douglas, and Geoffrey Palmer, the deputy prime minister, had left a meeting to get some coffee. "We had been told that it would take 40 acts of Parliament just to create a forestry corporation," Scott remembers. "We said that would never work; we have to find a way of going over the top." Palmer suggested a legislative shortcut. Instead of changing the innumerable laws, the administration would get blanket authority from Parliament to corporatize government entities; in return, it would notify Parliament before any specific corporatization was undertaken.

"It was decided that night, and it was government policy in a week," says Scott. Parliament adopted the legislation in 1986 and scheduled the first wave of corporatization for April 1, 1987.

On "Big Bang Day," nine state-owned enterprises came into

existence: coal, electricity, property management, land, forestry, the Post Office, the Postal Bank, telecommunications, and air traffic control. The change affected some 60,000 government employees—more than half the departments' and agencies' staff. For the first time, these organizations would face market pressures. With the exceptions of the Post Office, which maintained its monopoly on first-class mail, and the air traffic controllers, they lost their statutory monopolies. Although the government still owned their assets, SOEs had to pay taxes and could no longer draw free capital from the government. They reported to independent boards of directors instead of elected officials. The boards negotiated the corporate direction with ministers. They selected and contracted with chief executives, who were unshackled from government employment, budgeting, and procurement systems.

The changes were the equivalent of a hostile takeover in the business world, in which new management is installed to pursue goals entirely different from the previous management's. Almost immediately, the SOEs laid off huge numbers of civil servants in order to boost their productivity and competitiveness. The forest SOE cut salaried staff by two thirds; the railroad SOE cut employment from 21,000 to 11,000 in four years; the telecommunications enterprise dropped from 25,000 to 14,000. "The Post Office, the electricity, coal and forestry industries had been billing both taxpayers and consumers for thousands of workers who had never been needed at all," says Douglas. Within five years, the SOEs would cut employment by more than 50 percent.

Over those same five years, the SOEs registered astonishing turnarounds. Telecommunications increased its productivity by 85 percent and cut prices by 20 percent. The coal SOE maintained previous production levels with half the workforce, while cutting prices by 20 percent. The rail SOE cut freight prices in half, while turning a $77 million loss into a $41 million profit. The Forest Corporation turned a $70 million loss into a $53 million profit in just one year. The postal system, which had lost more than $38 million in 1986–1987 and was projected to lose more than $50 million the next year, instead made a large profit—without raising the price of basic mail. By 1995, it had cut the real cost of a standard letter by a third. (All figures are in New Zealand dollars, which have been worth 50–70 U.S. cents over the past decade.)

As a whole, the SOEs increased their revenues by 15 percent and quadrupled their profits during their first five years. By 1992, they were paying roughly $1 billion in dividends and taxes. The gains were far beyond anyone's expectations. "We couldn't believe it," says Scott, an architect of the policy. "We were all surprised."

Privatization and Much More

The economic effects of the Big Bang were spectacular—and they triggered even more fundamental shocks. After Labor increased its majority in the 1987 election, it began selling off SOEs and other public businesses.

One reason was to reduce the deficit. Another was that the SOEs had become a headache, because ministers now had public accountability for them but had given up control over them. For instance, the government chose not to set SOE prices, but when an SOE raised its rates, the ministers still got the flak. So ministers began asking: Why bother owning them? If we can't control them, why keep them in the public sector?

The third and most important reason was simple economics. Labor's experience with SOEs—and Margaret Thatcher's successful asset sales in the U.K.—convinced them that still greater efficiencies could be achieved by ending public ownership.

"We were getting increased efficiencies because we were exposing state monopolies to competition or the threat of it," says Douglas. "The outcome demonstrated that competition is far more effective than either ownership or regulation in extracting efficiency from business operations on behalf of the owner, and performance from it on behalf of consumers." Echoing an argument Treasury officials had raised since 1984, Douglas and his allies concluded that government was not a good owner of businesses; that keeping businesses in government's hands might generate pressure for additional public spending; and that ministers should spend their time on economic and social policies, not commercial activities.

The privatization process was not always smooth. Several times the sales process was reopened after a winner had been selected, because of political infighting within the cabinet. Another sale ended up in receivership and a legal squabble. And a public controversy erupted when the new private owners of the Rural Bank made a large profit in their first year.

These problems slowed but did not stop privatization. By 1991, the government had sold all or part of Air New Zealand, the Petroleum

Corporation, the Bank of New Zealand, the Rural Bank, the Post Office Bank, the Shipping Corporation, Government Life, the Forestry Corporation, the Tourist Hotel Corporation, the Telecom Corporation, and others. By 1995, it had sold more than 20 state organizations or assets, which represented more than two thirds of its commercial assets, by dollar value.

As they sold off SOEs, Labor ministers also thought about how to apply the lessons of their startling success to what they called the "core public sector." They assumed that waste and inefficiency were also rampant in defense, policing, criminal justice, health, education, environmental, and welfare agencies, where they could not create market discipline through privatization or corporatization.

As early as 1984, Scott and other Treasury officials had argued for fundamental changes in the bureaucracy. In their view, it was a bloated, unmanageable, inefficient drag on the nation's economy. Its conglomerate departments combined a hodgepodge of different functions: policy making, regulation, service delivery, and compliance. They lacked clearly defined objectives and had no management plans. They generated no information about how well they were performing. Managers had little real control over personnel or budgets, because a central civil service system set salaries, classification levels, and working conditions, while the Treasury controlled budgets and finance. Unionized public employees enjoyed automatic annual salary increases. The central administrative systems gave managers no incentives to perform well or to improve performance. In this system, it was extremely difficult to save money.

As Labor officials watched the success of the SOEs, says Scott, they began "to search for a framework that would bring analogous incentives for efficiency to the activities of other government entities and departments." In late 1987 they backed a Treasury plan to create explicit customer-supplier contracts between elected ministers and the departments. Ministers would determine policy goals and then purchase whatever outputs they thought would help achieve those goals, from departments or other providers. Departments would be accountable for delivering the specified outputs. In short, ministers would be responsible for steering—setting direction—and managers would be responsible for rowing—getting to where ministers wanted to go.

In order to make the departments truly accountable, Treasury added, managers should be given the freedom to decide how best to produce the outputs ministers wanted. That meant ending civil service, procurement, and most budgeting controls. In addition, managers and agencies should have economic incentives for improving their performance.

Labor's leaders were already deeply suspicious of the bureaucracy. They believed that in the mid-1970s, when Labor had a short term in office, senior managers had sabotaged Labor policies. Their suspicions had grown into frustrations when they encountered bureaucratic resistance to the SOE policy and to ongoing efforts to cut government spending. To the ministers, the bureaucracy seemed unmanageable. "We found that as a new government we weren't actually in control of [the departments] in any real sense, and that came as somewhat of a surprise," explains Geoffrey Palmer, then deputy prime minister.

Labor had not taken up Treasury's ideas before 1987 in part because some of the changes threatened the public employee unions, part of its political base. "The sensitive issue was always civil service reform," says Scott. In 1986 Labor adopted some modest internal deregulations. And in 1987 Labor's Stan Rodger, a minister and former public union chief, quietly tried to negotiate concessions from the unions. But the effort failed.

After the 1987 election, Labor decided to move anyway. "They'd obviously been waiting for the election to get out of the way," says Scott. "In two meetings of two hours each, all the key recommendations for civil service reform were decided. Then, there was a complicated dance between the government and the unions."

Without warning the unions, Rodger introduced comprehensive legislation—the State Sector Act of 1988—to change the basic industrial relations within government. Then he pushed it through Parliament at breakneck speed. "It's fair to say that I didn't consult on the bill," Rodger acknowledges. "The unions were very grumpy. They thought I had sandbagged them. . . . They stripped me of my union medal."

Changes at the Core

By adopting the State Sector Act and its companion, the Public Finance Act of 1989, Labor hoped to bring private sector management practices into the public sector. As Rodger announced when he introduced the 1988 legislation, "What is good for private sector employers, unions and workers should also be good for employers, unions and workers in the state."

The main reforms changed the organizational structure of government and the basic rules for managing public agencies. As in the U.K.'s Next Steps agencies, government managers gained great autonomy in exchange for increased accountability for performance.

The new laws separated policy-making or steering functions from rowing functions. In order to clarify roles, the reinventors decided to break their large departments up into discrete functions—"hiving off," they called it. Generally, policy-advising, regulatory, service-delivery, compliance, and funding functions were severed from one another. For example, the government broke the 4,000-employee Department of Transportation into six organizations. Five of them provided specific services such as maritime safety, accident investigations, and civil aviation. One, the Ministry of Transportation, provided policy advice to ministers. Once the corporate brain of an entire department, it shrank to fewer than 50 members. (Policy-advisory organizations are typically called ministries; others are normally called departments.)

Ministers would negotiate performance agreements with all departments and ministries, which would agree to produce a specified quantity and quality of outputs at a specified price. Ministers were free to purchase outputs from departments and ministries or from other providers. Typically, they would negotiate annual agreements with the organizations' chief executives. This gave them genuine control, for the first time, of what their departments and ministries produced.

The senior civil servant running each department or ministry would work on a fixed-term performance contract, rather than having permanent tenure. These chief executives—formerly known as "permanent heads"—now faced consequences for their performance. Job security and salaries would depend on their success in delivering the outputs they negotiated with ministers. Contracts could be for no more than five years. Chief executives would be recruited from the private sector, not just from the civil service, paid salaries more in line with those in the private sector, and given bonuses for high performance.

The new chief executives would have the freedom to manage their organizations' resources. The legislation transferred power over hiring, firing, salaries, and union negotiations from the 75-year-old civil service system to the chief executives. In effect, it eliminated almost all civil service rules. Public servants lost their guaranteed tenure; unions lost the ability to bargain uniformly for government employees in different departments. The State Services Commission's power over staffing numbers and the Treasury Department's control over day-to-day budgets shifted to the chief executives. Once budgets were set, in negotiated agreements between ministers and chief executives, agency managers could spend the money as they saw fit. Power over purchasing decisions shifted from centralized procurement offices to the chief executives; they could buy what they wanted, when they wanted it, at whatever price they were willing to pay.

Departments and ministries were given incentives to manage their finances effectively. The government charged interest on all administrative funds and assets held by departments and ministries. (This is called the "capital charge.") Since managers had to pay for their money, they had an incentive to manage it carefully. In addition, the government required departments to use accrual accounting, which forced once-hidden forms of spending such as future obligations or the declining value of assets into the open, by treating them as expenditures.

The role and function of central administrative agencies changed. The Treasury no longer specified how each department should use its internal resources; its role was limited to setting broad budgets, providing ministers with economic policy advice, and managing government-wide finances. The State Services Commission, stripped of its control over personnel systems, focused on a few remaining functions: it appointed chief executives, reviewed their performance, and set some basic personnel and labor-negotiation policies.

Another Political Shock

In 1990, as Labor implemented its new management framework, it had to face the voters. After six wrenching years of internal policy disputes, the party was in disarray. Roger Douglas and Prime Minister David Lange had engaged in a prolonged, messy public wrangle over fiscal policy, which culminated in Douglas's resignation—followed six months later by Lange's. Douglas had wanted more aggressive tax and spending cuts, including a flat income tax; Lange announced that it was time to slow down the pace of change. At the same time, Labor's privatization program and reductions in government financial support for health care and university students cost it support among its traditional constituencies.

Labor had made little progress on deficit reduction, and as the election approached, it lost fiscal control. "They started spending money like an old-fashioned Labor government of the past," says Scott. For all these reasons—and because the economy was heading into recession—Labor lost the election.

The incoming National Party ministers had been on the sidelines for six years. Because they had wanted government management to improve, they had not been a great obstacle to Labor's reforms. But they weren't sure if the changes were working. They immediately asked the former CEO of IBM New Zealand, Basil Logan, to chair a committee to review the changes.

After a five-month review, Logan endorsed Labor's framework. "It has already had a significant and beneficial impact on the effectiveness and efficiency with which the core Service operates," he reported. "The reforms undertaken over the past three years are at the leading edge of central government systems internationally, and should be given an opportunity to consolidate before major modifications are contemplated." The Logan report found that in addition to performance improvements, departments were more accountable to ministers and the quality of information given to elected officials had improved considerably.

Logan and others cite the National Party's success in cutting budgets in 1991 as a leading example of the new system's value. Initially, says Scott, the new ministers "tried cutting the old-fashioned way: giving instructions [to the departments] and waving their arms." It didn't work. "They found that the system could absorb that kind of punishment without saving money."

Then the ministers realized they could cut costs by renegotiating performance agreements with chief executives; all they had to do was eliminate or reduce agency outputs. "They found the new system of management offered them new levers they could pull," Scott says. They "went from being skeptics to being believers." Ruth Richardson, the finance minister, became an enthusiastic advocate of the new system.

Although the Logan Committee endorsed the reforms' basic framework, it also pointed out problems that needed work. Among them:

- ministers experienced difficulties in specifying performance objectives for chief executives;
- the central agencies' new roles were ambiguous, there was no way to monitor their performance, and they were not trusted by the departments;

- managers needed to develop new skills required by the new environment; and
- few qualified private sector candidates had been recruited for top management positions.

Most important, Logan reported that the ministers were having trouble steering the ship of state. They had not developed a clear process for articulating their long-term policy goals, so there were no agreed-upon outcome goals to guide them as they negotiated the outputs required of departments. (Outputs are what organizations produce: street sweeping, arrests, social security checks, or job training. Outcomes are the results: clean streets, low crime rates, satisfied senior citizens, and skilled individuals who find and hold jobs.) In addition, because departments were now held strictly accountable for outputs but given great autonomy, their managers had no incentive to focus on any goals beyond those outputs. No one was accountable for pursuing the government's collective interest. All in all, Logan reported, ministers were neither setting long-term, collective goals nor requiring departments to work on achieving them.

Improving Steering

In response to these concerns, National Party leaders struggled to develop a more strategic management system. First they tried a World Bank strategic planning model, but they found it too complex. They settled on a simpler alternative: the prime minister's political advisor, David Kirk, prepared a government statement setting out long-term goals. In mid-1993, four months before the next election, they published it as *Path to 2010*, a 35-page vision and strategy for New Zealand. It identified general goals—economic growth and social cohesion—and translated those into some measurable outcome goals, such as a 3.5 percent economic growth rate for 15 years.

The government still needed a way to translate *Path to 2010* into specific policies and priorities for departments and ministries, however. Working with the State Services Commission and top managers, it developed a set of three-to-five-year outcome goals—called "strategic result areas"—that would most contribute to its long-term outcome goals. Then it developed more specific outcome goals—called "key result areas"—for each department, which would contribute to the strategic result areas. (These are expressed primarily as outcomes, but some outputs have also crept in.) For each key result, milestones—or targets—were identified with which to measure progress. In early 1995 the government began to test the new system: there were some 40 strategic result areas to guide the government as a whole; about 200 key result areas for the 41 government departments and ministries; and many hundreds of milestones to judge progress. When ministers negotiated the outputs they would purchase from departments, they looked for outputs that would produce the key results they were after.

Aftershock and Aftermath

In 1993 the National Party almost lost its reelection bid, in part because it had forced deep, unexpected budget cuts. Although the economy was beginning to recover, voters were dissatisfied with their political leaders. "New Zealanders had had years of being pushed around by governments which appeared to be doing things for which they had little or no mandate," observes Scott. Both parties had forced deep changes through Parliament without consulting with the public or in contradiction to campaign pledges. By a small margin, voters in 1993 adopted a referendum that made it more difficult for a political party to unilaterally adopt such sweeping changes.

In the past, the candidate who received the most votes from each electoral district won a seat in Parliament. Winner-take-all systems like this produce electoral landscapes dominated by two major parties, as in the U.S. In New Zealand's unicameral parliamentary system, the party that won a majority of seats controlled both Parliament and the executive, and thus wielded enormous power.

Under the new system, seats are apportioned according to what percentage of the national vote a party wins. Hence minority parties are able to obtain more seats, and it is much more difficult for any party to secure a majority in Parliament. (In October 1996, the first national election after the change, none of the 23 parties running won a majority, though the National Party won the most seats.) The result will be more coalition governments, forcing compromises that will probably slow the pace of change.

Since 1984, one eruption after another has shaken New Zealand's welfare state. Reinvention hit the top of the political Richter scale, upending even the most entrenched government policies and agencies. It changed government's basic purposes, wiping away entire departments and privatizing about two-thirds of the government's commercial assets. It cut total employment in "core" national government agencies from 88,000 in 1984 to 35,000 in 1994. And it caused "a radical refashioning of the departmental landscape," as analysts at Victoria University put it.

Today, a set of small, sharply focused departments dominate the core public sector. Since 1984, the government has created 26 new departments or ministries and abolished, corporatized, or privatized 23. In 1984, only two of the 34 departments and ministries had fewer than 100 employees and a dozen had more than 3,000. By mid-1995, more than a dozen had fewer than 100 staffers and only three had more than 3,000.

It is widely agreed that these changes have contributed to overall economic improvement. The economy turned around in 1991, and by the mid-1990s it was humming. Real growth rates ranged from 3 to 6 percent a year, while inflation remained below 2 percent. Unemployment dropped from 11 percent in 1991 to 6 percent by 1995. New investment was growing rapidly, as were exports. In 1993 the World Competitiveness Report ranked New Zealand first among industrialized nations in quality of government and second in business community optimism.

Rapid economic growth coupled with constraints on government spending yielded a small budget surplus in 1994—New Zealand's first in 17 years and a rarity in the industrialized world. By 1995, government expenditures had fallen to 35 percent of GDP. Government-owned businesses, which had once absorbed 12 percent of GDP and 17 percent of national investment while losing money and paying no dividends or taxes, now absorbed only 5 percent of GDP but returned $1 billion in dividends and taxes. By 1996, public debt was down from 50 percent of GDP to roughly 25 percent, and the government was cutting taxes.

Few politicians now question the reforms. "No political party is making a fuss about any of it, really," says Graham Scott, who left Treasury to consult on reinvention around the globe.

Government managers like the changes, too. "There's no constituency for going back to the old system," says Derek Gill, a Treasury official. "You'd much rather be a chief executive under our system than under the old one." Agency executives say their organizations have a sharper focus and clearer missions, and that they must grapple with much less conflict over objectives.

New Zealand's reinvention—once so disruptive—is now embedded in the fabric of government. "It's just the way business is done here now," says Scott.

THE CORE STRATEGY

New Zealand's reinventors moved faster and more aggressively than any others in the world. In the process, they used the entire core strategy. They eliminated or privatized functions that were not consistent with the core purposes of government. They uncoupled functions with fundamentally different purposes—policy, regulation, service delivery, and compliance—and put them in different organizations, so each could more effectively achieve its mission. Finally, the National Party realized that while Labor had redesigned the core public sector, it had not built much capacity to steer the ship of state—to define long-term goals and focus the system on achieving them. Beginning in 1994, its leaders began creating the mechanisms they needed to steer more effectively.

In the process, New Zealand demonstrated the three basic approaches of the core strategy: clearing the decks, uncoupling steering and rowing, and improving your aim.

Why do we call these three approaches the "core" strategy? Because the most important role government plays—its *core* role—is steering. To a great extent, the core strategy focuses on improving steering, while the consequences, customer, control, and culture strategies focus on improving rowing. The core strategy helps define what direction you want to go, weed out functions that don't help you get there, and organize your government for the trip. The other four strategies help you reach your destination.

Achieving clarity of purpose, role, and direction does not in itself improve performance; it sets the stage. It creates the conditions for improved performance. One of the clearest patterns we have seen, however, is that once institutions have clarity about their purpose and goals, reinvention becomes much easier. That's why organizations with clear purposes, such as military organizations and revenue departments, often lead the way. It is also one reason why reinvention is easier in parliamentary systems and in local governments. In parliamentary systems the ruling party has the power, with few checks and balances, to clearly define and pursue its purpose and goals. And in small and midsize local governments, there is less political struggle over purpose and goals than in larger governments. Hence it is much easier for leaders to get some degree of clarity.

CLARITY OF PURPOSE: CLEARING THE DECKS

When leaders clear the decks, they eliminate functions that no longer contribute to their core goals—by abandoning them, selling them, or moving them to a different level of government. In today's environment of rapid change, this helps keep governments focused on what is important to the citizens now—not what was important 20 years ago.

Ted Gaebler, coauthor of *Reinventing Government*, describes the problem well:

There's no incentive in government to ever change your program of services. Most businesses would make 10 percent of what they produce each year obsolete the following year, and carefully winnow that out. They close plants and they make all those adjustments. The public sector never has any incentive to look at its product mix. And so it's always more, more, more, until there's a massive cutback, where everybody has to cut 25 percent, or a Proposition 13, which cuts off the funds, and then people go through the machinations of ugly blame-fixing and cutting back.

Some governments try to clear the decks all at once, using exercises such as blue-ribbon commissions and "program reviews." This only works when the politics are just right. In 1986, for example, Canadian Prime Minister Brian Mulroney launched a ministerial task force the day after he took office. Chaired by Deputy Prime Minister Erik Nielson, it was to review all programs, eliminate some, consolidate others, and recommend improvements in public management. It had 19 committees, drawn evenly from the public and private sectors. They recommended devolution, privatization, contracting out, deep cuts in some programs and many subsidies, and sweeping changes in procurement policy. But three months after Nielson released the report,

Mulroney dropped him from the cabinet for mishandling the resignation of another cabinet member. Without a champion, the recommendations died on the vine.

Seven years later, when the Liberal Party returned to power, it launched a similar exercise. Called the Program Review, it recommended slashing departmental spending by $17 billion—almost 19 percent—over three years. (We are using Canadian dollars, which were worth about 73 percent of U.S. dollars in 1994.) It recommended cuts in every department, some as high as 50 percent, and reduction of 45,000 positions, or 14 percent, through "accelerated attrition." And it proposed 60 percent reductions in corporate subsidies.

In transport, for example, the Program Review recommended privatizing the Air Navigation System and the Canadian National Railway System, devolving ownership of airports to local government, and replacing most transportation subsidies with user fees. It proposed shrinking Transport Canada from 19,000 employees and $19 billion in assets to 3,500 employees and about $1 billion in assets. The review also proposed to sell government's 70 percent interest in Petro-Canada, a state-owned oil company.

Because Liberal leaders were serious about cutting the deficit—and because they had an overwhelming majority in Parliament—they enacted the Program Review's recommendations. "Program Review is a tool that only works when the stars are in alignment," says Richard Paton, whose staff at the Treasury Board played an instrumental role in the exercise.

In Canada the stars were fiscal pressure—we had to deal with it. The government was relatively new. We got the right ministers and they were working as a team. They had the right information on the table. There was a certain willingness of the public to really deal with these issues; there was a concern about the deficit that was real. And there was a huge unhappiness among Public Service executives with earlier efforts to cut budgets across the board.

The same dynamics have occurred in other countries and states. When the Texas legislature asked the comptroller to do a "performance review" in 1991, for example, it faced a $5–$6 billion shortfall in its next two-year budget. When Comptroller John Sharp recommended $4.2 billion in spending cuts, increased use of federal subsidies, increased taxes or fees, and spending delays, the legislature passed $2.4 billion of them. Why? Because the law required it to balance the budget, it had only 30 days left to do the job when Sharp released his recommendations, and the option was a massive tax increase. In effect, the legislature had a gun to its head.

When Sharp convinced President Clinton to use his performance-review process for federal reinvention, however, the political stars were not so well aligned. Congress had no requirement to balance the budget, no 30-day deadline, and no gun to its head. Meanwhile the Clinton administration was busy bargaining with individual legislators for support of its budget and health care plan, so it had little interest in privatizing or eliminating functions if a member of Congress it needed opposed the move. The result: the administration quietly killed many proposals to eliminate programs before they saw the light of day, and Congress ignored most of the rest. The 1993 National Performance Review made progress on other reinvention fronts, but managed to eliminate only a few small agricultural subsidies.

Given how seldom the political gods do smile on exercises to clear the decks, the trick is to institutionalize the process so it happens gradually and continuously, not in painful megadoses. Societal problems and citizens' needs change fast enough today that we cannot wait for the stars to align to weed out functions that have become obsolete. The nation that has done the best job of this is the U.K., where—as we explained in chapter 1—every executive agency is now reviewed every five years.

During these prior options reviews, the department to which the agency reports asks a series of fundamental questions:

- Is there a continuing need for the activity?
- If so, does the government have to be responsible for it, or can it be privatized and left to the market?
- Where the government needs to remain responsible for an activity, does it have to carry out the task itself, or can it contract the task to one or more outside providers?
- If the latter, should the government contract out the entire activity, or should it be market tested, with civil servants competing with outside suppliers to determine which method provides the most value for the money?

- Should responsibility for the activity be transferred to or merged with another public organization?
- Finally, where the job must be carried out within government, is the organization properly structured and focused on the job to be done?

This process is taken quite seriously by many departments in the U.K. As the first 126 executive agencies were established, more than a dozen others were sold or transferred to the private sector. And from 1991 through 1995, departments and agencies contracted out or market tested £2.6 billion worth of services.

Institutionalizing the process of clearing the decks is far easier in a parliamentary system, where the party in executive power usually controls Parliament, than in a system in which the executive and legislative powers are separate. In the U.S., for example, any administration that wants to eliminate or sell an asset must secure majority votes in both houses of Congress. Typically, individual legislators can bottle these proposals up in subcommittee, strangling them long before they get to a vote.

To make a regular review of every function possible in an American-style political system, one would probably have to write a periodic sunset review into the authorizing legislation for every program. To survive, a program would need to pass muster. The sunset review would be done by an independent body with representation from the executive branch, the legislature, and major stakeholders, including program customers. To make the process effective, legislators would have to act on the recommendations within a limited amount of time. Perhaps the most promising version of this was devised to close military bases: first those with technical expertise in the Defense Department perform an independent review and make recommendations, then a commission appointed by the president and Congress reviews and modifies those recommendations and sends them to the president. Once the president approves them, they become law unless Congress passes a joint resolution opposing them—overriding the president's veto if necessary—within a specified period of time.

Some politicians think that eliminating, privatizing, and reorganizing functions is what public sector reform is all about. Unfortunately, they are wrong. Once you have eliminated and reorganized, there is much left to do to improve performance in the organizations that

---

Tools to Clear the Decks

Performance or Program Reviews are periodic exercises, normally involving large numbers of people, to develop recommendations for abandoning, privatizing, devolving, restructuring, or otherwise reforming public programs.

Prior Options Reviews, developed by the British government, examine every five years whether an agency and its functions should be abandoned, privatized, reorganized, or restructured.

Sunset Rules require that programs and/or regulations be reauthorized periodically (typically every seven years).

Asset Sales move government assets, such as businesses, airports, dams, or railroads, to private ownership. In most countries this is synonymous with the word "privatization," but in the U.S. privatization is also used to describe contracting out and other methods.

Quasi-Privatization Methods allow governments to preserve ownership of an asset but turn operation over to private owners for long periods of time. The typical method for an existing asset is a long-term lease; for assets a government wants constructed it can use "build-operate-transfer agreements."

Devolution transfers activities to a lower (state, provincial, regional, or local) level of government.

---

remain. But clearing the decks is a useful step. It keeps public officials from spending enormous amounts of time and energy reinventing organizations that should no longer exist, for one thing. It narrows and orders the universe on which to use the other four C's.

CLARITY OF ROLE:
UNCOUPLING STEERING AND ROWING

The second approach of the core strategy separates functions with fundamentally different purposes into different organizations. It uncouples the policy and regulatory roles from the service-delivery and compliance roles, and it separates distinct service functions into different organizations and distinct compliance functions into different organizations. This helps each organization concentrate on achieving one clear purpose.

In the traditional public organization, policy makers, advisors, and top managers run the show but rely solely on employees to deliver services or enforce compliance. In essence, the steering units are captives of monopoly suppliers: their own agencies and divisions. And as the British found in the course of their Next Steps study, the policy staffs typically don't care about or understand management, while most managers are so far down the chain of command that they lack the authority and flexibility they need to run effective organizations.

Uncoupling steering and rowing is the first principle outlined in *Reinventing Government*, where it was called "catalytic government." It is virtually identical to the method of organization Peter Drucker has long recommended for large corporations, known as "federal decentralization." It allows government to centralize and coordinate its steering functions, so policy makers can more effectively concentrate on policy and direction, while decentralizing rowing, so managers have the power to improve service delivery and compliance. Separating "purchasers" and "providers," as the British describe it, frees purchasers to look beyond public monopolies and choose many different providers. This creates what the New Zealand reformers call "contestability." It also allows steering organizations to develop contractual relationships with rowing organizations, through which they can exercise the consequences, customer, and control strategies.

Basil Logan, chairman of the Logan committee, explains why contestability is so important:

Road safety as an outcome is politically desirable. Politicians are prepared to invest resources in it. A traditional measure of road safety is the number of accidental deaths on the roads. But there are a number of outputs that can contribute to achieving the desired outcome, including more police patrols, improved road design and highway signage, the regulation/control of drinking and driving, better hospital treatment for accident victims and so on. The notion allows for consideration of the contestability of a whole range of otherwise unrelated activities in seeking to attain a particular outcome that politicians have decided is a political priority.

Reinventing Government listed 36 alternatives to public service delivery that policy managers sometimes use to achieve their goals. (See Appendix A of *Reinventing Government*.) In a decision tree we offer in chapter 9, we have boiled them down to the following 14:

- Contracting out
- Regulation of private sector activities
- Tax incentives or disincentives
- Franchising
- Subsidies to producers (grants, loans, equity investments, favorable procurement policies, favorable investment policies)
- Subsidies to consumers (vouchers, tax credits)
- Policies allowing use of public property
- Risk sharing (insurance, loan guarantees)
- Information for customers
- Technical assistance
- Demand management through fees or taxes
- Persuasion
- Catalyzing voluntary activity
- Public-private partnerships

While the British have uncoupled almost 75 percent of their civil service through the Next Steps process, they have only done so with service-delivery and compliance functions. New Zealand has even put policy advice functions into separate organizations, which negotiate outputs and performance agreements with the ministers to whom they report.

Ministers in New Zealand are free to buy the outputs they want wherever they choose—from the public or the private sector. Chief executives are accountable to them through two primary instruments, in addition to financial statements: annual performance agreements and annual purchase agreements. The former specify the key result areas (program outcomes) the agency will focus on for the next three to five years; the specific outputs it will produce for the next year; the chief executive's obligations to maintain and build the department's capacities for the long term; and the chief executive's personal training and development goals for the year. The purchase agreement summarizes the outputs to be purchased and specifies things such as funding methods, the department's powers and obligations, procedures for amending the agreements, methods of monitoring and reporting on performance, rewards and sanctions, and methods to be used to resolve disputes. At the end of the year, the department produces a statement of performance, which is audited for accuracy.

As the Treasury explained in proposing these reforms, they are designed to force leaders to be very clear about the purposes of their organizations and then hold them accountable for their performance. They help elected officials disengage from "detailed daily management decisions" and "concentrate instead on broad policy directions and initiatives." They help managers focus primarily on running their operations as efficiently as possible within policy parameters set by elected officials. And they avoid what Treasury calls "producer capture" of policy advice, in which the only input policy makers get is from public monopolies. As the State Services Commission explains, public service and compliance monopolies are often blind to many policy options; they typically fight off discussion of those that threaten their interests; and they often resist those that disrupt their current work or add to their workload.

By breaking up large, conglomerate departments, Graham Scott

Other Advantages of Uncoupling

- "Freeing policy managers to shop around for the most effective and efficient service providers helps them squeeze more bang out of every buck.

- "It allows them to use *competition* between service providers.

- "It preserves maximum *flexibility* to respond to changing circumstances.

- "Steering organizations that shop around can also use *specialized* service providers with unique skills to deal with difficult populations. . . .

- "[They] can even promote *experimentation* and learn from success.

- "Finally, [they] can provide more comprehensive solutions, attacking the roots of the problem. They can define the problem—whether it is drug use, crime, or poor performance in school—in its entirety, then use many different organizations to attack it."

—From *Reinventing Government*, pp. 35–36.

points out, uncoupling also created smaller, more focused organizations "with short chains of command." In addition, "Focused units have the advantage of being able to provide much more clear information about their resource use, as the separation forces the allocation of assets to specific activities. It is thereby easier to generate information about the real costs of services."

Virtually all discussion of uncoupling focuses on the separation of policy and service-delivery functions. But for obvious reasons, service-delivery and compliance functions should also be separated. When one organization must enforce compliance and deliver services, the two missions often work at cross purposes. The U.S. Federal Aviation Administration has long struggled with the fact that Congress asks it to be responsible for promoting commercial aviation and enforcing compliance with safety regulations, for example. Every time there is a major accident, critics wonder whether the first mission has received too much attention at the expense of the second.

Regulatory and compliance functions also benefit from separation. The main reason is quite simple: it is not a good idea to let the police write the laws. If the same organization writes rules and enforces them, the enforcement perspective may begin to color the way regulations are written, minimizing the rights of those who are regulated and maximizing the rights of enforcers. If a regulatory function is separate, it is more likely to balance the needs of both sides.

Producer capture can also be a problem. For example, those who work for environmental protection, workplace safety, or tax collection agencies are not likely to dream up market-based regulatory alternatives, such as pollution fees and private sector auditing systems. When outsiders suggest them, compliance organizations are likely to resist, both for ideological reasons—because their members genuinely doubt that the alternatives will be effective—and out of self-interest, to protect their jobs.

We call the basic model developed by New Zealand and the U.K. a flexible performance framework, because it creates a framework in which rowing functions are uncoupled from steering functions, given broad flexibilities, and held accountable for their performance. Because it combines three strategies—core, consequences, and control—it is a very powerful metatool.

Sweden has long kept policy and operations in separate organizations, and other countries have tried copying the flexible performance framework. Canada has created some 15 special operating agencies modeled on the Next Steps agencies, although Canadian leaders never made the initiative a high priority, as we noted in chapter 2.

In 1995 Vice President Al Gore also announced an initiative patterned after the British model. He called the uncoupled agencies performance-based organizations (PBOs). Because the administration felt it could not get blanket approval for such a radical reform from Congress, however, it sought approval agency by agency. Hence the process unfolded at Washington's typical glacial speed, and by late 1996 Congress had approved no PBOs. Gore also developed a version of a flexible performance framework between the federal government and state and local governments, called performance partnerships.

At the local level, the second basic tool of the uncoupling approach is more common: competitive bidding. Using this tool, governments add competition to the contracting process. A number of cities in Los Angeles County, for example, contract with public and private organizations for most or all of their services. This has become known as the Lakewood Plan, after the city that pioneered it. Its practitioners have banded together to form the California Contract Cities Association. Other American cities have developed less extensive versions, including Phoenix (in the Department of Public Works), Philadelphia, and Indianapolis. (See chapter 5.)

In the U.K., where the national government has forced local governments to competitively bid most services, the process has gone much

---

Tools to Uncouple Steering and Rowing

The Flexible Performance Framework is a metatool that separates discrete functions into different organizations and uses contracts to spell out their purposes, their expected results, their performance consequences, and their management flexibilities.

Competitive Bidding is a metatool that takes the process of uncoupling one step further by requiring that each rowing function be competitively bid out. Both public and private service delivery organizations typically bid for the contracts.

further. Many local councils now refer to themselves as "enabling councils," because their primary role has shifted from owning and operating service-delivery organizations to enabling (or catalyzing) public and private service delivery. Some, like the London boroughs of Bromley and Bexley, have gradually reduced their staffs by 50 percent. "I've seen so much improvement stem from simple realignment, from the purchaser/provider split," says Bexley Chief Executive Terrence Musgrave. "That very act will achieve 25 percent improvement. Competition will get you another 15 percent."

Keys to Successful Uncoupling

There are many keys to successful uncoupling, but the high points include the following:

If you want real results, combine uncoupling with the consequences and control strategies. Don't borrow the model, as Canada did, without buying the fundamental shifts in DNA required to make it work. Designating uncoupled agencies without giving them genuine control over their own management practices and genuine consequences for performance may help, but it won't yield transformation.

Reform your administrative systems to take control away from central agencies and hand it to uncoupled organizations. Most of the flexibilities needed to make uncoupling work lie within the budget, personnel, and procurement systems. If you don't change them, your uncoupled organizations will not have the freedom they need to make significant improvements.

Force departments and/or ministers to let go of their power to micromanage. The New Zealanders guaranteed this by removing every function save policy making and oversight from the ministers and leaving them with only small staffs. The British, who left many more functions within departments—including policy advice and central personnel and budget authority—had a real struggle forcing those departments to loosen their grip on uncoupled agencies. If you go this route, you will need a power center outside the departments constantly pushing them to let go, like the British Next Steps Team.

Embody the new relationship in a written agreement that forces the steering organizations to guarantee specific flexibilities and the rowing organizations to commit to delivering specific results. Without a contract, departments and central agencies may agree to empower rowing organizations in principle, but never relinquish specific controls. And rowing organizations may agree to performance accountability in principle, but never face specific consequences.

Help policy makers and implementors learn how to play the steering role well. (By policy makers and implementors, we mean ministers and their staffs in New Zealand; ministers, permanent secretaries, and their staffs in the U.K.; and chief executives, department heads, and their policy staffs in the U.S.) In every jurisdiction that has used uncoupling, from New Zealand to Indianapolis, policy makers and their staffs have had to learn how to define the outcomes and outputs they want, examine alternative methods to achieve them, and negotiate performance contracts with rowing organizations to provide them. These skills do not develop overnight. Governments need to invest carefully in helping their top people develop these new capacities.

CLARITY OF DIRECTION: IMPROVING YOUR AIM

Once reinventors have uncoupled steering and rowing, they typically realize that they need radical improvements in their capacity to steer. They discover, as the New Zealanders did in the early 1990s, that they need a third approach. They need to develop systems that help them constantly define and redefine their core purposes—the outcomes that are most important to them—and aim their organizations at achieving them. They need one set of tools to establish goals, another to develop and refine strategies to achieve those goals, and a third to connect each rowing organization to those goals by defining the outputs and outcomes it should produce to contribute to them.

This is a frontier area of reinvention. Only a few pioneers, including New Zealand, Sunnyvale, California, and the state of Oregon, are struggling to reinvent their steering mechanisms. Why? Because this approach does not come naturally to elected officials—but it cannot be done without them.

After two years of experience with their new system, however, both elected ministers and managers in New Zealand appear pleased with it. It seems to help politicians set broad goals, without forcing them to deal with enormous detail or piles of performance data. These broad goals are then translated into progressively more specific outcome and output goals, which drive departmental work.

Sunnyvale developed an approach similar to New Zealand's at almost the same moment in time. After 15 years of performance budgeting and management (see *Reinventing Government*, pp. 142–145), City Manager Tom Lewcock and his staff realized that their system was focused primarily on outputs, not outcomes. As a result, it took the existing service activities for granted. It measured the efficiency and effectiveness of existing services, but it didn't help the city council ask if those services were the best ways for the city to achieve its goals. It helped Sunnyvale do things right, but it didn't help the council figure out which were the right things to do.

Sunnyvale's leaders call their new system "outcome management." As they explain in a document that frames the initiative:

> *The structure developed is a fully integrated, outcome-oriented budgeting and management system. It is based on the premise that the entire structure begins with the highest level, core outcomes for the city, and flows from there.* These core outcomes should be developed before a program is created. *In other words, existing program structures and responsibilities might change dramatically if that is the best way to meet the city's core outcomes.* [emphasis in original.]

City Manager Tom Lewcock says the new system, which the city is gradually rolling out department by department, has had a profound impact. It has forced managers "to ask the fundamental questions about how their department or division is organized.

> *It forces much discussion and debate on appropriate strategies and tactics, and the appropriate blending of approaches that best meets the outcomes being sought in an economical way. It is hard to describe in an organization which has gone through so much service and cultural change over the past 20 years how different this approach is and how many questions are being raised regarding how we go about doing our business.*

Oregon came at the problem from the other end: it developed outcome goals first. In the late 1980s, Governor Neil Goldschmidt launched a process called Oregon Shines, to create a long-term economic strategy for the state. The legislature's Trade and Economic Development Committee, which had already seen several futures commission reports gather dust on the shelves, wanted some way to force governors and legislators to focus on the goals defined by these processes. It proposed a public-private council to keep them on everyone's agenda. A consultant to Oregon Shines proposed that such a group develop specific outcome goals for the state. Goldschmidt liked the idea, and in 1989 the legislature created a nine-member Oregon Progress Board, chaired by the governor, and asked it to develop the "Oregon Benchmarks."

The Progress Board is a steering organization. "It exists to do strategic planning, because legislators in the U.S. find it hard to do that," explains Duncan Wyse, the board's first executive director. It doesn't set policy, it advises the governor and legislature—as well as the private and nonprofit sectors.

Every two years, the Progress Board publishes several hundred benchmarks, or outcome goals, which it narrows down to about 35 "core benchmarks" and 15 to 20 "urgent benchmarks." In 1994, for example, the core benchmarks included the following:

- Reduce the pregnancy rate per 1,000 females ages 10–17 from 19.7 in 1990 to 8.0 in 2000.

- Increase the percentage of 11th grade students who achieve established skill levels in reading and math from 60 percent in 1992 to 99 percent in 2010.

- Increase the high school graduation rate from 72 percent in 1990 to 93 percent in 2000 and 95 percent in 2010.

In 1993 Governor Barbara Roberts began using the benchmarks to prepare her budget. But her successor, John Kitzhaber, did not follow suit. This is Oregon's Achilles' heel. While the benchmarks have had a remarkable impact on the private and nonprofit sectors—and many counties have imitated the effort and developed their own benchmarks—state government has not significantly reoriented its spending priorities to pursue the new goals.

Oregon needs another steering tool: performance budgeting. Most departments have developed performance measures, but few are linked to the benchmarks. Unlike Sunnyvale and New Zealand, Oregon has not forged a complete steering system, in which long-term outcome goals are translated into program outcome goals and output targets for departments and agencies. A few states (such as Minnesota and Florida) have imitated Oregon's benchmarks, and many states, cities, and counties are developing performance measurement systems. But holistic steering systems that start with overall policy outcomes and proceed to measure program outcomes, outputs, and processes are still rare.

Even rarer are systems that do this while forcing decision makers to look at the long-term implications of their decisions. Sunnyvale's long-term budget system, which projects the consequences of every spending decision out ten years, was described at length in *Reinventing Government* (pp. 237–240). In 1994 New Zealand created a similar system. It passed a Fiscal Responsibility Act designed to minimize politicians' tendencies to spend money and run deficits for short-term political gain and to maximize their long-term fiscal discipline. The act required the government to produce:

- A budget policy statement, due to Parliament three months before the annual budget deadline, to define the government's overall fiscal policy and frame the parameters of the budget debate. In Graham Scott's words, "This is intended to promote more informed trade-offs of strategic fiscal objectives by separating debate about them, at least temporarily, from the crush of detailed fiscal compromises and decisions in the final run-up to the budget."

- A fiscal strategy report, which includes ten-year projections of spending, revenue, debt, and net worth. The report publicly examines whether these long-term trends (and the annual budget) are consistent with the budget policy statement. "The long-term forecasts and scenarios that the act calls for are intended to expose the out-year effects of current decisions," says Scott.

- Fiscal reports, containing three-year economic and fiscal forecasts. These are required twice a year and roughly a month before any national election.

In addition, Parliament amended the Public Finance Act to extend requirements for accrual accounting and generally accepted accounting practices (GAAP) to all government spending. This was designed to ensure, in Scott's words, "that the financial implications of government decisions are highly visible." For example, "an appropriation is required when the government disposes of an asset below its recorded book value." In the past, cash-based accounting systems had hidden many of the government's losses and long-term liabilities. Accrual accounting makes that impossible today.

All of these measures were designed to make it harder for elected officials to make short-term decisions that create long-term fiscal problems. They still do, of course, but when it happens now it is much more visible to Parliament, the press, and the public.

Some people classify tools such as the Oregon Benchmarks and Sunnyvale's budget system under the umbrella of "strategic planning." We have deliberately stayed away from that label, because what we are

---

Tools for Improving Your Aim

Outcome Goals are long-term results the government wants to achieve.

Steering Organizations are boards, councils, and other organizations that set goals and choose strategies for public systems, or advise elected officials who do this. School boards are steering organizations in education; private industry councils (PICs) are steering organizations in job training; the Oregon Progress Board is a steering organization for the state of Oregon.

Strategy Development is the process of developing, choosing, and refining strategies to achieve outcome goals. Part of the discipline of strategic planning, this includes many techniques, from search conferences to design labs to gap analysis.

Performance Budgets define the outcomes and outputs policy makers intend to buy with each sum they appropriate.

Long-Term Budgets project current fiscal trends (spending, revenue, debt, and net worth) into the future, to indicate the long-term implications of current decisions.

Accrual Accounting is a system used by business, which depreciates assets and enters obligations on the books when they are incurred, not when the money is actually spent.

talking about is better described as steering than planning. Steering is about setting goals, choosing strategies to achieve them, choosing organizations to carry out those strategies, measuring how well those strategies and organizations do in achieving the goals, and making adjustments. This is what strategic planning is supposed to do, but the word "planning" mistakenly implies that the key is creating *plans*. Steering in a fast-changing world is not about making plans; it is about choosing and evaluating strategies to achieve fundamental goals. Planning is primarily operational: rowing organizations develop business plans to help them carry out the strategies and produce the outputs they have been assigned. This is important, but it is not what we mean by steering.

Improving Your Aim: Lessons Learned

This approach is a frontier area because it is so difficult. It is far easier in a rational, nonpoliticized environment than in the typical political environment one finds in a nation, state, province, or large city. In most political environments, elected officials are far more interested in achieving their short-term political goals—meeting constituents' pressing needs, satisfying key interest groups, getting reelected—than in increasing the government's capacity to choose long-term goals and strategies to achieve them. Indeed, many politicians don't want to articulate long-term goals, because the voters can then hold them accountable for achieving them. Far better to have no goals, if self-interest is the overriding factor!

Even when the steering approach works, the payoff for politicians is too far in the future to do them much good. "You don't get to measure success in your term, while you're in office," says former Oregon Governor Barbara Roberts.

In places like Oregon and New Zealand, leaders have learned some important lessons about how to overcome these obstacles. For example:

Focus on improving your steering capacity only after you have developed some momentum that supports the effort. In New Zealand, the success of the Labor Party's reforms in the 1980s led directly to the reforms of 1994. Without the confidence built by corporatizing public enterprises, clearing the decks, uncoupling steering and rowing, and introducing performance measurement and management—and the *demand* for better steering that these reforms triggered—the government might not have had the will to undertake its 1994 reforms. Oregon did not have this momentum, and it hit a brick wall when it came time for the legislature to take the benchmarks seriously in its budget decisions. (New Zealand also had the advantage of a parliamentary system in which the executive controlled the legislature, of course.)

The executive must take the lead in improving steering capacity, but it should involve the legislature in the process. Legislatures are notoriously reactive. Unless they have very strong and farsighted leadership, they don't focus on steering issues. It is up to the executive to lead, but if he or she does not involve the legislature in creating tools such as outcome goals, steering organizations, and performance budgets, legislators will develop no ownership of the new systems. This is precisely what happened in Oregon.

Keep the process bipartisan. Involve the leadership of all major parties, to ensure that when power changes hands the system is not abandoned. Many a governor has developed a set of goals and a strategic planning system, only to watch his or her successor ignore them. Despite political differences over short-term priorities and strategies, it is surprisingly easy to overcome partisan differences and agree on long-term outcome goals, steering organizations, and budgeting systems.

Build the whole system, not just a piece of it. New Zealand and Sunnyvale discovered what happens when you build performance budgets and management systems without outcome goals. Oregon discovered what happens when you build outcome goals and a steering organization without linking them to budget and management systems. To improve your capacity to steer, you need a holistic system that defines outcome goals and strategies, connects them to action through the budget system, monitors performance through a measurement system, and creates consequences through performance management. If you don't link goals to resource allocation through the budget system, neither legislators nor managers will take the goals seriously. To do things right *and* do the right thing, you need the whole strategic cycle.

INTEGRATING THE THREE APPROACHES

There is no correct order of play in unfolding the three core approaches. In New Zealand and the U.K., leaders began by clearing the decks, then moved to uncoupling, then (in New Zealand only) focused on improving their aim. This is the most pragmatic sequence, because it is politically easier to privatize and eliminate functions than to agree on long-term goals and build a system that forces everyone to stick to them. The first approach allows politicians to throw the voters red meat; the second requires them to put reason and the public interest above politics and self-interest.

In a nonpolitical world, however, the logical order would be to get clarity of direction by defining your goals and strategies; then clear the decks of functions that don't fit; then uncouple steering and rowing functions. To be even more logical, only then would one move on to the other four C's. But reinvention is normally driven by necessity, not logic. Reinventors start by solving their most pressing problems—even if they are Labor Party leaders and the most pressing problems include public organizations that should be privatized. The lesson is simple: start where you have the most political will and the best opportunity to make change. But don't forget to come back to the rest of the core strategy. At some point it will become indispensable.

STEERING AT THE ORGANIZATIONAL LEVEL

Because it is about steering, the core strategy is chiefly the province of elected officials and their top appointed officials, whom we call "policrats." However, managers often formulate goals and strategic choices and take them to executives and legislative committees for approval. It is not uncommon for managers to drive the process and elected officials to react and endorse their proposals.

Within their own rowing organizations, managers can also use the core strategy. As much as we talk about separating policy and administration, steering and rowing, the separation is rarely pure. Policy decisions remain to be made in many rowing organizations. For example, compliance organizations have to interpret the laws and regulations they enforce, and service-delivery organizations often experience budget reductions that force them to choose which policy goals are most important and which will be given less priority.

Managers can use all three core approaches within their rowing organizations. They can clear the decks of unnecessary functions, though they may have to get the permission of elected officials. They can use all of the tools of the third approach. Indeed, strategic planning was developed more for single organizations than for governments with multiple organizations, and its "planning" side makes more sense in that context. Finally, while they cannot uncouple steering and rowing, they can uncouple purchasing and providing, as the British have done through their market testing system. A rowing agency can purchase services from outside providers, thus splitting the purchasing role from the providing role. But this does not uncouple steering and rowing, as we have defined them. Thus the "purchaser/provider split," as the British call it, is similar to but not identical with the separation of steering and rowing.

Achieving clarity of purpose is a critical first step in any organization. According to Sonia Phippard, former head of the Next Steps Team in the U.K., the executive agencies that have made the most improvements are those that have focused on questions of mission, goals, and performance targets. "There is no doubt that agencies have done better when they have taken the time to think through very carefully their aims and targets," she says, "and how performance measures can be set against those aims."

QUESTIONS PEOPLE ASK
ABOUT THE CORE STRATEGY

Q: Which activities can be privatized—left to the market—and which cannot?
Functions can be left entirely to the market:

- If the market can provide them. If buyers will purchase them and nonpayers can be excluded from enjoying them, then private producers will supply them.

- If they primarily benefit individuals or groups of individuals, rather than society as a whole (if they are "private goods").

- If the community does not care whether everyone has access to them—if there is no concern about equity or universal access.

If all three of these conditions are met, the activity can be left to the market. In such cases the public sector may have to regulate the activities and enforce compliance with regulations, but it does not need to pay for or operate them.

Within these guidelines, there is much room for different communities to come to different judgments, of course. Some democracies leave ownership of railroads in private hands because they primarily benefit individual interests and voters do not feel every citizen should have access to rail transportation, for example. Others choose to subsidize rail transportation because they want to reduce highway congestion and air pollution, which are in the collective interest. Similarly, some democracies find it unacceptable that some people cannot afford basic housing, so they subsidize it. Others do not.

Q: Is there a core public sector that should always be operated by public organizations? Are there public functions that should never be carried out by private organizations?

Most steering functions—policy and regulatory activities—must be carried out by government. And many compliance functions normally remain in public hands, because the public is not comfortable with letting private organizations carry out functions such as those involving the courts, the police, and tax collection.

There are examples of private provision of all three of these functions: 30 Swiss towns and villages have contracted with a private company to operate their police forces; judicial functions such as dispute resolution are performed by private parties, and San Francisco uses Community Boards to resolve neighborhood disputes; and many governments use private firms to collect taxes. But in most communities, mixing these activities with for-profit organizations—or even nonprofits—makes people nervous.

The more sensitive and risky the function, the more likely it is that the public will want to see it operated by government employees. If it involves significant violence (as in police functions and high-security prisons), sensitive privacy issues (as in the administration of personal income tax collection), due process rights, or an absolute necessity of fair and equal treatment (as in the courts), citizens generally prefer to have public employees perform the function.

Though mercenary armies were common in the past, today most nations also insist that those who fight their wars and oversee their intelligence operations are public employees. Again, however, there are exceptions. During the Gulf War, the Joint Defense Facility at Nurrungar, Australia, tracked SCUD missile launches by satellite and conveyed information to Patriot missile batteries in the Middle East. Those who monitored the launches worked for Serco Australia, a subsidiary of a British company.

To our knowledge, all other functions can easily be operated by private organizations, when funded by government. Private companies run fire departments, operate the American space shuttle, manage low-security prisons, and handle nuclear fuel.

Q: Are there any situations in which steering and rowing should not be uncoupled?

This is a subject of significant debate in the U.K. and New Zealand. The New Zealanders have generally answered no, while the British have answered yes. We lean toward New Zealand's position, but not quite all the way. In our view, *almost* any function can benefit from the separation of steering and rowing and the creation of a contractual, arm's-length relationship. There are a few situations, however, in which either the control or the consequences strategy is impractical, so uncoupling may not be wise.

When an activity is extremely sensitive, requires a great deal of coordination, or involves great risk, policy makers may want to hold it very close. Examples might include defense, intelligence activities, and diplomacy. New Zealand tried uncoupling defense by creating a civilian defense policy ministry separate from the military. According to a number of respected academics, this led to problems. They report that the uncoupled model, "while retained in statute, is all but a fiction in practice."

When it is impossible to specify or measure outputs with any clarity, it becomes impossible to create consequences for performance. This might be the case with diplomacy, for example. Measuring the performance of diplomats appears to be almost entirely subjective. Peter Drucker's warning about federal decentralization in large corporations applies in government as well:

> *Indeed, wherever a federal organization gets in trouble ... the reason is always that the measurements at the disposal of the center are not good enough, so that personal supervision has to be substituted. ... To be able to give autonomy one must have confidence. And this requires controls that make opinions unnecessary.*

To be able to manage by objectives one must know whether goals are being reached or not; and this requires clear and reliable measurements.

Q: Won't uncoupling create many small agencies, all of which have to have personnel functions, procurement functions, and the like? Won't this duplication be inefficient? Isn't it more efficient to use larger organizations that can achieve economies of scale?

In a word, no. As General Creech argues, the key to high performance is to think big but organize small. Large organizations have many diseconomies of scale, because they tend to remove so many decisions from those who know the most about the issues in question. As for duplication of internal support functions like personnel and procurement, uncoupling allows for different policies in different organizations, which creates more efficiency, not less. And by using internal enterprise management, which we discuss in chapter 5, governments can allow organizations to buy many internal support services wherever they can get the best deal, rather than producing them in-house.

Q: Can radical reinvention as practiced in New Zealand work in smaller, local governments?

Yes. In fact New Zealand's Labor Party pushed through legislation in 1989 that completely restructured local government, shrinking the number of local and regional jurisdictions from more than 700 to 86 and imposing the same principles on them that Labor had imposed on the national bureaucracy. Policy, service-delivery, and compliance functions were separated, and elected councils now have direct authority only over policy. The reforms handed operational authority to chief executives, hired by councils on five-year performance contracts. All other local or regional employees work for the chief executive, not the council.

Councils must now prepare annual plans that specify their objectives, desired outcomes and outputs, performance targets and indicators, resources, and costs. In addition, they have to prepare general plans for the following two years. At the end of each year they must publish a performance report, showing how they did compared with their objectives and targets.

The reforms encouraged corporatization of commercial functions, many of which have been organized as local authority trading enterprises, the local equivalent of SOEs, or "business units," the equivalent of enterprise funds. These entities are encouraged to bid on work not just in their jurisdictions but in others, and some have been privatized.

Local authorities are not required to competitively bid out services, as in the U.K., but they *are* required to formally examine the advantages and disadvantages of different service-delivery options, public and private. This has led to a dramatic expansion of contracting: by 1994, the percentage of local services delivered by external providers had increased from 22 to 48 percent, according to a national government survey.

The reforms applied the new financial management and human resources frameworks to local government as well. They now use accrual accounting and general accepted accounting practices, as well as performance contracts for all salaried employees. Hourly employees can choose between negotiating their own performance agreements and designating a bargaining organization.

Did these reforms work? Apparently so. In 1993, after a worldwide search, Germany's Bertelsmann Foundation named Christchurch, New Zealand, one of the two best-managed cities—along with Phoenix, Arizona—in the world.

– 5 –

THE CONSEQUENCES
STRATEGY:
CREATING CONSEQUENCES
FOR PERFORMANCE

INDIANAPOLIS:
A MARKETPLACE FOR PUBLIC SERVICES

We are using competition to inject risk, believing that risk is an element that creates customer satisfaction and added value. We're dealing with organizations that don't believe risk should apply to them.
—Mayor Steve Goldsmith

Weeks after Steve Goldsmith became mayor of Indianapolis in January 1992, his new transportation director announced that a small portion of the city's street-repair work would be put out to bid. Local asphalt companies, which eventually stood to gain as much as $1 million worth of work, applauded the move.

The union representing city workers, the American Federation of State, County, and Municipal Employees, took a dark view of the decision. Alarmed by Goldsmith's campaign pledge to "privatize" up to 25 percent of city government (excluding fire and police functions), it had opposed his election. "Everyone knew Steve as the Prince of Privatization," says Steve Fantauzzo, executive director of AFSCME Indiana Council 62, whose locals represent more than 1,000 city workers. "It doesn't take a rocket scientist to figure out that he's coming after the people that I represent. . . . Initially we operated out of a high fear factor."

The union and the new mayor had been butting heads from day one. The bid for pothole and crack repairs threatened to escalate the skirmishing, until Transportation Director Mitch Roob (pronounced "Robe") told the union that its workers were welcome to submit a bid for the work. "We told the union, if you don't bid you could lose your jobs. If you do, you might maintain them," Roob recalls.

Roob's offer challenged the union's oft-stated claim that it could best any private bidder. "Mitch asked if we were prepared to walk our talk," says Fantauzzo.

We had for years been saying in a lot of places that if we were given a level playing field, the public employees providing day-to-day services were more than prepared to deal with private competition. . . . When the mayor changed the rules of the game to allow employees to participate in the [bidding] process, the union was able to take a much less adversarial position. . . . I thought we needed to position ourselves to be at the table and influence the factors that would determine whether we survived. We couldn't do that sitting on the outside.

The union first told Roob it couldn't compete fairly if it was stuck with the overhead cost of the department's bloated middle management. For 90 crew members, the department had 36 supervisors. Many of them were politically active Republicans—people who had helped elect Goldsmith. When the union raised the issue, Fantauzzo recalls, "We felt that we had thrown a grenade back into [the administration's] lap."

Without any warning, Roob laid off half the supervisors. "It just looked to me like if we had 90 truck drivers, we needed less than 36 supervisors," he says. "Probably 18 was a good number." His move— blessed by the mayor—produced an uproar in the local Republican Party. "My political party thinks I'm absolutely irrational," Goldsmith told a gathering several months later.

The union had a different view. "When the mayor actually laid off the middle managers," says Fantauzzo, "it was a positive message to our local leadership." AFSCME agreed to work with the slimmed-down management team to put together a competitive bid. Roob paid an outside consultant $20,000 to help the employees figure out their true costs—information no one had ever wanted before. Working hurriedly, they developed an activity-based costing model and determined that it cost the city team $407 per ton to get hot asphalt into potholes.

Then they figured out how to cut the cost. In the past, street-repair crews had consisted of as many as eight workers, including a supervisor. They normally used two trucks. Under pressure to compete, union members decided to cut down to four workers, without a supervisor, and one truck. This cut their projected costs more than 25 percent, without reducing service levels.

Seven local asphalt companies also bid for the first contract, to repair a ten-block section on the city's northeast side. "They were convinced that their day had come," says Roob. But they were wrong. The companies knew how to resurface entire streets, not how to fill potholes; the city had monopolized that business for years. The private bids "were absurdly high, all over the map," says Roob—from a high of $450,000 to a low of about $20,000. But even the lowest was three times higher than the public employees' offer of $6,700.

Some Goldsmith supporters pressured Roob to cancel the competition. They argued that awarding the first bid to city workers would damage the administration's credibility with the business community. And they worried that the city team had underestimated its costs and would not stay on budget—a potential embarrassment for the mayor.

Goldsmith left the decision in Roob's hands. Eager to preserve the cooperation he had built with the union, Roob gave the contract to the city employees. He will never forget the reaction:

I caught a lot of flak for this. I disappointed the people in the administration for whom public employees were by definition bad. I pissed off the people who were the Republican establishment of the city. My friends were in the union movement. It was as difficult a time as I've had in my career.

With the stakes so high, Roob also decided to hedge his bet. He hired private inspectors to monitor the quality and cost of the team's work. That contract cost more than the street repairs.

Drops in a Bucket

In the four years that followed, Goldsmith forced city employees to bid for their work more than 64 times. No one anticipated the powerful forces of change this would unleash—not the voters, not the union, not the local Republican Party.

As American cities go, Indianapolis had been a national showcase. Since 1968 it had been run by farsighted Republican mayors. It suffered from many of the economic and social ills that afflicted urban America, but it had a much milder case. "Most people were advocates for just incremental change," says Goldsmith. "They said, 'We're a successful city, why would we want radical reinventing?' "

The Republican establishment had anointed Goldsmith, a popular county prosecutor. But the new mayor believed his city was heading for fiscal and economic crisis. A persistent exodus of middle-class families and businesses was eroding its tax base. Inner-city neighborhoods were crumbling. The city was running a deficit; it couldn't keep up with demands for government to solve more and more problems.

"We viewed ourselves as at a real crossroads," says Charles "Skip" Stitt, an assistant to the mayor.

Goldsmith rejected the idea of a tax increase. "Cities today can't operate like they did 5 or 10 or 15 years ago," he says. "The tax bases are shrinking, the problems are exploding. You can't afford to tax your citizens more." Instead, he looked for a strategy that would "produce more services for less money." He chose competition.

Goldsmith acknowledges that competition is not the "privatization" he promised on the campaign trail. After he took office, he abandoned the simplistic view that business alone held the key to reducing government costs. He realized that private ownership and services were not the secret of success—*competition* was. It was the competition inherent in a market economy that drove businesses to innovate and improve.

Goldsmith's philosophical shift was driven home when he decided to turn the city's sewer billing process over to a private contractor. The private water utility offered to perform the work for 5 percent less than it was costing the city. Goldsmith was not impressed, so he decided to bring in other private bidders. Faced with competition, the water company offered *70 percent* savings—more than $2 million a year.

Goldsmith describes his shift to competition as a philosophical decision, but it was also pragmatic. He wanted to create change without disrupting city services. Letting city workers compete helped avoid a battle with AFSCME that might slow down or disturb services. At the same time, the bidding contests delivered the results he wanted.

Whether the employees won or a business won, government cut its costs without having to lower service levels or quality.

At times, the city refused to allow public units to bid because it thought they could not win. This so angered AFSCME, however, that Goldsmith finally relented, and city workers can now bid whenever they choose to. Sometimes, however, no public unit chooses to bid. In some cases the employees providing a service, such as courier runs, are spread across several departments, so there is no one unit to develop a bid.

The mayor did give city employees one major break: when creating a level playing field between public and private bids, he did not require in-lieu-of-tax payments in the public bids. Since city units don't pay sales, property, or income taxes, they start with an advantage. "If we still can't compete," says Fantauzzo, "shame on us."

To keep the entire bidding process open to public scrutiny and immune from charges of corruption, Goldsmith created a commission to identify government services that could be put up for bid. Calling it the Service, Efficiency, and Lower Taxes for Indianapolis Commission (SELTIC), he asked nine of the city's most successful business leaders to serve on it.

The commission and the mayor chose to start with the low-hanging fruit: services that did not involve large numbers of employees. With some quick successes, they hoped, they could build public support for larger, more controversial competitions.

Gradually, like drops in the proverbial bucket, the savings began to mount. Contracting out microfilm services saved nearly $1 million over three years; window washing, $45,000 over the same period; printing and copying, $2.8 million over seven years. Public-private competition to service the city's swimming pools and utilities saved nearly $500,000 over seven years. When the city bid out trash collection for 10 of its 11 garbage districts, city crews won all three districts in which they were allowed to compete. (No bidder—public or private—was allowed to bid on more than three districts, because the city wanted to prevent a single provider from gaining a lock on the service.) Overall the city was to save $14.8 million over three years, but city workers have driven costs down so fast that the savings will actually be closer to $20 million.

The Solid Waste Division produced such dramatic savings in part because it invented a second, more positive, source of consequences:

gainsharing. Union leaders proposed that if the division cut its costs below the level it had bid, its employees should share in the savings. Public Works Director Michael Stayton agreed, and they negotiated a deal in which employees would divide 10 percent of the savings—up to a maximum of $3,000 per employee per year.

Motivated both by this target and the competition, the Solid Waste Division beat its first-year bid target of $3 million in savings by a full $2.1 million. Though this entitled the 117 trash haulers and 26 administrative staff members to $3,000 apiece, department leaders balked at such a rich price. Ultimately they agreed to an average of $1,750 per employee, a sum that still set bells ringing throughout city government. Other units quickly copied the program, winning bonuses more in the $500–$1,000 per employee range.

Overall, says Deputy Mayor Skip Stitt, competitive bidding saved an average of 25 percent, no matter who won the bid. But it wasn't long before the low-hanging fruit was gone. In late 1992 Goldsmith reached for his first big plum—the city's wastewater treatment facilities. It proved to be a long and difficult stretch.

Wastewater Competition: "A Nice Piece of Change"

Goldsmith's first instinct was to sell off the Advanced Wastewater Treatment facilities, worth an estimated $300 million. But financial consultants told him no one would buy the plants unless sewer rates were allowed to rise to cover costs. Rates had not increased in eight years, and the city was losing $3–$4 million a year on the system. Without increased revenues, a business would also lose money.

Goldsmith didn't want citizens' sewer bills to increase, so he looked instead at bidding out the operation and management of the facilities. He hoped to save on the $30 million annual operating budget.

The two plants employed just over 300 people, nearly half of them union members. AFSCME objected vehemently to the possibility of losing jobs. Plant managers complained that such a radical move was unnecessary and risky—the plants were already award winners. Local environmentalists opposed the mayor, fearing private management would result in reductions in water quality. Even the city-county council had doubts about the idea; two of its members had been instrumental in developing the facilities. Then Goldsmith's own consultant, Ernst & Young, threw cold water on his plans. It reported that competitive bidding might generate only a 5 percent cut in costs, hardly enough to justify the political aggravation of a bidding process.

"It wasn't easy to sit in the council meeting and have AFSCME leaders read verbatim from consulting reports we had paid for," recalls Stitt, the mayor's assistant. "Nobody was clamoring for change."

But Goldsmith had a gut feeling. Deeply committed by now to competition, he was convinced that bigger savings were possible. "We were so wed to competition as a core strategy," says Stitt. "If in-house was the best way to go, they were going to have to prove it in the marketplace."

When the city announced the bidding process, plant employees reacted angrily. They confronted Stayton, the public works director. "We're well run," they told him. "Why are you doing this to us?" Stayton asked them to bid, too.

Division managers began to develop a proposal, and Stayton paid a local consulting firm to help them. But the union refused to participate. Fantauzzo complains that the city was late in inviting employees to join the process. "The bid team was put together," he says. "They had gotten far down the road, and *then* we were asked to participate."

To mollify AFSCME, the city made an unusual—but critical— decision. It specified in its request for proposals that if a private company won the bid, it would have to recognize the AFSCME local as the legitimate representative of the plant employees and negotiate with it in good faith.

Four private companies bid for the contract. Two of them, plus the public managers, survived the first round of scrutiny. Their bids reaffirmed Goldsmith's faith in competition: both private companies offered savings of about $50 million over five years—roughly 22 percent of projected operating and capital investment costs. Both planned to eliminate at least a third of all jobs at the plants.

Just a month earlier, the public managers had given Stayton a budget proposal for the next year that reduced costs by about 5 percent. Now, caught in a bidding war, they submitted a bid that cut another 10 percent, without eliminating any jobs. "After they gave at the office," Stayton wryly notes, "they still had 10 percent more to give."

Stayton rejected the internal-management bid and set the two private companies against each other. They eagerly sweetened their proposals with $6 million in additional cost reductions. Eventually, the White River Environmental Partnership (WREP) won by offering an additional package capped by a commitment to contribute 5 percent of pretax profits to the city and to invest $1 million to develop a wastewater training center in Indianapolis. It also pledged to help the city find jobs for workers it did not need. WREP was 51 percent locally owned—a partnership between the Indianapolis Water Company, a private business that had supplied the city's drinking water for more than a century, and a gigantic French wastewater treatment firm.

When the city added up WREP's package, the savings topped $65 million over five years. A 29.5 percent reduction in wastewater treatment costs, it was the biggest score yet for competitive bidding. It amounted to almost 3 percent of the city's annual operating budget.

Although Goldsmith had the authority to award the contract, he and Stayton sensed that the community was not ready for such a big change. Instead they created a review committee, including two city-county councilors who had opposed issuing the request for proposals, to conduct a one-month "due diligence" investigation into WREP's qualifications and proposal. The group visited other U.S. cities where the French company operated facilities. They came home believers, and they recommended that the city contract with WREP.

At that point, says Stayton, all hell broke loose.

All of a sudden, the union and the environmentalists came out of the woodwork. They asked, "Why is the mayor hurrying into this?" We had to do six weeks of damage control.

Environmentalists and AFSCME tried to get the council to block the contract. The union sued the city to stop the deal, but it did not succeed. The council held a heated public hearing that was broadcast locally on television. But by then, Goldsmith and Stayton had gotten their story out and calmed the waters. Stayton kept reminding people that the city's respected water company would be taking over the wastewater facilities. "You trust the water company for your water," he told them, "so why not for your sewer?" The council decided not to derail the contract.

Goldsmith signed the contract in November 1993, making the Indianapolis Advanced Wastewater Treatment facilities the largest privately managed municipal wastewater operation in the U.S. The process had taken nearly a year—a long time for the more than 300 wastewater workers who had lived with the stress of economic insecurity. Over Thanksgiving and Christmas, they faced a more concrete threat: many would lose their jobs at the plant.

When WREP took over on February 1, 1994, nearly 200 city workers made the transition to the new company. Their jobs with the private firm paid as much or more than they had earned with the city, and their benefits were better. Many of them were still represented by AFSCME. The new managers and the union had quickly struck an agreement—an unusual instance of a public employee union representing workers in a private company.

But 126 city workers did not make the shift to new management. The city offered to put all of them into a "safety net," which would guarantee them another job with the city or training and placement in a private sector job. It set up a job bank of vacant city positions and began moving people into them. About half chose this route, and WREP paid for placement and training for the rest. When the city got down to the last eight or nine people who had not been placed, it moved them into a new unit it was developing to improve overall customer service.

WREP has maintained wastewater quality, and in several respects it has improved on the city's high-quality performance of prior years. In its first year of operation it exceeded its discharge permit limitations only once, compared to 14 times in the city's last two years of operation. It cut the number and duration of overflows by 50 percent and the number of workplace accidents by 70 percent. Critics charged that it was responsible for two incidents in which fish died in the White River, but investigations by a county grand jury and an independent consultant hired by the city absolved WREP of responsibility. They blamed low water levels in the river and raw sewage overflows due to flaws in the city's sewer system. The state Department of Environmental Management charged that wastewater operations contributed to the problem, but local environmentalists disagreed. (Even if WREP had been responsible, the city-run system had experienced a much larger fish kill several years earlier.)

During WREP's first year, union grievances also fell—from 38 under city management to 1. Even sick time declined. "The majority [of former city workers] would say they don't want to come back," says AFSCME's Fantauzzo. "Economically, they've done better."

Managers who made the transition felt the same way. When Rick Farnham managed the wastewater facilities for the city, he was skeptical about using a private firm to do the job. "I had the same perceptions [as others]: that contract operation would lead to reduced water quality or cutting corners," he says. But a few months in his new job as WREP's technical services manager changed his mind: "I don't believe any of that is true at this point."

WREP met its contractual target for reducing the plants' operating costs. Changes in technology generated the majority of the savings. WREP substantially altered the plants' secondary treatment process, shifting more of the burden for processing fluids to less costly biotowers.

WREP also streamlined the top-heavy, overstaffed organization by eliminating supervisory positions and overly specialized jobs. "There were people who had fixed pumps in one area of one plant for ten years," says Douglas B. Reichlin, a senior manager for WREP. "That's all they did, they couldn't fix other pumps." So WREP trained workers for multiple tasks and gave them additional responsibilities. The company invests far more in training than a typical public agency does.

Careful use of electricity helped cut the annual utility bill by $1 million. Ending an unnecessary buildup of inventories saved millions of dollars. Renegotiating the labor contract converted half of the automatic cost-of-living increase into performance incentives for individuals and teams. And WREP trimmed planned capital expenditures, saving the city an additional $1.8 million.

Stayton believes that competition was the only way to force such dramatic changes. "People in the plants and the technical staff were not willing to break their norms," he says. "You couldn't do it by just appointing a new manager for the division."

In the spring of 1995, a WREP official telephoned Stayton. He explained that the company was holding $45,000 in an account for the city. It was Indianapolis' 5 percent share of the company's profits for 1994.

"They told us it'll be about that number every year," Stayton reports. "It's a nice piece of change."

Business as Usual

By 1996, the city had held 64 public-private competitions, putting up for bid more than $500 million in work on 27 separate services. Public workers had won 16 bids outright and split 13 additional bids with private contractors. The competition had cut the city's costs by more than $100 million, projected over seven years. An additional $20 million in projected savings had come from contracts on which city employees did not bid.

Goldsmith and the city council have used the savings to repair infrastructure in the city's inner-city neighborhoods—a move that helped turn some inner-city councilors from opponents to supporters of competitive contracting.

In 1996, the city had more competitive bids—and more savings—in the pipeline. It had begun final negotiations with a private company to manage the city and county's information systems, with projected savings of $37 million. It had launched bids for work in ice-skating rinks, mowing, buildings and grounds maintenance, solid waste billing, and sewer maintenance. And it was scheduling bids for street cleaning, tree removal, locksmithing, emergency shelter care, parks upkeep— and pothole repair, again.

By 1996, the mayor had eliminated more than 1,025 of the 4,416 city jobs that existed when he took office. Almost all of the reductions were outside the police and fire departments, where Goldsmith chose not to bid out work. The rest of the city's workforce shrank by more than 40 percent—much of it because of competitive bidding.

Although the city does not keep these figures, Skip Stitt guesses that about 20 percent of these 1,025 people were laid off. The rest went to work for private contractors, were moved into vacant city jobs, were placed in private sector jobs, or took early-retirement packages. Yet not one union member was laid off. Goldsmith never made a "no-layoff" pact with the unions, but his administration implemented a de facto no-layoff policy for the 20 percent of the workforce that belonged to unions.

Goldsmith's successes with competition attracted attention world-wide. Big-city mayors, governors, foreign officials, and journalists flocked to Indianapolis. The visiting traffic got so heavy that the city finally organized regularly scheduled conferences to share its story. Then it began to tell callers it could no longer host other visits.

The visitors found that competition had produced unexpected changes. City employees had feared competition but discovered they could win bids. "The bidding process is telling you that you've got to dig down and make every effort to maintain your job," explains Jeffrey Thomas, a ten-year employee in the Solid Waste Division. His unit increased daily workloads and redesigned trash-collection routes in order to win its bids. Through competition it even expanded its "market share" of the city's garbage-pickup routes.

Black politicians had feared that minority employees in government would be laid off, but local minority entrepreneurs found that competitive bidding opened up business opportunities. For example, George Pillow's fledgling courier service won a city contract that he says boosted his revenues by about 30 percent and gave him the credibility to land a handful of additional contracts. By 1996, according to Stitt, the city had increased its minority contracting 20 times over 1991 levels—to $40 million—in part because competition had opened up bidding opportunities.

And the public employee union found it could use competitive bidding to improve its members' pay and benefits, through gainsharing. The Solid Waste Division's $1,750 gainsharing payments sent a loud message to city employees. Another unit quickly submitted a bid that waived its right to a cost-of-living increase because it feared the pay boost would make its proposal uncompetitive, for instance. Instead, it convinced the city to agree to gainsharing, if it brought the work in under the proposed price.

By 1995, the combination of gainsharing, competitive bidding, and job security had begun to produce employee behavior that would be unthinkable in most governments. In Fleet Services, where the employees negotiated a 25 percent share of any savings below the price they bid, employees were beginning to *suggest* outsourcing when it would save money. In auto body work, for example, the city shop was not competitive with private shops. So it began outsourcing that work and moving the displaced employees into more competitive areas. In 1994 it outsourced only 15 percent of body work; in 1995 it increased the amount to 37 percent.

"The outsourcing issue used to be a big fight with the administration," says Skip Stitt. "But now it's not. There's no bickering if the employees can save—and make—money on the deal."

Fantauzzo confirms this change:

Those employees and their managers are determining what they do best, their core activities. We don't do body work best, so let's get out of the body work business. The next step is what they're looking at now: expanding what they do well and doing more of it.

Fantauzzo is referring to a trend that began to emerge in 1996. Motivated in part by the prospect of gainsharing, his members and managers such as Michael Carter in Solid Waste are teaming up to go after new business—from other city departments, from other public organizations, and from nearby governments. Solid Waste, which has already won contracts with municipalities in the neighboring county, is looking at private sector opportunities and pushing for the right to bid in more than three of the city's garbage districts.

Fantauzzo wants the city to allow other units to do the same. He finds himself in an unfamiliar position for a union leader: marketing his members' services.

> *Going after new business is something we've never done before. I find myself going to WREP and saying, "Why are you going to a private garage to get your trucks fixed? You should contract with the city garage for fleet services."*

Fantauzzo says that gainsharing has not changed employees' attitudes toward competition, which are still mixed:

> *On the one hand, there is a lot of apprehension about whether they'll be employed. . . . But on the other side of the ledger, for the first time in a long time, employees have been asked to stop parking their brains at the door when they come to work. They actually have been empowered to participate in the decision-making process. Workers are being asked how to do the job more efficiently and more effectively.*

But combine that empowerment with gainsharing and you get an entirely different attitude about *productivity,* he says. "Look at what happens in the eleventh month of a budget in traditional government: everyone is looking to spend the last dime to justify that plus more next year. Here, people are looking to save every dime because they figure a piece of the pie is going into their pocket."

In 1991, Fantauzzo was looking for ways to keep Steve Goldsmith out of the mayor's job. At his union's annual preelection convention, the members booed Goldsmith. But in 1995, at the same convention, they gave him a standing ovation. The city workers wanted to endorse him, but the teachers, who opposed a reform slate of school board candidates Goldsmith was promoting, did not. So the union endorsed no one. (Goldsmith won reelection with almost 60 percent of the vote.) Meanwhile, Fantauzzo partners with Skip Stitt at conferences to explain the city's competition process. "I suspect some union colleagues in other areas of the country are raising their eyebrows," he muses.

There's little doubt about that. But in Indianapolis, at least, competition seems to have become an accepted way of doing business. Following the success of the wastewater treatment competition, the city's airport authority bid out the operation and management of Indianapolis International Airport, where costs had risen 38 percent since 1984. No one caused a political ruckus; no environmental issues emerged; public meetings were sparsely attended. The union stayed out of the process because the 300 affected employees were not union members. Those workers submitted a bid. Like the city's wastewater division managers, they tried to compete by cutting costs sharply. But so did four private firms.

One bid came from BAA USA, Inc., the American subsidiary of BAA, the British company that owns and operates London's Heathrow, the largest international airport in the world. BAA had once been a government agency—British Airports Authority—but Margaret Thatcher's government sold it in 1987. It manages airports that serve 80 million passengers yearly—nearly 30 times Indianapolis's volume. "They've forgotten more than we know about airports," says Public Works Director Stayton.

In mid-1995, the airport authority's board of directors approved the British subsidiary's bid. The authority's May 11 press release crowed that "Private Management of Airport Could Save More than $100 Million, Improve Service." The savings will go to airlines that use the airport—not taxpayers—since landing fees fund most of the airport's operations. But they will help make the Indianapolis airport more attractive to airlines, which could lead to more jobs in the region.

When BAA assumed management of the airport on October 1, 1995, it took on the largest private airport contract in the U.S. This would have been big news anywhere else in the country. Four years earlier it would have been big news in Indianapolis, too. But by 1995 it was just another transaction—business as usual—in the city's bustling marketplace for municipal services.

THE CONSEQUENCES STRATEGY

Steve Goldsmith forced city employees to compete against contract-hungry private companies. Suddenly, public workers had to prove they were a better buy for the taxpayers.

This unwelcome risk pressured the employees. They quickly reexamined their traditional ways of doing things. Most learned for the first time how much it cost to do their work; many devised less costly, more effective methods. Even those who did not face competition took a second look at their operations—because, in Skip Stitt's words, they were "preparing for the prospect of competition."

Goldsmith was not the first to use competition between public workers and private firms to stimulate new behaviors in government. In the United Kingdom, Conservative Party leaders in 1980 and 1988 had forced local governments to put a wide range of services out for bid. By 1992, when the Conservatives extended "compulsory competitive tendering" to white-collar services, thousands of public-private competitions had been held for nearly £2 billion of local public services.

When Mayor Goldsmith took office, he told his managers to read *Reinventing Government.* It told the story of the Phoenix Department of Public Works, whose director, Ron Jensen, had spearheaded public-versus-private bidding for many services 14 years earlier. But in Goldsmith's hands, competition was more than a manager's tool for cutting costs in one department. It was part of a citywide strategy of introducing consequences for performance.

Goldsmith believed that a megadose of competition would be a powerful antidote to a key poison that causes government's inefficiency and ineffectiveness: *monopoly.* Public agencies should have exclusive control over certain activities, as we argued in chapter 4. But politicians overuse their power to create public monopolies. In response to community needs, they often turn without thinking to government agencies rather than private markets. They do this, in large part, because they are captives of the bureaucratic paradigm; some barely realize there is an alternative. They also do it because building monopolies enhances their power. It gives them direct control over the enormous resources of government agencies. By manipulating the use of public money, employment, and purchasing, they gain credit for responding to public needs and constituency demands. They can also reward allies and punish opponents.

Government employees support public monopolies for more obvious reasons. They and their unions have a direct economic stake in preserving or expanding their corner on the market.

The problem with government monopolies is that they have no real reason to improve their performance. They receive no reward for getting better. Because their customers cannot desert them, they risk nothing if they perform badly. And they rarely die. Their fate is independent of their performance. They seldom innovate, because they don't *have* to.

Goldsmith used competition to alter these dynamics, and it very quickly boosted government's performance. "We say it's 'antitrust' for government," explains Mitch Daniels, chairman of SELTIC.

Monopolies tend to abuse their customers, overcharge their customers. They're not pressured by any competition. . . . Competitive government means that whoever's providing the service knows they've got to keep on getting better, keep on serving the customer, or somebody will replace them.

Mayor Goldsmith used consequences—economic risks and rewards—as a *lever* to give government workers a stake in the outcome of their efforts. Competitive bidding and gainsharing forged a tight, unprecedented link between the quality of government's performance and the economic well-being of government workers. As a result, employees began to change management structures, work processes, union activities, and their own attitudes. No one had to mandate or specify these changes.

Once competition becomes the norm, explain Phoenix Auditor Jim Flanagan and Deputy Auditor Susan Perkins, employees become self-directed. "Discussions of unit costs, customer complaints, down time, and other production-line events occur with interest and energy. There is no need to build bureaucratic reporting, regulatory, and oversight devices."

These self-propelling dynamics are characteristic of the consequences strategy: reinventors introduce performance-based incentives, then let nature take its course. They make consequences an extremely powerful strategy.

Three Approaches to Introducing Consequences

Public leaders introduce consequences into government in three basic ways. The most powerful approach is to force public service-delivery organizations to function as business enterprises with financial bottom lines, preferably in competitive markets. We call this *enterprise management.* Rather than acquiring their revenues from government appropriations of tax dollars, these public enterprises earn money by selling goods and services directly to their customers. To earn their keep, in other words, they must succeed in the marketplace. Failure brings financial loss, which can lead to job loss. Success can result in increased economic rewards. When New Zealand replaced government bureaucracies with state-owned enterprises that operated like private companies, a process we described in chapter 4, it was using enterprise management.

Enterprise management is the most powerful of the consequences approaches, because the competition it creates is automatic and unrelenting. No contracting process is necessary; no one has to impose the consequences; the politicians are not even part of the decision making. Instead, the organization's customers impose the consequences directly.

However, enterprise management doesn't work for all public organizations. Sometimes a financial bottom line is not the appropriate indicator of success, because the activity—whether protecting the environment, managing the parks, or protecting the public safety—is not one that should be charged to customers in a marketplace. When this is the case, the next best choice is *managed competition,* the approach Goldsmith used in Indianapolis. Its consequences are less automatic than those of the marketplace, but they are still powerful. Managed competition requires potential providers of government services—private firms and/or public agencies—to compete against one another for contracts, based on their performance. When contracting is not possible, public officials can measure and compare the performance of similar organizations through competitive benchmarking, then create psychological and financial consequences.

When neither enterprise management nor managed competition is appropriate—whether for the rational reasons we will discuss later or because of political obstacles—the alternative is *performance management.*

This approach uses performance measures, standards, rewards, and penalties to motivate public organizations. The rewards and penalties can be financial, like gainsharing in Indianapolis. They can be quasi-economic, like the Air Combat Command's practice of giving three-day weekends to squadrons that hit their monthly performance targets. Or they can be strictly psychological, like recognition and award programs.

Performance management is less powerful than the other two approaches because the consequences it imposes are rarely as compelling or unavoidable as the consequences of competition. It also leaves the job of judging performance to public officials, who have an inherent interest in proclaiming the success of the organizations they fund and run. Finally, performance management sets relatively weak standards for performance. An agency's performance is usually measured against its past record or against a predetermined performance target. This tells us if it has improved, or if it has achieved an established objective. But because there are no comparisons with competitors, it doesn't tell us if someone else could have done better, nor just how good performance *could* be. Consider Mayor Goldsmith's experience with the wastewater treatment system in Indianapolis. After a long study, a respected private consulting firm told him the maximum savings from private management would be about 5 percent. Using managed competition, however, he generated savings of *29.5 percent.*

These three approaches are not mutually exclusive: organizations that operate as public enterprises or that compete for contracts typically use many performance management tools to maximize their competitive advantages. Indeed, we believe that every public organization should use performance management, whether it is a public monopoly, a competitive enterprise, or a competitor for contracts.

We have not listed performance measurement as an approach because we do not believe that the act of measurement itself has enough power to force fundamental change in most public organizations. It is a critical *competence* organizations need if they are to use the consequences strategy, and we will devote a chapter to it in our next book. But some public organizations have measured performance for years, with virtually no impact. Until the Guiliani administration began using New York's performance data, for example, the city's annual performance reports gathered dust on most shelves. To reinvent public bureaucracies, the key is to attach consequences to performance measurement.

Protecting Employees Who Are No Longer Needed

Both enterprise management and managed competition often force public organizations to downsize, sometimes rapidly. When they lose contracts or market share, they have to get by with fewer employees. How should they deal with this reality?

This is one of the most important questions reinventors face. We believe governments should protect employees from the threat of unemployment, unless they are in a fiscal crisis so deep they simply cannot afford to do so. Employees did not create the bureaucracies in which they work, and they should not pay the price of reinventing those bureaucracies. We recommend adopting a no-layoff policy and creating a menu of options for employees whose jobs disappear.

This is not only the right way to treat human beings, it is the pragmatic thing to do. As the Indianapolis experience demonstrates, it allows public leaders to use competition far more extensively, because it reduces resistance from employees and their unions. It also makes it far easier to change the culture of public organizations, because employees' minds are not riveted to the possibility of losing their jobs.

The key is to use attrition to downsize, shifting displaced employees into jobs vacated by those retiring or departing. The typical government has a 5–10 percent annual attrition rate, which fluctuates as economic conditions change. If your personnel system has too many rigid job classifications and rules, you will probably need to change it to give yourself the flexibility to move people around. The United Kingdom has shrunk its national civil service by 33 percent with few layoffs over the past 18 years, using a variety of techniques. The menu of options includes the following:

Shift dislocated employees into other public jobs. One useful method is a "job bank," through which organizations hold open a certain number of vacancies to be filled by dislocated public employees. In Phoenix, the city forecasts possible employee displacement; normally, unless budget cuts are forcing layoffs, it shifts at-risk employees into the new jobs. In Philadelphia, when a private contractor took over prison food services, the city gave displaced workers the opportunity to enter a new job classification—correctional officer trainee—and develop new careers in government.

When a government moves people to other jobs, it must decide whether to protect them from wage loss. Indianapolis and Phoenix don't guarantee equal wages, but they try to put people in roughly comparable positions.

If job dislocation is large and rapid, a job bank will not be enough. To ease the pain, some governments consciously manage the pace of dislocation. As Indianapolis's Skip Stitt explains, "If you recognize that you're going to take a big hit, you might postpone it a few months" to build up vacancies that can be filled.

Shift public workers into private firms taking over the work. Some governments build into any competitive bid a requirement that a winning private bidder must give preference to dislocated public employees in any hiring. In Philadelphia, Phoenix, and the U.K., virtually *all* contracts contain a "first hiring preference" clause, which requires contractors that need new employees to give displaced public employees the opportunity to be hired.

Require that contractors pay comparable wages and benefits. In the U.K., European Community policies require that in most cases, private contractors hire public employees to fill all positions they need to fulfill the contract, at the terms and conditions of their previous employment (with the exception of overtime pay). When they leave, the contractor does not have to replace them at the same wages and benefits. And if they do not perform, the contractor can fire them, using the same procedures required for any other employee. Some American governments require contractors to pay certain wage levels, and Phoenix now requires them to provide their employees with comparable health plans. In Philadelphia, when Mayor Ed Rendell contracted out work, he allowed some workers who were shifting to the private contractors to stay on the city payroll long enough to become vested for pensions—and got the contractors to pay the extra cost.

While we see no reason taxpayers should be forced to subsidize wages and benefits far above market rates, some communities will choose to protect the pay and benefit levels they feel their employees deserve, even after they go to work for private contractors. This is a question of values each community must decide on its own.

Help managers take their organizations private. Governments sometimes institute management "spin outs" to shift workers into the private sector. Usually, the government provides them with an initial contract for services to help them get established.

In the London borough of Bexley, the local authority's architects, street sweepers, grounds keepers, and refuse collectors had taken this self-privatization route by 1995, and other units were looking at it as well. Terrence Musgrave, Bexley's chief executive, describes how this developed. As a unit prepares for competition, he says, it usually experiences "about 15 months of complete anxiety." Then they win the contract, and "the anxiety is replaced by beads of perspiration."

Then about two and a half years later they knock on my door, and what do they ask for but freedom? They now know they are running a successful business. They've won the competition; they've worked hard to increase productivity; and they know the only way they can grow is to escape from being a local authority. Once they're in the marketplace, they can seek business anywhere.

Now as part of that process of freedom, all sorts of deals can be extracted by the council. They'll take all employees, so there's no redundancy [unemployment]. They'll give us a discount, so they can seek profits elsewhere.

Offer economic incentives and outplacement services to those who choose to retire or look for jobs elsewhere. Public officials often offer workers severance packages and early-retirement incentives, as well as placement services to help them find jobs in the private sector. These options cost extra money in the short run—a disincentive if departments are required to pick up the tab. In the U.K., the government set up a special fund to cover 80 percent of the departments' costs.

How to Make No-Layoff Policies Work

- Retrain workers and place them in other government jobs.
- Hold vacant positions open as a "job bank" for workers whose jobs disappear.
- Require private contractors to hire dislocated public employees before anyone else.
- Require private contractors to pay comparable wages and benefits.
- Carry people who are close to becoming vested with pensions—but make the private contractor pick up the cost.
- Help public managers take their organizations private.
- Offer severance packages or early-retirement incentives.
- Provide outplacement services.

ENTERPRISE MANAGEMENT

You *can't* run government like a business. But as New Zealand proved, you can run some public organizations like businesses. You can put them at the mercy of paying customers and aggressive competitors and make them accountable for their financial bottom lines. This is what enterprise management does. It makes government entities earn their income by selling their services. Like businesses, they can fail—and be forced to lay off staff, cut pay, or even liquidate. They can also make profits, which are distributed to the government (their "shareholders"), and/or to their managers and employees.

If a public organization produces goods or services that can be sold to customers, it can be structured as an enterprise. This applies to agencies that serve "external" customers, like citizens and businesses. But it also applies to government's "internal" providers—agencies that supply other public organizations with printing, vehicle maintenance and fleets, data processing, and other services. Enterprise management forces even these long-standing internal monopolies to become more productive.

Enterprise management is enormously powerful, because it combines four strategies. To create a public enterprise, you must first uncouple government's commercial activities and give them institutional structures that hold them financially accountable. You then make them dependent on their customers for their revenue. Next you give them the flexibility to respond to their customers and markets, freeing them from the usual administrative control systems that set rigid rules for most public agencies. Finally, unless they are natural monopolies, you make them compete. (If an enterprise is a natural monopoly, you use regulation to create consequences.)

As we described in chapter 4, reformers in New Zealand used enterprise management to wring enormous inefficiencies out of more than half of their national bureaucracy. Australia began reforming its public enterprises at about the same time—requiring them to pay taxes like businesses, eliminating protective regulations, and giving their directors and managers more freedom to guide day-to-day operations without political interference. By 1992, analysts reported widespread gains in productivity, profitability, and service quality. While reducing prices, the enterprises had returned $4.7 billion in taxes and dividends to the government, and the numbers were growing annually. (We are using Australian dollars, which were worth about 75 American cents from 1988 through 1992.)

At about the same time, reinventors in Minnesota, Australia, New Zealand, and British Columbia pioneered the use of enterprise management on internal service units. Australia broke 60 percent of its $1.2-billion-a-year Department of Administrative Services (DAS) into 13 independent businesses, eliminated their monopolies, and forced them to compete with private companies. Three years later it took away their subsidies, turning them into enterprise funds dependent upon their customers for all revenues. In response, these units cut staffing from 14,000 to 9,900 between 1987 and 1991—mainly through attrition and voluntary severance—and turned a $100 million loss in 1988 into a $46.7 million profit. In the same period, DAS's productivity increased 5.6 percent a year, double the average for the rest of the Australian government.

Tools for Enterprise Management

Corporatization turns organizations into publicly owned businesses that are quasi-independent of government. Public corporations focus on business goals, such as maximizing profits and return on investment. Usually they have nongovernmental boards of directors and top managers who set the organization's direction and policies and are accountable for their performance. They operate outside of government's budget, personnel, planning, and procurement systems.

Enterprise Funds, also known as "revolving funds," "trading funds," and "enterprise centers," are public organizations funded primarily with customer revenues rather than tax dollars. Like public corporations, they are accountable to their customers. But unlike public corporations, they do not have independent governance.

User Fees are financial charges to customers of government services—either outside consumers or other public agencies. The money is used to defray all or part of government's costs for providing the service.

Internal Enterprise Management is the application of enterprise management—including corporatization, enterprise funds, user fees, and the withdrawal of monopoly status—to make internal service units accountable to their customers, the line agencies they serve.

The Advantages of Enterprise Management

Enterprise management uses market forces, not contract bids or administrative performance targets, to create consequences for performance. This gives it a number of advantages over the other two approaches.

Enterprise management makes agencies directly accountable to their customers. A public enterprise's success or failure depends on its customers' decisions. Because customers can go elsewhere (or, in the case of natural monopolies, buy less), public enterprises are forced to listen carefully to what they want. In contrast, managed competition and performance management rely on decisions by government officials.

Enterprise management forces continual improvement, because the competition is constant; it doesn't just happen at contract or review time. Agencies that compete for contracts have to beat the competition—but only once every few years. Agencies that must meet performance standards also face only periodic reviews. But agencies that depend on their customers for their income have to please those customers every day. They face continuous pressure to increase their quality and lower their costs.

Enterprise management sharpens the consequences of an agency's performance. If a public enterprise does a good job for its customers, it thrives. If it does not, it shrinks and potentially dies. The bottom line profit-and-loss numbers provide a simple, elegant, and accurate measure of the efficiency and effectiveness of the agency. The legislature doesn't have to wonder whether a unit is performing well: the financial statement says it all.

Enterprise management empowers public enterprises to make the long-term financial decisions necessary to maximize value for their customers. Public enterprises use financial methods customary in business, not government: long-term business plans, accrual accounting, depreciation of assets, borrowing to finance investments, and calculation of the return on those investments. Because they retain part of their earnings, depreciate assets, and borrow money, they can make the long-term investments in technology, training, and productivity improvements that are so difficult to make in the public sector.

Enterprise management saves money because it is simple to administer. It creates competition without creating a time-consuming bidding process to administer. In addition, the constant war between the budget and personnel offices and the operating agencies—over what they can spend, how many people they can employ, and what investments they can make—virtually disappears. Nor does the legislature have to spend time wrestling with appropriations levels and investment decisions; the competitive market creates accountability.

Finally, enterprise management radically simplifies the politics of improving performance. No one has to vote to eliminate or privatize an enterprise activity that is not performing well; the competitive market takes care of it. No one has to vote for a special appropriation to invest in new technologies. No one has to choose which bid wins a contract; no one has to defend the contracting process from cries of favoritism; and no one has to withstand a lobbying assault from disappointed contractors. Customers decide who offers the best deal, not administrators and politicians.

Politics or Markets?

Using enterprise management leads inevitably to a tug of war between political and market forces. It creates public-but-private enterprises that inhabit what political scientist Donald F. Kettl calls "a murky in-between world." They live with one foot in the public sector and the other in the private sector. Sometimes these contending forces destabilize them.

The tugging is about two basic issues. One is over who controls the public enterprise, elected officials or managers. If elected officials are unhappy with the prices that an electric utility or city parks department or community college training center charges its customers, can they override the market and order a reduction? In other words, should market forces or political forces control the enterprise?

The other tension is over how completely to unleash market forces. If the enterprise is in trouble, will taxpayers bail it out instead of letting it fail? If certain services are unprofitable, can the enterprise stop selling them? Will the enterprise enjoy any regulatory advantages over private competitors? Will enterprise employees be protected from downsizing and other management efforts to reduce costs?

Confronted with these fundamental tensions, many public leaders vacillate when they use enterprise management. They thrust an enterprise into the marketplace, but then intervene in its operations when political advantage or concerns beckon. In effect, they put their faith in the market, but reserve the right to change their religion.

As a result, public enterprises occupy a continuum that stretches from extensive public control at one end to significant market control at the other.

At the public end of the continuum, elected officials fully control the enterprise. They determine what the product or service will be and the price that will be charged. They still subject the activity to government budgeting, personnel, and procurement systems. They make the enterprise at least partly dependent on paying customers, but do not give it the flexibility to respond to those customers the way a business would. Many enterprise funds inhabit this end of the continuum. They are barely distinguishable in their performance from other public agencies.

At the market end of the continuum, enterprise activities are run by independent directors, appointed by elected officials. They negotiate a basic charter with the politicians that spells out the enterprise's purpose and government's financial expectations. The directors hire managers, who decide which products and services to offer. Managers set prices and determine their own administrative systems, usually adopting private sector practices. State-owned enterprises (SOEs) in places like Australia and New Zealand inhabit this end of the continuum. The further toward true market discipline they go, the more their performance improves.

Between the ends of the continuum, there is a world of difference. Unfortunately, where an enterprise lands on this continuum usually depends more on circumstance and politics than on rational analysis. In some cases, as in New Zealand, public leaders consciously push government activities into the marketplace. (Occasionally they even use enterprise management to prepare public organizations for sale to private owners.) In other cases, public officials back into enterprise management; because money is short they ask public agencies to start charging for services. And sometimes governments take over bankrupt private enterprises because they want to preserve their services.

Given their many different origins, public enterprises take on enormous variety. "No two are exactly the same," says Kettl. Most land somewhere in the broad middle of the politics-to-markets continuum. If you want to harness the enormous power of this approach, however, you should minimize politics and maximize market discipline. In some cases, you should go even further and privatize the organization. As the Labor Party discovered in New Zealand, creating an enterprise often clarifies whether a function needs to remain public or can be performed just as well by the private marketplace.

MANAGED COMPETITION

When you cannot structure a public service-delivery organization as an enterprise, you can still usually make it compete. Where governments use competitive contracting willingly and enthusiastically— as opposed to being forced into it—they typically save 20–25 percent in their first round of contracting. Indianapolis saved 25 percent; the national government in the U.K. has saved 21 percent. "No reporting process, auditing procedure, or budget procedure has ever gotten a public organization to put anywhere near the energy into improvement that competition has," says Phoenix auditor Flanagan. "Enormous energy goes into getting prices down for competitive bids."

But competitive bidding creates more than a onetime windfall. As services are rebid, the competitive pressures reoccur. Because every bid can be a new roll of the dice, service providers must strive repeatedly to get their costs down and quality up.

No one knows this better than Phoenix's garbage collectors, who began competing for their work when Jimmy Carter was still president. After losing the first few competitive bids, they won back all five of the city's districts. During the first ten years of competitive bidding, they cut the cost per household in half. But in 1993, their remarkable winning streak came to an end. When the city bid out its largest residential district, the north side, the Department of Public Works (DPW) added only the cost of inflation to its winning bid of six years earlier. That bid, for $3.90 per household per month, had been much lower than the private competitors', says Public Works Director Ron Jensen. He thought the new bid was a sure thing.

It wasn't. Waste Management, a private company operating nationwide, bid $3.77 per house per month. DPW employees were shocked: Waste Management's bid was $1.13 *less* per household than it had bid six years earlier. The company's bid was $5.2 million lower over the seven-year contract than the city employees' bid. The city accepted the bid, then used the savings to open a recycling transfer station it had planned but not yet funded.

Competition not only saves money, it helps bolster public confidence in government. When taxpayers are treated to the unexpected sight of public employees and private companies scrambling to give them the best possible deal on services, it changes their attitudes. In Phoenix, this positive signal has clearly helped improve public perceptions of city government.

Tools for Managed Competition

Competitive Bidding forces organizations to compete to provide goods and services paid for by the public sector. There are three basic varieties: private-versus-private competition, known as "contracting out" or "outsourcing"; public-versus-private competition, as in Phoenix, Indianapolis, and the U.K.; and public-versus-public competition, in which only public organizations are allowed to bid.

Competitive Benchmarking measures and compares the performance of public organizations. It publicizes the results in "report cards," "performance tables," and other types of scoreboards. This creates psychological competition between organizations, appealing to public officials' and employees' pride and desire to excel. It can also be used as the basis for financial rewards.

Designing an Effective Bidding Process

We call this approach *managed* competition to stress that we are not suggesting cutthroat competition for every public service. To make competition work, government needs to structure it fairly and manage it carefully. This is not easy, and few governments do it well. It requires a significant investment and a great deal of work, and there are pitfalls at each step—one reason enterprise management is often a better approach if you can use it.

The first step is to create a process that all sides can trust. Particularly in public-versus-private bidding, everyone worries that the process will be rigged against them. "You never know what hangs in the shadows," says AFSCME leader Steve Fantauzzo. "You may have somebody trying to whisper into a council person's ear. You may have people making pledges—you know, I'll donate to your campaign if, when you get into office, you don't forget that I was there for you."

Private bidders worry that insiders will manipulate the process to ensure that government providers win. This occurs, for example, at local levels in the U.K. Howard Davies, a former Audit Commission controller, says that in response to compulsory competitive tendering, "Many local authorities have sought . . . to rig the system in favour of their in-house workforces." Often, he charges, local officials have increased service specifications to make it more difficult for private providers to submit effective bids. By 1991, the national government had intervened with 16 local authorities that were acting in an anticompetitive manner. In several cases it had required local public service bureaucracies to "cease trading."

To keep the process free of manipulation, you need to give control over the bidding process to a neutral, nonpolitical party—for example, a civil servant auditor or purchasing chief. You should not let the government organization performing the services control the bidding process. "The key to a bid with credibility is the requirement that it be prepared or certified by an independent third party or 'cost referee' without a vested interest in the outcome of the bid process," explains Phoenix's Ron Jensen.

Phoenix's solution has held up well for nearly two decades. First, it has a division of the city finance department, which is independent of the operating departments, prepare bid specifications. This avoids the problems the U.K. has experienced when the agency bidding for the service designs the specifications. The division holds a preproposal conference to address questions from city staff and private vendors, then amends the specifications based on their feedback.

Second, the city auditor's office, which plays an independent watchdog role, evaluates the city's bids. The audit staff checks to see if the costs in the city's proposals are reasonable and accurate. It looks at historical cost data, and it makes sure that inflation adjustments and future increases called for in labor agreements or the city's merit pay system have been included. It identifies costs that should not be included, especially those that will be borne by the government even if the private sector wins the bid. And whenever a city department wins the bid, within 12 months the auditor's office conducts a post-implementation audit to check on costs and service levels.

It also makes sense to use an oversight board, ombudsman, or inspector general to investigate complaints about bids. Bidders need a confidential body that will do an objective investigation of their complaints, without taking them public. Bidders often refrain from complaining publicly, for fear of alienating the very office that will be reviewing all future bids. They need a way to register complaints with confidentiality.

The best defenses against corruption are maximum competition, solid performance contracts, a good system to track performance information and complaints, a capacity to investigate problems, and the threat of prosecution. The competition and performance information will expose and penalize firms whose contracts were not awarded for the right reasons, and the threat of investigation and prosecution will discourage fraud.

The second major challenge is to create a level playing field for all bidders—particularly for public and private bidders, who bring entirely different cost structures and accounting systems to the competition. One contentious issue, for example, is how to allocate government's overhead costs, since they are rarely included in an agency's budget. Another is how to treat the cost of capital investments: Should public agencies be charged for interest payments on their capital, as private companies are?

We believe governments should go into competitive systems with two basic objectives: to maximize value for the taxpayer and to make sure that both sides are fairly treated. Sometimes, when governments let private companies bid *below* their costs, just to get into the market, the latter objective is sacrificed to the former. This saves the taxpayers money in the short run, but if it happens too often, public employees' anger may lead them to exercise whatever political muscle their unions have to attack the entire competitive process. In the long run, therefore, we believe bidding below costs should not be allowed. It is not only unfair, it is likely to undermine the competitive bidding system.

This means public and private bidders should be required to calculate their costs in the same fashion, and all financial advantages should be neutralized. Hence public bids should include pension costs, all operating costs, capital costs, in-lieu-of-tax charges, interest charges on capital depreciation, and charges for all overhead that is directly tied to the service.

PERFORMANCE MANAGEMENT

Performance management creates less urgency for change than either managed competition or enterprise management. Because it maintains rather than breaks up government's monopoly power, it poses less of a threat to employees and politicians. No employees lose their work to private competitors. And politicians continue to allocate public resources, rather than letting customers make those decisions.

Thus, performance management usually improves performance more gradually than either of the other approaches. It also takes longer to implement—often three or four years. Still, reinventors worldwide have found it can produce remarkable, sustained growth in government's productivity. Sunnyvale, California, the American pioneer of performance management, says performance management increased its productivity by 44 percent between 1986 and 1993—*6 percent per year.*

Performance management gives public employees a direct stake in their organization's results. Hampton, Virginia, is a good example. It conducts a random telephone survey of citizens every October to learn how satisfied they are with city government's performance. Employees bombard City Manager Bob O'Neill to find out the results, because they have money riding on the answer. If citizen satisfaction levels are high enough, each city employee gets a bonus check in early December. In 1995, the bonus was $250.

In Hampton, in Sunnyvale, in the U.K., and in New Zealand, performance management sends employees unmistakable signals about which results matter, and it rewards them when they produce those results. Elected officials and top managers spell out what they want public organizations to accomplish, then create incentives to "pull" behaviors toward those goals.

Designing Incentives: Lessons Learned

To use performance management, you must design a new incentive system. In doing this, you will face at least four basic decisions: What kinds of incentives should you use? Who should get the incentives? Should you create negative incentives—punishment—as well as positive incentives? And should you use subjective or objective measures to assess performance? Our research yielded the following lessons:

Don't underestimate the power of psychological incentives. Many people assume that financial incentives have the most powerful pull. Money is important to most employees, but it isn't everything. For many, it's not even at the top of the list. For decades psychologists have reported that people need and want other things more. Abraham Mas-

Tools for Performance Management

Performance Awards provide employees with nonfinancial recognition for their achievements. This lets workers know their performance is appreciated, respected, and valued.

Psychic Pay provides employees and/or organizations with quasi-financial incentives such as paid time off and new equipment.

Bonuses are one-time cash awards in addition to salaries. They go to individuals or teams that achieve specified performance targets. They do not become a part of an employee's compensation base.

Gainsharing gives employees a guaranteed portion of the financial savings their organizations achieve, as long as they meet specified service levels and quality. It gives workers a clear economic stake in increasing their productivity.

Shared Savings is gainsharing for organizations. It allows them to keep a portion of the funds they save during the fiscal year (or biennium) to use in the future. It creates an organizational incentive to save money.

Performance Pay, also known as "merit pay," revamps traditional compensation systems to link a substantial portion of employee pay to performance. Rather than offering financial add-ons such as bonuses or gainsharing, it ties pay schedules and raises to performance.

Performance Contracts and Agreements put managers and their organizations on the hook for performance. They build in rewards and penalties, and they give public leaders the freedom to get rid of top managers—or entire organizations—that do not deliver the desired results.

Efficiency Dividends reduce agencies' administrative budgets a small percentage each year, but require the organizations to maintain their output levels. This forces them to achieve productivity gains that at least offset the lost revenues. Because reductions occur every year, the pressure for productivity improvements is constant.

Performance Budgeting inserts required performance levels into budget documents. When the executive prepares a budget and the legislature passes it, they specify the outputs and outcomes they intend to buy with their money. As we noted in chapter 4, this is a metatool.

low described a hierarchy of human needs that begins with the basic need for physical safety and security and moves up through a sense of belonging, love, status or esteem, and self-actualization. Much earlier in the century, William James, a pioneer of psychology, wrote that "the deepest principle of human nature is the craving to be appreciated."

The seminal study on what motivates employees was done by Frederick Herzberg at Case Western University in the 1960s. When he and his colleagues studied a large sample of public and private sector employees, they came up with the following list, in order of importance.

The Seven Motivating Factors

1. Achievement
2. Recognition
3. Challenge
4. Interest
5. Responsibility
6. Advancement
7. Salary and Benefits

In Australia, when researchers asked public managers what kinds of rewards they preferred for doing an outstanding job, money ranked third behind personal recognition from senior managers and career development opportunities.

In short, we recommend that you use financial incentives. But while you do so, don't forget to tap into the impact of praise, recognition, and other forms of psychic pay.

Magnify the power of incentives by applying them to groups as well as individuals. Results rarely depend on the work of just one person; they are normally created by groups of employees. An important part of improving performance, therefore, is to increase cooperation and collaboration among workers. Unfortunately, incentives for individuals may undercut this.

Usually, team-based incentives are preferable. In Indianapolis, Hampton, and the ACC, many employees must pull together in order to win the rewards. As more and more government organizations shift control and accountability to work teams, they should use performance incentives that reinforce the value of teamwork.

Individual incentives have their place when individual performance can be distinguished and measured. This is possible with some jobs: keypunch operators, CEOs, highly trained professionals such as physicians, and many others. Individual incentives may also make sense in organizations that cannot organize themselves around stable teams. The Employment Service in the U.K. found that many of its work teams had very high turnover rates, for instance. As unemployment fluctuated, the organization constantly brought people in and out. When its leaders researched private sector experience, they discovered that team incentives when teams were not stable created turmoil, because of debate over how much someone who arrived or departed partway through the year should receive. So they decided to reward employees on an individual basis.

Use negative as well as positive incentives, but select and target them carefully. Although you should rely primarily on positive incentives, it is difficult to create a truly entrepreneurial, innovative, high-performance organization if that is all you use. This is because you need effective ways of signaling that performance is not good enough. Still, you must be very careful that penalties are fair, sure, and swift, and that they do not create barriers to risk taking and experimentation by employees.

We suggest that you stay away from using *financial* penalties for poor performance. The threat of losing income fuels fierce employee resistance to performance management. Employees object strenuously to giving managers the power to cut individuals' pay. In Sunnyvale, for instance, this led the union to block performance pay for non-managerial employees.

Financial sanctions also tend to curb employee innovation. If failure means losing pay, employees are less likely to take risks and try new things. Managers in Sunnyvale, for example, sometimes avoid experimenting for fear that the effort might fail and drive up their costs, leading to a pay cut. "I've had discussions with people—'maybe you could do it this way'—and the big fear is, what if my unit cost goes up?" says Jim Masch, Sunnyvale's fleet manager.

Finally, financial penalties are not necessary. The opportunity to make money is a powerful enough signal, even in the absence of a financial downside.

Organizations do need some form of sanctions, however. Most organizations already use some type of "progressive discipline" to address unacceptable behaviors such as substance abuse, theft, absenteeism, and sexual harassment. But these personnel processes are not very good at dealing with employees who consistently perform poorly but have not crossed the line behaviorally.

One important answer is training—making sure employees have the skills and knowledge they need to perform well. Another is motivating them with incentives. If these options don't work, you need to impose negative consequences. The first might be to move employees to other jobs in the organization that better fit their skills. In some cases this might result in a pay cut; in others you might prefer to freeze their pay. (There is no right answer for something like this; the best solution depends on the situation.) We have also seen organizations respond to chronic failure by reducing an employee's autonomy to make decisions—for example, taking away a manager's control over his or her budget—while also providing the coaching and/or training the person needs. The reduction of autonomy can be very effective in getting an employee's attention and making him or her receptive to coaching.

If none of this works, you need to bite the bullet and let the employee go. Otherwise you will have an organization that includes people who simply cannot perform—a reality that will undercut all your efforts to motivate employees and create a culture committed to high performance.

Organizations that use work teams find that peer pressure can be a powerful disciplining force. "It's one thing to be called in by your boss—and another when five of your colleagues ask to meet with you to discuss why you haven't held up your end of the bargain," explains Tharon Greene, Hampton's human resources director. It's important, she adds, to provide employees with "nonpunitive exit routes" so they can move to other jobs in or out of government.

We should make clear that there is a big difference between chronic poor performance and occasional mistakes. The occasional error does not require discipline. Sometimes, when performance suffers because employees tried something new and it didn't work, they should be rewarded, not disciplined. At a minimum, your evaluation system needs to create room for innovations that fail. If employees feel they might lose out on a bonus because they spent money on an innovation that failed and their unit costs went up, they may not take that risk.

Tie financial incentives to objective measures of performance, not to managers' subjective appraisals. Performance appraisals are the Achilles' heel of incentive programs. They rely on subjective assessment—a manager's judgment—rather than indisputable performance data. It is difficult—perhaps impossible—for individual managers to be consistent in the way they rate employees. For instance, the first-year appraisals of 18,000 managers in Australia's federal government resulted in the use of substantially different standards by managers in different agencies. Although there was a five-point rating scale ("unsatisfactory," "adequate," "fully effective," "superior," and "outstanding"), managers had different interpretations of what it meant.

Often, employees and their unions object to subjective appraisals because the process can be abused by managers. If workers suspect that a supervisor's personal feelings or biases influence the ratings, they will not accept his or her judgments.

Subjective appraisals also put managers in the difficult position of delivering bad news to employees. It's tough enough to tell workers that they aren't performing well—and many managers don't do it particularly well. But it's even harder to tell them they won't be getting a raise or bonus. Many managers don't feel confident justifying why they are rewarding one person and not another. Many want to avoid disappointing or angering workers.

Typically, the result is "rating inflation." Managers end up rating practically everyone above average—a result that is by definition impossible. This happened in the first year of Australia's bonus program, when 94.4 percent of the eligible senior officials got a bonus. It was also the norm in the U.S. and Canada, where most managers spread merit pay increases equally. Duke professor Robert Behn calls this the "Lake Wobegon syndrome," after Garrison Keillor's mythical town where "all the children are above average."

The best solution is to use objective measures of performance, like productivity and customer satisfaction. Objective measures have an added benefit: they can withstand public and political criticism. People may argue over which measures should be used, but they can't complain that incentive awards are unrelated to demonstrable improvements in performance.

CHOOSING THE BEST APPROACH
FOR EACH FUNCTION

Which approach works best for which government functions? Enterprise management works only for services that can earn all or part of their revenues by charging their customers, whether those customers are citizens, private organizations, or other public organizations. Hence it is not appropriate for "public goods" that benefit the community as a whole more than specific customers. These include policy-making functions, regulatory and compliance functions (like environmental protection and public safety), and services that are consumed collectively (like national defense, public health services, and fire prevention). Since customers cannot be charged for collective services, the market will not produce them on its own. Governments can produce these services themselves, contract with private companies to produce them, or give grants to private companies to produce them, but they cannot create enterprises that charge customers for them.

As we noted above, enterprise management is inappropriate for compliance functions. It makes no sense to put a compliance organization in a market and let its compliers fund it through fees. Imagine an environmental permitting agency funded through permit fees, or a police department funded by traffic tickets, and the problem becomes obvious. The agency would have a powerful financial incentive to crack down on every infraction, real or imagined.

When delivering "private" goods, which benefit individuals or discrete groups, you can use enterprise management as long as you meet several criteria. You must be able to exclude nonpayers from benefiting; collect fees efficiently; ensure that customers have enough information to make intelligent choices; and minimize equity problems. For example, if low-income people cannot afford the fee but the community wants to give them access to the services, there must be a practical way to identify them, so you can admit them for free or give them vouchers.

Moving to managed competition, any organization that can measure its performance can use competitive benchmarking, a tool that compares the performance of organizations. And virtually any *service* can be contracted, as long as you can define fairly clearly what you want done; generate sufficient competition; measure or evaluate performance; and replace or penalize poor performers. If you want to include private firms in the competition—as most governments do—you must be willing to trust them with the service. As we argued in chapter 4, most communities prefer that highly sensitive functions—those involving state-sanctioned violence, due process rights, security and privacy issues, or an absolute necessity of fair and equal treatment— remain in public hands. Governments can use competitive contracting for these functions, but most communities are more comfortable when only public organizations compete.

Some compliance functions can also be contracted out to competing organizations. For instance, revenue departments often contract with private companies to collect overdue tax payments. And a few communities in southern California contract with police departments in other communities—or from Los Angeles County—to provide their police services. There is no reason such contracting cannot be done competitively. It is often wise in such cases to contract with only one organization at a time, but to rebid the contract regularly to ensure competition. If a revenue department contracts with three firms and each treats people differently, some compliers will feel they are being discriminated against. In other activities, such as police work, the solution is to contract only with public organizations—and only one at a time.

Finally, performance management can be used with any public organization. It is far more difficult with some than with others, depending upon how well the outputs can be measured. But the New Zealanders have even managed to use it with their ministries that supply policy advice to ministers.

QUESTIONS PEOPLE ASK ABOUT
THE CONSEQUENCES STRATEGY

Q: Doesn't creating consequences cause fear in government organizations, undercutting efforts to develop innovative organizational cultures and to support innovators?

Employees of any monopoly—public or private—fear the imposition of new consequences for their performance. They worry that they will not generate enough revenues from customers; that they will not compete successfully against other organizations; that they will lose their jobs.

However, these anxieties have desirable effects. Government organizations take a new interest in pleasing their customers. They pay much more attention to how they spend taxpayers' money and what elected officials and the public want them to accomplish. These effects—caring about customers, efficiency, and effectiveness—are important drivers of a healthy organizational culture. They create pressures that push a bureaucratic culture to focus on accomplishment and improvement, not procedures and compliance.

There are several keys to minimizing employee anxiety and maximizing improvement. One is to take away the fear of job loss, as we explained earlier in this chapter. Another is to use the control strategy to give ownership of the improvement process to the employees. If employees feel in control of their organizations—if they feel like owners, not victims—they will more quickly move past their anxieties and make the most of their opportunities to succeed. A third is to give them a meaningful "upside" for improving their performance. Tie bonuses and promotions to improved performance, or let employees keep part of the money their organizations save by increasing efficiency, as Indianapolis does.

Q: Won't making employees compete with one another prevent collaboration and teamwork?

Public employees facing competition may hoard information about their successful innovations to keep their competitive edge, rather than sharing the knowledge with others. Of course, they will still work harder to find the secrets to better performance than if they faced no competition. But you can get the benefits of competition and collaborative learning at the same time, if you structure the incentives carefully. If done right, competition can stimulate greater information sharing and learning.

First, make organizations and teams—not individuals—the competitors. This promotes the cooperative behaviors that are part of teamwork. Indeed, the most intense teamwork we have ever seen takes place in teams that have to compete.

Second, be careful how you define success in competitive situations. For example, sometimes you can reward all teams that show improvement, or that exceed a specified performance target. This way everyone can win, if they all improve. Hence every team has an incentive to learn everything it can from other teams that are performance leaders. And those leaders have no reason to hoard their secrets. Indeed, by sharing information they can usually learn something that will help them improve as well.

Q: When public organizations become intensely focused on their own performance, don't they quit collaborating with other public organizations for the greater good?

Results-oriented governments from New Zealand to Sunnyvale, California, have wrestled with this problem. If you give organizations powerful incentives to produce specific outputs, they will concentrate all their energies on doing just that. In the process, they may start ignoring the needs of other public organizations, or the larger collective welfare. Sunnyvale Personnel Director Liz Birch puts the problem into concrete terms: "One of the criticisms of our system is that it has not fostered cross-departmental assistance, because whenever you ask someone to do something for you, they want a task number."

The solution, as we argued in chapter 4, is to focus the entire system first on key collective outcomes, then make sure the outputs you want organizations to produce contribute to those outcomes. This is precisely the challenge Sunnyvale is struggling with, as it revamps its performance management system. If your incentives are forcing narrow, noncollaborative behavior, you need to broaden your output and outcome targets. You may even need to create some funding that policy makers can use to purchase collaborative work from a variety of organizations.

TAKING COMPETITION TO A NEW LEVEL

In 1996, Indianapolis put managed competition to use in a new way.

Several years earlier, city leaders had realized that the U.S. Navy would probably shut down the Naval Air Warfare Center on the city's east side. Established during World War II, the center employed about 2,550 people, more than half of them engineers and scientists who developed electronics and software systems for the military and NASA. Mayor Goldsmith estimated that losing the center would cost the region $1 billion in payroll, contracts, purchases, and economic ripple effects. He appointed a 20-person public-private task force to explore options for keeping the facility alive.

Hundreds of American communities have faced similar threats. Most have struggled in vain against the death sentence, calling press conferences and calling in political favors. Indianapolis, whose leaders were now in the habit of using competition, instead made the government a novel offer.

The Navy's plan to give the facility to the city and disperse its workforce to bases on the East and West Coasts would cost an estimated $400 million. Why not, Indianapolis asked, let businesses compete to take over the facility and perform the Navy's work at reduced cost?

Since the Navy had no experience doing something like this, Indianapolis volunteered to handle the process. The city persuaded the federal Base Closure and Realignments Commission to overturn the center's death sentence and recommend privatization.

After President Clinton and Congress approved the change, Indianapolis issued a request for proposals. It asked companies how they would use the center and its workforce to spur the city's economic development and to save the Navy money. Seven companies submitted proposals, and the city invited four of them to develop more detailed bids. Fairly quickly, it became a bidding war between two firms.

The winner, Hughes Technical Services, got a 10-year lease on the center and its equipment for $1 a year. In exchange, it guaranteed that it would cut the Navy's costs by $225 million over five years. (The Navy would also save its $400 million in closing costs.) It pledged to keep nearly all the center's employees on for at least five years, at no loss in wages or benefits, and to relocate four divisions from California— adding 730 jobs and $100 million in annual business to the Indianapolis economy. Hughes also agreed to invest at least $7.5 million in capital improvements annually; to set aside $500,000 to assist workers in finding new jobs; and to invest 1 percent of its gross revenues (or at least $3 million annually) to upgrade its workers' skills.

The company will pay taxes on the center's property and equipment, which were tax-free when operated by the federal government. Hughes will also reimburse the city for the $1 million it spent to develop the privatization plan and contribute 1 percent of its gross revenues to charitable grants, gifts, endowments, and economic development projects in Indianapolis.

Announcing the agreement in May 1996, Goldsmith claimed it was the first full-scale privatization of a U.S. military base. The mayor thanked the federal officials who allowed him to use competition to keep the Naval Center viable. And he welcomed to town Hughes Electronics—the newest player in the city's marketplace for public services.

– 6 –

THE CUSTOMER STRATEGY: PUTTING THE CUSTOMER IN THE DRIVER'S SEAT

MAKING SCHOOLS ACCOUNTABLE TO PARENTS

In the late 1980s, a group of parents in Minnesota's Forest Lake school district, about 30 miles north of the Twin Cities, began talking about creating an elementary school that used the Montessori method. Their children were in a Montessori preschool, and they were excited about the hands-on, self-directed learning style the school used. Joni Callahan, who knew the local public school well because her older child attended it, was concerned about what would happen to her preschooler there. "We were very worried that the self-initiating, the self-challenging, the self-evaluating skills that our children had developed in the private Montessori school would be squashed," she remembers.

First the parents investigated starting a private elementary school, but they decided the tuition would be too high. Then they approached their school district, meeting repeatedly with top administrators. Mark Gilchrist, a teacher in another district who also had a child in the Montessori preschool, remembers the frustration he experienced as these talks dragged on over several years:

> Every meeting resulted in, "No, we can't do this." And the reasons weren't that it was an educationally poor concept. In fact, every school administrator and teacher we talked to agreed that this was very sound educationally. But it was, "We don't know how we

*would arrange the busing," or "We don't have magnet schools, we
have neighborhood schools," or "How would we train teachers?"
It was "Yes, this is a good program, but we can't do it, we can't do
it, we can't do it."*

Finally, in 1991, a glimmer of hope appeared. The state legislature
passed the nation's first charter school law. In general, charter schools
are public schools created by groups of parents, teachers, community
members, or—in some states—even by institutions such as businesses
and universities. They sign a charter with their sponsor, typically a state
board of education, a school district, or a college, giving them the right
to operate the school for three to five years. In essence, the charter is a
performance contract: it spells out the results the school will produce,
while granting it waivers from virtually all rules and regulations governing public schools. Minnesota already had statewide open enrollment, which allowed students to attend schools outside their districts.
Reformers pushed through charter schools—though the legislature
passed a fairly restrictive version—to give students more alternatives
from which to choose. When families choose any public school outside
their district or a charter school, most of their public education dollars
move to the new school or district.

To the Forest Lake parents' group, the charter option looked like
their salvation. They hired a consultant to help them draft a plan to start
a charter school and began meeting with administrators and school
board members, who, under Minnesota's new law, would have to
approve their proposal. They passed the hat to raise money to finance
their efforts. Finally, they took their formal proposal to a school board
meeting. The board was receptive to the concept, but reluctant to let a
charter school take funding away from the district.

"They said, 'We're gonna lose too much money if you guys do this
charter school,' " remembers Jane Norbin, one of the parents. "You
could see them adding and subtracting the amounts of money that each
child represented, and once it looked like we had some economic force
and we'd reached a critical mass number of students, we really had
their ears."

Finally one board member asked, "Why don't we find a way to do
this in the public school?" The board directed the administration to
work with the parents to find some way to make it happen. When they
met, says Norbin, it was as if night had become day.

One at a time, all the barriers that just weeks before were there, we started finding ways around. It was just amazing how those could be taken down when you wanted to take them down. And so the administration came back to the board several weeks later and said, "Yes, we found a way. We can put this in the public school and we can make it happen here."

The result was a small Montessori school within a school at Columbus Elementary, in which parents were intensely involved. When her two older children went through school, Norbin says, "My experience was that parents were always welcome into the school if you wanted to help raise money for special projects." But when the Montessori program began, parents were asked to choose a representative to sit on the search committee for teachers—something "that was unheard of before." "We have meetings now, as the program grows, to work on each particular problem as it comes up, to figure out how we are going to handle this and how we are going to handle that," Norbin adds. "And we really feel more a partner in the educational process than I ever felt before."

Julianne Carver, a teacher in the Montessori program, agrees that choice and charter schools have changed the role parents play. "The parents who choose the program are very much aware of what we're doing, and because they've made that choice, they get very involved," she says. "So I am accountable in different ways than I was in a traditional program."

Has choice made principals more accountable? "I don't think there's a question about that," says Larry Carlson, principal of Columbus Elementary.

You can't toe the straight, narrow line. When there's choice out there, you have to keep yourself aware, you have to keep yourself updated, you have to keep yourself informed as to what is going on and what the choices are out there. If you don't keep yourself aware, I'm afraid you're going to get pushed to the side. There's always somebody looking over your shoulder that—hey, they know about it, they'll take the job from you.

Bringing School Choice to Minnesota

The Forest Lake story is one of many similar stories in Minnesota, the first American state to give the customers of its education system their choice of public schools. As *Reinventing Government* reported, Minnesota gradually withdrew the monopoly status held by school districts between 1985 and 1991, because its leaders believed that when customers could choose, they would have the power to force districts to improve their schools and diversify their offerings. They believed that the key to transforming schools was changing the system of incentives, accountabilities, and control within which they operated. By giving customers choices, making districts compete for their students and dollars, and encouraging teachers, parents, and others to create new schools free of the red tape that constrained most principals and teachers, they believed they could create a system that would produce not just a few excellent schools, but thousands of excellent schools.

"The object of charter schools is not just to create a few good new schools," explains Ted Kolderie, a leader in the reform effort.

The object is to improve all schools. Districts do not want to lose kids and the money that comes with them. They will make improvements themselves to attract kids back from charter schools, or they may make improvements before a charter even appears.

Kolderie and his colleagues were successful because they found a governor with the courage to champion cross-district public school choice at a time when only 33 percent of adults in the state said they supported the idea. Rudy Perpich, who served as Minnesota's Democratic-Farmer-Labor (DFL) governor from 1976 through 1978 and 1983 through 1990, grew up on the edge of an iron pit in northern Minnesota's Iron Range. One of four sons of immigrants from Croatia, he didn't speak English until he was five. Like many immigrants, his parents saw education as a ticket out of the mines for their sons, three of whom became dentists and state senators and one of whom became a psychiatrist. Rudy, the eldest, began his political career by running for the local school board in Hibbing.

"Rudy Perpich was the first governor in Minnesota to take his oath of office on the stage of the high school in which he graduated," says Dan Loritz, who was Perpich's key advisor on education reform. "That's how seriously he took education. He used to talk about education as his passport out of poverty."

Perpich had also experienced firsthand the frustrations of a parent faced with an unresponsive public school monopoly, as he told us a year before his death in 1995:

I've often been asked why I emphasized this choice program. I always felt, as a member of the board of education for six years, that education in Minnesota was equal in every district, that we had the best educational system in the United States, and that wherever you went, the system was good.

And then when I was elected to the state senate and my children were of school age, I moved to the Twin Cities, which is 200 miles south of where my home is up in northern Minnesota. I just went and found a home and I figured, "Okay, this is it." I enrolled the children in school and in a short period of time, the children were saying, "This is like a review for us. We're really not learning anything."

Then my wife and I, we went to the school and said, "For us, for our children, this is repetitive. We would like to enroll our children in another school." We had gone and talked to the Department of Education and asked for a listing of what they thought were some of the more creative and better school districts. But we couldn't move them. You live there, that's it. And that's where I first began giving some real thought to a) people should have some choice, and b) we have to do a better job of equalizing and improving education in Minnesota.

Taking office for the second time in 1983, the year that the seminal report *A Nation at Risk* was published, Perpich began looking for a strategy that would improve the schools. They were already well funded, and coming out of a deep recession, Minnesotans were in no mood for a tax increase. The governor said, " 'You know, we can't really order them to improve,' " remembers Loritz. " 'We can't pay them to do it. I think we need to find a reason for them to continue to see improvement as something they should strive for.' "

When the reformers pitched their strategy of customer choice, Perpich bit. It was exactly what he had been looking for. He instinctively understood the argument that different kids needed different kinds of schools, and that by making the schools accountable to their customers—by making them compete for their customers' dollars—he could give them all a powerful reason to improve.

At the time, it was a radical new idea, pushed mainly by People for Better Schools, an activist group founded by a public school administrator and author named Joe Nathan, and by a group Kolderie had once led called the Citizens League. In January 1985, at an annual Citizens League breakfast, Perpich shocked the education establishment by proposing that every student in Minnesota be allowed to change districts—and take their public dollars with them.

The teachers unions, principals, and superintendents were aghast. And they wielded enough power in the legislature to knock out Perpich's "open enrollment" provision. But they passed another provision he and House Majority Leader Connie Levi had inserted in the broader education bill for fear of offending both the DFL governor and the Independent Republican majority leader. Called "Postsecondary Enrollment Options," it allowed juniors and seniors in public high schools to take courses at any college in the state, with their high school funding following them to pay for tuition, fees, books, and in some cases transportation.

Postsecondary Options quickly became wildly popular with students: those who were bored with high school; those who needed more demanding courses; those who were worried they wouldn't be able to afford college; and those who just didn't fit in in high school. Some took only a few college courses, while others attended college full-time. Within two years, 5,700 students were participating: 5 percent of all juniors and seniors in the state, and 10 percent in the Twin Cities, where so many colleges were concentrated.

Not all were high performers in high school—60 percent were B, C, and D students. At the University of Minnesota, 50 percent were from the inner city. "Some of our students just can't function anymore in high school," says Darryl Sedio, who runs the University of Minnesota's program for these students. "A lot of our kids come here because they need to learn faster; they're just bored stiff."

Not surprisingly, surveys showed that both the high schoolers and their parents loved the program. But it was not so popular with teachers, principals, and superintendents, who watched it drain money from their high school budgets. In 1986, after just a year, the teachers unions and the School Boards Association tried to gut it. But students and parents descended upon the legislature en masse to protect what for them had been a lifesaver. "I've never had in the ten years as governor any program that had as much support," Governor Perpich told us. "I mean, people kiss me on the street, literally."

After their aborted attempt to strangle the initiative in its crib, the school administrators had no choice but to compete with it. They quickly doubled the number of advanced placement (AP) courses they offered and began contracting with colleges to train their teachers to offer courses for college credit, at their high schools.

In 1995 a superintendent quietly mobilized another attack on the program, and again Sedio and his allies called out their students and parents to beat it back. After the House defeated the effort by a 102–31 vote, its members requested that the Legislative Auditor's Office do a review. Published in March 1996, its report was overwhelmingly positive.

The auditor's office found that by the 1994–1995 school year, participation was up to 6 percent of Minnesota juniors and seniors (12.5 percent in the Twin Cities). Most took their college courses very seriously; on average, they had a higher grade point average than college freshmen at all postsecondary institutions except technical colleges. Some 73 percent of Postsecondary Options students said they were "very satisfied" with their experience, and 95 percent of parents said they would "probably" or "definitely" encourage their children to participate again.

Even more impressive was the effect the program had had on the high schools. By 1996 almost two thirds of secondary schools provided at least one course for college credit, and 38 percent of high schools provided courses under contract with colleges. Overall, the percentage of Minnesota juniors and seniors who took an advanced placement exam had tripled.

Reframing the Debate

The overwhelming popularity of Postsecondary Options gradually weakened the resistance to school choice, particularly in the legislature. Meanwhile Governor Perpich, Commissioner of Education Ruth Randall, and the reformers went to work to bring the teachers unions around. After Perpich's 1985 defeat in the legislature, says Kolderie, "He got really ticked and he went downstairs and had a press conference, and told everybody that when he ran for election again next year he would neither seek nor accept the endorsement of the teachers unions."

That shook up the unions. When they and the school boards,

superintendents, and principals associations approached the governor to try to heal the wound, Perpich made them an offer. He proposed that they participate in a "governor's discussion group," to come up with an education reform package on which they could all agree. To their surprise, however, he also invited the reformers: Kolderie; Joe Nathan; Citizens League Executive Director Curtis Johnson; John Cairns from the Minnesota Business Partnership; former Republican governor Al Quie; and several others. By the end, there were 61 participants, representing 24 groups with a stake in education reform.

As Kolderie explains, the governor cleverly boxed the unions in.

> *Perpich made it very clear to the education groups that there were going to be no end runs. He was not going to take to the legislature in 1987 anything except what came through the governor's discussion group. So if you had anything else you wanted, like more money, or whatever else, you had to get it through the governor's discussion group.*

The group met once a month for 18 months. The reformers gradually reframed the terms of the debate. Their most effective argument had to do with equal opportunity for disadvantaged students. Verne Johnson, one of the reformers, pointed out that for most families choice already existed.

> *You can go to private school, or you can move your place of residence to another district, and people in fact do this all the time. So choice exists. But it's related to your personal family wealth. It costs money to move into a different kind of suburb, to get a different kind of house, it costs money to pay tuition. You can even go to a different public school without moving, if you're willing to pay tuition. If you have a lot of money you have a lot of choice. If you don't have a lot of money, you don't have a lot of choice.*

The reformers were prepared to take that argument to the people of Minnesota and let the unions fight to deny equal opportunity to poor and working families. "I think it became clear to the unions for the first time how vulnerable they were," Kolderie says.

Still, the negotiations were not easy. Perpich had set a deadline of December 19, 1986, for the group to produce a reform plan, but deadlock loomed on the issue of choice. Finally, during a stormy meeting as the clock ticked down on December 19, the two sides came to a compromise. Their reform plan would give districts the right to offer choice on a voluntary basis, give schools more freedom through site management, and establish mandatory statewide testing to measure performance. The reformers also managed to shame the teachers unions into an agreement in principle—with no specifics—to do something to give at-risk students more choices.

In January, when Perpich put together his budget, he called the group back together to reiterate their agreement. At that point, he fleshed out the proposal for at-risk students: it would give students who had dropped out or were at risk of dropping out their choice of public schools.

Mandatory statewide testing failed to pass the legislature, and the site management bill that passed was voluntary. But with all sides now backing the compromise on choice, the other bills passed easily in the spring of 1987. Perpich and his allies then pushed hard for districts to participate voluntarily. They succeeded beyond their adversaries' wildest dreams: 96 districts—22 percent of the total—opened their borders.

By 1988, the opposition to choice had wilted. Though Perpich chose to take a back seat this time, DFL Senator Ember Reichgott introduced an amendment to make open enrollment mandatory. After all the Sturm und Drang of the previous three years, there was an almost eerie lack of debate on the issue. In February the state Department of Education had released an extremely positive evaluation of the Postsecondary Options program. The teachers unions and administrators associations were split, because so many districts were already offering choice voluntarily. Parents testified in support—particularly those disappointed that their districts had not yet agreed to open their borders.

The final bill required large districts to allow interdistrict transfers (except when student departures would hurt desegregation efforts) in 1989–1990, but gave smaller districts, which faced more financial risk, an extra year to prepare. With the departing students would go most of their public dollars.

On the strength of little more than good ideas and the convictions of a courageous governor, the reformers had won.

The Scramble to Survive

Open enrollment had an immediate impact on school districts in Minnesota, just as Postsecondary Options had. Two academicians at

Northwestern University, James Tenbusch and Michael Garet, did a survey of 126 high school principals in the spring and summer of 1990, after the large districts had opened their borders and just as the small districts were about to. Most of the principals said they were making changes to compete: lengthening their hours, adding more counseling, and developing new educational programs, new after-school programs, new career programs, and new programs for gifted and talented students. Smaller schools were working to specialize in particular academic areas to attract students.

In addition, Tenbusch and Garet concluded, "Open enrollment has stimulated an increase in parent decision-making power, which is characterized initially by administrators involving parents more in school planning efforts and day-to-day operations. School administrators were seen to become more responsive to parent wishes and demands in an effort to keep them satisfied."

Small rural districts faced the greatest consequences, because the loss of just a handful of families could force them to cut back their meager course offerings and trigger an even greater exodus. Indeed, all three schools that closed in their sample were rural. Not surprisingly, Tenbusch and Garet found rural districts listening the most intently to what parents wanted and making the most dramatic changes. Rural school administrators, they said flatly, "have been forced to expand their educational programs in order to stay competitive."

Perpich was elated by the changes taking place. He saw schools suddenly doing—on their own initiative—many things he had been unable to get them to do before choice. He had long pushed both the legislature and the school districts to lengthen the school day, for example. The legislature had refused to appropriate any new money, and the schools had refused to lengthen their days without compensation. By 1988 only a handful of schools had an extended day. Choice changed their attitudes quickly, he explained.

In a short period of time, before I left the office of governor, 90-some districts had an extended day. Now, we didn't pass a law that said you have to have an extended day; we didn't appropriate any money. But because choice was there, the parents or the family could decide, "I think I will change and go to this school because it has an extended day and I won't have to worry what's happening to my children after 3:00 in the afternoon."

Perpich also pointed to foreign language courses, which he said were traditionally among the first programs cut when money tightened up. By the time he left office, he said, there were almost three times as many foreign language courses taught in the state. "Program after program is initiated because if you don't make that offering, students are going to go elsewhere. It's market forces at work."

Rather than cutting language and arts programs, districts were cutting their administrative costs. "Before, as programs were closed down, it was kind of circle the wagons, and administrators were safe," Perpich said. "I think that's changing. I believe that programs are safer under choice than are management people."

The proof of the pudding was a great flowering of alternatives to the traditional public school. Joe Nathan, who runs the Center for School Change at the University of Minnesota's Humphrey Institute, does a regular survey of nontraditional schools in the state. He found that between 1986 and 1994 the number increased from 108 to 300, and he says it has continued to grow.

Expanding Choice for the Disadvantaged

Opponents of school choice often argue that it will help the brightest and most affluent students, but leave poor students behind in inferior schools. In Minnesota, that didn't happen. Because of the 1987 legislation for at-risk students, the greatest number of alternative public schools have sprung up to help them.

The High School Graduation Incentives Act, known informally as the "second chance" program, let students aged 12 to 21 who had dropped out or were at risk of dropping out (two or more years behind academically, pregnant or a custodial parent, or expelled from school), choose any traditional or alternative public school in the state. In 1988 the governor got the legislature to remove the age cap, so any adult who has not graduated from high school can go back to school for free.

A companion bill passed in 1987, the Area Learning Centers and Alternative Programs Act, allowed people to create innovative schools for at-risk kids. These schools tend to be very small, work on an intensely personal level with students, and offer very nontraditional services. One of the models, for example, is called City Inc. Built around individualized education and personal relationships between students and teachers, it offers a group home for girls, family counseling, day care for the children of teenage mothers, a job program, and a night-course program.

By 1996 there were more than 140 alternative schools for at-risk students. Thousands of dropouts had returned to school to attend them. Indeed, in 1994–1995 alone, roughly 3,000 of their 42,749 students were adults.

There is little hard evidence available, at this writing, on the outcomes for second-chance students. An early survey did find that after students enrolled at second-chance schools, the percentage who said they planned to graduate and go on to further education jumped from 19 to 39 percent.

A group at the University of Minnesota School of Education, led by Cheryl Lange and James Ysseldyke, has done a series of studies of the second-chance students and schools. They found that many students who were labeled "emotionally disturbed" and placed in special education classes, at enormous expense to the taxpayer, were suddenly no longer emotionally disturbed after they enrolled in area learning centers. "You just don't see disruptive behavior; you don't see disrespectful behavior," says Lange. "And we've been in these schools a lot."

She believes there are four reasons for this. First, "Students tell us they are treated differently; they are more respected by staff." Second, the schools offer more counseling and related services. Third, "If you look at area learning centers and alternative schools, their characteristics are close to what the ideal special education service-delivery system would be—individual learning plans, contracts with students, one-to-one tutoring, and so on." Finally, "If the student does not conform to the rules or their contract, they're out. They do kick kids out. That's what a choice system allows you to do, because the kid chose to come, and there are other alternatives he or she can go to if they aren't willing to meet the terms the school sets."

Lange and Ysseldyke recently completed an in-depth study of 60 students at three alternative schools. They surveyed the students at enrollment and again a year later, and they did in-depth interviews with many students and teachers. It is very clear, Lange says, that these students are more satisfied than they were in their traditional schools. Their attitudes and commitment are better. Based on test scores, those who have stayed in school are making progress in math, reading, and writing. In math and reading, they fell within the average statewide range. Perhaps more important, "Half of the students surveyed report they would not be attending school if they were not in the alternative school."

"There's a theme that comes out of all of our surveys and interviews with students and teachers, and that is the importance of relationships," says Lange.

These students really desire an environment that fosters relationships between staff and students. It emerges in every element of our research—from the teachers and directors, from the students, when they talk about why they left their school and are attending this one. And you see it in the outcome data.

The second thing is that school choice for these students is, I believe, a very great motivator for retention. If we look at all the information we have, that piece is very important. If you're going to set up programs for at-risk youth, allowing them the choice is very important.

The third theme is flexibility. We have a group of students that needs a lot of flexibility in programming and schooling, and these programs provide that.

Another set of alternative schools—some 19 by 1996–1997—are charter schools. Some of these focus on at-risk youth, like area learning centers. Others are for more typical kids, but use progressive teaching techniques. The New Country School in LeSueur, Minnesota, for instance, offers year-round operation, extended daily hours, flexible scheduling, "active learning," personalized learning portfolios, and "performance/product based assessment." It has no courses and no classrooms. Its learning activities include community service, youth apprenticeships, a youth entrepreneurship program, and heavy use of computer technology.

One of the most interesting charter schools is the Metro Deaf School. It teaches in American Sign Language, which allows for much faster communication than English translated into sign language, the method most public schools use with the deaf. A group of parents and teachers created the school because they wanted a place where children could communicate quickly and fluidly, in their first language. Marcia Passi, one of the founding teachers, describes what happens to many deaf kids in normal public schools:

What we've seen a lot of times, a child is in one particular classroom and they use some sign system. It might be sign system A. And then the next year, within the same building, they'll move on to another classroom and that teacher will use sign system B. Can you imagine going through a system—by the time you've gotten to high school, you might have seen 17 different sign systems?

With the traditional school system, most of the time, our students will get up to the third-grade reading level and then plateau out.

At the Metro Deaf School, students do not plateau out. Metro Deaf was created to fit the particular needs of its customers—not to force them to fit the needs of a school district. Marcia Passi says it eloquently:

Here at MDS all of us are responsible for what these kids learn. Within the other education system, we were accountable for making sure all of the t's got crossed and the i's got dotted. And the child's learning was secondary. We had to make sure that all the paperwork was taken care of, that the IEP's [individual education plans] were filled out, the proper forms were used. Here, for some of our kids, we don't have all of the paperwork just so. However, the child's education is most important. That's what we're most accountable for.

The Bottom Line

By the 1995–1996 school year, 19 percent of all public school students in Minnesota—more than 150,000 students—attended schools chosen by their parents. (This includes most students in Minneapolis and St. Paul, which offer choice within their districts.) "Most of the studies indicate that academics is, in fact, the factor named most frequently by parents who request a switch—about one-third of them," says Joe Nathan. Perhaps the second biggest reason is convenience: parents often choose to send a child to a nearby school in a neighboring district rather than a faraway school in their own district, or to send them to school near where they work rather than near where they live.

The most in-depth study of the effect of open enrollment in Minnesota was conducted by Cheryl Lange at the University of Minnesota. Using surveys and interviews, she examined its impact in 8 of the state's 435 districts. She found that, in most of these districts, "Administrators and school board members take open enrollment's potential impact into account when deciding on buildings, programs, services, extracurricular activities, student discipline plans, and staffing. Seven of the eight school districts reported several instances of how the transfer of students or the threat of transfer affected their planning."

All four districts that worked to make improvements gained students. "Districts whose superintendents and school boards took a proactive role towards open enrollment, were aware of the implications for their district, and implemented strategies to attract or retain students gained students," Lange writes. "Districts in which these strategies and actions were not taken lost students."

One district, which had a serious fiscal crisis on its hands, provides a good example of how choice forces administrators to make different decisions than they would if they still enjoyed monopolies. Lange quotes the superintendent at length:

> We have just gone through massive restructuring and a reduction of our budget. We were very concerned. When we first came out with an approach of [making change] the traditional way, we were going to wipe out two thirds of our extracurricular activities. We were going to wipe out a lot of the electives the kids in the upper levels had.

Because they knew that would cost them students—at $3,050 per student—they figured out other ways to save money. The superintendent had to lay off teachers. But, says Lange, he sent other "teachers out around the country to get new ideas, and he said, 'We're going to restructure our school around these new ideas.' They changed all kinds of things."

The superintendent of the smallest district, which lost 22 of its 117 students and was only able to stay whole because its community passed a tax increase, made a similar comment:

> Open enrollment has a lot of impact on us. One of the things it does is that we don't dare, even under budget constraints, we don't dare curtail programs. We don't dare curtail. In almost anything we say we won't do anymore, you have to consider if we lose one family as a result of that, where are we at?

Lange is careful to point out that parents move their children for many reasons, including convenience—and some small districts get hurt in the process despite the high quality of their programs. (Overall, studies show that more students are moving into small districts than out of them, according to Joe Nathan.) Despite the fact that not all the competition is based on quality, however, she reports that it does drive administrators to do what they can to maximize customer satisfaction.

Open enrollment impacts the parent-educator dynamic by subtly changing the degree of power held by each player in the system. . . . Rather than the debate occurring at the legislative level, it is occurring at the district level. Parents are flexing their political muscles by demanding desired programs and services. If the requests are not honored, many threaten to leave the district. Findings suggest that it doesn't take a large number of families threatening transfer for administrators to take seriously the requests.

It is impossible to say yet whether choice has improved student learning in Minnesota. In all three charter schools whose charters have come up for renewal, student test scores have improved. But the state only began requiring standardized tests in all schools in 1996, and only at one grade level. Even if more test scores were available, however, standardized tests are a relatively limited barometer of student learning. And in any case, many of the reformers believe it will take more time to see significant improvements in student outcomes, because it will take time for schools to make dramatic changes in the way they teach. John Brandl, who led the charge for choice in the state senate, told us in 1995:

I think that even if we did have the measurements, the measurements wouldn't show much yet. We have not implemented anything ambitious enough yet. When we did let people choose, there still wasn't much variation in what they could choose from.

This is gradually changing, and the reformers continue to push for more charter schools and a more competitive system. The second-chance schools are already an exception. With more than 40,000 students attending at least 140 of these schools, Minnesota may already have changed those students' educational experiences fairly dramatically. Unfortunately, with no standardized testing or other assessment, we do not have enough data to know the impact for certain.

We do know two things. First, choice has not led to the negative outcomes its opponents predicted, such as increased racial segregation, the decimation of small districts, and widespread shifting of schools for "frivolous" reasons like the pursuit of better sports teams. Second, the people of Minnesota think it is a big success. By 1994, 86 percent of adults surveyed said parents of public school children should be allowed to send their children to a public school in another district and 71 percent said increased competition from choice would improve the quality of education.

Even public school teachers have accepted choice. As early as 1989, 61 percent of teachers surveyed supported choice. Hundreds have used it to create charter schools, second-chance schools, schools within schools, and the like. Even some of those still teaching in traditional schools find that it relieves them of the burden of trying to meet every student's needs in the same classroom, because kids who don't fit in can find different schools that suit them better.

But the last word should be reserved for parents, hundreds of thousands of whom have used school choice to pursue what their children need in a school. Jane Norbin speaks for many when she tells the following story:

> My oldest child is now 21 years old, but when she entered the school district in second grade, she went to the second-grade teacher and said, "I've already finished these reading books in my previous school." And the teacher told her, "Well, I'm sorry, that's all we have, you'll have to read them again." At the time, I was blissfully flying through public school education and didn't really realize what was happening. It wasn't until she graduated from high school and she told me that story that I was horrified. And that's when this sort of a choice meant so much more to me. My son does not have to go through that.

THE CUSTOMER STRATEGY

Minnesota made its schools accountable to parents like Jane Norbin. It did so by giving parents the power to withdraw their children from their district and take most of their public dollars with them. The schools are still accountable to their school boards and to the state, which set their overall rules and standards. But now they are accountable to parents as well.

In the past, teachers and principals were responsible for delivering the required curriculum in the required number of days, following the required rules. "As traditional teachers, we've always been accountable in a traditional sense," says Bob Holewa, a teacher at Columbus Elementary School. "We've always had the reporting formats. We've always had to make sure that we've covered certain components in the curriculum."

Once school choice hits home, teachers and principals are accountable in a new way. They may teach the curriculum and follow the rules, but if they don't please their customers, they will face consequences.

Education is not the only arena in which governments are using customer choice. It is common, for example, in health care, housing, job training, day care, and recreation programs.

Nor is Minnesota alone in having applied choice to public education. In New Zealand, the Labor Party introduced full school choice and shifted most school funding to a per capita basis, so dollars follow children not just to the district, but to the school their parents choose. It gave most governance authority over each school to a board made up of elected parents, and it allowed groups of parents to create new schools, much like charter schools in the U.S.

The British have taken similar steps. All parents can choose their children's schools—if their school of choice has room—and roughly 80 percent of the money follows the child to the selected institution. For four-year-olds, the government now provides vouchers parents can use to pay for nursery school, public or private. It also offers low-income students full or partial tuition at nearly 300 independent private schools, and provides "youth credits" that 16- and 17-year-olds who are not in school full-time can use to pay for part-time education or training.

British schools are run by "governing bodies": boards of directors made up, typically, of about 20 people—one quarter elected by parents, one quarter appointed by the local council, and the rest teachers and volunteers from the community and local businesses. The governing bodies control school budgets and hire and fire head teachers (principals). Local councils—the equivalent of city and county councils in the U.S.—must hand over at least 85 percent of their education budgets to governing bodies, leaving only 15 percent for central services. (As we write, the government is considering increasing the percentage to 95.) If they are not satisfied with their powers and a majority of parents vote to do so, governing bodies can apply to "opt out" of their local education authority—the local government's education department—and receive funding directly from the central government. (About 90 percent of these applications are approved by the education minister.) By 1995, 1,100 of the nation's 25,000 state schools had opted out, to become what they call "grant maintained schools."

In addition to encouraging schools to withdraw from their districts, the government has pushed the formation of new "city technology colleges"—inner-city secondary schools focusing on science and technology, set up through partnerships with business—and "technology schools," which are centers of excellence with enhanced technology facilities and a vocational emphasis. Recently it added programs to stimulate the creation of specialized secondary schools focused on language, arts, and sports. (Since 1944, churches have also sponsored roughly one quarter of all state schools.) And in 1993 Parliament gave voluntary bodies, whether existing schools, universities, nonprofit organizations, or groups of parents, the right to set up the equivalent of charter schools.

In the U.S., some 17 states had passed laws by mid-1996 creating some form of interdistrict choice, and 25 states had passed charter school laws. A few states with strong versions of choice or charter schools have begun to achieve some degree of leverage.

Massachusetts is one example. Several years ago the Boston School Committee and the teachers union were discussing an initiative to create five "pilot schools" free of many regulations and union contract rules. They had not been able to reach agreement when the state passed a charter school bill, allowing the creation of 25 charter schools statewide. Faced with the reality that 18 of the first 64 charter school proposals had come from Boston—and that charter schools would take money out of the district—the school committee and the union quickly resolved their differences and announced the pilot school initiative.

In Marblehead the school committee and teachers reacted to a group of parents who created a charter school as if they had declared civil war. But forced to compete, the local middle school site council began implementing many of the same reforms the charter group was planning.

In Essex, a small town that has no high school, the school committee voted in 1995, when its existing high school contract with a neighboring district was about to expire, to sign a contract with a district that was 30 minutes away by car. Though many parents objected, the school committee pushed ahead. Only when parents organized a survey showing that all but one or two families would use school choice to send their children (and their dollars) to closer high schools did the school committee relent.

When public organizations become accountable to their customers, it alters their behavior. It is a powerful lever of change. The customer strategy builds on the consequences strategy by making organizations accountable for their performance not just up the chain of command, but also to their customers. This could be viewed as simply one approach to creating consequences. As we said in the previous chapter, the consequences strategy does change both the incentive system and the accountability of public organizations. But in our research, we have found that when governments that already use the consequences strategy build in accountability *to the customer,* it adds a powerful new dimension. While the core strategy defines *what* organizations are accountable for and the consequences strategy changes *how* they are held accountable, the customer strategy changes *to whom* they are accountable.

In the U.K., for example, the Next Steps initiative used performance management to create consequences, but performance was defined primarily in terms of efficiency. Even when Next Steps agencies measured effectiveness, few of them asked their customers how they would define effective services. It was only when John Major launched the Citizen's Charter that most British agencies began surveying their customers and measuring their performance in terms of whether they were satisfying those customers. It added a qualitatively different dimension to British reinvention.

The same thing happened in Sunnyvale, California, the American pioneer of performance management. In the early 1990s, during a severe recession, a couple of businesses moved out of Sunnyvale. With the state already slashing local government funds, the loss of tax revenue hit home. This led City Manager Tom Lewcock to start asking questions. Since Sunnyvale measured the performance of every unit, Lewcock knew that 85 percent of the people who came in for a permit from the Community Development Department got one the same day.

It seemed like an impressive statistic. But for years, businesses that were frustrated in their efforts to get permits had been the number one source of complaints to the city council. Why, Lewcock asked, were there so many complaints?

"We did focus groups with our customers," he remembers, "and found what we thought was important was not what they thought was important."

"They told us we were too slow, too inconsistent, and what happened in the office wasn't followed through in the field," adds Director of Community Development Bill Powers. "That we had an attitude of creating problems rather than solving problems." Businesspeople also complained about having to visit several different departments, where they got different treatment and conflicting information. "Generally we got the feedback that Sunnyvale was a very hard city to do business with—and that's not the impression we wanted to give."

So Powers began making changes. He created one-stop shopping for all development and permitting issues. The department cross-trained its electrical, plumbing, and other building inspectors, so one inspector could do all the inspections. It turned the inspectors into project coordinators, who were responsible for making sure customers got what they needed through the entire course of a project. It created customer service standards and built customer satisfaction measures into its performance targets. It encouraged businesspeople to complain directly to Powers, who did his best to solve their problems. It began surveying its customers, and it created a customer focus group to suggest further improvements. Out of that came an "advantage plan check" process. "If we have a company that wants to move in in a hurry, or wants to expand in a hurry, we will pull together a team of experts, and we will plan-check that project in a day—two days max," says Powers.

"Now we have a great reputation," adds Lewcock. "We were rated by the Chamber of Commerce in California as the number one community in which to do business." The entire experience taught him, however, that "a satisfied customer is the ultimate performance indicator. I only learned after the fact that it's not just the measures that are important, it's the attitudes of the customers you're dealing with."

Sunnyvale now requires that every service it provides, external or internal, have some customer feedback mechanism in place. It has built customer service and satisfaction measures into its performance targets in every unit. One unit, called Leisure Services, has even adopted a customer satisfaction guarantee: if you are not satisfied with a recreation program or course, you get your money back, no questions asked.

Like Minnesota, Sunnyvale has discovered that when an organization empowers its customers, whether through choice or service standards or satisfaction guarantees, they become the engine of change. They keep the pressure on to improve—not once or twice a year, but constantly and forever. As Dan Loritz says of school choice, "I can think of no higher level of accountability than the fact that if the program is not performing, parents—who above all else want their children well educated—simply aren't going to stand for it. They're going to take them out of that program."

Dual Accountability

As we said earlier, accountability to parents does not mean that schools are no longer accountable to elected school boards, governors, state legislators, or the courts. It means they are accountable to elected officials and the courts for complying with the basic rules and meeting the basic standards of the system, *and* they are accountable to parents for meeting their children's needs. In Minnesota, for example, the rules set up by the legislature and the courts do not allow parents to make choices that further segregate the schools along racial lines. Minneapolis can let minority students leave the district for other districts, but not white students. Within the bounds set by the legislature and courts, however, parents can choose and schools are accountable to parents.

People who manage businesses in competitive markets also have dual accountability. They are accountable to their customers, but they are also accountable to their owners, usually through a board of directors that represents shareholders. When there is a conflict, accountability to owners trumps accountability to customers. When a company has products that customers love but is still losing money (think of Apple Computer in recent years), the board often steps in to replace the management. Similarly, if a public organization is pleasing its customers but not achieving what elected officials (or the courts) want, accountability to those officials takes precedence. They represent the organization's owners, the public.

The customer strategy works best when elected officials can define their goals for public organizations in terms of customer satisfaction and hold service providers accountable for satisfying their customers. In the long run, businesses are successful only if they are able to produce what both their customers and their owners want. The same is true of public organizations. There are several ways that elected officials can create this kind of alignment. They can give customers choices and set the rules of the market so that their choices force organizations to produce what the elected officials want. Or they can translate their definition of success into standards of customer service and satisfaction. These basic approaches, outlined below, align accountability to owners with accountability to customers—a powerful combination.

Some conflict between what customers want and what elected officials want is inevitable. Again, a good example is racial integration. Individual families may make choices that lead to more segregated schools, while the "owners" of the school system have integration as a goal. In such cases, the owners, who represent the collective interest, must overrule the customers, who represent individual interests. (Experience has proven, of course, that mandating something like integration of schools is most effective when the owners can give customers choices that let them exercise their self-interest in ways that do not undermine the collective interest. Otherwise most people use any means to pursue their self-interest, regardless of the collective interest.)

When customer choices are aligned with the goals set by policy makers, a system of competitive choice forces managers to take seriously what their customers want. If parents think a particular class has too many students, for example, the principal must listen carefully and try to resolve the problem. Our argument is that elected officials will find that their goals are met more often when they make that principal accountable to those parents, through choice.

In a nutshell, the reinvention paradigm asserts that systems in which accountability only flows up the chain of command are not as effective as systems in which a great deal of the accountability flows to customers—within a framework of rules and standards set up by those who steer the system.

Defining the Customer

When public organizations try to sort out who their customers are, it can get very confusing. Sometimes the customer is the public at large.

This is always true when the product is a "public good" such as police protection, defense, or environmental protection. With "private goods," such as recreation programs, the customer is an individual, family, or group. Many public services combine both public and private aspects, however. Public education serves individual students and families, for instance. But it also serves the public at large, by creating an educated population with the skills necessary to sustain a competitive economy and the values necessary to sustain a civilized society. This is why we long ago made education compulsory to age 16 and set minimum standards for curriculum, length of school day and year, teacher qualifications, and the like.

Another source of confusion is the fact that some organizations serve members of the public, while others serve other public organizations. As we said in chapter 5, internal service units such as print shops and maintenance units exist to serve other public organizations. General Loh remembers what it was like when he began asking members of the Air Combat Command who their customers were.

I said, "Okay, what business are you guys in? Who are your customers?"

"Well, gee, we've got a lot of internal customers and we've got some external customers, we've got macro customers and micro customers."

"Well," I started asking everybody, "who are your macro customers? Who is it that we're really trying to serve?" And I got some wild answers: "Well, the president, the members of Congress, the American people."

I said, "Wait a minute, they're really not; you don't go talk to the American people every day to find out whether they like your product." So I said, "Who is it you're really talking to?"

"Well, in an operational context it is those commanders out in the field that we are supporting that are responsible for conducting operations." Okay, good. For example General Schwarzkopf and his group in Saudi Arabia. We provided all the airplanes to people for the Gulf War.

Once we understand who that macro customer is, well, let's go visit them and see if they like our product, if they like the way we fly, the way we operate, and how frequently we do it, and whether we're satisfying them. For the Middle East, for Europe, wherever we have to deploy our air power to operate, let's go out there and ask those guys if they're happy with our product.

In our view, Loh has it right. *In the public sector, your primary customer is the individual or group your work is primarily designed to help.* Your customers give your work its purpose. The Air Combat Command is there to help military commanders in the field. Those commanders, in turn, are there to help the American people. Hence the commanders' primary customers are the president and Congress, the elected representatives of the people.

Sometimes an organization's primary customers may not even use its work. They may not know anything about it. But if it is designed to help them directly, they are the primary customers.

For example, if you work for the Department of Community Development in Sunnyvale—or most other permitting organizations—you interact constantly with developers and businesses. But your work is designed primarily to help the community at large: the residents of Sunnyvale. Hence they are your primary customers. The developers are "compliers." To be effective, you often need to understand what they want and meet many of their needs. In other words, you need to treat them like customers. But if their needs conflict with the community's needs, the community's needs should take precedence. And who represents the community's needs? The elected officials. Hence you are accountable to the community by being accountable to the elected officials. (Occasionally a court steps in and overrules the elected officials, in which case you become accountable to the court.)

If you run a public school, we would argue that your work is primarily designed to help students and their parents. They are your primary customers. But as is often the case in the public sector, you have several secondary customers as well—groups that benefit from your work, but less directly than students and their parents do. They include the community at large and the employers who will someday hire the students you graduate. Both have a stake in your performance. In the long run, you serve them as well.

Some people prefer to call these secondary customers "stakeholders," but we think that can be confusing, because stakeholders and secondary customers are not identical groups. Some stakeholders are not secondary customers. For example, teachers are extremely important stakeholders in the public school system. Their unions are also stakeholders. But neither are by any stretch of the imagination *customers* of the system. The schools do not exist to serve teachers; teachers exist to serve schools.

Other people use different definitions than we have. There is no universally accepted practice, because most people in the public sector have only begun thinking in terms of customers in the past few years. Those involved in total quality management usually define the customer differently than we have, for example. Using a private sector model, they define the customer as the person or people who use the outputs an agency creates. In *Total Quality Management in Government*, for example, Steven Cohen and Ronald Brand say, "We define customers as the people who use the things that you produce." President Clinton's 1993 executive order, "Setting Customer Service Standards," uses the same definition: "For the purposes of this order, 'customer' shall mean an individual or entity who is directly served by a department or agency."

The problem with this definition is that it tells compliance organizations that compliers are their most important customers. It tells the police and prison wardens that criminals are their customers; it tells

---

Definitions: Customers, Compliers, and Stakeholders

Primary customers: The individual or group your work is primarily designed to help.

Secondary customers: Other individuals or groups your work is designed to benefit—but less directly than your primary customers.

Compliers: Those who must comply with laws and regulations: for example, taxpayers in relation to the Internal Revenue Service; developers in relation to a permitting agency; or drivers in relation to the Highway Patrol. They are not customers.

Stakeholders: Individuals and groups that have an interest in the performance of a public system or organization. For example, teachers in the public schools, or unions and business groups in relation to a workplace safety agency. Some stakeholders may be customers; others are not.

environmental agencies that the businesses they regulate are their customers; and it tells the IRS that taxpayers are their customers. Most of the time, as we said above, compliance organizations can improve their performance by treating compliers like customers, because that increases voluntary compliance. But it is dangerous to confuse compliers and customers. Obviously the safety of the public should be more important to the police and prison wardens than the satisfaction of criminals, and the safety of the public should be more important to environmental protection agencies than the satisfaction of business executives. Finally, consider what would happen if the IRS really made the satisfaction of taxpayers its highest objective. Tax revenues would plummet!

This is just one more example of the difficulty of bringing private sector practices into the public sector without any translation. Because so many public organizations exist to serve the public interest, not private interests, their customers are not always those they deal with day in and day out. We have taken pains to build these complexities into the definitions presented above.

Defining an organization's primary customers is a critical step, because it helps the organization understand exactly whom it is there to serve and who should define what effective service means. Defining the secondary customers and compliers is also important, for the same reasons. When the needs of primary and secondary customers (or customers and compliers) are different, organizations must consciously determine what their priorities are and how to balance any conflicting needs. If the community wants less pollution but an agency's compliers demand less burdensome regulation, for example, the agency must figure out how it can more effectively limit pollution while also minimizing and streamlining the red tape that frustrates the compliers. By reengineering processes, compliance agencies can often accomplish both goals. But when they cannot—when the goals conflict head-on and the win-win solutions have been exhausted—the agency needs to know who its primary customer is, because that is where its priority must lie.

The Customer Strategy's Three Approaches

Reinventing Government discussed at length why public organizations should be customer driven. It presented many of the ways they could deliver more value to the customer. This chapter asks a different question: How can we use accountability to the customer as a lever to force public organizations to change? Our purpose is not to explain all the ways in which public organizations can deliver better services to their customers. It is to help you understand how you can use accountability to the customer as a driving force of reinvention, to produce organizations that are more innovative and more entrepreneurial.

There are three basic approaches that make public organizations accountable to their customers. The first is to give customers a choice of public organizations. Choice has inherent value for the customer, as *Reinventing Government* explained. But as a lever to force change in public organizations, it is weak unless it is paired with consequences. The simple reality that one's customers can go elsewhere sometimes forces organizations to pay more attention to what customers want— even if they cannot take dollars with them. This is common: many of us can choose the motor vehicle offices we use to renew our drivers' licenses, or the public parks we frequent, or the library branches we prefer.

Some of us can choose the public schools our children attend. But public education provides a good example of why choice needs to be wedded to consequences to have real power. In many school districts parents have choices, but when they choose to leave a school, there are few negative consequences. The district simply fills that school up with other children. If enough customers leave a school, the district will probably look into the problem and try to help the school improve. If things are really bad, it may even transfer the principal. But until things get desperate, customer choice alone doesn't bring many consequences—or many changes.

Hence the second approach is to combine the customer strategy with consequences, by letting customers control the resources and take them to competing service providers. We call this *competitive choice*. It is quite similar to the enterprise management approach we described in chapter 5. But it stops short of organizing public units as enterprises that can determine their own prices. It allows parents to choose among schools and take their public school dollars with them when they move their children to a different school, for example—but it doesn't turn that school into a public corporation or enterprise fund.

The third alternative, called *customer quality assurance*, sets customer service standards and creates rewards for organizations that do a good job of meeting them and penalties for those that don't. It is the customer version of performance management. We introduced it in chapter 1, when we described John Major's Citizen's Charter.

Finally, there is an important competence every organization must have if it is to use the customer strategy: the ability to listen to its customers. We call *customer voice* a competence rather than an approach because, like performance measurement, it is necessary but not sufficient to force change. Many organizations survey their customers, use focus groups, and the like. (For 17 methods you can use to listen to your customers, see *Reinventing Government*, pp. 177–179.) But knowing what their customers want is not always enough to force them to provide it. Change is often painful, and public monopolies have many ways to rationalize their unwillingness to endure the pain. School officials in Forest Lake listened sympathetically for several years to parents who wanted a Montessori school, but there were always reasons they couldn't create one. Only when they realized that their customers could depart, taking their money with them—only when they became accountable to their customers—did they suddenly find the will to take action.

Some reinventors believe that customer voice is powerful in its own right. These same people often view the customer strategy as the central, most powerful, reinvention strategy. Much of the management literature from the private sector points in this direction: some of it reads as if honing in on what your customers want is *the* key to success.

In the private sector, there is some truth to this. Most private companies already face consequences in competitive markets, and few are embedded in administrative systems (budget, personnel, procurement) imposed from above that inhibit their ability to respond to their customers. They have administrative systems—but they have the power to change them.

In the public sector, as we have explained before, most organizations are monopolies, and most are part of larger systems that use bureaucratic rules to control them. Hence, using the customer strategy without also using consequences and control is rarely enough to produce significant change. Customer choice and quality standards usually add value for the customer. But to *force* public bureaucracies to transform themselves into more entrepreneurial organizations, they need to be wedded to consequences and decentralization of control.

Several years ago education consultant Michael Alves, who had helped design and implement choice plans in 14 American school districts, made a statement that accurately captures the limited power of choice to force organizational change:

> We have found that there is no independent effect of choice on educational improvement. But we have found, however, that choice can identify schools that parents want and schools that parents don't want. In Boston, for example, we have fourteen schools that are overchosen by everybody (blacks, whites, Asians, Hispanics), and we have fourteen schools that nobody wants.

Alves might have added that if consequences were attached to parents' choices—by closing the schools parents didn't want and asking principals and teachers to replicate the schools parents did want in those buildings—most principals and teachers would try harder to please parents.

But these principals and teachers must also be empowered to make the changes necessary to improve their schools. If they are hamstrung by centralized budget and personnel systems and overly restrictive management and union rules, they will not be free to innovate. That is where the control strategy comes in.

Minnesota's experience illustrates the point. It has liberated teachers who have the imagination and courage to start a charter school, an alternative school, or an area learning center. But not all of those who have stayed within traditional schools have been empowered to make significant changes. Cheryl Lange's study of eight districts found that Minnesota's competitive choice system had a significant impact on school boards, superintendents, and principals—but not on most teachers. Only in one of the eight districts did teachers tell her they had changed their teaching methods or classroom offerings because of open enrollment.

In the other seven districts, Lange writes, "It was as if they were outside the cause and effect dynamic. Even if they acknowledged that parents' reasons for transfer may be program centered, they did not report any change of behavior." One teacher explained it this way: "Teachers were not given the power to make a difference, so they were incapable of it."

Because they had little control over how their schools were run, most teachers were, in effect, outside the loop. As a result, their behavior didn't change. This is a rather dramatic illustration of why the customer strategy must be wedded to the control strategy to be effective. Unless frontline employees feel it is in their power to make changes, they will not do so—even when their organization is accountable to customers and has clear financial incentives to change.

Paul Pryde, a veteran consultant on public sector redesign, says it well:

> *Freeing parents to choose is only one half of a well-designed choice system. The other, equally important, half is freeing teachers and principals as well. Allowing "producers" of education to innovate, to do what they uniquely know how to do, is vital to the success of choice. It is the combination of producer choice and consumer choice, not one without the other, that will produce improved educational outcomes.*

CUSTOMER CHOICE

Customer choice works primarily with service functions. It does not apply to policy functions, and it is of limited utility with respect to compliance functions. A revenue department or permitting agency can let compliers deal with their choice of offices; some motor vehicle departments let motorists apply for a license at any of their offices; and the Environmental Protection Agency lets some polluters choose whether to clean up their smokestacks or buy pollution credits. But these choices are not designed to pressure compliance organizations to improve.

In the service arena, we would recommend using competitive choice whenever possible, because choice without consequences does not create significant leverage. But many reinventors do not have this option, because their elected officials do not have the courage or imagination to create competition between schools or training programs or other service providers. In these situations, reinventors can combine customer choice with performance management, to create enough leverage to drive change.

Practitioners have learned a number of other lessons about the customer choice approach. To make customer choice systems effective, there are a number of basic criteria that must be met:

There must be enough suppliers to give customers real choices. If a service is a natural monopoly—if it is far more efficient to have one provider than many—choice is the wrong approach. If there are only two or three suppliers, choice may or may not be useful, depending upon the service.

Customers must have sufficient resources to generate the demand necessary to produce an adequate supply of service providers. If money is a limiting factor, governments can increase demand by subsidizing low-income people, through vouchers or other mechanisms.

Customers need useful, reliable, accessible information about the quality and cost of different service providers. This is particularly true in services that seek to provide human development, such as education, day care, health care, and job training, because the difference between low and high quality is not always obvious at first blush. Governments can solve this by measuring the performance of service providers and making that information accessible to customers, if necessary through brokers who help them find and use it.

The British are developing a fairly useful collection of information parents can use to choose their children's schools, for instance. Students take national exams in English, math, and science at ages 7, 11, and 14 (most also take exams when they are 16), and schools are required to publish the aggregated results. The government publishes performance tables every year, which include comparative data on each school's exam results at ages 11 and 16 through 18. They also include rates of authorized and unauthorized absences, results in pre- and post-16 vocational qualifications, and percentages of students receiving baccalaureate diplomas. (The Department for Education and Employment is working to develop further measures.) In addition, teams of professionals and nonprofessionals inspect each school every four years. They issue reports with both qualitative and quantitative assessments, and the schools must publicize them and develop plans of action in response.

Governments need to structure the rules of the marketplace carefully, then enforce those rules. In any market, unscrupulous people will try to sell shoddy services to unsuspecting customers. Fly-by-night proprietary schools have long collected Pell Grants from the federal government, then delivered second-rate courses to their students. To control such abuses, government must police the market.

Governments must pay particular attention to the question of equity in structuring the market. Left to their own devices, choice systems will at times produce less-than-equitable results, because those who have more education and money will be better able to find the information they need to make good decisions. They will also have more access to transportation and more ability to talk themselves into the schools or day care centers or hospitals they prefer. Hence the rules that govern any choice system must be set down with care, as we argued in *Reinventing Government* (pp. 101–104).

Tools for Customer Choice

Public Choice Systems allow recipients of public services to choose between different providers, whether all public or both public and private.

Customer Information Systems and Brokers give customers who are choosing service providers—with public resources, their own resources, or a combination—information about the quality and cost of each provider, so they can make informed choices.

COMPETITIVE CHOICE

Competitive choice has far more power than choice alone, but its use is limited primarily to services. With compliance functions, the customer is the public at large, represented by elected officials. These officials may want to contract with multiple organizations—such as multiple service stations to perform vehicle emissions tests. But if they let compliers choose between compliance organizations and let those organizations compete for their revenues based on their volume, they create incentives to relax standards so as to attract more compliers.

Consider what happens in states that use private service stations to check automobiles' compliance with emissions standards. Since the service stations earn more by attracting more compliers, they have a financial incentive to cheat. To get the kind of compliance they want, states have to invest heavily in efforts to monitor them. It makes more sense for the state to contract with multiple service stations and pay them based on both the quantity and quality of their inspections, to limit the incentive to cheat.

Within service functions, competitive choice is often the best option

for services that are not purely "private goods." For private goods—
services that primarily benefit and can be charged to the individuals or
groups that use them—enterprise management is typically a better
approach. It gives providers maximum flexibility but makes them
directly accountable to their customers, normally in a competitive
market.

But many services are public goods, or combinations of private and
public goods. This is true of education, as we noted earlier. It is also true
of health care: when individuals are immunized against contagious
diseases, for example, all members of society benefit. Hence we all
have an interest in making sure everyone is immunized.

As we explained in chapter 5, enterprise management is not appropriate for public goods, because their costs should not be charged to
individuals. When we want all or most members of society to have
equal access to a service, we normally either provide it free or subsidize
consumers and fix its price so they can all afford it. We do the former
with public education and the latter with Medicaid and Medicare, for
example. Neither option is compatible with enterprise management,
because the providers are not free to set their prices.

Competitive choice is the next best option in such situations. There
are several ways to do it. You can fund the service directly out of the
public purse but let the dollars follow the customer to his or her chosen
provider, as Minnesota and others do with public schools. You can give
some or all customers vouchers and restrict the price providers can
charge, so as to guarantee equal access, as some communities, states,
and nations do with day care or early childhood education. Or you can
reimburse providers for services at a set price, as Medicaid and Medicare do. In all three cases, the government sets the price, to ensure
equal access for all.

In effect, when we use competitive choice we are saying, "Since this
service is in part a public good, we don't want to put it into a pure
market. But to get some of the advantages of the market, we will put it
into a 'social market.' We will make the customer king, but within a
marketplace structured to ensure equal opportunity and other collective
needs."

All of the lessons that apply to the customer choice approach,
outlined above, also apply to competitive choice. Governments that use
competitive choice must be especially vigilant about several additional
problems.

They must guard against "creaming"—the tendency of providers to select the best or easiest customers. If schools want to attract more students, they may covet those who can score well on standardized tests or star in athletic competition—since some parents look at schools' average test scores when making their choices and some students look at their sports teams. When job training providers are reimbursed based on the number of people they can train and place in jobs, they have a clear incentive to select those who will be easiest to place in jobs and avoid those who will be difficult.

Given these realities, governments need to build protections into their competitive choice systems if they want to preserve equal opportunity. In public education, for example, districts and states often require schools to select their students by lottery if more students apply than they can accept—so the schools can't choose the best test takers or athletes. In job training, governments can set different reimbursement rates for different groups of trainees. They can pay more for those who will be difficult to train and place in jobs, because they have been out of the workforce for a long time or have poor work histories or backgrounds of crime or drug abuse.

They must guard against deceptive marketing. In a competitive market, clever service providers will learn to market their services. In the process, some will distort reality and deceive prospective customers. To prevent this, governments need to police their advertising and provide the objective information customers need to make rational decisions, as we argued above.

They must guard against increased segregation by class or race. Competition heightens the tendency of uncontrolled choice systems to increase segregation, because it creates incentives for providers to attract the most desirable customers, from the point of view of other customers. Michael Alves, who has as much experience wrestling with this issue as anyone in the world, puts it this way:

> *After implementing controlled choice in fourteen districts around the country, we feel confident that there is no conflict between choice and integration, if you control for it. And we are equally confident that if you don't control for race and social class, then choice will have no positive effect [on integration]. If anything, history shows that uncontrolled choice will make things worse. So you need to design the ground rules of choice programs very carefully.*

Tools for Competitive Choice

Competitive Public Choice Systems, such as Minnesota's interdistrict choice system, encourage customers to choose their providers and let the public dollars follow the customer.

Vouchers and Reimbursement Programs give those eligible for certain services the resources to purchase them themselves, or reimburse providers when they do.

CUSTOMER QUALITY ASSURANCE

Bromley is one of the better managed boroughs in London. During the 1980s, its employees worked hard to improve their performance. But to most of them, that meant cutting costs, increasing efficiency, and reducing debt. It was not until the 1990s, after John Major announced his Citizen's Charter, that Bromley began listening carefully to its customers. "When we went out and listened to the public," says Chief Executive Nigel Palk, "we found they were more interested in quality than in these hard finance numbers." People were less concerned about efficiency than about crime, the borough's physical environment, and a "sense of place" and "community" in their local village, of which there are about 30 in Bromley.

Many British organizations have suddenly discovered their customers' priorities in the wake of the Citizen's Charter, the single most sweeping example of customer quality assurance we have seen. Though Major wrapped other reforms under the Charter umbrella, at its heart the Charter simply asks all public organizations to define the standards of customer service—the levels of quality—they will guarantee to their customers.

The National Health Service set maximum waiting times for different services. Police forces set maximum times for answering emergency telephone calls and responding to emergency incidents. The courts set maximum times for issuing summonses, sending judgments, and keeping witnesses waiting. British Rail lines defined what percent of their trains would arrive on time and what kind of discount they would offer passengers if they missed their targets. The London

Underground—the subway system—set standards for reliability, cleanliness, security, and passenger information.

The Citizen's Charter applies to almost every public organization in the country—and to some monopolies that have been sold to private owners, such as gas and electric utilities. It requires them to publish both their standards and their progress in reaching them. As the 1995 Citizen's Charter report says, "This makes them more accountable to their users: the public can see their strengths and weaknesses and seek changes where improvements are needed."

The Citizen's Charter articulated six principles, which "every citizen is entitled to expect":

Standards: Setting, monitoring and publication of explicit standards for the services that individual users can reasonably expect. Publication of actual performance against these standards.

Information and Openness: Full, accurate information readily available in plain language about how public services are run, what they cost, how well they perform and who is in charge.

Choice and Consultation: The public sector should provide choice wherever practicable. There should be regular and systematic consultation with those who use services. Users' views about services, and their priorities for improving them, to be taken into account in final decisions on standards.

Courtesy and Helpfulness: Courteous and helpful service from public servants who will normally wear name badges. Services available equally to all who are entitled to them and run to suit their convenience.

Putting Things Right: If things go wrong, an apology, a full explanation and a swift and effective remedy. Well publicised and easy-to-use complaints procedures with independent review wherever possible.

Value for Money: Efficient and economical delivery of public services within the resources the nation can afford. And independent validation of performance against standards.

The Citizen's Charter used a series of mechanisms to bring these principles to life, as we explained in chapter 1. The most important were the individual charters themselves. The Charter asked each public organization to consult its customers to find out what was most important to them, then to publish its own charter. Those charters spell out customer service standards, give customers the information they need to get the most out of services, tell them how to file complaints, and explain how the organization will "put things right" when it fails to meet its standards. Several major services now pay compensation to their customers when they fail to meet their standards, including British Rail, the London Underground, British Gas, public electricity suppliers, water companies, and water/sewerage companies.

The Citizen's Charter also called for better information for customers. As a result, the government asked the independent Audit Commission to publish performance tables comparing the performance of local government services, police forces, and fire brigades. The national government publishes comparative performance tables on schools and hospitals itself.

In addition, the Charter asked public organizations to provide better information to those who used their services. By 1996, national organizations had created more than 50 telephone help lines for customers. For example, the National Health Service's toll-free Health Information Service provides a range of information, from advice on medical conditions and treatments to the maximum waiting times at local hospitals. It received 106,500 calls during the first three months of 1995.

The Charter also asked public organizations to improve their procedures for handling complaints and to establish an independent review mechanism, such as an ombudsman, for people who complained and were not satisfied with the response. It promised "tougher and more independent inspectorates" in areas such as police, prisons, schools, and social services, where inspections were used to check on the quality of professional services. The government pushed existing inspectorates, which had been staffed exclusively by members of the profession they were inspecting, to include more lay members, "to ensure [that] professional expertise is balanced by the practical concerns of the general public."

Finally, the Citizen's Charter created a new award for outstanding customer service. Public organizations can apply for the right to display the Charter Mark on their publications and signs for three years. To win that right, they must demonstrate that they fulfill the six principles listed above, plus three others: "customer satisfaction," "measurable improvements in the quality of service over the last two or more years," and introduction of "at least one innovative enhancement to services without any extra cost to the taxpayer or consumer." To continue to display the Charter Mark after three years, they must demonstrate continued improvement.

The effect of all this has been to push public managers to become more conscious of what their customers want—and then to deliver it. Some organizations have taken this challenge more seriously than others, of course. In chapter 1, we described improvements in the National Health Service, British Rail, and the Passport Office. Other examples include the following:

- The Royal Mail raised the percentage of first-class letters delivered in the U.K. by the next workday from 85.5 percent in 1990–1991 to 92 percent in 1994–1995. In a 1993 Citizen's Charter survey, 91 percent of those surveyed said postal services had improved or were at least as good as in the previous year.

- The Driving Standards Agency brought the waiting time for a "large goods" vehicle driving test down from four weeks in 1990–1991 to one week in 1994–1995.

- The Driver and Vehicle Licensing Agency processed 90 percent of applications within 16 days in 1991–1992; by 1994–1995, it processed 95 percent within ten working days.

- Customer satisfaction with local government services increased from 51 percent in 1991 to 61 percent in 1995, on a National Consumer Council survey.

The Citizen's Charter has inspired imitations in the U.S., Canada, France, Belgium, Australia, and Italy. After a 1993 visit from Diana Goldsworthy, then the deputy director of the Citizen's Charter Unit, President Clinton's National Performance Review recommended that the U.S. government do something similar. On September 11, 1993, only four days after receiving the NPR recommendations, the president issued an executive order requiring all executive agencies and departments to:

a. *identify the customers who are, or should be, served by the agency;*

b. *survey customers to determine the kind and quality of services they want and their level of satisfaction with existing services;*

c. *post service standards and measure results against them;*

d. *benchmark customer service performance against the best in the business;*

e. *survey frontline employees on barriers to, and ideas for, matching the best in business;*

f. *provide customers with choices in both the sources of service and the means of delivery;*

g. *make information, services, and complaint systems easily accessible; and*

h. *provide means to address customer complaints.*

The president proclaimed that "the standards of quality for service provided to the public shall be: Customer service equal to the best in business."

By 1995, 214 federal agencies had established customer service standards. As in the U.K., the early ones suffered from a lack of teeth. But also as in the U.K., they are beginning to have an impact.

Tools for Customer Quality Assurance

Customer Service Standards are quality standards—for example, "a customer will not wait longer than five minutes in line"—that public organizations commit to and publish.

Customer Redress gives customers some form of compensation—usually financial—when an organization fails to meet its customer service standards.

Quality Guarantees commit organizations to give customers their money back or redeliver services for free if customers are not satisfied the first time around.

Quality Inspectors, often working in teams that include both professionals and nonprofessionals, inspect public services and rate their quality. Sometimes they do so by going through the system anonymously, like "mystery shoppers" in the private sector.

Customer Complaint Systems track and analyze customer complaints, ensure prompt responses, and create methods by which organizations can learn from complaints to improve their services.

Ombudsmen help customers resolve their disputes and get services or information they need when they are not satisfied with the system's response to their complaints.

Lessons Learned About Customer Quality Assurance

If you want customer service standards to be powerful, use redress and guarantees to make them consequential. As we have argued, the customer strategy needs consequences to achieve its real power. Customer service standards will help managers and employees understand what is expected, but consequences will give urgency to the task of changing the way they do business.

Be ready to invest in developing the capacity to improve customer service. When public organizations first listen to their customers, they often discover that those customers don't think much of the service they're getting. So to improve quality, managers and employers have to develop a series of new capacities, such as total quality management and business process reengineering.

Don't try to sell customer service standards to the public as an innovation until organizations have committed to achieve high standards and provide redress when they fail. As we explained in chapter 1, John Major's Citizen's Charter got off to a rocky start because he announced it with great fanfare, long before there were any charters with real teeth. Until organizations such as British Rail and the London Underground began setting high standards, meeting them, and offering compensation when they failed, the press and the public treated the Charter as a joke. People are not impressed by good intentions, particularly those of politicians and bureaucracies. But they are impressed by documented improvements in service quality. They are even more impressed by quality guarantees and refunds.

Use a customer council to lead the quality assurance effort, so the push for high standards has the urgency and credibility that outside customers can lend it. Remember Mayor Goldsmith's SELTIC Commission in Indianapolis, which he used to drive his managed competition strategy? By using an outside group to select the services for competition, he gave the effort credibility, neutrality, and urgency. When establishing customer service standards, it helps to do the same thing. If public managers lead the effort, they will not have the credibility that an outside group like SELTIC has, particularly with the media.

Diana Goldsworthy says this is one of the lessons she and her colleagues learned in creating the Citizen's Charter. As civil servants reporting to a minister, they had little credibility with the press when they talked about forcing public organizations to deliver better services to the public.

QUESTIONS PEOPLE ASK
ABOUT THE CUSTOMER STRATEGY

Q: Is the customer always right?

No. As we emphasized earlier, when a customer's desires conflict with the policies set by elected officials, those policies must take precedence. Customer empowerment should not mean letting racist families that want their children in segregated public schools have their way, for example. In the private sector the customer may be king, but in the public sector, things are more complex. Elected officials, who represent the citizens at large, set the overall rules of each service delivery system. Within those rules, providers should be accountable to customers and customers should be king. But customers must obey those rules.

Q: How do you get the politicians to care about customers, rather than just interest groups and constituencies?

Rudy Perpich and John Major cared about the customers of public services for personal reasons: because they had had bad experiences as customers themselves. Most elected officials do not have the same passion. They care about *voters* and *interest groups* and *constituencies*, not customers. If voters get angry about their schools or police force or the condition of their roads, their elected officials will develop an intense interest. But how can you get them interested in customer service all the time?

The best way we know is to turn customers into constituencies. You can do this by empowering them: giving parents their choice of public schools, for example, or giving neighborhoods some control over police services. Once customers have power, they will defend it and use it to demand better services. Customers will also organize themselves as constituents whenever that power is threatened, as Minnesota legislators discovered when several of them tried to gut the Postsecondary Options program.

You can't always turn customers into constituents, of course. They must care a great deal about a service before they will mobilize as a constituency. Another way to get politicians to focus on improving customer service is to give them information about what customers think of their public services. Customer surveys can be very useful in calling problems to the attention of elected officials. But the most effective tactic we have seen is the use of *comparative data* to show how one jurisdiction's services are rated compared with those of others. This can embarrass public officials into paying attention, if their services look bad, or give them reason to be proud, if their services outrank the competition.

Q: Can we use the customer strategy in compliance organizations?

Yes, but with one big difference: the primary customer of compliance organizations is the community at large, represented by its elected officials. As we said earlier, those it deals with day in and day out are "compliers." Compliance organizations can use customer standards and customer voice to improve their service to compliers, as a means to improve their voluntary compliance—which helps the community at large. But in doing so, they need to balance the interests of both groups. Making things too easy for developers, for example, may sacrifice the needs of community members for a healthy environment.

A number of public organizations, including the Minnesota Revenue Department, the Madison Police Department, the U.S. Environmental Protection Agency, and the U.K.'s Inland Revenue, have used an approach we call "winning compliance." Rather than concentrating on catching noncompliers, as most compliance organizations do, they have put more energy into encouraging voluntary compliance. According to the Public Strategies Group, a consulting firm that pioneered this approach, it involves the following steps:

- Involve compliers in helping make the rules.
- Educate compliers about what is expected of them.
- Provide services that facilitate compliance, such as telephone help lines and complier choice of methods of compliance. (For example, American taxpayers can file their federal tax returns by mail, phone, or electronic mail.)
- Establish quality standards, guarantees, and redress for service to compliers.
- Give compliers feedback on their level of compliance.
- Create incentives and consequences for compliance and noncompliance.

Inland Revenue in the U.K., which is switching from a system in which it calculated what most people owed to one in which taxpayers calculate their own payments due, as in the U.S., has used at least four of the steps outlined above. It has done extensive surveys and focus groups to get taxpayers' views on the rules and methods of the new system. It has worked hard to educate taxpayers. It has set up help lines and many other mechanisms to help taxpayers make the transition. And it has established customer service standards.

Q: Is the customer strategy useful in policy and regulatory organizations?

Absolutely. Policy and regulatory organizations need to know what their different sets of customers think and want. These organizations can use customer quality assurance and customer voice. A school board, for instance, can benefit greatly by listening to its customers and setting customer service standards, such as the quantity and quality of information it will provide to the public.

Q: What do you do when not all customers have adequate access to service providers or access to quality services?

This situation is common in the public sector. In education, for example, inner-city families and rural families often have fewer good schools within a reasonable commute than suburban families. There are a number of ways in which to minimize these problems and maximize equal opportunity:

- Governments can subsidize low-income customers, to increase the number of options they can afford or their ability to commute.
- Governments can encourage the creation of new service providers in underserved markets, through policies such as charter school laws.
- Governments can divide large service providers, such as large public schools, into smaller organizations to create more choices.
- Governments can create incentives that encourage low-quality providers to improve their services and provide assistance to hurry them along.

■ Governments can provide information and counseling to customers to help them find quality service providers.

Q: Are government employees customers, too?

No, employees are employees. As we noted above, some public offices and agencies serve other public units, not the public. In this sense, one group of public employees can be the customer of another group. But when organizations call all their employees customers, we believe they confuse the issue of where their accountability lies. The organization does not exist to serve its employees; it exists to serve its *customers*. Employees are important stakeholders, and we will discuss the necessity of empowering them in the next chapter. But they are not the organization's reason for being—and never should be.

THE POWER OF COMMITMENTS TO THE CUSTOMER

The idea that public organizations have customers is a new one. If you read public management literature published prior to the 1990s, you won't see the word "customer." In 1990, it was a radical new idea, associated mainly with total quality management.

Even today, a great deal of confusion still surrounds the notion of public sector customers—and for good reason. In government *citizens* are ultimately more important than *customers*, and accountability to the elected representatives of those citizens is more important than accountability to customers. This dual accountability makes the customer strategy more complex and confusing than other strategies. As we noted earlier, even the White House got its definition of the customer wrong!

The customer strategy also needs to be paired with consequences and control to achieve real power. Despite these qualifications, however, it is a critical element of reinvention. When organizations listen to their customers, learn what they want, and commit themselves to producing services those customers value, they often turn themselves upside down.

Consider the U.S. Postal Service. When the National Performance Review cajoled the Postal Service into publicly committing to deliver local first-class mail overnight, in September 1993, the Service fell flat on its face. By December 1993 it delivered only 58, 52, and 66 percent of first-class mail overnight in Washington, New York, and Chicago, respectively. But with the spotlight on, those numbers rose to 89, 89, and 86 percent by May 1996. Nationally, the number rose from 74 to 90 percent. A simple promise to the customer made a big difference.

– 7 –

THE CONTROL STRATEGY: SHIFTING CONTROL AWAY FROM THE TOP AND CENTER

THE SPIRIT OF THE FOREST

Most Americans know about the National Forest Service through its fire-prevention mascot, Smokey the Bear. Smokey is a septuagenarian, and the service is even older. Teddy Roosevelt and Gifford Pinchot, the governor of Pennsylvania, invented it at the turn of the century to promote forest conservation and to supply clean water and timber products. Pinchot became its first chief. Nearly a century later, Forest Service officials still post his short list of commonsense rules for managing the organization.

By the mid-1980s, Congress had expanded the service's original mandate to include protection of wildlife and wilderness and provision of recreational opportunities to the public. The agency controlled more than 191 million acres of federal land—holdings as big as all of Texas and Louisiana combined. It employed more than 40,000 people. Most of them worked in ranger districts, subdivisions of the system's more than 150 forests. Each forest had a supervisor who reported to one of nine regional offices, which reported to the national office in Washington. It took more than $2 billion a year to run the organization.

And it took a few more rules than Pinchot had laid out—a 17-foot-high stack of them. That's what a deputy in the national office, F. Dale Robertson, found when he gathered all the books of rules, regulations, procedures, and policies. Each rule had a proud author—in the Congress or the Washington office or the regional offices or a forest supervisor's office. But no one had ever considered the cumulative effect of the regulations on the organization. When a consulting firm assessed the Forest Service's condition in 1985, it found little of which Robertson and his colleagues could be proud. Pinchot's innovative, pathbreaking organization had vanished. A stodgy, rule-bound bureaucracy had grown up in its place.

The problems extended all the way down to the ranger districts. Employees had learned to "follow the book," says Floyd "Butch" Marita, a 30-year veteran who ran the Eastern Region until early 1996. "They were manual-driven, not much into risk taking. It was a mind-your-own-business mentality. Everyone waited for someone else—at the top—to make the decisions."

The result was enormous inefficiency. If a rancher needed a special-use permit to graze cattle on Forest Service land, for instance, it could take as long as three months to get approval. The rancher asked the district ranger. The ranger sent a written request to the forest supervisor. The supervisor sent it to the regional office. There, the staffer in charge of such matters wrote a recommendation. That went to the regional forester. When he signed off, the district ranger finally got his approval.

If a ranger had to respond quickly to an emergency—a destructive rampage by wild hogs, for instance—he first had to ask the forest supervisor for money. Even if the request was for just a few thousand dollars, to change a single line item in the forest's annual budget, the supervisor had to go up through the chain of command to get approval. The supervisor had to ask the regional office for "reprogramming authority." The regional office asked the Washington office, which asked the Office of Management and Budget, which asked the congressional appropriations committees. Once approved, the decision worked its way back down the chain.

Standard operating procedure was to kick every decision upstairs and then wait for orders. This concentrated decision-making authority in the iron fists of a few top managers—regional foresters and Washington office staff. It bred "hierarchical, ego-driven, dictatorial leadership," says Larry Payne, a seasoned forester in the national office. "The first regional foresters I ever met—one wouldn't speak to me; I was a nobody. The next two would scare you to death; you would quake in your boots even seeing them come near you."

The rigid hierarchy existed for a reason. "The process was designed to ensure minimum error and limited judgment by the district ranger," explains Marita. It sent an unmistakable message to Forest Service employees: "Don't embarrass the outfit. Don't make any mistakes or we're going to shoot you."

But it meant employees took little initiative. "The forest ranger had no authority to do anything," says Eric Morse, a longtime forest supervisor. So they stopped caring about the quality of their work; they just did what they were told. They learned to live with a slow, unresponsive organization. Top managers rarely noticed these problems; they were too busy making all the decisions.

No one worried much about the organization's overall performance until the mid-1980s, when Congress slashed its budget. At that point Max Peterson, then Forest Service chief, started wondering if getting rid of all the rules would increase productivity. He had his associate chief, Dale Robertson, order up a field test.

On the Mark Twain

The Mark Twain National Forest in southern Missouri is a patchwork of 1.5 million acres of Ozark foothills and plateaus—overlogged forests and worn-out farmlands when the federal government began buying it up in the 1930s. It is one of the largest forests in the Eastern Region, which stretches from Missouri to Minnesota and Maine. Its headquarters is in Rolla, Missouri, a small, bustling town.

That's where Forest Supervisor Eric Morse was in 1985 when he got a call from the regional forester in Milwaukee. "He says, 'You're a pilot,' " Morse recalls. "No one knew what that was." A while later details arrived: from faraway Washington, Peterson and Robertson had developed a pilot program freeing the Mark Twain Forest, two other forests, and a research station from many Forest Service rules. Their plan allowed these organizations to shift money around without seeking reprogramming authority. It removed their personnel ceilings. It let them keep money they saved through efficiency and spend it on other priorities. And it encouraged them to request waivers to rules that got in their way.

The moment of truth came in a St. Louis conference room. Robertson had invited pilot leaders to St. Louis to ask a committee of Washington staffers for the waivers they needed. Morse wanted about 50 waivers. "It was hotter than hell," Morse remembers. "We sat down there and started going around the room offering proposals."

Right away there were problems. "They were saying no to every-thing," recalls Morse. "Absolutely we cannot do that." Robertson stopped the meeting and asked the pilot participants to leave. "For two hours we waited out in the hallway," says Morse. "We didn't know what to do." They don't know exactly what Robertson said. But when the meeting started again, says Morse, "Everything was approved—absolutely everything. And there was enthusiasm. We walked out of there with four different ways of approaching budget and spending."

Morse felt unleashed. "We were free to operate any way we wanted," he says. There were only two conditions: they had to operate in accordance with the law, and they had to meet the performance expectations specified in their forest-management plan.

Morse's instinct was to push the freedom down to his lowest-level employees, the nearly 300 workers toiling in forest districts. But, again, barriers emerged—in Rolla this time. Headquarters officials clung to their power. "Our staff officers had a terrible time," he remembers. "Their role as staff officers was control of the money, control of the districts through policy and review." It turned out, much to everyone's surprise, that the forest's own bureaucracy—not Washington—had created nearly three-quarters of the rules that tied their employees' hands. "We had more authority to do things than we knew we did," says Morse.

He stripped his headquarters staff of their power. "We took all that away from them, all of the money away," he says. "It took some pain on their part to begin trying on a new role." He threw out the rule books and—with his staff—drafted a slim handbook to replace them. It emphasized that employees were expected to solve problems and make decisions, not simply comply with rules.

Morse gave each district its own budget and the same flexibility he had received from Washington. He encouraged district rangers—the system's supervisors—to help their employees organize into self-managed teams. He let district teams select their own rangers. And he told the rangers to stop asking him for permission to do what they wanted to do.

All this took some getting used to. When ranger Art Wirtz trans-ferred into the forest, he couldn't believe the freedom he was given. "This is the first district I've ever been on where I've felt empowered to do my job, and there wasn't somebody watching over my shoulder," he says. Two months after starting, Wirtz tested Morse's new system. He called up Morse to find out what his boss thought about a small matter. The conversation took an unexpected turn:

Wirtz: *What do you think?*
Morse: *What the hell you callin' me for? You feel like you can make that decision?*
Wirtz: *Yeah.*
Morse: *You think you looked at everything about it?*
Wirtz: *Yeah.*
Morse: *Call me on something you really need.*

That was enough for Wirtz. "From that point on," he says, "I was empowered."

And it wasn't just Art Wirtz; most employees enjoyed their new freedom. When Wirtz arrived at his new job, the 15 employees he was brought in to supervise told him *they* had selected *him*. The team "was so proud that they got to select Art as their ranger," says Morse. "My God, whether he was good or bad, he was going to succeed!" Some team members teased Wirtz: Did he want to see the selection criteria they had used?

Wirtz's team set the district's priorities and its members' work assignments. Before long, Wirtz was working on project teams directed by his subordinates. "This unit has absolutely flattened the hierarchy," says Morse. "It said, 'We have a common job to do,' and then organized itself to do it."

Employees across the Mark Twain Forest used their new power to achieve results no orders could ever have produced.

Forest Ranger Donald "Pepper" Martin and his team decided to use $25,000 of their budget to upgrade the Pinewoods Recreational Facility near Poplar Bluff, for example. They had completed other projects under budget and stashed the savings in "the Big Bucket," Morse's nickname for the lump-sum budget. The team could do what it wanted with the money, even award bonuses to team members. All it had to do was vote.

"We took those dollars and plunked them into a project that we really wanted to do," says Martin. They purchased lumber, cement, and pier floats and built a floating wooden pier, concrete sidewalks, two 20-car parking lots, barrier-free restrooms, and a 125-person shelter at the 34-acre lake. None of the work had been approved by the old chain of command.

Budget savings and new projects sprouted like well-nourished seedlings. At Mark Twain and the three other pilot sites, productivity grew an average of 18 percent in the first two years. And in the Mark Twain Forest, the improvement kept going. The staff did more and more with less and less: by 1995 it was operating with 12 percent fewer employees than it had in 1986, while continuing to meet performance targets that were getting tougher.

This was only possible, insists Morse, because "the people who know how best to do the work"—the employees—had been given the authority to make decisions. A 1991 assessment by a private firm, SEC, Inc., backed him up. "The Forest is meeting most of its targets . . . with a less than planned level of funding," it said. "This is a tribute to the dedication and effort of [Twain] personnel. It may also reflect the benefits associated with changes the Forest has been able to implement as a result of . . . being designated a 'Pilot Forest.' "

Another Bureaucracy Catches the Bug

Thanks to its impressive early results, the Mark Twain experiment spread like a potent virus up the chain of command. At the regional office in Milwaukee, it found a willing host in Butch Marita.

Marita was a lifer who had never bought in to the system's bureaucracy. Within a few weeks of signing up in the late 1950s, he was in trouble. "I go to work for the Forest Service and, holy mackerel, I find this bureaucratic process," says Marita. "I spent three years as an angry young man. The ranger was mad at me because I would challenge these stupid systems." Negative entries grew in his personnel file. His wife and friends warned him that he'd lose his job if he kept it up. So he changed. "I modified my behavior, but never lost my passion to change things."

Three decades later, after running two forests and taking the obligatory tour in the Washington office, Marita got his big chance. In late 1986 he was appointed to run the Eastern Region, also known as Region 9. He took over an entrenched bureaucracy with 300 employees, which controlled 15 national forests. "It was a traditional regional office— very conservative," says Marita. "The staff was comfortable, not very energetic, prone to be safe, prone to not experiment." It was a "massive control mechanism" set up to tell the forests what to do.

When he arrived, Marita found that he was expected to read and sign every outbound letter. Each night he took home, read, and signed up to 20 letters. He quickly concluded that this had the perverse effect of letting staffers off the hook for what they wrote. "If you don't sign the letter, you don't really care too much about it," he explains. "If you sign it, by God, you're accountable, and that has a very distinct impact on you." So he changed the rule: with a few exceptions, the person who wrote the letter had to sign it.

At Robertson's prompting, Marita went on to change almost everything else about the regional office. He issued a 14-point vision statement that called for the regional office to serve, not control, employees in the forests. He took the unprecedented step of sharing his own power with the two like-minded deputies he brought in. Together, they formed a leadership troika. "All three of us had equal authority, power, and responsibility," says Larry Payne, one of the deputies. "It had never been done in the Forest Service before."

The shared leadership shocked the Washington office. "They asked, what is that?" says James Jordan, the other deputy. "There's only *one* regional forester. Where does the buck stop over there?" But Robertson, now the Forest Service chief, protected the Milwaukce troika.

Marita took his top staffers to visit every forest in the region, where he personally delivered his message of empowerment. At each stop they swapped bureaucratic horror stories with the workers. Then, Marita says, he urged the workers to take control of their forests.

We'd have a symbolic handing off [of control] to the forest supervisor. . . . We said, "It's now handed off to you, you in this forest. We're going to come back a year from now. We want to know what you've done."

Marita quickly dismantled the regional office's control mechanisms. He eliminated more than half of the office's top administrative positions and made everyone work in teams. As positions needed to be filled, he hired only people he thought were committed to his management approach. He ended the regional office's control over the forests' hiring, budgeting, and purchasing. He gave every forest a Big Bucket budget just like the Mark Twain had. He scrapped the old regional office inspection tours of forests; instead, he or a deputy would visit and ask the employees, "How can the regional office do a better job of helping you?"

When Marita asked employees for suggestions about how to improve the region, they responded with more than 12,000 ideas in four years—50 times the number generated in the previous four years. The region implemented about 70 percent of the new suggestions. Suggestions led the region to adopt flex-time work schedules, to let workers select supervisors, to give district rangers the authority to approve special-use permits (which cut average processing time from two weeks to one day), and to let employees make routine purchases directly from retailers rather than use the organization's procurement processes. When the national Forest Service adopted this purchasing innovation, it saved $500,000 a year.

Managers up and down the line resisted Marita's initiative, unwilling to give up power. In his first year, he says, he replaced seven district rangers—10 percent of his frontline managers—because "they were generally authoritarian and control oriented."

When employees flooded the region's personnel director with more than 250 suggestions for improvements, he reacted defensively. So Marita took him along on the next round of visits to the forests.

We got up there on stage, and when I got a personnel question, I'd let him answer that. Then he could see it wasn't fabricated. He could see no one was going to kill him and everybody wanted to make it better. It turned him around.

It proved much more difficult to turn around persistent opposition from the Washington office. Marita and Morse took Washington staffers on field visits in the region and gave them impressive performance data. But they still had trouble getting proposals through the national bureaucracy. Most of the time, Marita and his colleagues fought Washington to a draw. "With the results we've been producing, we have been fairly immune [to interference]," says Jordan.

But in 1993, the region lost the Big Bucket—its lump-sum budget mechanism. It died in a cross fire over fiscal control between Congress and the Forest Service chief. Key members of Congress had complained for some time that the entire Forest Service was too loose in tracking its budgets. Their concerns boiled into anger when they learned in 1991 that the service had diverted more than a third of the wilderness preservation budget they had substantially increased three years earlier—at the service's request. They pressured Robertson to tighten up his budget controls. As he gradually complied, the Big Bucket disappeared.

This hurt Marita's effort, but it didn't change the fact that Region 9 was racking up impressive gains in efficiency. Because Marita had eliminated many of the control functions in the regional office, he gradually—voluntarily—cut the office staff and budget. By 1995, the regional office had 33 percent fewer employees and 20 percent less budget than in 1989. It ate up only 7 percent of the region's budget—far below the 12.6 percent average of the other regional offices. If Marita's productivity levels were matched by the other eight regions, the Forest Service would save more than $54 million a year, according to regional staffer Karl Mettke. That's almost enough money to operate four Mark Twain Forests.

"Just think what would happen if each unit in the service would turn their people loose," muses Marita. He worries, however, that this will not happen. "The old structure in Washington is being assertive," he told us, just before retiring in February 1996. "The bureaucracy wants to go back to controlling everything."

THE CONTROL STRATEGY

If angels were to govern men, neither external nor internal controls on government would be necessary.
—James Madison

Beginning in the rolling hills of Missouri, Region 9's reinventors blazed a path into an unfamiliar land in which the rules of organizational gravity seemed to be reversed. Decisions flowed *up* from the bottom of the organization rather than *down* from the top. Day-to-day control shifted from administrators in Washington, Milwaukee, and Rolla to frontline workers in the forests, the people closest to the action. Supervisors became coaches; administrative staffers became servants. The top managers—the Maritas, Paynes, Jordans, and Morses— provided overall direction and guidance, but issued few orders or rules. And somehow, this bottom-up organization was far more efficient and effective than the traditional bureaucracy had been.

The Forest Service was a battleground for control. All of government is—perpetually. Politicians fight each other on a regular electoral schedule for the right to wield the power that flows from "the people." When they have it, they try mightily to impose their will on their institutional creations. Legislators appropriate detailed budgets and often set specific personnel levels. Executives select the top managers, who create within their institutions layers of managers, middle managers, and supervisors—the well-known "chain of command." Legislators and executives set up the central agencies that tell managers exactly what they can and cannot do and then check for compliance.

The control strategy shifts both the *locus* and *form* of control in public systems and organizations. It pushes control down through the ranks, and sometimes out to the community. And it replaces the traditional bureaucratic system of controls with a new system built upon shared vision and values and explicit performance expectations. Marita and Morse shattered the chain of command, tore up the rule books, stopped issuing orders, eliminated many administrative positions, and ended inspections for compliance. They developed new methods to guide employees. Workers knew the organization's mission, objectives, and performance targets; with these in mind, *they* could decide how to use public funds, how to respond to customer requests or emergencies, and how to organize to get their work done.

"Our people should use common sense and their best judgment, and then go ahead," wrote Dale Robertson in a 1989 statement of management philosophy. In Region 9, it worked.

Trust Is a Key

Roger Douglas remembers encountering the absurdity of bureaucratic controls when he took over as New Zealand's minister of finance in 1984. One of his first tasks was to authorize a $300 expense payment to an air force officer stationed in Fiji. New to office, Douglas had national currency and fiscal crises on his hands. He didn't care about trivial expenditures thousands of miles away in Fiji. "I had no way on earth of knowing whether they were justified or otherwise," he writes. "The system was preposterous." But the rules said the minister's signature was required.

Those rules—and others like them—exist because someone decided that government employees should not or could not be trusted to take responsibility for their own actions. Instead, someone had to make rules to tell workers what to do and how to do it, then set up compliance systems to make sure they didn't violate the rules. Thus government became a rule factory, with layers of managers and inspectors. The result has paralyzed and dehumanized public organizations.

"It was ridiculous," says David Couper of the system he inherited in the Madison, Wisconsin, Police Department. "We said we needed police officers who respect people's rights, are sensitive to people's feelings out there on the street. But we had an internal control mechanism which said [to officers] that you don't amount to anything, you're dumb, you're stupid, and if we catch you breaking the rules, we'll fire you or suspend you."

Government employees hate bureaucratic controls. Most would loudly echo the observation of Michael Masterson, a Madison police captain, that "the problem is, when you create rules and try to micromanage the 5 percent, you catch the other 95 percent of the good." If families acted like government, when one of the toddlers wet his pants, the whole family would have to wear diapers.

In 1986, David Packard's Commission on Defense Management published a seminal critique of bureaucratic controls in government. It studied the management problems at the U.S. Department of Defense, one of the world's largest public bureaucracies, and concluded that "the nation's defense programs lose far more to inefficient procedures than to fraud and dishonesty. The truly costly problems are those of overcomplicated organization and rigid procedure, not avarice or connivance."

An early generation of reinventors—among them David Couper, Butch Marita, and General Bill Creech at the Tactical Air Command—decided that bureaucracy's restraint on human initiative would have to end. News from the private sector reinforced this belief; in 1982, Peters and Waterman's *In Search of Excellence* argued that excellent companies used shared vision, values, and goals, not bureaucratic rules, to achieve control.

Instead of seeking compliance with rules, these reinventors hoped to achieve commitment to organizational goals. Control from on high can't do that.

Instead of forcing problems up to the top of the organization, these reinventors wanted people with the greatest stake in solving the problem and the best local knowledge to make the decision. As Creech put it in his 1994 book: "The less the authority vested in those closest to the problem, the more the problem lingers and spreads."

Instead of distrusting workers, these reinventors assumed that people wanted to do well. They believed that people wanted control over their work lives. When employees had more control, they would be happier and—it didn't take a rocket scientist to figure this out—they would perform better.

"I get more results from people who are having fun," says Butch Marita. "I want people to enjoy their work."

Trust, but Verify—And Hold Accountable for Results

Sin is the other side of freedom's coin.
—Charles Handy

"You're letting the lunatics run the asylum." That's the charge Madison Police Captain Mike Masterson has heard the most—even from his own father, a retired police chief. "I began talking about employee empowerment," he recalls. "He just couldn't understand it. His response was, 'It sounds like you're letting the monkeys run the zoo.' " The implication is that when bureaucratic controls are removed, chaos and corruption will fill the vacuum. Elected officials fear that newly empowered employees will make mistakes, ignore basic requirements for fairness and equity and, even worse, take advantage of the relaxed vigilance to steal the people's money.

Advocates of the control strategy offer several responses. One is a belief in self-control: most employees *can* be trusted to control themselves, they argue. Most people are not crooks, so why treat all of them as if they're trying to rip off the taxpayers? Most people are not slackers, so why treat them as if we suspect they're doing as little work as they can get away with? Most people value the principles of due process, fairness, and equity, so why treat them as if they would readily trample these beliefs?

A second response is that bureaucratic controls have not been especially effective at limiting undesirable behavior. "Discretion does not ensure corruption, nor do rules guarantee its absence," note professors Martin Levin and Mary Bryna Sanger in *Making Government Work*.

A third response is that not all forms of control should vanish. Government should still conduct financial audits and investigations to uncover inappropriate and criminal behavior. Indeed, computer technology makes it far easier to monitor spending and detect fraud than it was just a generation ago.

But the most important answer is accountability. As we've said, the control strategy changes the *locus* of control—where decision-making power lies. But it also changes the *form* of control, from prescriptive rules to shared vision and values and accountability for performance. In a decontrolled environment, people become accountable for the results they and their organizations produce, not for following rules. *The control strategy only works when an organization's people are clear about and committed to its mission and goals and accountable for what they achieve.*

Thus, the control strategy can be depicted as a five-step exercise:

1. Get clear on the mission and values of the organization, and get buy-in from employees.
2. Determine the results you want.
3. Trust people with the decision-making power and resources to produce those results.
4. Verify whether or not they are producing the results.
5. Hold them accountable for how well they do in producing the results.

In *In Search of Excellence*, Peters and Waterman called this approach a "loose-tight" system. It is loose on rules and regulations and tight on vision, values, and goals.

Rather than controlling what people do, reinventors try to influence what people want to accomplish. They help them understand and embrace the organization's goals and values. Until this happens, empowerment may lead half your teams to march off boldly in different directions, while the other half remain paralyzed, unsure of what to do with their new freedom.

They also have to get employees to *care* about achieving the organization's goals. When this happens, leaders obtain far greater command over results than they would by using bureaucratic controls. This is a crucial change, says Bill Creech.

Many people believe that decentralization means loss of control. That's simply not true. You improve control if you look at control as the control of events and not of people. Then, the more people you have controlling the events—the more people you have that care about controlling the events, the more people you have proactively working to create favorable events—the more control you have within the organization, by definition. . . .

I am convinced that I had far more control of TAC on the day I left than the day I took over, despite the massive decentralization. Actually we had the control. TAC ran far better because more people were exercising control, including people at the lowest levels. Decentralization, empowerment, and ownership created great improvement in our control of events, products, and outcomes. That, in the final analysis, is what organizational control is all about.

When employees don't know or care about their organization's objectives, you have trouble. As Creech puts it, "The fewer the people who care whether it goes right or wrong, the greater the certainty it will go wrong."

Once people care about reaching the organization's goals, you have to make sure that they are accountable. *The buck should stop with whoever has the control.* Power has its price; accountability must accompany authority and responsibility. Everyone should be clear about who has the authority, and there should be no way for them to shift the responsibility by pointing up, down, or sideways.

Finally, *those in control should face consequences for their performance.* Shifting control is not enough to guarantee better performance. As officials in Phoenix put it, when given autonomy, "Sometimes the good get better and the not so good stay about the same." Without incentives for performance, the "not so good" have no reason to improve. To be effective, marry the control strategy to the consequences strategy. A powerful metatool you can use to do this is the flexible performance framework, discussed in chapter 4.

Graham Scott, one of those who invented New Zealand's version of the flexible performance framework, makes this point well:

A system which gives a lot of freedoms to managers without strengthening their accountabilities is inferior to both the traditional bureaucratic model and the empowerment models exemplified by New Zealand and being used in a number of countries. No political system would tolerate the results for long. At each step in the evolution from centralism to decentralism there should be a balance between the freedoms granted and the accountabilities imposed. This can be thought of as a ladder in which each step balances freedom and accountability and maintains the functionality of a management system. The system will not work if people are held to account for things they cannot control, or if they are given freedom without clear expectations of performance.

General Creech's former organization provides a good example of how to combine the control and consequences strategies in a large, highly decentralized entity. The 150,000-person Air Combat Command is organized around more than 500 autonomous squadrons. Each one has measurable performance standards. ACC managers and employees can study the latest information on how the units performed. To General Michael Loh, the quality performance measures (QPMs) are the organization's bottom line:

They are the indicators of whether or not we can produce combat capability, which is our mission. I don't tell them how to do it. But if they're not producing those QPMs, if they're not delivering, then we're going to do something about it.

Three Approaches to Shifting Control

The first approach reinventors use applies the control strategy at two levels: governing systems and administrative systems. We call it *organizational empowerment* because it empowers organizations by eliminating many of the rules and other controls that central administrative agencies, legislatures, executives, and higher levels of government impose on them. One example is the "Big Bucket" budget that temporarily freed the Forest Service's Region 9 from the constraints of line-item budgeting.

The next logical step is to apply the control strategy at the organizational, process, and people levels. The second approach, *employee empowerment*, does this by reducing or eliminating hierarchical management controls within organizations and pushing authority down to frontline employees. Reinventors replace authoritarian controls with employee self-control and commitment to the organization's direction and goals.

These two approaches should, whenever possible, be used in combination. Freeing organizations from overbearing central controls produces far better results when top managers pass their new power down to their employees. Similarly, when an organization empowers its employees, it will reach a point where administrative system controls impede further progress. Employees may become frustrated and cynical, because their hands are still tied on the big issues—budget, personnel, and procurement.

The third approach is far more radical, and often far more difficult than the first two. But its impact is often far more profound, because it shifts the bureaucracy's power out into the community. Reinventors use *community empowerment* to hand control to neighborhoods, public-housing tenants, parents of schoolchildren, and other communities.

ORGANIZATIONAL EMPOWERMENT

A rule is a screw that can only be tightened.
—Ben G. Watts, Florida secretary of transportation

As the Mark Twain National Forest and Region 9 started experimenting with a "Big Bucket" budget, reinventors in Australia applied a similar idea to their *entire federal government.*

For years the Australian Department of Finance had zealously controlled the budgets of federal agencies. To stay on top of spending, it forced departments to use line-item budgets. These broke down administrative or operating expenses into 20 or more lines—one each for salaries, travel, equipment, supplies, computer services, rent, and so on. To increase a line or to transfer funds between lines, departments needed permission from the finance agency.

Studies dating back to 1976 had blamed the government's unsatisfactory performance in part on bureaucratic controls such as this. They found that managers in the 160,000-employee Australian Public Service focused primarily on complying with rules and following specified procedures, rather than on producing results and improving performance.

In 1988 reinventors ended the use of these financial fetters. They rolled the line items up into a single amount for each agency, known as a "running costs" budget. (As in the U.K., running costs are operating costs; they do not include funds that go to beneficiaries, such as benefit checks, vouchers, and grants, or funds passed on to other organizations or governments.) Then they told agency managers to use the funds as they saw fit to accomplish their organizations' objectives. To create further flexibility, they allowed departments to carry forward into the next fiscal year up to 3 percent of their running costs. They even let agencies borrow against future costs to invest in increasing productivity. At the same time, they told finance officials to become consultants to the agencies, to help them improve—rather than dictating—their finances.

Australian reinventors also shifted a great deal of control over purchasing and personnel practices to line agencies. Departments gained responsibility for recruiting, appointments, probation, retirement, discipline, transfers, and promotions, as well as greater discretion to determine their own procurement processes.

For the first time, line agencies were in charge of managing their own resources. "We've come an enormously long way," says Derek Volker, secretary of the Department of Employment, Education, and Training. "There's a lot more autonomy and independence and power for departments to be run their own way, really to determine their own futures in whether they succeed or fail." He could have added that for the first time agencies were also clearly responsible for producing results. With the taste of freedom came a dose of accountability, in the form of performance targets and in-depth, periodic evaluations.

This has become an international trend. The United Kingdom, New Zealand, and Canada have also "eliminated detailed central control of departments' operating expenditures and staffing levels and provided departments more authority to manage their resources within overall budget ceilings," the U.S. General Accounting Office reported in 1995. "[They] encouraged top department management to extend as much flexibility as possible to their line managers. [They] also began to simplify personnel rules and transfer control of human resource management functions, such as hiring, position classification, promotion, and pay, from central personnel agencies to departments and from departments to line managers." In the U.S., Vice President Gore's National Performance Review has recommended similar changes. The administration has responded with internal reforms, but so far Congress has passed only procurement reform.

There are many ways to free public organizations from the stifling controls of administrative and governing systems. In Australia and New Zealand, decentralizers took on the entire system at once, rapidly liberating all organizations. In Edmonton, Alberta, School Superintendent Michael Strembitsky did the same. He shifted administrative control to his 200 public schools and gave them roughly 85 percent of the district's money to spend as they decided. New Zealand and the United Kingdom did much the same for *all* their schools.

Other tools for organizational empowerment focus on liberating some, but not all, agencies. When they cannot transform entire administrative systems, reinventors pick their spots, much as the Forest Service did when it created its four pilots. In fact, these pilots were predecessors of the 200 "reinvention laboratories" the National Performance Review has unleashed. These agencies, designated by their departments, are encouraged to experiment with new methods and to apply for waivers when rules stand in their way. In Great Britain and the U.S., increasing numbers of grant-maintained and charter schools have been allowed to operate outside most system controls that public schools face. The U.K.'s Next Steps initiative, detailed in chapter 1, offers another example: it allowed central agencies to let go gradually, as each executive agency committed to a performance contract and then proved itself able to perform.

Convincing Elected Officials to Let Go

As we argued in chapter 3, most elected officials will only let go if they get something in return. The key is to negotiate a deal. Give elected officials more accountability for performance and many will in return give agencies more flexibility. This equation worked in Australia, the U.K., and New Zealand, because politicians were desperate for better results and reformers were committed to making public organizations accountable for results.

The same deal has been struck in many American governments. General Creech used it to pry loose the flexibility he needed. The Minnesota Department of Administration used it to win legislative support for internal enterprise management. Once it proved that it would shut down enterprise units that performed poorly, it won full legislative endorsement of its approach, which required enormous freedom for internal service units.

In Oregon, the Department of Transportation had a similar experi-

Tools for Organizational Empowerment

Decentralizing Administrative Controls shifts to line agencies the authority to manage their own personnel, finances, and purchasing, with a minimum of mandates from and oversight by central administrative agencies.

Organizational Deregulation repeals many of the other internal rules and regulations created by legislatures, central agencies, and departments to dictate the behavior of public organizations.

Site-Based Management shifts control over resources and day-to-day decisions from the central office of a system, such as a school district or a national employment service, to the many frontline organizations in the system, such as schools or local employment offices.

Opting Out or Chartering allows existing or new public organizations, such as charter schools, to operate outside the jurisdiction of most government control systems.

Reinvention Laboratories are public organizations that receive permission to temporarily break administrative rules and procedures and experiment with new ways of improving performance. Typically, they are granted waivers and protected from interference.

Waiver Policies are a mechanism that central agencies use to temporarily exempt organizations from rules on a case-by-case basis.

Beta Sites are public organizations that implement new ideas, such as employee empowerment, that are to be adopted throughout a government system. The organization's experiences generate lessons for effective implementation by organizations throughout the system. This is sometimes called "pioneering."

Rule Sunsets build a time limit into any rule or regulation controlling organizations' administrative behaviors, after which the rule dies unless it is reapproved.

Intergovernmental Deregulation involves waiver agreements among multiple levels of government, usually negotiated on a case-by-case basis.

ence. The key "is building an envelope of credibility," says former director Don Forbes. At one point, the department launched a reengineering project it believed would save $15 million. Forbes asked his committee chairman to hold him accountable for producing those savings in a budget note—a rider attached to the budget. "That is so different from what most administrators do," Forbes says.

> They don't give back $15 million. And they don't want budget notes. So this was a strong message to [legislators] that we wanted them to play the policy oversight role. It created a love-in, as one person put it.

To strike a deal you will need performance data. Without it, it is difficult to prove anything; with it, you can usually defend your need for flexibility. This was the second key in the Oregon Department of Transportation. "One time in 1993 we were testifying about the [performance] benchmarks, and one of the legislators said, 'That's fine, but I was never part of that, and I don't relate to these benchmarks. If I went out to a maintenance shop, could they show me their measures?' " recalls Craig Holt, who ran the Office of Productivity Services.

> We went that night and pulled up the measures and performance information for maintenance for their districts. We brought it in the next day. One senator said, "I don't understand this." And the chair explained it to him, using the documents. For 30 minutes, they talked among themselves.
>
> Another representative said, "Now, if I were to go to maintenance people in my district, could they tell me their measures?" I said yes. And before I got back to my office he called them, and they could explain what their measures were and how they used them, well enough to satisfy him.
>
> After that, a representative called a press conference and said, "DOT has set the standard of standards for managing in government."

Holt sums it up this way: "They feel very good about us managing, so they've stepped out of management issues to focus on policy."

To further bolster the case for organizational autonomy, you can take elected officials to visit places such as Oregon's DOT and the Air

Combat Command, to see for themselves how flexibility leads to higher performance.

Finally, if you cannot implement organizational empowerment system-wide, ask the politicians to let go in only a few places, where they trust the managers, as an experiment. In Florida, Governor Lawton Chiles persuaded legislators to let the Revenue and Labor Departments launch pilots that upended administrative controls, in part because lawmakers had faith in the two departments' directors. When those efforts succeeded, lawmakers gave greater autonomy to two additional agencies, including the state's largest.

Convincing Headquarters to Let Go

The Forest Service's Butch Marita fought battle after battle for control with the headquarters staff in Washington—until his retirement in February 1996. They just wouldn't give up the bureaucratic power they had built, he says. "They've worked a career to get where they are. They are the experts, the specialists that have the knowledge. Most of them wrote the regulations."

When General Bill Creech began to empower employees in the Tactical Air Command, he knew he'd have to fight with the Department of Defense's central office staffers—"the zealous champions of Centralism in Washington, who I was sure would swoop down on us with a vengeance when they got wind of what we were doing." He was right:

> What we were doing was so out of step with the centralization catechism and the philosophy, that all the centralizers in Washington were constantly sniping. Every time I tried to change a regulation, it had to go up there for approval. They had to throw sand in my face. I got a lot of sniping from the Congress.

As with legislators, the only reliable way to convince headquarters to give up power is to demonstrate results. Creech developed data on TAC's performance, proving that the centralized system he inherited was a failure: productivity was getting worse every year. His data also demonstrated that where he had decentralized, performance was improving dramatically. "They'd never seen numbers like that before," says Creech. Then he got key Defense Department managers to visit

TAC bases and see the positive benefits of his employee-empowerment approach up close. When they saw the results, many converted.

Perhaps the best example we know of conversion-through-experience occurred at the United Kingdom's Treasury Department, which controlled budgets and personnel. As we reported in chapter 1, the Next Steps initiative called for Treasury to negotiate framework agreements that gave executive agencies more management control in exchange for commitment to specific performance goals. At first, Treasury was reluctant to give the agencies much freedom. But as agency after agency delivered on its agreement without overspending its budgets, Treasury leaders became convinced. Gradually they abandoned many of their controls.

It also helps if you can offer the central headquarters or administrative agencies—like the politicians—something they need in return for flexibility. In Australia, for instance, top managers in the Finance Department worried that if they loosened their grip spending would explode. So when they allowed agencies to manage their own costs, they also imposed an "efficiency dividend," which automatically cut running-cost budgets by 1.25 percent every year. This forced the agencies to control their costs.

EMPLOYEE EMPOWERMENT

Empowerment is in the mind. You can't be afraid to trust. That's what it comes to—trusting the people below you to do the job. You kind of orchestrate, and then you step back and let them do their jobs.

—Lynn Corbitt, district ranger
Mark Twain National Forest

When organizations gain autonomy from the center, it goes to their heads—literally, to the managers at the top of the agency hierarchy. All too often, that's where it stays. "The fact that power was given to you doesn't seem to make it any more likely that you'll give it up," says Doug Ross, a former director of commerce in Michigan and assistant secretary in the U.S. Department of Labor. "Every level of government bureaucracy seems to be its own separate battle."

After Australia's federal government shifted control from central agencies to departments, reinventors found that many of the departments' top managers used their new power to *tighten* their grip over employees. Mike Codd, secretary to the Department of the Prime Minister and Cabinet from 1986 to 1992, says his "greatest disappointment has been the unevenness with which these reforms have been carried through within departments, too many of which have retained excessive central control."

Most reinventors discover that a majority of the constraints they rail against originated in their own organizations. Few administrators hold a darker view of the center's pathologies than Marita. But even he found—much to his surprise—that many of the controls that frustrated him and his allies had been developed by his own regional office, before he took over, or by managers at the forests.

Marita and his fellow reinventors wanted their employees to think for themselves. So they eliminated many management jobs designed to command workers and check for their compliance. They expected employees to figure out how to achieve the organization's goals, not just to follow the rules. So they reduced the importance of detailed job descriptions and eliminated many regulations. Instead, they put workers into teams, where they could pool their skills to get the job done.

When Bill Creech took a similar step in the Tactical Air Command, he had to first break down the rigid functional silos that the organization's bureaucratic designers had created. Because Creech, Marita, and Morse expected workers to take control of their own work, they also developed new roles for managers to play, as coaches, facilitators, strategists—as practically anything but controllers.

Most organizations that embrace employee empowerment take these types of steps. Some also use total quality management and business process reengineering, metatools we discuss in chapter 9, to let employees redesign their work processes.

Pass the Power Down, Please

There are several ways to encourage managers to deregulate their own agencies and pass the power they receive on to frontline employees:

Create consequences for passing power down. First, make managers accountable for achieving ambitious performance improvements. Then, to encourage them to empower their employees, make the degree to which they let go of control a factor in assessing their performance. Make it a measurable goal of their performance contracts and appraisals. Ask the people they control how well they're doing at it.

Tools for Employee Empowerment

Management Delayering eliminates layers of middle managers—supervisors, inspectors, and assistants—between frontline workers and top management. In the process, it increases the span of control of managers. This makes it much more difficult for managers to act as order givers and reduces costs without cutting service levels.

Organizational Decentralization shifts control from top-level managers to frontline units in the organization. It is site-based management *within* an organization. An excellent example of the use of this tool is the Air Combat Command, an organization of more than 500 autonomous squadrons.

Breaking Up Functional Silos eliminates bureaucratic units and work processes based on functional specialization, moving those functions into frontline work teams that are accountable for producing results for their customers.

Work Teams are groups of employees who collaborate with one another to achieve common performance goals.

Self-Managed Work Teams are work teams that handle their own supervision.

Labor-Management Partnerships are agreements between managers and unions to collaborate on improving organizational performance and working conditions. Typically, they agree to work in partnership to solve problems.

Employee Suggestion Programs give employees a formal mechanism for sharing with managers their ideas about how to improve performance. Often, employees receive a portion of financial savings realized by their suggestions.

Establish a driving force. Create a unit outside the central agencies, but close to the top executive (president, minister, governor, mayor, city or county manager), whose mission is to keep pushing the agency heads to let go. In the U.K., the Next Steps Team played this role. In the U.S., the National Performance Review does the same.

Teach managers the benefits of letting go. Take them to see organizations that practice employee empowerment, so they can talk with practitioners. Help them test its approaches and tools without having to commit entirely to them. Use management development courses to consciously teach them how to let go. Create experiences that challenge them to break their habits of control—as Butch Marita did by exposing his personnel director to employees who had ideas about how to change the personnel system. When some of them buy in and try letting go, reward them and hold their efforts up as models for the entire organization. And if you are a top manager, teach by example. Show your subordinates how to let go of power by visibly doing it yourself.

If they can't let go, let **them** *go.* Pressure, opportunities, and teaching don't always work. Sometimes you have to force the issue—as when Butch Marita eliminated more than half of his region's top administrative positions and moved 10 percent of his field supervisors out of their jobs.

Lessons Learned About Empowering Employees

Combine employee empowerment with other strategies, particularly consequences and culture. To make employee empowerment work you must not only dismantle bureaucratic, hierarchical controls but create alternative ways of guiding and supporting employees. You must embrace all five steps described on page 215, establishing clear goals and marrying the control and consequences strategies. As much as possible, you must do this in ways that involve the employees.

All this is often difficult at the outset, because you run up against the formidable power of bureaucratic culture: the habits, hearts, and minds of public employees have been shaped by their years of experience under bureaucratic controls. Hence, many workers and managers will be skeptical about the prospect of change, even if they want it. And some will be very anxious about taking more responsibility, because it comes with potential consequences for performance. Thus, leaders using employee empowerment also must focus on changing their organization's culture, a strategy we address in chapter 8.

Design employee empowerment to foster effectiveness, not democracy. Employee empowerment does not mean every decision in the organization must be made democratically or through consensus. There will still be levels of responsibility, although fewer of them. The military will still have generals and privates, with officers—middle managers, really—in between. Orders will still come down from the top ranks, but there will be fewer of them. A fire chief will still require firefighters to follow safety procedures, whether they want to or not.

"There's still 'yes, sir—no, sir.' You cannot get away from some of that," explains ACC General Michael Loh.

After all, our mission is to send people in harm's way, which is different from any other private company or enterprise. . . . So there has to be a certain obedience level. When we get in the middle of combat we don't say, "Oh, let's stop and think about this and see if there's a better way." You think about the better way before you get into those circumstances.

Determining how much hierarchy an organization needs is an art, not a science. It depends largely on how confident leaders are about the employees' commitment to organizational goals and their capacity to take on greater responsibilities. Many leaders start with a built-in bias against empowering employees; they are trapped in bureaucratic assumptions. But even leaders committed to empowerment don't propose to do away with all management roles. Nor do public employee unions.

Stop lower-level managers from hoarding power. Just because you want power to flow to frontline workers doesn't mean it will get there. You must push it through middle management's ranks. Leaders must do more than let go and get out of their people's way, advises Bill Creech. They must "help *find the way, show the way, and pave the way.*" You will have to lean on, reward, and educate managers to help them let go, and move those who won't out of the way.

Embed empowerment in your organization's structure. Even when employee empowerment has taken hold in an organization, reinventors should worry about recidivism. "It took me 20 years to change this place, it'll take a long time to go back," observes former Madison police chief David Couper. "But we have this incredible relationship with the authoritarian structure. We're quick to fall back into that. It's simpler, it's less work, it's the lazy person's way to lead."

The best solution to this problem is to institutionalize administrative decentralization and work teams—to permanently change your bureaucratic structures. If you strip the central controllers of their authority and then greatly thin their ranks, it will be difficult for anyone to reimpose centralization. And if you reorganize work around permanent teams of collaborative, cross-function employees, it will be hard for managers to micromanage.

COMMUNITY EMPOWERMENT

In the typical community, government experts do the urban planning, and citizens learn to live with the plans. The experts work hard to minimize opposition. The public gets a shot at them in hearings, but usually the planners are only looking for ratification of decisions they want to make. For the citizen wading into a comprehensive urban development plan, the challenge is daunting. So residents normally get involved only when they are outraged. If opposition grows large and loud enough, it can force changes in the plan. But even then, the professional planners remain in charge; they will control the next round of planning.

In the early 1990s, Hampton, Virginia, a city of 130,000, stopped being typical.

Joan Kennedy remembers when the traditional planning process stopped making sense. She was the city's planning director. Her agency had just finished drafting the city's comprehensive plan, she recalls.

We had gone through a kind of normal, traditional citizen participation thing where you put an ad in the newspaper and tell everybody to come to a meeting. Then you tell them what you're thinking about doing. So we claimed that this plan was going to be the community's vision of where we were going next.

The next step was a public hearing before the planning commission.

I had just done my spiel about how the comprehensive plan is the community's vision. But when I looked around, there was just this sea of angry faces out there. I thought, this must come a lot closer to being these people's nightmare than their vision.

Kennedy was right. Many citizens were angry over a proposal to construct a road through residential neighborhoods in order to ease traffic congestion. Kennedy agreed to scrap the proposal and to work with citizens to develop an alternative recommendation. That opened the door to community empowerment—putting the bureaucracy's power into the hands of citizens. First, city planners agreed that an alternative proposal had to meet with the neighborhoods' approval. Then they agreed to redraft the entire comprehensive plan in partnership with the neighborhood groups. "We totally redid the comprehensive plan from *A* to *Z*," says Michael Monteith, the assistant city manager who facilitated the process.

The planners were amazed; the results were more creative than anything they had done previously. When the community has an equal voice with you, you have to really debate the planning issues, to figure out how to meet everybody's requirements. That's when you get really creative.

But it wasn't long before the neighborhoods were complaining that the city still had too much control. Its planners set the agenda for planning; *they* identified the problems and convened the stakeholders. The neighborhoods wanted this power too. "They're the people who live with the problem, not the city staff," says Kennedy.

Take the example of a residential neighborhood with a road that carries 3,000 cars a day. Our traffic engineer says there's no problem: the road is built to handle that much traffic. But to the neighborhood, 3,000 cars a day sounds horrendous.

So Hampton let the neighborhoods define their problems and their preferred solutions. That caused a different problem: power had shifted too far into the neighborhoods' hands. "They defined the problems, mailed us a list of solutions, and said to implement them," explains Kennedy. The city became the "bad guy," telling neighborhoods their solutions cost too much or couldn't be used because they had negative effects on other parts of the city.

So the city changed the process again. "Now," says Kennedy, "we say to the neighborhoods, 'We'll accept the problem as you defined it. Then, let's go through the planning process as partners.' "

The Many Uses of Community Empowerment

Community empowerment involves handing to communities substantial control over the decisions, resources, and tasks of public organizations. In Hampton, Dayton, and other cities, neighborhood groups—

not elected officials—decide how to use public funds appropriated for neighborhood development. In Denver, Savannah, Roanoke, and other cities, thousands of citizens have participated in large-scale collaborative planning—steering—for their communities. In Kansas, state government gave a consortium of corporate, charitable, union, and neighborhood leaders the power to allocate more than $250 million in social services funds targeted for Kansas City families. In hundreds of cities that have adopted community policing, residents share responsibilities with police departments; they help implement crime-prevention strategies. In hundreds of public housing developments, residents have formal corporations to manage the property.

In Chicago, reformers shifted control over nearly 600 public schools to local school councils made up of parents and community members elected by voters in neighborhoods. The councils allocate portions of their schools' budgets, set school-improvement goals, and recruit, select, and negotiate performance contracts with their principals. In New Zealand and the United Kingdom, every school has a community governing board that performs similar functions. Many cities, business districts, and, increasingly, residential neighborhoods, are forming self-taxing improvement districts to enhance their physical, economic, and social conditions. These community governance mechanisms decide what to do with the special revenues they collect and often manage the work and services that are needed.

Community empowerment is used typically to shift public control to place-based communities—neighborhoods in a city, or residents in public housing projects, for example. But a community may also be defined as stakeholders who, whatever their geographic links, share an interest. In Florida, a nonprofit partnership led by the business community, called Enterprise Florida, has taken over functions of the state's Department of Commerce. In Montreal, the local Chamber of Commerce has taken responsibility for operating the government's Business Assistance Office.

Chapter 2 of *Reinventing Government* explained why this is happening: because people are more energetic, more committed, and more responsible when they control their own environments than when some authority outside the community does. It described the advantages of community empowerment this way:

■ *Communities have more commitment to their members than service-delivery systems have to their clients.*

- *Communities understand their problems better than service professionals.*

- *Professionals and bureaucracies deliver services; communities solve problems.*

- *Institutions and professionals offer "service"; communities offer "care."*

- *Communities are more flexible and creative than large service bureaucracies.*

- *Communities are cheaper than service professionals.*

- *Communities enforce standards of behavior more effectively than bureaucracies or service professionals.*

- *Communities focus on capacities; service systems focus on deficiencies.*

Making Community Empowerment Work

Community empowerment often meets with more resistance than the other approaches for shifting control, because it so radically undermines the power of elected officials and institutional managers. Indeed, many politicians and public executives can't imagine community empowerment—it is outside of their paradigms. Of those who can, many argue that communities lack the knowledge, professional expertise, or commitment to solve their own problems. Often, this is nothing more than a self-serving rationalization, says Doug Ross, a former state senator and top manager of state and federal agencies.

Most of us are not comfortable consciously or unconsciously with saying, "I love the control, I like to lord it over other people and I'm not going to give it up without a fight." Instead, we frame it more paternalistically, as the need to protect those who are less able to fend for themselves. The claim is a modern, more politically correct version of the white man's burden.

Typically, it takes a large amount of sustained public anger—like the "sea of angry faces" that Joan Kennedy saw—to get the political sector to even consider community control. It is a rare public official who, without prodding, initiates the shift.

Tools for Community Empowerment

Community Governance Bodies shift control over the direction of public organizations from elected officials and civil servants to members of a community. Usually, they are allowed to steer within parameters set by government. For instance, a school district may mandate a core curriculum for all schools, but allow school governance bodies to decide which additional academic topics and extracurricular activities it will offer, who should be principal, and how to spend its budget. This is a metatool that combines the control and core strategies.

Collaborative Planning allows stakeholders, such as neighborhood residents or advocacy groups, to join government officials in consensus-based planning for their community.

Community Investment Funds are public funds controlled by community-based entities, such as neighborhood groups. Typically, they are allowed to use the resources to improve a community's physical infrastructure. Recently, the U.S. has seen a boom in community investment funds that finance business development.

Community Managed Organizations are organizations that perform public services but are managed and operated by community groups, not government agencies. Sometimes, these organizations also become the owners of public assets, such as housing stock.

Community-Government Partnerships are joint ventures between communities and public agencies that share common goals and operations.

Community-based Regulation and Compliance shifts control over regulatory and compliance functions to communities, such as businesses or neighborhood associations.

Even when community empowerment gains support and momentum, it is risky. Sometimes community-based initiatives fail. Sometimes they become paralyzed by factionalism and conflict. Sometimes corruption sets in. A few efforts are even hijacked by authoritarian leaders, who re-create a bureaucracy *they* can control. (Of course, all these ills befall government organizations as well.)

These difficulties can be addressed by applying the same kinds of lessons we have discussed regarding the other control approaches:

Give communities a clear charter. Just as flexible performance frameworks work best when they use written contractual agreements, so does community empowerment. The charter should spell out which decisions and tasks are shifting into the community's control and which are not, and it should specify the performance expected of the community. Ambiguity will lead inevitably to confusion and ineffectiveness, and possibly to conflict between the community and government officials. It will also stymie accountability. Sometimes getting clear about a community's charter involves an evolutionary, negotiated process, as we saw with Hampton's planning function.

Use the consequences strategy to establish genuine accountability measures. Unless a community is accountable for its performance, politicians will be very reluctant to give it control over public decisions and resources. Use the customer and consequences strategies to make communities directly accountable to their customers and to elected officials. In Britain and New Zealand, for example, governing bodies run public schools, but parents have their choice of schools, and public dollars follow the children. Thus the governing bodies have powerful incentives to respond to their customers' needs and concerns.

Invest in the competence of communities to manage their own affairs. If you empower communities but don't also help build their capacity, you are condemning some of them to failure. Many poor communities have depended on government for so long that they don't have the capacities needed to exercise control. They need strong leadership, as well as organizing and technical skills. These don't materialize the instant communities are empowered; they must be developed.

That's why Hampton created a Neighborhood College in 1995, to offer neighborhood residents free courses in "City Hall: Behind the Scenes," "Neighborhood Organization," "Public Speaking," and other topics. Governments in Dayton, Chicago, the United Kingdom, and other places have made similar investments—training, resources, and technical assistance—to help community residents become more effective in using their new powers.

Change the culture of government agencies so they can be better partners with communities. As power shifts to communities, public managers and employees must adjust their roles, attitudes, and expectations. This is rarely easy, because it involves changing government's organizational culture.

In Hampton, for example, city planners were not used to having to listen to and share power with neighborhood residents. They didn't know how. Terry O'Neill, who succeeded Joan Kennedy as the city planning director, had to redefine their jobs. He assigned them as liaisons to neighborhoods, and he asked them to attend meetings and survey neighborhood groups regularly. They worked with residents, schools, and children to design six neighborhood parks that met the specific needs of each neighborhood. All of this, says O'Neill, required big changes in his organization's culture—the way employees thought and felt about their work.

Use organizational empowerment to free communities from the bureaucratic requirements of government's central administrative agencies. Just as public organizations and employees need the freedom to manage their resources, so do community-based organizations. When you give them control, don't handcuff them with bureaucratic budget, personnel, and procurement systems. You still need safeguards such as audits and investigations. But if you wrap communities up in bureaucratic controls—a common mistake—you will greatly diminish the advantages of community empowerment.

QUESTIONS PEOPLE ASK ABOUT
THE CONTROL STRATEGY

Q: If you give people more control, won't they make mistakes?

Yes, they will. It's inevitable. But if you don't decentralize control, the organization will still make mistakes. More of them may be mistakes of omission than commission, but the results will be the same— or, more likely, much worse.

Rather than asking if people will blunder, a better question is: What will you do when they do? "A mistake is not a crime, and a crime is not a mistake," says Bill Creech. Foul-ups are opportunities for lessons. If you punish people who make mistakes, they will try to hide them from you.

Never admitting you goofed is standard operating procedure in bureaucratic organizations. Butch Marita remembers the day a deputy from the Washington office came to visit him.

He challenged me when I referred to the mistakes [we were mak-
ing]. "They weren't mistakes, Butch. Don't call them mistakes,
don't admit they're mistakes." And I said, "Well, they were mis-
takes, by God, and if you don't agree with it, then take 'mistake'
out of the English language."

Once you acknowledge a mistake, you can figure out what went
wrong—and then decide how to make sure it won't happen again.

Q: Can compliance agencies use the control strategy?

Yes, but not in every situation, and not always as fully as service
organizations.

Compliance organizations can empower employees. They can also
empower other agencies. For example, the Nuclear Regulatory Agency
allows about half of the states to regulate nonreactor nuclear materials.

Compliance agencies can even hand some degree of control to the
community. One way is by negotiating regulations with stakeholder
groups before submitting them for legal approval. Another is by letting
the stakeholders do the inspections. When the federal Occupational
Safety and Health Administration in Maine gave control over workplace inspections to the nearly 200 businesses in the state with the
highest injury rates—in partnership with their employees—the
improvements were astonishing. According to the 1995 National Performance Review report:

Industry's response was immediate and positive. . . . Employer/
worker safety teams in the participating firms are identifying—
and fixing—14 times more hazards than OSHA's inspectors ever
could have found, including hazards for which the agency didn't
even have regulations. After all, who knows where the problems
are better than the workers themselves?

Compliance organizations can also partner with the community to
prevent problems. An example of this is community policing, which
gives neighborhoods some say over how law enforcement resources are
used.

Still, there are limits to decontrol in many compliance organizations.
Some controls exist to protect citizens' rights. When citizens must be
treated identically, for instance, it makes sense to remove discretion
from employees. A good example is the reading of Miranda rights to a

suspected criminal. Police officers have no discretion about when and how this must occur (unless their well-being is endangered).

Tax agencies face a similar issue: they must respect everyone's rights and treat everyone fairly. But if they want high compliance rates, they must also allow employees to deal with habitual compliers and habitual noncompliers very differently. In some areas standardization is imperative; in others it is to be avoided. "Getting that right—what they can change and what they can't change—is the trick," says Clive Corlett, director general of Inland Revenue, the U.K.'s tax agency.

Getting the delegation right is difficult. You've got to understand what it is you're empowering them to do, and make them accountable. Otherwise you've got chaos. There's a lot of discussion that has got to go on between different levels of management. People have to understand what the constraints are within which they can do different things.

In general, compliance organizations must spend the time necessary to sort out where employee discretion is appropriate and where it is not.

Q: Can policy and regulatory organizations use the control strategy?

Certainly. Organizational empowerment is just as important in policy and regulatory organizations: there is no more reason to tie them up in rules and red tape than to tie up service and compliance organizations.

Even community empowerment can be used with policy and regulatory activities, though to a more limited degree. Communities can be brought into the policy-making process, as advisors and as decision makers. The progress boards that have sprung up throughout Oregon, which consult closely with their communities and advise elected officials, are made up primarily of community members. School boards are policy-making bodies directly elected by their communities.

Some regulatory functions can also be delegated to communities. Local neighborhood associations often set rules for their members, for example. Housing cooperatives and resident councils in public housing developments do the same. Governments often let professions regulate their own members, to a degree. In all cases the society's laws, passed by elected officials, apply. But the community in question sets rules that go beyond these laws. This makes perfect sense, but there are limits to how far it should go—as years of inadequate self-regulation by the legal, medical, and journalistic professions attest. Common sense would suggest that government should impose those rules the nation, state, or community feels it cannot live without, but leave more specific matters to the narrower community. The trick is to get the balance right.

CAN A DEVELOPING NATION AFFORD TO DECENTRALIZE CONTROL?

This book is based on public sector experience in five English-speaking democracies with information age economies. Although we have had consulting experience in democracies that are still industrializing, such as Brazil and Argentina, we have not done research in those countries.

The social, political, and economic realities faced by developing nations are very different from those found in the countries we have analyzed. They are in many ways similar to the conditions faced by reformers in the U.S. 100 years ago. Corruption and influence peddling are often widespread. Patronage is often the norm: many get jobs because of their connections, not their abilities. The public sector is often used as the employer of last resort for the unemployed. And in some countries, the courts and police departments are not fully independent of political control, so legal prosecution of corruption is difficult.

In such countries, leaders must pick and choose their reinvention strategies with care. Certainly there are elements of bureaucracy they can discard with impunity. And there are many elements of entrepreneurial government—including competition, privatization, and customer choice—they can introduce without qualms. After all, these approaches worked well in the U.S., when used, even in the heart of the bureaucratic era. But other elements of bureaucratic government were invented precisely to deal with problems like corruption, patronage, and political manipulation of public employees. Many of the rigidities of our central administrative systems, from civil service to procurement to budget and finance, evolved to solve these problems.

Developing democracies can clearly use the core, consequences, and customer strategies—indeed, many have already embraced asset privatization, competitive contracting, and customer choice. They clearly need the culture strategy. The one strategy that becomes tricky is the control strategy.

As information age democracies have loosened their bureaucratic systems of control, they have shifted to other forms of control—performance measurement and rewards, competition based on results, information systems that track financial transactions, careful auditing, and rigorous prosecution of illegal activity. Many developing democracies can do this as well, leapfrogging decades of the bureaucratic era. If they cannot, however, they should probably loosen the old controls with great care.

This is one of those frontier areas that will be clarified only through experience. Fortunately, developing nations are beginning to experiment. Singapore has introduced many elements of entrepreneurial government, including performance budgeting, activity based costing, and empowerment of organizations through a step-by-step process similar to the U.K.'s Next Steps reform. Malaysia has initiated a management system in which public managers are held accountable for producing results and rewarded for excellent performance. Like the U.K. and New Zealand, it is drafting formal agreements in which departments specify the outputs they will produce—although it is not giving organizations and their managers as much flexibility as New Zealand and the U.K. have. Malaysia is also developing an accounting system to track the cost of each output, and it has adapted the Citizen's Charter idea from the U.K.

In Latin America, Brazil is struggling to reinvent on a broad scale, and Argentina, which launched a very successful asset-privatization initiative in the early 1990s, is trying to figure out how to reform the organizations it does not privatize. Costa Rica is developing performance agreements with its department heads.

Should governments such as these decentralize authority if corruption and patronage are still the norms in their countries?

In our view, the answer depends at least in part on what other reinvention strategies these governments are willing to use. The best defenses against many types of corruption are full information, consequences for performance, and prosecution of illegal activity. If everyone in a system faces consequences when performance suffers, outright stealing will trigger those consequences, because it will drive costs up. This is one advantage of highly competitive markets—a fact that makes asset-privatization, corporatization, and the rest of the enterprise management tools very effective and relatively safe in developing countries.

Managed competition and performance management, the other consequences approaches, can only be effective if information systems reveal full and accurate information about costs and quality. Yet part of the problem in countries suffering from corruption is the almost complete absence of management information systems. Managers cannot detect fraud when it occurs.

The best answer we can give is the following: as reformers loosen the old systems of control, they should construct new systems in their place—management information systems, systems that impose consequences, auditing systems, and systems that will prosecute corruption. When they cannot use market competition to create consequences, perhaps their best option is to grant flexibilities organization by organization, as the British Next Steps process did. Using this approach, they would grant an agency freedom from overly centralized controls only after the agency had proved its capacity to detect and control corruption, patronage, and political manipulation of employees. The freedoms could even be granted in stages, as agencies gradually strengthened and demonstrated the effectiveness of their new control systems.

For those who fear to take these steps, we will close with one last question. Clearly centralized controls have not eliminated corruption in many countries. Yet they have hurt the performance of public institutions. Isn't it time to try another path?

— 8 —

THE CULTURE STRATEGY: CREATING AN ENTREPRENEURIAL CULTURE

"THE MOST LIVABLE CITY IN VIRGINIA"

In 1996, many city employees in Hampton, Virginia, didn't do their jobs.

Mary Bunting, an assistant city manager, worked instead in the ditches with a city sewer crew. The heavy-construction team in the Public Works Department put in weeks developing a new city park for another agency that didn't have enough money to get the job done.

Donald Gurley, the chief housing inspector, organized an exhibition about city services for the city's Neighborhood College, a training program for residents.

Kevin Gallagher, who runs the city's recycling programs, spent long nights helping street crews clear away snow and ice. "When we have a snow- or ice storm, everyone comes in so we can get the job done," explains Ed Panzer, the public works director.

Most of the city's approximately 1,300 employees participated in one or more of its 115 task forces, advisory groups, self-directed teams, committees, and councils—work that was not covered in their job descriptions.

Why did Hampton's employees behave in these ways? Bunting was on a job rotation. City Manager Bob O'Neill had decided that his assistants needed to know more about how agencies really worked. So beginning in January, Bunting spent time in the field with public works crews, to prepare her to run the agency temporarily when Panzer retired. The field work changed her assumptions about employees, Bunting says. They were much more skilled and flexible than she had expected. "I assumed that many of our people were more concerned about their job description, that when something came up they'd say, 'That's not our responsibility.' " But over and over she was proven wrong.

The heavy-construction team took on the park development project after the parks director asked Ed Panzer for help. Panzer agreed because he knew the park was a community priority. It wasn't the first time his team had gone beyond the call of duty. Several years earlier the city had wanted to convert a landfill into a golf course, but private bids for the contract were far above what it had budgeted. Panzer told O'Neill his crew could do the job within budget—and they did.

Donald Gurley ran the exhibit for the Neighborhood College because, as he puts it, "I opened my big mouth." Two years earlier he had attended a Neighborhood College session in which department heads made speeches to attendees. "It didn't keep their attention," Gurley says. "So I spoke up at a meeting. I suggested we do something like a career day, letting people rotate around to workstations for each department. The idea caught on."

Then Gurley volunteered to make it happen. He also served as chairman of the department's awards team and as a member of three interagency reengineering teams.

Kevin Gallagher turned up during snowstorms to help clear the streets for the simple reason that it needed to be done. "My job description is recycling manager, but my duty is customer service for the citizens of Hampton," he says.

> My motto is, "Whatever it takes." People say, "You're the recycling manager." And I say, "Not when I'm the follow truck behind the snow detail." I like the challenge. It makes life more interesting.

Hundreds of employees joined the city's numerous teams and groups because they were given the chance. "If you want to get involved in something, there's something out there for you," says Gurley. "There are newsletters letting everybody know what's going on. You put your name on the list and get involved." In fact, participation in groups has grown steadily since 1990.

Gallagher enjoys working on teams because it connects him to other employees. "It lets me know who's who in the organization," he says. "I invite people into my world, and I dabble in theirs."

This is true for many employees, says Tharon Greene, the director of human resources.

Many of us get things done through informal networking and connecting with people. At the emotional level this means we're more than just organization charts and boxes. A lot of us feel that by working this way you have a voice in where the organization is going. It's a feeling like no other.

In short, an extraordinary number of Hampton employees collaborated avidly with one another and routinely went the extra mile for citizens because they wanted to. They thought it was what they should do. It made them feel good. Ed Panzer recalls a spring day when he met with members of the heavy-construction team. They were just finishing a project, so he started talking about which project they might tackle next. "Their reaction was 'We hope it's a very big one.' That's the mind-set we have in this organization."

Hampton employees weren't always so flexible. City government in Hampton used to be a standard-issue bureaucracy with a standard-issue culture.

The city manager was the boss. Three assistant city managers told the 35 or so department heads what to do. The department heads protected their turf, hoarding decisions and information. They commanded mid-managers and supervisors, who in turn controlled the day-to-day work of employees. In this pyramid of control, everybody micromanaged the next layer down.

It had been this way for quite a while. Ed Panzer was hired in 1973 as an assistant director of public works. He remembers that before he got the job, he was taken to the city manager's office for a quick interview.

There he was, sitting behind a long table that was totally covered with papers of one kind or another. He was preparing the city budget. . . . He was running the city, every aspect of it. Nothing was done, except routine tasks, without going through him.

Managers and employees focused on complying with detailed operational procedures. Communications followed the chain of command: up, over, and down. It was hard to get things done in this environment, says Chris Snead, who joined the city manager's secretarial staff in 1977. "You had to go through three or four different departments to get resolution to an issue."

People stayed in their institutional boxes and worried about pleasing their bosses. They waited for orders or permission to act. The organization prized loyalty, stability, certainty, and control. "Employees did not take risks," says Gurley, who in 1970 got his first city job as a zoning inspector. "They more or less relied on their supervisors to tell them what to do, and they did it."

Things began to change in 1984, after the mayor and council conducted a major review of the city's condition. Its population was stagnant at 130,000. Its tax rate was one of Virginia's highest. Its home values and per capita income were the lowest in the region. Its budget was strained by debt repayments; the council had balanced it by tapping one-time sources of revenue. It was losing business to nearby communities. And federal spending cuts were imminent.

In short, the big picture was not pretty. "The statistics scared us," says Mayor James Eason. "We knew that we could not continue this decline. Otherwise we were going to be like some cities in Virginia that we didn't want to be like."

Then the council asked a question: If we don't do anything, where will we be in three or four years? Given the trends, says Eason, "The answer *scared us to death.*" Hampton was dying in slow motion.

When this realization sunk in, Eason adds, the politicians developed "a sense of urgency and a bias for action." They developed an aggressive economic development agenda, including the acquisition and development of land, improvements in the city's physical appearance, and tax cuts.

To implement it, they needed a city government that was more responsive to the community's needs, more innovative and flexible, with a bias for action and an ability to do more with less. Eason says that when he read several years later about "entrepreneurial government" in *Reinventing Government*, the concept captured exactly what he had wanted to create in Hampton.

When the city manager retired, Eason and the council went looking for a successor who would change things. They found someone right in town. Bob O'Neill knew the bureaucracy from the inside. A dozen years earlier he had begun working for the city as a young, longhaired intern and risen quickly to the post of assistant city manager. But he was also an outsider; in 1979 he had left government to work as a business consultant.

O'Neill was cerebral, an ideas man. And he had the right demeanor. "Bob has no visible ego," says Eason. "He's very satisfied with staying in the background." Those who worked with O'Neill in the 1970s describe him as shy and unemotional.

Although many people in city government knew O'Neill, they weren't sure what to expect from him. The council wrote a performance contract for him that spelled out specific goals for city government. It emphasized the need for lots of action, embracing what Eason calls "the Noah Principle" of management: "No more prizes for predicting rain; only prizes for building the ark."

O'Neill got the message. "Their charge to me was do more, do it faster, change internally, handle multiple agendas, be a much better organization." He didn't have a blueprint for the ark he was supposed to build. "The only grand plan I had was that I had a great deal of confidence in the organization."

O'Neill believed that city government had to do more than just respond to what the mayor and the council wanted, however. It also had to anticipate and adapt to future changes in Hampton's environment. "The issue is whether one can be excellent over time, not whether you can do it one time," he says.

We tried to build adaptability so we would maintain a high degree of excellence and success. I really believe that organizations have to adapt to changes in their environments. If they don't, they die.

To make the organization more adaptable, O'Neill would have to change the way it did business. He would have to change people's assumptions, attitudes, and norms—the organization's deep-rooted culture, its basic character. In the hearts and minds of employees, entrepreneurial instincts would have to replace bureaucratic instincts.

O'Neill recognized that he couldn't just order up a new culture. People don't change themselves on command. They only change voluntarily, and few people give up their old ways very quickly—even when their situation warrants it.

"You can manage culture, but you can't control it," says O'Neill. "You can manage a process that produces a statement of values for the organization, but you can't control how people respond to the fact that you want to do that."

From the beginning, O'Neill's emphasis was on employee participation, says Mike Monteith, then an assistant city manager.

When we started out, we said, "We're all in this together, we're all going to be a part of the process." Bob modeled a way of dealing with people. He had a respect for them, a belief in them.

To get employees involved in change, O'Neill adds, "We had to figure out what everyone's stake in our success would be." That meant tapping into a number of motivations.

For some people, it's money. For some people, it's enhanced professional opportunities. For some, it's the contribution they make. It's different in different individuals.

O'Neill's commitment to getting everyone involved didn't mean that business-as-usual was acceptable; from the start, his message was that the organization had to change. He used performance management and organizational empowerment as his key approaches. He put his department heads on performance contracts that spelled out the results they were expected to produce, then tied their bonuses to their achievements. "That sent a message," he says.

He also told his assistant city managers to stop micromanaging the departments. He reassigned them to work on long-term strategic issues, such as the city's relationship with the local schools, and gave the directors full control over their agencies. "Bob gave us the latitude and authority to do the job," says Panzer.

I recall talking to him about it. I asked, "Bob, what do you want me to report to you on?" He said, "Ed, run the department. I know very little about the public works department, and that's the way I want it."

Then O'Neill created a handful of interdepartmental task forces to focus on major common functions, such as physical infrastructure, public safety, and citizen services. "I told the directors, 'We're paying you a lot of money, we expect you to build cooperative relationships with those people you need to support your department's mission,' " says O'Neill. Department heads decided who should participate in the groups and chaired them. The task forces had the power to allocate resources across departmental lines.

For a while, employees weren't sure what to do in the task forces, O'Neill says. "When we said to the departments that they could structure the task forces any way they wanted, they waited. They said, 'What's the answer? Tell us what you *really* want.' " O'Neill assigned Monteith to help the new groups—but not to tell them what to do.

After a while, the task forces evolved into problem-solving groups. "Someone would say, 'I've got a problem,' and the group would deal with it," O'Neill explains.

When Walt Credle joined city government as social services director in 1990, he found that the task forces had fostered a great deal of work across departmental lines.

Over time it had built very strong collaborative relationships. It was amazing. It created an environment that was like nothing I was in before. There's no sense of competition, of hidden agendas, of politics. People of different philosophies and different backgrounds talk with each other about the city.

For Don Gurley, the change in control was inspiring. "Information was filtering down to my section," he says. "They wanted my input. That wasn't done before. I was becoming more involved with the process because I was being consulted on different things."

O'Neill also used his performance contracts to push department heads into collaboration. Each year he asked his task force chairs to review the performance contract reports of the other directors. "He'd put them into a big pile and give them to the task force chairs," says Credle.

He'd say, "You go through them and comment on them. Are they truthful? Do they collaborate? Do they work together? Give me feedback." It gradually dawned on me that if I went to task force

*meetings and behaved like a jackass, I was sinking my own ship.
But if I went to meetings and tried to facilitate and work with
people collaboratively, they would tell Bob that.*

A Vision and Mission for City Government

O'Neill's performance contracts, task forces, and initiatives to
empower departments began to change the culture. But he, the mayor,
and the city council decided that employees also needed what Eason
calls "a compelling vision of a desired state of affairs." By envisioning
the future you want, Eason explains, "You can more easily achieve
your goal. Vision is the link between dream and action." He wanted
Hampton's elected officials, city managers, and public employees to
share the same mental picture of the organization's purpose. "If you
can get this alignment, where everybody knows where you're going to
go, you create a synergy that enables you to do far more than you can do
on an individual basis."

O'Neill worked with the council to develop vision and mission statements that described the purpose and role of city government. The
process was bottom-up as well as top-down; hundreds of city employees
got involved. "There was a lot of iteration between the organization and
the council," says O'Neill. "By the time we ended up with a nice clean
statement, as much had come from below as from the council."

Monteith remembers how difficult the process was:

*The vision statement didn't show up the way the textbooks say it
should. We didn't all sit down and say, "What is it we're trying to
create?" We had a set of meetings. We'd been into it for a year. Bob
and the assistants met four or five times, agonizing and word-
smithing. We never came up with anything that anybody really
liked.*

Finally, Monteith drafted a vision statement and showed it to several
groups. It pledged that Hampton would become "the most livable city
in Virginia." The new mission statement said the city would "bring
together the resources of businesses, neighborhoods, community
groups, and government" in order to realize that vision. The mission
embodied the council's view that government should become a broker
of the community's resources, not just a provider of services and

regulations. The council embraced both statements, and O'Neill used them to develop measurable objectives and action plans for each department—which he wrote into department directors' performance contracts.

"Over time," says Monteith, "the statements became very important and dear to us."

In 1988, 23 parks department employees were taking a class called "Making Winners of Your Employees." Their instructor, a state government contractor, asked them to write down what their mission was. In a memo to O'Neill, then-parks director Thomas Daniel explained what happened next:

> *[The instructor] didn't really expect to get anything, but was amazed when most of the people in the class wrote, "To make Hampton the most livable city in Virginia." During the follow-up discussion, it was pointed out that not only do we have a mission, but we have specific goals. We have objectives attached to those goals with a reporting mechanism to ensure completion or progress. . . . We have contracts to ensure concentration on the accomplishment of these objectives.*

Daniel could not resist adding a punch line: "He has questioned his employer, the State Department of Education, what their mission is, and can get no answer."

" 'The most livable city in Virginia'—everybody knows those words," says Kevin Gallagher. They were hard to miss when he started his first city job with the parks department in 1987. "Everywhere you looked, there it was—all the offices had our mission statement. It was even on our paycheck stubs."

"Employees don't see themselves working for the department, but as working for the organization to achieve its mission," adds Mary Bunting. That's why the heavy-construction crew worked on developing a new city park, even though it was the parks department's project.

The statements shape employee thinking about how to get their jobs done, O'Neill says. For example, the city was under pressure to create community centers in several neighborhoods. But instead of building and operating new centers—the old service role—the city brokered two centers into existence. In one case, officials enticed the YMCA to establish a branch in the wing of a closed high school. The YMCA rehabilitated two gyms and the outside athletic fields, then began raising money to build an extension with an indoor swimming pool. In a second neighborhood the city renovated a facility, then turned it over to the neighborhood to operate.

Growing a New Culture

The changes O'Neill put in place created both anxiety and enthusiasm among employees.

Many employees were unsettled by the new emphasis on performance, autonomy, accountability, and change. "For a long time," recalls Human Resources Director Tharon Greene, "there would be lines of people outside the door who wanted to come in and say, 'Is it okay if we do this?' "

Others, including a few top managers, couldn't survive in the new environment. "We've lost a few department heads along the way, who just weren't able to manage in this environment," says Monteith.

Most employees liked the changes, though. "There was a big hump in the front end" of the change process, says O'Neill. "In our experience, some [employees] require remedial work, but the vast majority feel like all the constraints have been freed and they can finally do what they've always dreamed about doing."

About a year after O'Neill began, the city conducted a "temperature check," its first survey of organizational climate. "We got off-the-scale responses," says Monteith. "There was a high level of excitement about the changes: a new city manager, new roles, new structure. Everybody had high hopes."

But as O'Neill's efforts took hold, employees raised all kinds of issues. "They tested whether we were going to be consistent about building a new culture," he says. They complained that there was no way of recognizing people who did extraordinary work over time. So the city created a program that allowed each department to develop awards for employee innovations and productivity improvements. The agencies shared 10 percent of annual savings with employees and provided awards such as office equipment, time off, dinners, and premium parking spaces.

Employees also complained that their compensation did not reward them for customer service. So O'Neill instituted an annual citizen-satisfaction bonus. If satisfaction with government performance reached certain levels, every city employee would get a bonus check.

In response to other employee challenges, the city:

- created "venture teams" that visited other governments to learn what they were doing to initiate change;
- allowed employees to manage education funds for employees;
- provided small amounts of seed capital to test innovative ideas; and
- drafted a set of organizational values: responsiveness to citizens, quality, integrity, teamwork, professionalism, and innovation.

The values statement helps "employees keep management honest," says O'Neill.

If your actions aren't consistent with the values, the employees will tell you that. They will tell you, "Wait a minute, you say innovation is a value, but every time I try to do something differently, you've got a rule that stands in my way." From the employee's standpoint, it's a contract: if I behave in this way, I'll prosper.

Each challenge employees threw at him was an opportunity to reinforce the culture he was trying to develop, O'Neill points out. "Once you pass these tests enough times and people see things happening differently, they build a commitment to the new culture. The way they think about things and the way they behave changes dramatically."

Kevin Gallagher remembers how difficult it was to believe in a new culture.

I figured it was just the latest management buzzword. When Bob would say something or make a policy change, you'd wait for it to collapse. And it never did. I thought, "This is really happening. We were this way before and now we're this way." I started getting more involved.

By the late 1980s, many new ways of working had emerged. Often, says Tharon Greene, the organization had to "change the rules to catch up with new practices."

When the city's building and environmental inspectors realized they would save time in the field if they had cellular phones, Mary Bunting went right out and bought 29 phones for them. "She caught us off guard," says Don Gurley. "We were surprised that the phones were made available that quickly."

When the city decided to reengineer the way it responded to requests for information, a dozen employees met with a half dozen citizens every Friday for several months. Together they came up with radical changes for the city to consider.

When city officials became worried about how many of Hampton's youth were not succeeding in school, they asked the community what should be done. The answers surprised them. "We ended up with a conversation about how the whole community was part of raising a child," says Monteith. "It was all about the importance of neighborhoods and family." So the city organized a community-wide coalition of parents, businesses, community groups, youth advocates, and teenagers, which brought more than 5,000 people into a three-year process to develop comprehensive recommendations that became part of the city's strategic plan.

When city leaders worried about the health of Hampton's neighborhoods, they decided to share control of the city's planning process with neighborhood groups. The planning agency required developers to meet with neighborhood groups before they requested zoning changes and use permits, and it worked with residents, schools, and children to design six neighborhood parks. Then the city created a Department of Neighborhood Services, as recommended by the community coalition, to meet the unique needs of each neighborhood and harness the energy of neighborhood leaders. It provided small grants for neighborhood development, launched an institute to train neighborhood leaders, helped develop neighborhood groups, linked neighborhoods to each other so they could exchange services, and leaned on other city agencies to support neighborhoods. In short, it brought the neighborhoods into city government.

In these and other cases, city employees converted challenges into opportunities. They behaved like entrepreneurs.

Success . . . and Stress

By the mid-1990s, Hampton was a big success story. Citizen satisfaction with city government hovered around 90 percent. The city's financial indicators remained strong even during the recession of the early 1990s. Downtown development had leaped forward. Property taxes, once high, were now among the lowest in Virginia. Debt payments had been cut in half. Mayor Eason had been reelected three times, and his allies on the council had also worn well with voters. On a variety of indicators, such as employees per capita, Hampton usually ranked better than comparable cities. Employee morale, measured annually, was consistently good, and employees were supportive of the changes O'Neill had unleashed.

The city's performance had also begun to be recognized. In 1993, for instance, it won the President's Award for Entrepreneurial Government from the Virginia Municipal League, for its "new approach to management and decision-making and a new view of the citizens as customers."

Many employees believed a new culture had emerged. "My grandfather worked for city government in Hampton for 20 years," says Don Gurley. "He would be overwhelmed and amazed because of the changes in the attitude and culture of the people."

But Hampton's culture was not perfect. Many frontline employees still didn't care about customer service, says Kevin Gallagher, and many were still afraid to make changes.

The big thing that the organization can't seem to get across to the line workers is that change is not scary, it's a challenge they need to embrace. It's going to change them, but it's not going to hurt them. They could learn a lot by being open to it.

Many employees note that the new culture shortchanges important emotional needs of employees. "We don't do enough celebrating," says Mary Bunting.

We haven't really taken the time to step back and say, 'Gee, look at what we've done.' We're so caught up in trying to accomplish all we need to. One of the complaints you hear is that we've lost a sense of family around here.

Gallagher agrees: "I'd like to see the emotion back in the organization. I'm a big proponent of the fact that you can work your ass off but you can still have fun."

"It's a fair criticism of our organization," admits O'Neill. "We probably give substantially less attention to celebrating than we should. But we just don't come to it very naturally." Instead, after each success, O'Neill turns to the next hurdle. That's his personality.

Tharon Greene is the same way. "I focus on getting things done," she says. "I'm almost obsessed with it."

The drive to perform has also left the organization exhausted. "People are tired," says Chris Snead, now the budget director. "They're kind of tired of change."

Greene and O'Neill agree. "People are feeling wrung out," says Greene. "We've done more with less for years."

In 1995, O'Neill met with his department directors to talk about the problem. He wanted to rally them.

> I told them, "I'm just as worn out as you are. I wouldn't mind taking a break either. But the environment out there is moving rapidly. If we aren't prepared to stay in front of the curve, we will lose our edge. As much as we'd like to take a break, it's not doable."

Then he launched a new wave of changes.

Adapting Again

O'Neill had his eye on two challenges. One was the fact that many problems the city faced could not be solved within its perimeters. "A whole range of issues—air quality standards and employment, for instance—transcend the organization's boundaries," he says. The other was that Hampton's citizens still didn't think city government was responding adequately to their neighborhoods' needs.

City government was not well prepared to deal with either challenge. It didn't have strong connections with other entities in the region, and its departmental structure got in the way of achieving strategic objectives, such as creating healthy neighborhoods.

"We had trouble getting department heads to buy in to the fact that [neighborhood service] was their priority," says Joan Kennedy, who ran the fledgling unit created to help neighborhoods. "They viewed it as an add-on to the regular job." As a result, she spent most of her time "jumping organizational hurdles."

In response to these concerns, O'Neill asked his department heads to figure out how to realign the organization around the city's major goals: healthy families, healthy neighborhoods, healthy businesses, and a prospering region. They recommended permanently dismantling the remaining walls between departments and shifting resources to the strategic areas. "We're talking about department boundaries disappearing within a year," says Greene.

Because the organization had used teamwork, performance incentives, and collaborative planning with great success, O'Neill applied those tools to his senior managers. He gave them group goals and told them their pay would depend on how well they performed as a team.

No one knew where the process would lead. But in Hampton's change-oriented culture, this was not unusual. "We have a measure of adaptability," says O'Neill. "We're not uncomfortable with the questions we're asking."

"It's just the next big change," adds Monteith, who finds the challenge exciting. "Given that we are continually looking for the better way to make things happen, this organization is going to keep on changing."

THE CULTURE STRATEGY

You probably know the story about the elephants who are tied to very small stakes. The western visitor asks why they don't pull up the stakes and walk away. The local people reply that when the elephants are babies, they are tied to the stakes and learn they can't walk away from them. Even when they grow up to be big and powerful, and could easily walk away, they don't because they have accepted the idea that they can't.
—Otto Broderick, former auditor general of Canada

Organizations have distinctive cultures, much as people have distinctive personalities. Like people, some organizations are energetic, creative, or caring, while others are depressed, compliant, or neglectful. And like personalities, organizational cultures are very hard to change.

An organization's culture is a set of behavioral, emotional, and psychological frameworks that are deeply internalized and shared by the organization's members. It has a tangible, physical dimension:

people's habits and routines; their rituals, customs, and conventions; even the stories they tell. It also has an intangible, hidden dimension: people's beliefs, assumptions, ideas, hopes, and dreams. Every aspect of an organization—its structure, its job descriptions, its standard operating procedures, its language, its policies, even its technologies—contributes to its culture.

An organization's culture signals to people the appropriate attitudes and behaviors for success in the organization. It is a social reality, an ongoing phenomenon from which people consciously and unconsciously draw guidance. It provides powerful guideposts that tell people what they should do, feel, and think. In Hampton, for instance, many city employees use their organization's vision and mission statements to guide their behaviors. And when they collaborate with each other or provide good customer service, the organization rewards their behavior.

You can tell an organization's culture right away if you know what to look for. When Tom Glynn took over as general manager of the Massachusetts Bay Transit Authority, he saw photographs of trains, trolleys, and subway cars all over the walls of the main office. No pictures of employees, none of passengers. He knew from these clues that his new organization's people—dominated by engineers—cared and thought more about machines than people. Their focus was on managing and maintaining the equipment.

When Doug Ross took the helm at the Employment and Training Administration in the U.S. Department of Labor, he immediately visited the agency's ten regional offices, some of which had not seen a director in years. "As I met with the employees at each one, invariably there was a whole group of middle-aged white men sitting in the back rows with their arms folded," Ross says. "It was a very defensive posture. Right off the bat, it communicated to me: we don't know who you are, and we're not interested."

When Peter Hutchinson's firm, the Public Strategies Group, was hired to function as superintendent of the Minneapolis schools, he immediately began visiting schools. The teachers complained bitterly about the district's central office. They told him "a lot of stories of people being very badly treated," he says. "People being demeaned in public, openly yelled at, of people in the central office using fear as their principal tool."

They told him no one even had a copy of the curriculum, which had not been printed for ten years. They made him pick up the telephone and listen. "You couldn't get a dial tone," he recalls. "They were literally cut off from the central office."

Over and over, the staff talked about the curriculum and the dial tone. They were feeling like they were on little islands out there by themselves. People were absolutely certain that you couldn't try anything new; that if you did, you'd get punished whether it worked or not. They were certain that you could get fired for trying, but no one could ever name someone who had been. There was a ton of fear.

The Culture of Public Bureaucracies

Glynn, Ross, and Hutchinson encountered their organizations' cultures much like anthropologists visiting a remote tribe. As outsiders, they brought new eyes and ears.

What they found was a distinct phenomenon: call it "public sector bureaucratic culture." Many public organizations share it, though they may have variants and multiple subcultures. Employees express it in many ways: when they tell new workers to "follow the rules and stay out of trouble"; when they joke that a decision is "above my pay grade"; when they say something is "good enough for government work."

Why is this culture so widespread? Because most public organizations share certain fundamental characteristics, which shape their cultures.

Government organizations are creatures of the political sector. Inevitably, they are the target of incessant public demands channeled through elected officials. They become footballs in political contests, kicked from one end of the field to the other. They undergo hostile scrutiny from legislators, lobbyists, interest groups, and the media. Public employees live in "an atmosphere of investigation," writes Bill Godfrey, former commissioner of the Australian Taxation Office.

In response, organizations learn to defend themselves. Sometimes they ignore and ward off the outside world; at other times, they kowtow and please. Typically, they blame elected officials and interest groups for whatever is wrong with government. And because they are afraid they will be blamed when things go badly, they take few chances. Duke University's Robert Behn, a leading public management scholar, once described the Ten Commandments of Government this way: "Thou shalt not make a mistake. Thou shalt not make a mistake. Thou shalt not make a mistake. . . ."

Government agencies are almost always organized as multilayered hierarchies. Rank rules. It determines authority, compensation, and career opportunities. It separates people into order-givers and order-takers, and it values those in command and those who obey. In response to this concentration of power, government workers tend to be fearful. They stay in their cages. If they want to try to change something, they ask permission first. But most don't even try.

Government is organized bureaucratically. Thinking is separated from doing. Doing is compartmentalized by function. Functions are separated into units. Units are broken down into jobs. Jobs are reduced to specific tasks and codified in rigid classifications and descriptions. The tasks are performed by specialists. The specialists occupy cubicles and offices that wall them off from one another.

This model has been in place for so long that it is routinely accepted as the received wisdom of the last generations. It is the way things are supposed to be—not just the way things became in response to certain conditions. But it devalues people. Like cogs in a machine, they play a static part in a grand design that does not need their capacity to learn and does not have room for their hopes and dreams. The effect is numbing: people caught in the monotonous bureaucratic machinery become unimaginative and unresponsive.

Government organizations usually have monopolies or near monopolies. They face little pressure from their customers or from competitors. Because there are no consequences for their performance, they are inwardly focused. Their people often worry about budgets and personnel levels and bureaucratic status rather than about how to improve results. They put no premium on effectiveness or outcomes. Employees are more likely to be rewarded for living through another year than for performing well. As a result, many employees have low expectations and take little pride in their work. Outsiders come to feel the same way about them.

These fundamentals—politics, hierarchy, bureaucracy, and monopoly—give rise to organizational cultures in which the inhabitants:

- blame each other and outsiders, rather than taking responsibility for their actions;
- live in fear of making mistakes, rather than trying to innovate;
- compliantly accept mediocrity, rather than creatively reaching for excellence; and
- resist change rather than adapting to it.

Changing Government's Culture

To change these kinds of behavior, you must change the culture of public organizations. The most powerful methods to do this are the first four C's: clarifying the purposes of public organizations; creating consequences for performance; making organizations more accountable to their customers; and shifting the locus and form of control. In Hampton, Eason and O'Neill built consensus around a clear purpose and goals, initiated performance contracts with senior managers, rewarded workers for satisfying their customers, and empowered employees to participate in decision making. This began to loosen the hold of bureaucratic culture, but it was not enough.

Organization after organization has discovered the same thing. As reinventors use the first four C's, they find that the old culture slows down and deflects the strategies' power. They also discover that culture does not obediently bend to the shape imposed by the other strategies. Instead, it takes forms they did not expect—quiet resistance, disengagement, even depression.

Sooner or later, successful reinventors learn that the changes they are making by using the first four C's will not stick until they become part of the organization's culture. As Harvard Professor John Kotter explains, "Until new behaviors are rooted in social norms and shared values, they are subject to degradation as soon as the pressure for change is removed." Thus, reinventors need explicit strategies to reshape their cultures.

The U.K. provides a good example. As we outlined in chapter 1, British leaders used the core, consequences, customer, and control strategies to change the DNA of their entire system. Yet they found that organizations still clung to their old cultures. In 1994, after six years of Next Steps and three years of market testing and the Citizen's Charter, William Waldegrave, then the minister in charge of public service reform, told us, "There is a terrific tendency of the bureaucracy to respond to the more devolved structures—rather like an organism in microbiology—by mimicking in the new-style organization what is being done in the old-style organization."

The Australian federal reformers had the same experience. After a decade of reforms in the Australian Public Service (APS), Steven Sedgwick, the finance secretary, noted:

> *What we have to do yet is to embed cultural change within agencies and within the working lives of managers and staff to empower them to make [the] best use of that framework. This is in fact the hardest part of the reforms, the stage where . . . we have to change some deeply ingrained elements of culture which are not amenable to direct regulation. This will be a slow, painstaking process, and one which will be played out in individual workplaces across the APS.*

Sunnyvale, California, provides an even more concrete illustration of why the first four C's are not enough. For more than 15 years, Sunnyvale's leaders have used the core, consequences, and customer strategies to transform their organization. They have produced extraordinary results—increasing their productivity 6 percent a year, year after year. Their employees work very hard. But the last time we visited, in 1994, employee after employee told us performance could be even better if the culture were different.

City Manager Tom Lewcock had pushed to organize the culture around results, and he had succeeded. Employees described it as "results oriented," "bottom-line," "hard driving," and "high pressure." They were well paid and proud of their organization. But no one described it as a culture that produced continuous improvement and innovation. That was the managers' job, not the employees'. In other words, Sunnyvale had created a culture in which line employees worked hard but did not take responsibility for innovation. When managers asked them to come up with ideas to improve things, they were met with relative silence. "We've had some meetings; we've got a couple of ideas," Fleet Manager Jim Masch said about his own efforts. "But I'm seeing their reluctance to put something out there."

Part of the reason was that Sunnyvale had not fully implemented a control strategy. It had empowered managers, but not their employees. But even managers were sometimes loathe to experiment, because they were running so hard to keep up and felt so much pressure not to make mistakes. Gail Waiters, a manager who had just left Sunnyvale to take a job in Bakersfield, explained the problem.

> *Sunnyvale touts itself as an organization that believes in risk takers and innovators and creative thinkers—which is true. However, because of the leadership, people are reluctant to take the risk, because they're afraid of the consequences. So there is a gap somewhere. While Tom and I and a few others continued to reassure people that that's what we wanted to happen, our actions did not portray that. In other words, if a person stuck their neck out and tried to do something that they thought was pretty innovative, Tom might shoot them down—and they would forever be gun-shy and never take another risk.*
>
> *People did not really believe that it was an organization of risk taking, because they felt that they couldn't make a mistake. Well, you could make those mistakes, but you were going to pay for them. And I think that's different—if you read about HP, or Xerox, or 3-M, they say, "We applaud mistakes." Sunnyvale is not into applauding mistakes.*

Sunnyvale was one of the best managed, most productive public organizations we had ever seen. Yet it clearly needed a strategy to change its culture. Sooner or later, so will any organization. The culture strategy is weaker than the other four C's, but it is necessary all the same.

The culture strategy is weak in part because it is so slow to produce results. Many leaders start out assuming that if they can only get their people to understand the need for change, big changes will follow. Gradually they discover that the conversion process proceeds almost person by person. Changing organizational culture is "like being a Hoover salesman," says Nigel Palk, the veteran chief executive of the London borough of Bromley. "I've got to convince a lot of people to do things that they haven't done."

"Changing government culture is Kafka's Great Wall of China," adds Bob O'Leary, one of Governor Lawton Chiles's key reinventors in

Florida. "By the time the message gets to the outer provinces of the department, there will be a new administration."

Glacial speed is not the only problem. Changing people's habits, hearts, and minds does not ensure that their organizations will become more effective and efficient—only that their members will want to. Unless you use the other C's, your culture strategy will eventually run into a brick wall, because the organization's purpose, incentives, accountabilities, and power structure will continue sending opposite messages.

So a culture strategy is essential but insufficient. In the end, it takes all five C's to transform the public sector.

Factors that Shape a Culture

Changing an organization's culture is not a science. The process cannot just be planned and implemented; it cannot be engineered. It contains too many variables. Indeed, there are at least a dozen key factors that shape culture.

The first four ingredients listed below are the systemic DNA reinventors change with the core, consequences, customer, and control

---

Factors Shaping Organizational Culture

1. Purpose
2. Incentive Systems
3. Accountability Systems
4. Power Structure
5. Administrative Systems
6. Organizational Structure
7. Work Processes
8. Organizational Tasks
9. External Environment
10. History and Tradition
11. Management Practices
12. Leaders' Predispositions
13. Employees' Predispositions

strategies. Factors 5–7 are the changes in systems, structures, and processes that must follow from the first four C's if the new DNA is to be institutionalized.

The next three factors—the organization's tasks, its external environment, and its history and traditions—are more difficult to change. Reinventors can change the tasks their employees do, through employee empowerment, business process reengineering, and the like. But there are limits to how far they can go; they can't turn a benefits agency into a policy think tank. Similarly, they can alter the external environment—the political climate, the attitudes of legislators, the positions taken by interest groups—but it is rarely easy. (Bob O'Neill and James Eason did it in Hampton, by bringing elected leaders and senior managers together to do visioning and strategic planning.) Finally, reinventors cannot change an organization's history and traditions, although they can reinterpret them.

After you use the other four C's and change administrative systems, structures, and processes, most of your remaining leverage will lie in the last three items on our list: changing your management practices and your leaders' and employees' predispositions. Here you will confront the most fundamental challenge of the culture strategy: changing people's paradigms.

A paradigm is a set of assumptions about the nature of reality. Thomas Kuhn introduced the notion into social science in 1962, with the publication of his book *The Structure of Scientific Revolutions*. The scientific paradigms he described were highly rational: they had explicit rules, recorded in scientific literature. Cultural paradigms are different: they are often unwritten, unspoken, even unconscious.

A cultural paradigm is like an identity: it is so much a part of each of us that we are not even aware of it. If someone asked us to write down the basic assumptions of our cultural paradigms, few of us could do it. And yet we could not operate without them. They tell us what is important and what is not; the unwritten rules of behavior in our organization; how to relate to our peers, supervisors, employees, and customers; and what constitutes success and status. They even tell us the meaning of particular words and actions. People operating out of different paradigms often misunderstand each other completely, just as people from one culture often misunderstand the actions and words of people from a foreign culture.

Our paradigms even shape our perceptions. Kuhn argued that

"something like a paradigm is prerequisite to perception itself. What a man sees depends both upon what he looks at and also upon what his previous visual-conceptual experience has taught him to see."

He described a psychology experiment in which people were briefly shown a series of playing cards and asked, after each one, to identify it. Most of the cards were normal, but a few were abnormal: a red six of spades, for instance, or a black four of hearts. The results captured the way in which people are blind to realities that do not fit their paradigms:

> For the normal cards [the] identifications were usually correct, but the anomalous cards were almost always identified, without apparent hesitation or puzzlement, as normal. The black four of hearts might, for example, be identified as the four of either spades or hearts. Without any awareness of trouble, it was immediately fitted to one of the conceptual categories prepared by prior experience. . . . With a further increase of exposure to the anomalous cards, subjects did begin to hesitate and to display awareness of anomaly. Exposed, for example, to the red six of spades, some would say: That's the six of spades, but there's something wrong with it—the black has a red border. Further increase of exposure resulted in still more hesitation and confusion until finally, and sometimes quite suddenly, most subjects would produce the correct identification without hesitation. Moreover, after doing this with two or three of the anomalous cards, they would have little further difficulty with the others. A few subjects, however, were never able to make the requisite adjustment of their categories. . . . And the subjects who then failed often experienced acute personal distress.

In his book *Paradigms*, Joel Barker describes other experiences which show that people will rearrange their perception of reality to fit their expectations. For instance, a scuba diver once told him a puzzling story.

> Quite often he dove to the depths of 100–150 feet to check out fish traps. . . . Because the area is well trafficked by expensive yachts, lots of garbage is strewn along the ocean floor, especially beer cans. His problem had been caused by the fact that when he saw

Budweiser beer cans down at the 150-foot level, he clearly saw their red labels.

Why did that bother him? If you understand the physics of light, you know that the color red cannot penetrate through 150 feet of water. All that you have left at that depth is green and the few other colors far toward the ultraviolet end of the spectrum. There is no color red at that depth!

. . . He saw the red label because he knew the "correct model" of the Budweiser beer can. That is, he knew the color it was supposed to be, and, in order to make it fit the rules, he literally colored the can in his mind.

Shifting Paradigms

To change a culture, you have to change people's paradigms. You will need to change most of the assumptions we described above: that rank rules; that risk is to be avoided at all cost; that every mistake will be punished; that decisions must be kicked upstairs. This is extremely difficult, because people cling ferociously to their paradigms.

The first thing you have to do is get people to let go of their old assumptions. How? In science, the key is what Kuhn calls "anomalies"—problems the old paradigm cannot solve, realities it cannot explain, facts it cannot admit to be true. As these anomalies pile up, people begin to lose faith in the old paradigm. Some become so uncomfortable that they leave the field. But at some point someone articulates a new paradigm, and people begin making the leap.

Guidelines for Leading Paradigm Shifts

1. Introduce anomalies and help people perceive them.
2. Provide a clearly defined new paradigm.
3. Build faith in the new paradigm.
4. Help people let go of their old paradigm.
5. Give people time in the neutral zone.
6. Give people touchstones.
7. Provide a safety net.

With cultural paradigms, the process is similar. People begin to let go of their old paradigms when they run into experiences, facts, and feelings that cannot be explained by the old set of assumptions. These anomalies provoke what psychologists call "dissonance"—conflicts between what one has experienced and what one knows to be possible. Often people cope by refusing to see the anomalies, just as people in the experiment Kuhn described could not see the anomalous cards. When anomalies appear, they immediately define them as something else. When they see managers rewarding employees who innovate, for example, they define that as management rewarding its favorites. When they see their union leaders working with management to improve performance, they define that as "selling out." When they hear someone advocating charter schools, they define that as privatization of public schools. Often they will swear that someone talked about, say, privatization—despite all evidence to the contrary—because that is the only way they can interpret the message within their old paradigm.

To break through this paradigm blindness, you must not only introduce anomalies into your organization, you must actively help people perceive them for what they are. As they begin to experience the resulting dissonance, they will become uncomfortable, just as those confronted with a black four of hearts became uncomfortable. Asking people to give up their most basic assumptions about life in their organizations is like asking them to play a new game without knowing the rules—a game that will determine whether they have a job, how much they earn, and what their colleagues think of them.

Hence you must give them a new set of rules. You must provide a new way of understanding the anomalies—a new paradigm—they can embrace. They will not be able to tolerate the ambiguity for very long: they will either make the leap or retreat to their old paradigm. To help them make the leap you need to define the new paradigm for them as fully as possible, so they have something clear to embrace. Nobody abandons an old cultural paradigm without having access to a new one—because nobody can function for long without one. William Bridges, the author of *Managing Transitions: Making the Most of Change*, uses the analogy of a trapeze artist, who lets go of one trapeze in faith that she will be able to grasp another one. Unless she can see that new one very clearly, she is not going to let go—because she can't survive long in midair. So one of the first things you need to do is paint a clear picture of the new culture for all to see.

Third, you must help people build the faith necessary to make the leap. Every paradigm shift is ultimately a leap of faith. Just as you cannot prove to the trapeze artist that she will catch the new bar, you cannot prove to people that everything will be fine once they embrace the new culture. Kuhn makes this point nicely:

> The man who embraces a new paradigm at an early stage must often do so in defiance of the evidence. . . . He must, that is, have faith that the new paradigm will succeed with the many large problems that confront it knowing only that the older paradigm has failed with a few. A decision of that kind can only be made on faith.

To build people's faith, you must first earn their trust. We cannot emphasize this enough. None of us put our faith in people we don't trust. You must then prove to them that others who have made the leap before them have flourished, and assure them that they too will flourish in the new culture.

Fourth, you must recognize that, as Bridges puts it, a paradigm shift begins with an ending. It begins when people let go of their former worldview—a frightening process that creates much of the resistance to change. If you understand how difficult it is for employees to let go, and use tools that make letting go easier, you will get much further.

Fifth, you must accept the fact that it will take time before people fully internalize the new paradigm. After they let go, Bridges tells us, they move into the so-called neutral zone. "This is the no-man's-land between the old reality and the new. It's the limbo between the old sense of identity and the new. It is a time when the old way is gone and the new doesn't feel comfortable yet."

If you don't understand how long and difficult the neutral zone can be, Bridges points out, "you're likely to try to rush through it and to be discouraged when you cannot do so." But, he adds:

> People make the new beginning only if they have first made an ending and spent some time in the neutral zone. Yet most organizations try to start with the beginning rather than finishing with it. They pay no attention to endings. They do not acknowledge the existence of the neutral zone, then wonder why people have so much difficulty with change.

Many of our lessons later in this chapter give leaders techniques to mark the ending, support and guide people through the neutral zone, and celebrate the new beginning.

One of the most important things you can do to help people get through the neutral zone and make a new beginning is to give them touchstones—guidelines and reference points they can hold onto as anchors, while they struggle to internalize the new culture. *The American Heritage Dictionary* defines a touchstone in two ways. One is "a criteria or standard." But the more literal definition is even more useful: a touchstone is "a hard black stone, such as jasper or basalt, formerly used to test the quality of gold or silver by comparing the streak left on the stone by one of these metals with that of a standard alloy."

Touchstones, in other words, were first used to tell if pieces of gold or silver were the real thing. Cultural touchstones perform a similar function. They help people figure out if a particular action is the real thing: Is it consistent with the new paradigm, or not? There are many kinds of touchstones. The city of Hampton used vision, mission, and values statements; other organizations have used symbols, stories, slogans, and even rituals.

Finally, you can help people work up the courage to let go by providing a safety net. As trapeze artists learn their art, they know that when they try something and fail, they will not perish. They will simply land in the safety net and have to climb back up the ladder and try again. This is exactly the attitude leaders must take as they try to change a culture: let people know that when they give it their best shot and fail, they will not be punished.

Three Approaches to Cultural Transition

A culture can be thought of as a product of experience interacting with emotion and reason. Consider our bureaucratic cultures. No one set out intentionally to create a bureaucratic government culture; it grew up because people experienced bureaucratic government realities. These experiences produced a set of unspoken, often unconscious emotional commitments: expectations, fears, hopes, and dreams. Together, these experiences and emotional commitments shaped a set of ideas, assumptions, and attitudes—mental models of reality.

These three elements, then, hold the keys to cultural paradigm shifts.

If you can change people's experiences, their emotional commitments, and their mental models, you will change their cultures.

When there is dissonance between these elements—when new experiences conflict with one's mental models or emotional commitments, for instance—people either reject the new experience (reinterpreting it or simply denying its significance) or they change their ideas and emotional commitments. The process of changing culture is the process of provoking this dissonance by exposing people to new experiences, new emotions, and new ideas—then working with them to help them adjust the other elements to align with the new one.

Using this framework, we have defined three basic approaches you can use to change your organization's culture: changing habits, touching hearts, and winning minds.

CHANGING HABITS: CREATING NEW EXPERIENCES

This approach immerses employees in new experiences that challenge their workplace habits and push them to behave in new ways. When Mary Bunting, Hampton's assistant city manager, joined a sewer team, she was plunging into a new experience that changed her perception of city workers.

Our experiences shape and reshape us. They form the deep-rooted emotional commitments and mental models—the paradigms—that guide our behaviors. We constantly test new experiences against our paradigms. When experiences reinforce them, we find it comforting. But many experiences don't resonate with our inner rules. When this happens, we may reject the dissonance and retain our paradigms, even though they fail to account for our experiences. Or we may adapt our paradigms—broadening, deepening, and restructuring them to adjust to the lessons of our experiences. When this happens, we learn.

Immersing people in new experiences is the most powerful way to change an organization's culture. It reopens their hearts and minds. But more important, it changes what they do. This is not easy to accomplish. People often have new feelings and thoughts without ever changing what they do. That is because what we do has a power of its own—the power of habit.

A habit is defined in *The American Heritage Dictionary* as "a recurrent, often unconscious pattern of behavior that is acquired

Tools for Changing Habits

Meeting the Customers exposes employees to the people their work is designed to help, whether through focus groups, conversations, or frontline work.

Walking in the Customer's Shoes asks employees to go through their own system as customers—to apply for benefits, or apply for a permit, or take a course—so they can experience the world from the customer's point of view.

Job Rotation moves employees through different jobs within an organization; they take full responsibility for the work and stay in each position long enough to learn its intricacies.

Internships and Externships bring in outsiders for stints of up to several years, to expose the organization to new experiences, and send members out to work in other organizations for similar periods, to immerse them in new environments.

Cross-Walking and Cross-Talking get employees to cross their bureaucratic boundaries by working with or engaging in dialogue with people from other units, agencies, or even businesses.

Institutional Sponsors establish formal processes that attract, support, protect, and celebrate innovative behaviors in public organizations.

Contests promote behaviors leaders want to see in their organizations by rewarding those who best exemplify those behaviors.

Large-Scale, Real-Time Strategic Planning immerses most if not all of an organization's employees in an intensive, multiday retreat, during which they participate fully in identifying important changes in the organization's strategy and commit to implementing them.

Workouts are intensive, short-term group exercises in barrier-free climates, designed to inspire the free flow of ideas about improving targeted work processes. Often groups implement improvements on the spot.

Hands-On Organizational Experiences are other large events in which hundreds of employees share new experiences that build the habits, emotional commitments, and attitudes leaders want.

Redesigning Work, whether through reengineering business processes, reforming administrative systems, or introducing new technology, permanently changes employees' experiences.

through frequent repetition." As we repeat behaviors many times, they become automatic. This is efficient: confronted with a familiar situation, we don't need to rethink our moves or stir up feelings anew; we just do what we've done before. But because habits allow us to turn off our minds and hearts, they blind us to changes in reality.

Changing our habits is not easy. We are unaware of some of them. We would deny that others existed if they were called to our attention. Habits "have tremendous gravity pull—more than most people realize or would admit," writes leadership development guru Stephen R. Covey. "Breaking deeply imbedded habitual tendencies . . . involves more than a little willpower and a few minor changes in our lives."

Reinventors employ a range of tools to help organizations escape the gravitational force of bureaucratic habits. These tools immerse public employees in new experiences, which pose new problems that cannot be solved by using career-long habits. They must find new ways of acting.

TOUCHING HEARTS:
DEVELOPING A NEW COVENANT

In the fall of 1993, the Minneapolis School Board asked the Public Strategies Group (PSG), a consulting firm, to fill the role normally played by the superintendent and his key deputies. Peter Hutchinson and Babak Armajani, managing partners of the firm, decided to begin by asking everyone involved with the schools—students, teachers, administrators, even parents—to sign a "new covenant."

First company members spent weeks meeting with students, parents, teachers, and interest groups, asking them what they needed from the system and what they would pledge to improve it. The idea, Hutchinson says, "was to have a personal dialogue with students and families about why they were in school, what they expected, and what they needed." Then they drafted the Minneapolis Covenant, which articulated what they had heard. It had sections for students, parents, staff people, the superintendent, the school board, and members of the community. Each one listed promises ("I promise to find a quiet place for school work and make sure work is done") and needs ("I need clear and frequent communication with school"). It then left a blank space for a "personal promise."

The district distributed tens of thousands of these covenants—long documents on blue parchment—and asked students, parents, teachers, administrators, school board members, and community members to sign them. Several weeks later, it staged an Olympics-style parade, in which students from each school delivered the covenants to a mass meeting attended by the mayor, business leaders, and other politicians. The local media covered the event heavily, and it even made Cable News Network. Hutchinson read a letter from President Clinton—who had talked often about a new covenant between citizens and their government during his campaign—congratulating the students, their parents, and their teachers.

This ritual announced to the entire community that there was a new way of doing business in the school district. It signaled a new beginning: a new openness, a new relationship of mutual responsibility between the system and its customers, and a new commitment to every student in the system.

Finally Hutchinson and the school board signed the covenants—more than 27,000 of them. "I personally signed every single one of them and they know that," says Hutchinson. "It was beautiful."

Hutchinson and his colleagues were trying to begin the process of changing the school district's culture. They were attempting to shift the *emotional commitments* of public employees, customers, and stakeholders: their hopes and dreams, their expectations, their unspoken assumptions, their commitments to one another.

Organizational cultures are rooted in emotional commitments, many of which are barely even conscious. In bureaucratic cultures, many people are committed to their status in the hierarchy. Others are committed to deep resentments—toward management, toward unions, toward politicians. Still others are committed to their own victimhood: they operate out of fear and blame others for all their problems.

To create an entrepreneurial culture, you must convince employees to let go of their old commitments and develop a new and different set. This process of touching hearts is intensely personal. It requires leaders to acknowledge and satisfy peoples' innermost needs—for praise, for peace, for belonging. It requires that they make many small gestures and give many small gifts. And it requires that leaders do this every day, every month, every year. As former Austin, Texas, city manager Camille Barnett says, "It is the little things that happen between people that make a great family, a great organization, or a great city."

Tools for Touching Hearts

New Symbols communicate at a gut level the culture you want to build. As they buy into organizational symbols, people create new emotional bonds.

New Stories create new cultural artifacts: anchors that help bind employees together around a common set of values, expectations, hopes, and dreams.

Celebrating Success, through both regular and spontaneous events that honor the achievements of individuals, teams, and the organization as a whole, reinforces the culture leaders want to build.

Honoring Failure means using innovations that fail as opportunities to improve performance and to promote innovation—not as occasions for blaming and punishment.

Rituals are special events that embody and reinforce the new culture. Often repeated regularly, they give people new touchstones. When they are participatory, they also draw people in, helping them make the emotional commitments required by the new culture.

Investing in the Workplace—upgrading the quality of the standard-issue working environment—proves to employees that the organization's leaders value them and value quality.

Redesigning the Workplace reinforces the emotional commitments leaders want, such as a sense of teamwork or a commitment to customer service.

Investing in Employees proves to them that their leaders are serious about the changes they advocate by investing in their capacity to make those changes.

Bonding Events develop powerful new relationships among groups of employees based on trust, collaboration, and taking shared responsibility for producing results.

Valentines are group exercises in which employees tell other work units what they would like them to do differently. They help people speak the truth to one another without getting hung up in workplace rivalries and antagonisms—and ultimately change their commitments to one another.

WINNING MINDS:
DEVELOPING NEW MENTAL MODELS

The third approach to changing culture works on the conscious, rational terrain of the new culture. It helps employees forge new understandings of the organization's purpose, role, goals, values, principles, and strategy—of where the organization needs to go and how to get there. The city of Hampton depended heavily on this approach.

In 1990, Walter Credle interviewed for the job of social services director in Hampton. Although he worked in a nearby city as a top welfare administrator, he didn't know much about Hampton's city government. During his first interview with a panel of employees, he could tell there was something different about the city. "Right away there was a real emphasis on their mission," he recalls. "They asked me how I would tie my goals and objectives to the mission and how I would get my managers to do the same thing."

After Credle won the job, the performance contract he negotiated with City Manager Bob O'Neill set departmental goals that tied in to the city's mission. When Credle began participating in interdepartmental task forces, he found that although the chairs rotated among "people with different philosophies and outlooks," it didn't matter, because agency directors were "all still trying to move toward the same mission." When he and several fellow department heads crafted a new welfare "prevention" strategy with the community and asked O'Neill for funding, money was so tight that the city had reduced its staff. Yet O'Neill and the city council came through with $162,000 for the pilot program. "I was stunned," Credle says. "It was the only new initiative in the budget." When he asked O'Neill why the project got funded, "He said it was because it was so consistent with his and the mayor's long-term vision for the city."

As Credle found, Hampton's employees didn't just memorize the mission and vision statements and regurgitate them on command. They found meaning in them. The ideas became what Peter Senge, author of *The Fifth Discipline*, calls the "governing ideas" of the organization: compelling new touchstones people use to guide their behavior and decisions.

Creating governing ideas has important effects on organizational culture:

It helps employees align their energy toward common goals. The importance of this cannot be overestimated. A widely shared understanding of what the organization is trying to accomplish stimulates collaboration and coordination among its employees; it glues people together.

It energizes the organization, because it speaks to employees' dreams—their need for meaningful achievements. "Most employees will come to work almost every day for a paycheck," notes Doug Ross, former head of the U.S. Employment and Training Administration. "But if our goal is to enlist the creativity and the souls of the members of our organization to bring about great change, we have to offer something more ennobling and meaningful than the money to pay your bills."

By engaging people in developing governing ideas for their organizations, you raise their sights. "When you elevate the discussion to a question of their broader purpose and mission, the mechanical tasks people perform take on a higher calling," says Ross. "This inspires and energizes."

It helps organizations shift from bureaucratic control to employee self-control. When compelling ideas rule, bosses don't have to micromanage employee behavior. In other words, winning minds goes hand in hand with employee empowerment.

When Walt Credle arrived in Hampton, he was shocked by the autonomy he had. He assumed that Bob O'Neill or one of his assistant city managers would start telling him what to do.

> *I kept waiting for the phone to ring. You wait for somebody to call up and raise Cain about something. But after weeks, the phone didn't ring. I started thinking I was out of the loop, that there was something wrong here. It took me months to become accustomed to the fact that Bob's approach was to say, "You're the director, if you need something, call me." It was a huge culture shock for me.*

New governing ideas have real power when they become part of peoples' mental models: the rational part of their paradigms. The authors of *The Fifth Discipline Fieldbook* describe mental models as "images, assumptions, and stories which we carry in our minds of ourselves, other people, institutions, and every aspect of the world." Mental models are the rational frameworks on which our inner world

Tools for Winning Minds

Surfacing the Givens is a group exercise in which people identify the unspoken, often unconscious assumptions that shape their system or organization, then discuss which of those assumptions need to change.

Benchmarking Performance compares the performance of different organizations to dislodge outdated mental models by undermining faith in the old ways of doing business.

Site Visits give people a chance to see, feel, and touch organizations that exhibit the culture, behavior, and results leaders want. This helps dislodge their old mental models and introduce new ones.

Learning Groups change employees' minds by helping them learn new things together. The groups undertake disciplined study processes—identifying what they want to learn, who they will learn with, and what they will do with what they learn.

Creating a Sense of Mission uses a participatory process to develop a mission statement, thus giving an organization's members a widely shared understanding of its basic purpose.

Building Shared Vision gives employees pictures-in-words of the future they seek to create—their collective image of what the organization is there to accomplish.

Articulating Organizational Values, Beliefs, and Principles gives employees nonbureaucratic standards to guide their actions in the workplace.

Using New Language to replace the language of bureaucracy—phrases, ideas, metaphors, entire new vocabularies—gives employees touchstones that help them navigate the neutral zone and internalize the new culture.

In-House Schoolhouses give organizations the internal capacity to educate and train change agents to become carriers of the new culture.

Orienting New Members helps incoming employees understand the organization's mission, vision, and values—the basic mental models that are shared throughout the agency.

hangs. They are built up over time, shaped by our experiences, our emotional commitments, and our reasoning processes. They become lenses through which we see and interpret reality.

The process of shifting mental models can be sudden or gradual. For individuals, it is often sudden. Most of us have experienced the sensation of a sudden shift in paradigm—of the scales falling from our eyes. But for organizations the shift is usually gradual, because so many scales must fall from so many eyes.

USING ALL THREE APPROACHES

We realize that a person's experiences, emotions, and ideas are entwined, integrated aspects of their psyches. Separating them analytically is a useful but risky fiction. It allows us to develop a framework you can use to design a culture change strategy, but it runs the danger of overlooking the inseparable connections among the three. These three approaches are not like the approaches we have outlined under other strategies: you cannot choose one or two of them and hope to succeed. You will need all three.

Often reinventors identify with only one or two approaches, because of their own personalities and paradigms. The rationalists among us, who value analysis and reason above other things, instinctively focus on changing people's mental models—they work with people "from the neck up." The humanists focus on the emotional side, because they are most concerned with people's feelings; they "share the pain." Others try to change what people *do*—because they themselves are doers.

It doesn't matter where you start, as long as you incorporate all three approaches. You can provoke new habit-changing experiences and then help people adjust their emotional commitments and mental maps. Or you can help people change their emotional bonds, then help them develop new mental models and behaviors. Or you can shift peoples' thinking by introducing new ideas and winning allegiance to them, then help them adjust their emotions and actions.

Each of these three approaches impacts the others. But we believe that changing habits is the most powerful of the three, because getting people to do new things can most easily disrupt their existing mental models and emotional ties. It most forcefully creates dissonance—

provoking the endings that Bridges says are the first step in making cultural transitions.

LEADING CULTURAL TRANSITIONS: LESSONS LEARNED

The culture strategy begins in most organizations when a leader visibly signals a break with the existing culture. In fact, unless leaders proclaim and demonstrate their total, sustained commitment to changing the culture, little is likely to happen. An organization's people need good reason to let go of the old culture. In the past, they've been cowed by old-culture leaders. Why take the risk, they ask, if the leader hasn't demonstrated total commitment to the change?

The good news is that most organizational leaders are relatively free to act. They don't need permission from the political sector to break with the old culture. The only real constraint is their own predispositions. Many of them operate in a bureaucratic paradigm. It is difficult for them to step outside of that box.

That's why many organizations seeking cultural change often look for new leaders—someone not caught up in the old ways. Sometimes, however, an "insider" emerges—like Butch Marita, a lifer who learned how to get ahead in the bureaucratic culture while preserving his deep hatred of it. When he got a chance to run the Eastern Region of the National Forest Service, Marita pushed the culture strategy as well as the control strategy.

Often one leader is not enough. Teams of leaders form because so much energy is required to push on the many fronts of cultural change. In this case, too many cooks do not spoil the broth.

In general, people respond in three distinct ways to leaders' efforts to change the culture. Some rapidly embrace opportunities to change. They are *pioneers*. They want a new beginning and are ready to let go. They are motivated by a new vision or relationship, or by career opportunities. Usually no more than one-fifth of an organization's members are pioneers—and often far less.

Others—typically 5–10 percent of the organization—oppose changes. They don't want to let go of the past. They think the changes are wrongheaded, or they believe that their own economic or organizational interests are in jeopardy. They are *resisters*. Usually their opposition is passive, but sometimes they turn to sabotage.

The bulk of most people in organizations are *fence sitters*. They adopt a wait-and-see posture. They aren't ready to let go; they fear change and uncertainty; they suspect, as the saying goes, that "this, too, will pass." So why, they ask themselves, should they get on board?

Most of these straddlers are persuadable. Eventually, some will join the pioneers. Hampton's Kevin Gallagher started out as a fence sitter; he was skeptical about Bob O'Neill's efforts. But he became a pioneer when he found that O'Neill kept delivering on the changes he promised. Some fence sitters will stay neutral for as long as they can, and a few will become resisters.

Given this bell curve, the main tasks of leaders are to liberate the pioneers and convert the fence sitters. Adding fence sitters to the early pioneers builds a critical mass of people who come to act, feel, and think in new ways. They become the powerful seed of a new culture, which grows in the shell of the old culture. Eventually, the effect snowballs and overwhelms the old culture.

Sy Fliegel, the former deputy superintendent of Community School District 4 in East Harlem, tells a story that illustrates the effect on a group when a critical mass of its members adopt a new practice.

> *Scientists observing a Pacific island with fifty thousand rhesus monkeys saw them pulling fruit off trees and eating it. Then one mother washed a piece of fruit in the water before eating it. Slowly the other monkeys in her clan took up the practice, until there were nearly thirty monkeys washing before they ate. The practice spread, still at a slow rate, until the hundredth monkey began to wash his food before eating it. And at that point the entire population of fifty thousand monkeys rapidly adopted the technique.*

This conversion process can take several years. "I used to worry more that we were taking forever to operationalize these concepts," says Barry Crook, a former budget officer who helped push cultural change in Austin, Texas.

> *But as I have observed this process over and over again, it seems to me this is the way it gets done. . . . It takes a while for all those things to gel, for a consensus to be built around ideas and for a*

critical mass of the right people to enthusiastically get on board so you can move forward.

Our research has yielded a number of lessons that leaders should take to heart in changing their organization's culture.

A Dozen Lessons for Leaders of Cultural Transition

1. Don't control employees—involve them.
2. Model the behavior you want.
3. Make yourself visible.
4. Make a clear break with the past.
5. Unleash—but harness—the pioneers.
6. Get a quick shot of new blood—and a slow transfusion.
7. Drive out fear—but don't tolerate resistance.
8. Sell success—but don't make the new culture politically correct.
9. Communicate, communicate, communicate.
10. Bridge the fault lines in the organization.
11. Change administrative systems that reinforce bureaucratic culture.
12. Commit for the long haul.

---

1. Don't Control Employees—Involve Them.

The employees are not the enemy (except for a few resisters—see lesson 7). Leaders must not give in to the instinctive feeling that employees "tainted" by the culture are hopeless cases. And they must not interpret fence sitting as resistance.

An organization's people need a chance to change, not an order to do so. As Martin Levin and Mary Bryna Sanger write in *Making Government Work*, the trick is not to get people to do what you want them to do, but to get them to want to do it.

You do that with incentives, using the consequences strategy. But you also do it with the control strategy: you get employees involved. Give them projects they can own—projects that embody and build the new culture you want. In Visalia, California, for instance, one of the most successful culture-changing events during Ted Gaebler's tenure as city manager was an annual street fair. Teams of employees put together exhibits to explain to citizens what their agencies did. To draw residents, they staged a one-day fair in the center of town, with food and crafts booths, a chili cook-off, a string of special events, and a dance that lasted until 2:00 A.M. Some 25,000 people turned out. It so thoroughly captured the teamwork and entrepreneurial spirit Gaebler was trying to build that he gave bonuses to the teams that created it.

"There is no such thing as going too far in trying to involve staff," says Steve Banyard, head of the Change Management Team for the U.K. Inland Revenue agency. "If employees don't get involved, they will feel suspicious, they will be alienated, and they will not own the change."

Keep wooing the fence sitters with opportunities to participate, as Bob O'Neill did in Hampton. Recognize that they expect—even hope—that leaders will give up. Then prove them wrong. Alleviate their fear and anxiety about trying new things; give them small, relatively safe chances to explore change. And make them welcome—no matter how long they have been on the fence before coming over. "Accept all converts," says David Couper, the former police chief of Madison, Wisconsin.

2. Model the Behavior You Want.

People will only trust leaders who walk their talk—figuratively and literally. The leader must come as close as possible to modeling the new culture, because every misstep will be read by employees as a sign of lack of commitment to the change. When President Clinton met with 400 federal employees at a 1993 conference on total quality management, their top recommendation for spreading TQM was to "train top down." In other words, make sure the organization's leaders understand it and do it before anyone else must.

In 1993, Don Sargeant, chancellor of the Crookston campus of the University of Minnesota, faced a major challenge. The university president had let Sargeant know he wanted to close Crookston, a two-year agricultural school. Sargeant pleaded—successfully—for a chance to prove the value of his campus. He hired the Public Strategies Group and began a strategic planning process to reposition the school.

To survive, Crookston needed to differentiate itself from other campuses. Sargeant and his staff developed a vision of a four-year technology-based institution. "But he couldn't get everyone to understand it," remembers PSG's Peter Hutchinson, "until he hit on the idea of laptop computers for every student.

> *We spent a lot of time with them on the question of value—the difference between cost, price, and value. We convinced them that if they made this transformation they could raise the price. This drove people crazy. They said, "Enrollment's falling, you can't raise the price!"*
>
> *Sargeant said, "We're gonna die unless we do something radical." So he went out and leased computers, and gave them to students, by imposing a technology fee of about $250 a quarter. This was a big increase in price—about 25 percent—and people thought this was lunatic. He had to go to the Regents twice, to get approval to spend $10 million to buy the machines.*

When Sargeant finally got the second approval, on a Friday afternoon, the students had already been in class for two days. So he faxed the order to IBM, in North Carolina. "Then we had to find a trucker coming from North Carolina," he says. "We found a trucker, got him to pick up the computers on Saturday morning in North Carolina. When he got to the Wisconsin line he called me." It was about 6:00 P.M. on Sunday, and he was six hours away.

> *So I called about five or six people to come and meet me about 2:30 in the morning, and we started unloading these computers. Then I organized a group to come in at eight o'clock, including four or five people from IBM, to distribute them to the students. We had a list of the students, all 900 or so, and we used a highlighter. Somehow they knew the computers were there. We had people unboxing the computers, writing the serial numbers down, and giving them to the students. By 5:00 P.M., we had 90 percent of them out—and we hadn't even sent a notice out that they were there.*

That story is still a legend among some people at Crookston. What impact did it have on the culture? "Hey," Sargeant told us when we asked him that question, "the leadership has to be committed." This event communicated to everyone that their leader was very, very committed and very hands-on. It modeled the behavior he wanted.

*I'm committed, and the employees know it. I take every training
session, I use my computer every day. There's a couple of other
institutions that have come close to what we've done, and I see that
the quality of what they're getting is about half of what's possible,
and the reason is that there's not as much direct involvement of the
leadership. The secret isn't that leaders know so much—I only
know enough to be dangerous—but if you just get in there and
muck it up with the employees, then you get a lot done.*

Despite the tuition increase, Sargeant's gamble paid off. By 1996 the
computer fee was up to $900 a year (on top of tuition of $3,000). But
full-time enrollment had jumped 22 percent, and student satisfaction
had soared. The number of high school students taking courses on
campus, through Minnesota's Postsecondary Enrollment Options program, had jumped *tenfold*.

Many leaders find that practicing their new-culture preaching is a
trying experience. "For most persons in command positions," write
David Couper and Sabine Lobitz in *Quality Policing*, "it is a process of
'unlearning' all that they know about leadership." In addition to letting
go of certain controls, leaders must react appropriately to critical
incidents or organizational crises. At these times, especially, the entire
organization is watching. If leaders rush to assign blame, or blow up
inappropriately, or act before they know all the facts, they are likely to
spread fear throughout the organization and undermine the culture they
are trying to build.

3. Make Yourself Visible.

As Sargeant demonstrated, it helps if leaders are willing to put their
bodies on the line. Call it "management by walking around" or "being
visible"—the point is to be *out there* with people of the organization,
not in the front office. You cannot delegate this.

Obviously, this requires a great deal of time, especially when the
agency's "empire" is a large one. When Derek Volker ran Australia's
Social Security Department, he was in charge of 300 regional offices
spread around a nation nearly as big as the U.S. "Getting around the
troops is crucial," says Volker. "You've got to get out there and see
what the feeling is. You'll always find that there is a lot of worry about
ongoing change which you can easily drive into the ground." He and

his top lieutenants shared responsibility for visiting the offices at least once every two years.

Region 9 of the U.S. Forest Service extends from Maine to Minnesota and Missouri. Yet every year, Butch Marita visited each of the region's more than 100 ranger districts. The first time he toured the region, it lasted for months. "We rented a motor home and spent eight weeks going around and talking about what was going on," says Jim Jordan, a deputy in the region. "It was an extremely important step for us because it really gave us that condensed look at every one of our units."

4. Make a Clear Break with the Past.

Leaders must send a loud, clear, unmistakable signal that they are initiating culture change. This should happen once they have deciphered what the old culture is and what they want to build in its place.

New leaders often choose to send the message immediately. "You get one window, and if you don't go through it, you're done," says Evan Doubelle, former chancellor of San Francisco City College. In his inaugural speech to employees on November 5, 1990, Doubelle challenged the institution's old, unruly culture:

The games that people play every day and every way now are over. No more rumor; no more mind games; no more misconception; no more half truths; no more accepting less than the best. From now on, it's going to be leadership by empowerment, by honesty and by passion. If you find joy in domination and believe that leadership means control, do me a favor—type a letter of reassignment, date it March 15 and let me sign it today. You'll save us both a very unhappy five months.

When Peter Hutchinson began running the Minneapolis schools, he wanted to signal the advent of a culture in which leaders listened to the schools and served them. Right away, he began to visit each of the district's 100 schools and 7,000 employees.

I wanted to try to touch every classroom, every employee. It was a campaign—door to door, room to room, child to child; reading books, talking to custodians, meeting principals. And listening, real hard listening.

This went on for three months nonstop. It was backbreaking. Almost no meetings were in the central office. . . . Meetings first thing in the morning, last thing at night.

But the signals got through. People recognized that something new was in the air, Hutchinson says.

It was completely different from what people were expecting and experiencing. They could have a voice. They could get right to the person that they think has the answers.

5. Unleash—but Harness—the Pioneers.

Pioneers are always in a hurry. They rush to embrace the new culture; they rush to get other people on board. The trick is to channel their energy. Don't just encourage and reward them and turn them loose—plan how to use them to change the organization's culture. Use them to generate early successes that you can market to the rest of the organization. Put them in positions where they can change the culture in their part of the organization. Assign them to redesign the organization's systems and to run important projects. Teach them how to help other employees make the cultural transition. Groom them for leadership, and promote them.

General Creech was a master at this at the Tactical Air Command. In 1981, he added Michael Loh to his headquarters operation at Langley Air Force Base. An engineer and operations expert, Loh studied in Creech's classes on leadership and organizations. He fit in well. "Creech was looking for guys who were smart and could expand his philosophy," says Loh. "I understood his philosophy, I understood his concept of decentralization down to the working level very, very well."

Creech gave Loh a long leash. "He gave me great latitude in laying out plans and making recommendations on how to get things done," says Loh. About ten years later, long after Creech's retirement, Loh got Creech's job at Langley. And he launched a new wave of culture-changing activities throughout the organization.

When David Couper began changing the culture of the Madison, Wisconsin, police department, he used promotions to reward pioneers and send signals to his organization. "Who gets promoted sends a louder message than any words from management," he later wrote. In March 1987, Couper sent a memo to all employees declaring that in the future he would only promote "people who have strong interpersonal and facilitative skills, and who [are] ... totally committed to the mission of the organization, able to work in a team, be a coach, accept feedback, ask and listen to others on the team, facilitate employee input . . ."

6. Get a Quick Shot of New Blood—and a Slow Transfusion.

If you don't have enough early pioneers, bring in some people who already carry the new culture. If you don't have vacancies, create room by offering old-culture employees attractive exit routes, such as early-retirement incentives and severance packages. You can also use consultants, loaned executives, or partnerships with businesses or other public agencies to inject fresh blood into your organization. But above all, make sure your key positions are occupied by true believers who are permanent employees. If possible, promote employees who embrace the new approach into these jobs.

Robbie Stokes, director of leisure services in the London borough of Bromley, is a leader of what Bromley calls its "customer revolution." His department was the first in Bromley to win a coveted Charter Mark for outstanding customer service. When he took over in 1989, Stokes says, "I took the view that the best way to effect change quickly was to bring in new people at the higher level." Within about six months, he had laid off most of the organization's managers and brought in 30 new ones.

A shot in the arm is good for the short run, but you will also need a slow transfusion of new blood. The key here is your recruiting and hiring process. Employee turnover is a slow but steady opportunity to bring in people receptive to the new culture.

"You really have to pay attention when it's time to hire people," says Ed James, assistant city manager in Sunnyvale. "That's probably your biggest opportunity right there: when you bring somebody on board. Are they going to flourish here? Are they going to take this stuff and run?" Sunnyvale's leaders hired an industrial psychologist to interview and profile applicants, to see if they would fit well in the bottom-line, results-oriented culture they were building.

Change who you're looking for, where you look for them, and the way you screen them. Make clear to applicants what the culture will be like and what it will take to succeed. And aggressively use a probationary period to check out the "incoming."

Unattended, the opportunity to hire new blood can become a liability. Every time you hire someone who carries the traditional bureaucratic culture you signal the troops that you don't consider cultural change that important.

7. Drive Out Fear—but Don't Tolerate Resistance.

Fear is in the air of most bureaucratic organizational cultures. Managers routinely use fear of repercussions to control employees. People are afraid to say what's on their minds or to try new things. They are afraid of being criticized or of making mistakes. They are even afraid of trying to change what they are afraid of.

Leaders must take responsibility for breaking the cycle of fear, because no one else can. They must publicly identify the invisible fears; root out management behaviors that create and perpetuate fears; and encourage and model new behaviors.

The best antidote to fear is information. Let employees know everything you can about the change process you plan. Make the unfamiliar familiar right from the start. In the U.K., for example, the Surrey County Council published and distributed to employees "Your Guide to Management of Change"—a 31-page booklet that described the changes under way and planned; how they would affect employees and their jobs; how they would affect the public; and how employees could get help with managing the effects of change.

Leaders should also use positive incentives to reward the kind of behavior they want and protect risk takers by tolerating their mistakes. At the same time, leaders must figure out how to deal with people who resist making a transition to a new culture. Every organization has a few "blockers" and "saboteurs." They won't let go of the old ways. In the hallways and bathrooms, they badmouth the new direction. They don't participate in new activities. They wage guerrilla warfare against change.

Leaders are often tempted to ignore this problem, because it seems relatively small. But leaving resisters alone can do severe damage. It undercuts the leader's signals to the organization's fence sitters: if resistance is tolerated, then maybe the leader isn't really serious about change. It poisons the atmosphere for those who do take on the difficult transition to a new culture. And, when resisters are supervisors, it may prevent those who report to them from participating in the transition.

In the Eastern Region of the Forest Service, leaders worried that punishing resisters smacked of old-culture behavior. "If you jump in to remove someone or try to make the change faster than that person is going to change," says Jim Jordan, "then you're perceived as reverting to the old way of doing business—just hammer the hell out of 'em if they don't agree. [This] is counter to what we're trying to do in saying, 'You can be open, you can make some mistakes, and you can go on and learn from those.' "

So Jordan and his colleagues made a common mistake: they repeatedly gave resisters "one more chance." And they paid the price. "We've been overly conservative in intervening in situations where we probably should have been in earlier," says Jordan.

Practically every leader we talked with has the same lament: they wish they had been quicker to deal with resisters. The humane solution to resistance is not to turn a blind eye. It is to make it clear that resistance will not be tolerated, then offer exit routes—transfers, reassignment, early retirement, severance, or outplacement—to those who continue to resist.

The best policy is to give people one chance, then move them out, says General Michael Loh of the Air Combat Command. "I'm mostly talking about the middle managers and senior managers and leaders. Those that won't buy in at that level are the ones who you really need to get rid of."

This is *not* old-culture behavior. In bureaucratic cultures, leaders typically pressure resisters but never move them out. In the Tactical Air Command, for instance, General Creech's predecessors were known for their "merciless browbeatings," as author James Kitfield puts it. When Creech took over this behavior stopped. But his subordinates soon noticed that "Creech was in his temperate and reasoned fashion giving an inordinate number of officers the ax."

You don't have to fire all the resisters; only a few. The others will see you are serious and either get on board or take one of your exit routes.

8. Sell Success—but Don't Make the New Culture Politically Correct.

Success builds success. When fence sitters see pioneers succeed because they have embraced the new culture, it makes them more willing to follow.

"Once you get some people buying in and understanding [the new culture], you publicize those excessively, you get the word out," says former ACC commander Michael Loh. To accomplish this, leaders use an array of communications methods: internal newsletters, annual reports, awards ceremonies, local cable television channels, and so on.

Vice President Gore regularly visits federal reinvention labs that are making progress. National Performance Review staffers precede the vice president, find a big success story, videotape it, and show the videos to the department secretary at a town meeting, in front of the employees. Then they bring the people responsible for the initiative up onstage with Gore and the secretary and give them a "Hammer Award," for their efforts to smash bureaucracy.

When Clive Corlett, CEO of the U.K.'s Inland Revenue, visits units, he listens to presentations on their change efforts. The events "reinforce the message that what they are doing is right," he says. "Other people who are coming more slowly see that you are endorsing the people who are taking the initiative."

But rewarding success should go on every day, not just when the top banana visits. "You need to reward the behavior when it happens— say, 'That's what we want, you're hitting it now, this is what we meant,' " explains Ed James, assistant city manager of Sunnyvale. "And you need to point out what is not appropriate behavior. And that is just day in and day out, living and breathing it."

You can go overboard marketing success. When you do, you run the risk of creating a new political correctness in the organization, rather than an open dialogue. People learn to mouth the leader's mantras when the leader is around, but once he or she is out of sight, they say what they really think. Instead of honestly discussing differences, they just comply—the old behavior pattern.

Even as they sell success, leaders must honor honest disagreement and stimulate constructive discussions. They must be serious about making change, but not deadly serious. They should not punish employees who criticize or poke fun at the change.

They should also keep widening the circle of acclaim. If they lavish praise on a select group of superstars, some in the organization will view them as the leader's "boys" and will see the leader as playing favorites. Others will feel that they can never be as good as the superstars, so they won't try. The solution is to showcase the achievements of fence sitters whenever they step forward and embrace change.

9. *Communicate, Communicate, Communicate*

Every reinventor we know says the same thing: you cannot communicate too much. The less employees know about your change strategy, the more likely they are to perceive it as a threat. The more they know, the more comfortable they will feel. "I've found that no matter what you say, you have to say it over and over and over again," says Joe Thompson, who runs the Veterans Affairs regional office in New York City.

Twice a year I'll meet with all the employees in small groups—I'll spend a couple of weeks, go through everything I know that's going on, and answer all their questions. You just have to keep doing it.

Common Excuses for Not Communicating

Many leaders latch onto rationales for not communicating with employees, says William Bridges. In *Managing Transitions*, he exposes some of the most common:

"1. *They don't need to know yet. We'll tell them when the time comes. It'll just upset them now.* For every week of upset that you avoid by hiding the truth, you gain a month of bitterness and mistrust. Besides, the grapevine already has the news, so don't imagine that your information is a secret.

"2. *They already know. We announced it.* OK, you told them, but it didn't sink in. Threatening information is absorbed remarkably slowly. Say it again. And find different ways to say it and different media (large meetings, one-on-ones, memos, a story in the company paper) to say it.

"3. *I told the supervisors. It's their job to tell the rank and file.* The supervisors are likely to be in transition themselves, and they may not even sufficiently understand the information to convey it accurately. Maybe they're still in denial. Information is power, so they may not want to share it yet. . . .

"4. *We don't know the details ourselves, so there's no point in saying anything until everything has been decided.* In the meantime, people can get more and more frightened and resentful. Much better to say what you do know, say that you don't know more, and tell what kind of schedule exists for additional information. . . ."

*And you have to do some of it directly. There is no substitute for
that. Well-intentioned people will not say what you want to say just
the way you would say it.*

Nor will they say it with your emotional commitment—which is
perhaps the most important thing employees need to see.

Inland Revenue, the U.K. version of the IRS, learned this lesson the
hard way. A 65,000-person organization with 800 offices, it launched a
massive, ten-year change effort to reengineer its basic processes in
1991. Two years later its leaders surveyed their employees. What they
heard shocked them. "A lot of people didn't understand what was
going on, were not happy with it, and weren't getting a clear message,"
says Director General Clive Corlett. The message was being distorted
on the way down, and people were hearing a lot of rumors. They were
particularly worried about downsizing.

Leaders underestimated the difficulty of communicating to an organization with 800 offices, Corlett says, as well as the necessity of
spending a lot of time face-to-face with people. "People at the top of
the organization have to get out and spend a lot of time talking with
people, being seen," he concluded. They also have to make sure their
top managers get the message and pass it on.

Once they understood this, Corlett and his colleagues started over.
They launched a huge communications campaign to help everyone
understand their vision, plus a "team listening" effort to make sure
they were hearing what people said in response. Their first step was to
involve hundreds of people in developing a mission statement.

10. Bridge Fault Lines in the Organization.

Government organizations are not monolithic. Indeed, they are
divided along many occupational, social, and economic lines: civil
service lifers versus short-time political appointees; administrators
versus professionals versus technicians versus support staff; labor
union officials versus managers; young, upwardly mobile managers
versus "peaked out" managers nearing retirement; men versus
women; blacks versus whites versus browns.

These fault lines often lead to tensions. The leader must be inclusive;
culture building is not like trying to win 51 percent of the vote in an
election. Leaders should personally reach across the organizational
lines—and down into its ranks. They should identify the stresses and

develop processes for creating better understanding and relationships across the lines.

11. Change Administrative Systems that Reinforce a Bureaucratic Culture.

We cannot emphasize this lesson enough. Bureaucratic administrative systems—personnel, purchasing, budgeting, planning, and auditing—send powerful signals that undercut a leader's efforts to move the organization through a cultural transition.

Bob O'Neill's experience in Hampton was typical—he had to change the city's compensation system to make it an enabler of, not a barrier to, the new culture. Working in the Forest Service, Butch Marita went after his organization's budget system. In Madison, David Couper started by changing the procurement system, which his employees despised.

There is no way around this problem. Sooner or later, these systems must be changed. What Michael Hammer and James Champy, authors of *Reengineering the Corporation*, write about the private sector goes for government, too:

> *Unfortunately, too many managers still believe that all they have to do to shape their employees' belief systems is to articulate some high-sounding values and then make speeches about them. . . . Without supporting management systems, most corporate value statements are collections of empty platitudes that only increase organizational cynicism. To be worth the paper it's printed on, a value statement must be reinforced by the company's management systems.*

12. Commit for the Long Haul.

Because cultural change is a slow process, leaders must commit for the long haul—and they must make that commitment very public. Otherwise, the fence sitters will worry that when leaders leave—which, in employees' minds, always could be soon—the next boss will dismantle the new culture. And the resisters will know they can outlast you.

There are no exceptions to this rule. It takes five to ten years to transform a bureaucratic culture. If you are not willing to stay for this long, you'd better make sure that your successor is fully committed to your culture strategy—and that the employees know it.

When Butch Marita, Jim Jordan, and Larry Payne decided to change the Forest Service's culture, they knew they were getting into a long-term commitment. "Between the three of us we had 80 years of experience," says Jordan.

We knew this outfit; we'd worked every level of the organization. We felt we had enough knowledge to say that this organization was not going to make change easily. The culture was so strong. If we attempted to make this kind of change, we had to be in it for the long haul. We made a career decision: that as long as we were around, we were going to be involved in making this change come about.

QUESTIONS PEOPLE ASK ABOUT
THE CULTURE STRATEGY

Q. Should all types of government organizations develop more entre-preneurial cultures?

Yes, but the degree to which they should become entrepreneurial depends upon their function. In compliance and regulatory agencies, for example, a cultural focus on customization may not be appropriate. When the police or courts enforce the law, they should be consistent, treating everyone alike. On the other hand, compliance agencies can learn to focus more on problem solving and continuous improvement. The police department in Madison, Wisconsin, developed a culture based on improving quality, preventing crime, and building strong relations with the community. In Minnesota, the Department of Revenue decided to win the voluntary compliance of taxpayers, rather than simply enforcing the tax code. This change required agency employees to think more entrepreneurially about how to assist taxpayers. The Internal Revenue Service and Inland Revenue in the U.K. are making a similar shift in strategy.

Q. Can you change the culture in hard times—during budget cuts and downsizing?

Yes. The pressure to cut costs disrupts an organization's equilibrium, giving leaders openings for the growth of a new culture. It becomes easier to convince people that change is inevitable, and that the organization should be proactive, not reactive; it should determine what will change.

Leaders can also use new-culture values to help the organization get through the pain of reductions. When Phoenix's city government faced its first budget crunch in decades and had to lay off workers in the early 1990s, public leaders worked hard to help people get new jobs. Even though some people lost their jobs, proof of management's commitment to the well-being of employees drove overall employee satisfaction up.

When organizations are in a fiscal free-fall, however, it is much tougher to develop a new culture. People are so concerned about their economic survival and other basic needs that nothing else matters to them. In the Air Combat Command, employee surveys indicated significant cultural change—increased awareness of the organization's mission, increased teamwork and cooperation, and support for quality principles. But these trends were not visible among employees affected by the trauma of base closings.

Q. What is "organizational development"—OD—and does it work in government?

"OD" is a phrase used to describe a coherent set of diagnostic and prescriptive tools used to create healthier, better performing organizations. It was popular in the 1960s, 1970s, and early 1980s. During those years, organizational transformation efforts of all kinds were typically referred to as OD. Then TQM became the favored approach. Then reinvention swept in. Each concept has different emphases. Seen in light of the five C's, practitioners of OD tend to focus exclusively on control and culture, while TQM tends to limit itself to the customer, control, and culture strategies.

OD's tools were effective, but limited. The demands for change have grown stronger, the scope of changes that are needed has expanded, and practitioners have learned about other strategies, approaches, and tools. Although we have included some OD tools in the culture strategy, we find OD inadequate as a frame of reference for reinventors. It leaves out the most powerful forces for change: the core, customer, and consequences strategies.

Q. Does the size of the public organization affect the use of the culture strategy?

Massive organizations—such as the Air Combat Command—can make the transition to an entrepreneurial culture, but only if they are broken down into much smaller, largely autonomous units. Follow Bill Creech's central precept: think big, but organize small.

In school districts in New York City and other big cities, education reformers are applying this doctrine to big high school "factories" with thousands of students. In order to let go of bureaucratic culture and develop a "learning culture" in schools, they are breaking high schools up into smaller schools of no more than 300 to 400 students.

THE CULTURE STRATEGY'S BOTTOM LINE: PERSISTENCE AND COMMITMENT

The culture strategy is not like the other four C's. It has much less leverage, for one thing. For all we have written in this chapter, the best way to change your culture is still to use the other C's. When you introduce enterprise management, managed competition, or customer quality assurance, your culture will change.

Still, there will come a day when you discover that the first four C's are not enough. Craig Holt, who spent eight years reinventing the Oregon Department of Transportation, says it well.

I think people get excited, start implementing, and then they see it starting to get tough, because they're hitting the culture. So they start looking for another direction instead of just slogging through it. That's where a lot of people fail. They hit the culture, and they go looking for another way, rather than beating on it and beating on it and beating on it. All doors lead to it.

A second critical difference is that the culture strategy requires extraordinary persistence, as Holt implies. There are no home runs hidden in the culture tools. They produce only walks and singles, and you will need dozens of them to win the game. Because culture change is a retail process, in which you must convert people one by one, there is no one lever that changes everything. "Culture isn't one thing," says Peter Hutchinson. "It's everything."

Doug Farbrother, who has spent 15 years working on culture change at the Defense Department and the National Performance Review, describes the challenge this way:

There are 30 things you should do and you ought to try them all. The brain is mysterious, and it's hard to say what's going to resonate with one person. I guess my observation is it just takes a long time. And in most cases you don't see a dramatic shift—it takes repeated exposures for most people.

Veterans Affairs' Joe Thompson, one of the most successful reinventors in the U.S. federal government, has a similar message:

There's no one thing and there's no short-term thing. The only thing I know that works is total commitment and unbelievable patience. It just takes time. There are a lot of techniques that you can apply along the way, but the sustained change only comes with patience and determination. Most of those I have seen that have struggled—it's usually because they gave up too soon. They run into a little difficulty, and the tendency is to back off and not see it through.

Ultimately, success and failure in culture change will come down to the quality of your leadership. If your leaders are committed; if they are willing to stick it out; if they are willing to invest the time it takes to communicate their vision; and if they can prove themselves to their employees; they can succeed. "I couldn't push commitment enough," says Thompson.

Not just that you're committed, but that your people know that. I don't think they'll go any further than they know you're committed to going. Because all of it involves risk. If you're changing the organization and the pay system and everything else, there's an enormous risk for them. And they won't trust it if they don't think the managers are committed. They just can't let go enough, if they think the managers are in it for themselves, or if they suspect you're going to bail out.

Once you convince your employees that you are deeply committed, however—once they know you will put your entire career on the line for what you believe in—you will gain the power you need to shape their habits, hearts, and minds.

Bill Creech's first command, back in the 1950s, was of an aerial demonstration unit called the Skyblazers—the European version of the Thunderbirds, for whom he had flown. He loved the precision of their supersonic barrel rolls, loops, and other maneuvers—four planes doing acrobatics as one, wingtip to wingtip. It was there that he learned his most important lessons about trust and empowerment and teamwork. In his four years as leader of the Skyblazers, the unit never lost a plane or pilot.

A quarter of a century later, in Creech's early years at TAC, the Thunderbirds suffered a tragedy. James Kitfield tells the story in his book, *Prodigal Soldiers*:

> *A Thunderbird flight lead drove his aircraft into the ground, followed in split-second succession by three other aircraft in his flight. It was the third major accident for the Thunderbirds that year, one more example of Nevada Freestyle in the minds of many, and it led to a movement inside the Pentagon to disband the flight team forever.*
>
> *To save the Thunderbirds, Creech had driven from Langley to Washington, D.C., to personally promise the Air Force leadership and Congress that if the Thunderbirds suffered so much as one more accident, he would hand in his resignation. He had then gathered the Thunderbirds together to talk in a very reasoned way about the value of adult supervision, and there had been steel in his voice and new admiration in his audience.*

This level of commitment was at the heart of Creech's success. The Thunderbirds had no more tragedies on his watch. And the governing ideas Creech instilled penetrated TAC to its core. A dozen years later, TAC put on a performance in the Gulf War that dazzled even its own leaders. Kitfield's book, the story of the military's return to glory after the debacle of Vietnam, is told in part through the eyes of Gulf War Air Commander Chuck Horner—a daredevil pilot who had long resisted Creech and his doctrine of quality, accountability, and empowerment. Horner's Gulf War saga ends this way:

> *"How did we do this?" Horner said, looking over at Hal Hornburg. The subtext needed no explanation. Tactics that anticipated the threat, pilots trained to fight on the first day of a war, technology and tactics that leveraged lives, unprecedented operationalreadiness figures for their aircraft. Above all, the synergism that was created by the combination of all of those things. "How did we make all this come together?"*

Both men looked at each other. The answer was there in the emphasis on high technology and precision-guided munitions, just as it was there in the port-o-toilets the Air Force used in the desert while the Army was digging holes in the dirt. The name came to their lips almost at the same moment, and they shook their heads in unison. "Creech."

The staying power of the culture Creech had instilled is even more striking in the story Kitfield chooses to close his book. Horner, a rumpled, hard-drinking man, had initially detested Creech's fanaticism about spotless facilities and equipment. But as the book closes, he is on the phone with a friend who has gone to work for the Military Airlift Command:

"John, I was flying on one of your airplanes the other day, and I noticed where someone had leaned back in their seat and left these dirty old boot prints on the ceiling of your airplane," Horner said.
  "You noticed what?"
  Horner knew he sounded like some raving anal retentive, but he didn't give a damn. Everyone in Air Force blue could mouth slogans such as "total quality management" and was happy to faithfully repeat the rhetoric about pride in ownership. Somehow Chuck Horner had to make the man see how it all came down to a pair of dirty footprints on a ceiling.

– III –

USING THE STRATEGIES

– 9 –

ALIGNING THE STRATEGIES

In 1988, when Margaret Thatcher's government began creating Next Steps agencies, a member of Parliament asked her if these new agencies would be exempt from her privatization program. She answered that Next Steps was "primarily about those operations which are to remain within Government." But, she added, "I cannot rule out that after a period of years Agencies, like other Government activities, may be suitable for privatization. Where there is a firm intention of privatization when an Agency is being set up, this should be made clear."

As it created executive agencies, the Next Steps Team made it clear that if they were not being actively considered for privatization, they would be given a number of years to "settle down" before the issue was raised again. The policy was sufficiently vague that most agency civil servants breathed a sigh of relief, assuming their organizations had dodged the bullet.

Then, in November 1991, John Major's government released its "Competing for Quality" white paper. It announced, among other things, that agencies would periodically be put on trial for their lives. Before negotiating a new framework document every three years (later changed to every five years), departments would conduct a prior options review—investigating whether the agency or pieces of it should be abolished, sold, contracted out, or moved to another organization.

This new initiative wreaked havoc with morale in the agencies. Most civil servants found it "threatening and offensive," says John Oughton, who ran the Efficiency Unit. Many saw it as a downright betrayal. It undermined employee confidence and slowed the pace of improvement in some agencies for several years.

To transform public institutions, we have argued, leaders must use most or all of the five strategies we have described. Reinventors in the U.K., New Zealand, Phoenix, Hampton, and the Air Combat Command have used all five strategies, while their counterparts in Australia, Sunnyvale, and Indianapolis have used three or four of the five. Along the way, however, these reinventors have also learned that they must be careful to unfold their strategies in ways that create synergy rather than conflict. They must avoid what happened to the British, who undermined the Next Steps initiative by unleashing privatization in the midst of their efforts to create executive agencies.

Knowing how to sequence and coordinate the strategies for optimal results is an important part of the craft of reinvention. The Canadian Auditor General's Office emphasized this point in 1995, when it compared Canada's lackluster track record with the successes of New Zealand:

> *The wider international experience . . . illustrates that a significant reform program, to be successful, must jell as an integral whole; the pieces must come together. Some governments have succeeded in putting the pieces together reasonably well; others have not. The international experience also makes clear that coherence and consistency in a major reform program are unlikely to be forthcoming without a strong and sustained commitment from political leaders. Perfunctory political commitment will not suffice.*

To optimize implementation of the strategies, you must anticipate how they will affect each other, and how they will work together most powerfully. Although in this book we have separated them conceptually, in practice things are not so neat: the strategies sometimes overlap, and some tools use more than one strategy. Some strategies naturally go together, almost like matched sets. Our research identified the following patterns of alignment.

1. When you use the core strategy to uncouple steering and rowing, also use the consequences and control strategies to transform the behavior of rowing organizations.

It is useful to separate steering and rowing functions, because organizations can then focus more clearly on their purposes. But you will have much greater impact if you then give these organizations control over their own resources and incentives for improving their performance. Reinventors in New Zealand and the United Kingdom understood this well. As they uncoupled functions, they used the flexible performance framework metatool to incorporate the consequences and control strategies into their plan. (See below, pp. 306–307.)

2. Use the consequences and control strategies as a matched pair; don't use one without the other.

The consequences strategy puts intense pressure on organizations to improve. But they cannot do so if they are bound up in rules and red tape. If employees don't have the power to change how their organizations work, they can't improve performance—they can only complain when they face the risks of not performing well.

Similarly, giving employees more power without creating consequences for their performance makes little sense. As we explained in chapter 7, the control strategy should replace centralized, hierarchical controls, which dictate what organizations and employees do with their resources, with clear goals and incentives.

In New Zealand, departments that were not corporatized were given two years to develop acceptable output measures that could be used for performance agreements. Only then were they released from central controls. "This avoided the danger of removing input controls without having the new system for output control in place," says Graham Scott, who as Treasury secretary helped engineer New Zealand's organizational empowerment.

> The risk was a real one. Some chief executives tried to gain excessive freedoms through vague output definitions. In one case a department sought to have only one output for a huge and complex government agency. The result would have been no control whatsoever.

3. When you make organizations accountable to their customers, also create consequences for their performance and give them control.

If public organizations want customer service standards to be effective, they should introduce rewards and penalties for employees' success or failure in meeting those standards. Otherwise, the standards will provide only temporary motivation for improving service.

To get and sustain employees' attention, you need to give them financial and psychic rewards when they produce high levels of customer satisfaction. The same lesson applies when organizations offer their customers more choices. As we said in chapter 6, choice without consequences—though fairly common—is weak. The best way to put teeth into choice is to add competition for customers' dollars.

For the reasons discussed under number 2 above, it makes no sense to do this if you cannot give managers and employees the freedom they need to make dramatic changes in the way they do business.

4. When you use the core strategy to improve steering, also use performance management (the consequences strategy) to translate the outcomes you want into goals for rowing organizations.

To improve your aim you must establish clear goals for government. Once they are set, you must then get public organizations to pay attention to them. The best way to do this is by introducing consequences for achieving the goals. Performance budgeting ties budget allocations to the goals, while performance management rewards or penalizes organizations and employees for their performance in meeting the goals. One without the other is incomplete: to be effective, a performance system should start with outcome goals and move down through output and process goals for every unit and employee, in a way that links the smallest job to the most ambitious long-term goal.

5. Don't bother trying to develop an entrepreneurial culture without also shifting control to employees.

You can change your organizational culture without empowering your employees. As we noted in chapter 8 (see pp. 260–261), Sunnyvale had developed a hardworking, businesslike culture, but not—by the last time we visited—a culture in which employees constantly innovated. One reason was that Sunnyvale had not empowered most of its line employees. Because workers had little power to make decisions, they had little reason to dream up new ways to do their jobs. And the less they innovated, the less they developed the habits, commitments, and mind-sets of innovators.

In Hampton, by way of contrast, City Manager Bob O'Neill understood that empowerment and an entrepreneurial culture went hand in hand, because people's habits, hearts, and minds are heavily influenced by the bureaucratic controls that affect them. "If your locus of control and culture are in conflict, then whatever is the most powerful system will win," O'Neill says. Because the most powerful controls are the fiscal ones, "You have to change people's ability to allocate, get, and commit resources."

THE POWER OF METATOOLS

The simplest method to bring multiple strategies together in a coherent, complimentary way is to use a tool that brings two or three strategies into play at once. We call such instruments *metatools*.

We have identified a dozen metatools, although others undoubtedly exist—and still more will be invented in the years to come. Precisely because they bring multiple strategies into play at once, these metatools pack the greatest power in the reinventor's tool kit. They are reinvention's heavy hitters. If you want to make big changes, use them. Don't hesitate to use more than one: By our count, British reformers have used them all.

While powerful, most metatools also require the expenditure of

Metatool	*Strategy Used*
Performance Budgeting	Core, Consequences
Flexible Performance Frameworks	Core, Consequences, Control
Competitive Bidding	Core, Consequences
Corporatization	Core, Consequences, Customer, Control
Enterprise Funds	Core, Consequences, Customer, Control
Internal Enterprise Management	Core, Consequences, Customer, Control
Competitive Public Choice Systems	Consequences, Customer
Vouchers and Reimbursement Programs	Consequences, Customer
Total Quality Management	Customer, Control, Culture
Business Process Reengineering	Customer, Control, Culture
Opting Out or Chartering	Core, Consequences, Customer, Control
Community Governance Bodies	Core, Control

substantial resources, time, and political will. With the exception of total quality management, their implementation requires the permission and support of elected officials.

We will discuss each of these metatools at length in our next book.

Performance Budgeting

Policy makers use performance budgeting to specify the outcomes and outputs they intend to buy with each sum they appropriate. For example, cabinet ministers in New Zealand negotiate "purchase agreements" with department executives that detail the quantity, quality, and cost of an agency's deliverables. As we said in chapter 4, performance budgeting improves steering (core), because it requires policy makers to be very clear about what outputs and outcomes they are buying, and it allows them to see the results they are getting for their money.

This also creates consequences. It allows elected officials to check the performance of past expenditures before making further budget allocations. These officials should not automatically cut funding for organizations that perform poorly and increase funding for organizations that perform well. Indeed, sometimes they may decide that organizations are performing poorly precisely because they have *too little* money. In general, organizations should be rewarded or sanctioned for their performance not by increasing or decreasing their funds, but through enterprise management, managed competition, or the performance management tools outlined on page 146: bonuses, gainsharing, shared savings, and the like.

Over time, performance information should lead elected officials to shift money to programs that provide better value for the taxpayers' dollars. Hence performance budgeting should, in the long run, create consequences. But this is different from automatically raising or cutting budgets each year in response to performance levels.

Flexible Performance Frameworks

This metatool embodies the most common deal made by reinventors: a trade of flexibility for accountability. Reinventors in the United Kingdom and New Zealand pioneered it, but we have seen the same basic arrangement so many times that we have given it a name. It grows out of a basic demand for better performance. Reinventors often turn that impulse into performance contracts that spell out exactly what they expect each organization to accomplish and what the consequences will be if they succeed or fail. They quickly realize, however, that this is a bit like tying their managers' hands and then asking them to work harder. It won't work unless they liberate their managers, giving them freedom from cumbersome rules, red tape, and central administrative controls. If managers are not given flexibility, they can always blame their failures on lack of control over budgets, personnel, and other resources.

The solution, perhaps most clearly embodied in the British Next Steps initiative, is to hive off rowing functions into discrete organizations; create performance contracts that spell out the organizations' purposes, expected results, and consequences for performance; and give them management control over their resources.

A flexible performance framework can be applied to any public organization. New Zealand even applied this metatool to its policy advice organizations. (For more on flexible performance frameworks, see pp. 25–30, 83–85, and 99–102.)

Competitive Bidding

Indianapolis and the United Kingdom have used this metatool to great effect, as we described in chapter 5. It forces private vendors and (often) public organizations to compete to perform services. If they can deliver quality services for the lowest price, they win. If not, they suffer the consequences.

Competitive bidding also uses the core strategy. It uncouples rowing functions from steering functions, so that competitors who bid to perform the rowing are not burdened with the costs or problems of steering. Steering functions are usually exempted from competitive bidding, although discrete steering functions can also be competitively bid. For several decades, Arizona has competitively bid out the job of setting local mental health service priorities and contracting with providers to local governments and community organizations. These "administrative entities" then turn around and competitively bid out the actual service provision.

Competitive bidding does not require that governments decentralize control, but it usually creates pressure to do so. When public employees bid for work, they become intensely interested in controlling the factors that will determine their success. Hence competitive bidding creates the perfect opportunity to use the control strategy.

Corporatization

Corporatization turns government organizations into publicly owned businesses that are quasi-independent of government and must meet business bottom lines, such as maximizing profits and return on investment. It uses the core strategy to uncouple rowing functions that can be organized as public corporations, such as air traffic control, postal delivery, and forest land management.

Corporatization also forces organizations to get their revenues by making sales to customers, usually (but not always) in a competitive marketplace. Like businesses, they shrink or grow based on their performance. Finally, corporatization frees organizations from bureaucratic controls such as civil service systems and government budget and finance systems.

Because it brings four strategies into play—core, customer, consequences, and control—corporatization is a very powerful tool. As we discussed in chapter 5, however, it is only appropriate for services that can be charged to paying customers.

Enterprise Funds

A weaker form of enterprise management, enterprise funds are public organizations financed by customer revenues rather than tax dollars, but not organized as quasi-independent corporations. Like public corporations, they are accountable to their customers, but unlike public corporations, they do not have independent governance. They also bring the core, consequences, customer, and control strategies into play, but few enterprise funds are given as much freedom from central control as most public corporations. They normally operate within government personnel, procurement, and auditing systems.

Internal Enterprise Management

This is the application of enterprise-management tools to government's internal service units, such as print shops, computer services, and vehicle fleets. Internal enterprise management makes those internal services accountable to their customers, the line agencies they serve. It takes away most of their long-standing monopolies and transforms them into public business enterprises. Since their customers can choose whether and how much to buy from them, they must improve quality and prices in order to keep business. They also gain new freedoms: most internal enterprises are allowed to set their own prices (unless they remain monopolies) and develop new products and services as they see fit. Accordingly, their managers gain some autonomy from traditional centralized control systems. (For more, see chapter 5, pp. 137–139.)

Competitive Public Choice Systems

When enterprise management is not appropriate, reinventors can often still give customers a choice of service providers and make those providers compete for their income. This is what Minnesota did when it created interdistrict school choice, as we discussed in chapter 6. This forces providers to be responsive to their customers, and it creates consequences for their performance.

Vouchers and Reimbursement Programs

One way to maximize both accountability to the customer and performance consequences is to give customers vouchers (or credit cards that are backed by government reimbursement) to purchase goods or services such as housing, health care, child care, or even groceries. When providers must compete for their customers, this metatool combines the customer and consequences strategies.

Total Quality Management

TQM is one of the best known and most commonly used metatools. It has the power to help public organizations continuously, incrementally increase the quality of their services and compliance functions. It empowers, trains, and equips employees to redesign their work processes. In doing this, TQM combines three strategies:

- **Customer:** TQM is rooted in the belief that only the customer can define the quality an organization must achieve. It relies heavily on listening to the voice of the customer to set quality standards for services and products. As we noted in chapter 6, this is an important new competence for government. When done well, TQM also sets customer service standards, a central tool of customer quality assurance.

- **Control:** TQM empowers teams of employees to analyze, redesign, and monitor their own work processes. In short, they do work once reserved for managers. Indeed, the hallmark of a TQM organization is an abundance of teams working to improve many processes.

- **Culture:** In quality organizations, employees value their customers' needs; recognize the need to constantly adapt their work so they can satisfy their customers; and get into the habit of collaborating with one another. These habits help build strong, nonbureaucratic cultures.

Although TQM is a powerful metatool, its leverage to force widespread change is limited by the fact that it focuses mainly on work processes. Normally, it produces continuous, incremental improvement at the process and people levels, by changing work processes and cultures. If used systematically throughout an organization TQM can also have powerful effects at the organization level. But it rarely impacts administrative or governing systems.

Business Process Reengineering

BPR also focuses on improving work processes, but it does so by redesigning them from scratch, to produce dramatic increases in efficiency, effectiveness, and quality. Usually, reengineering eliminates or alters the work many people do and changes the organizational structure of functional divisions and units.

Developed in the private sector, this metatool was popularized by Michael Hammer and James Champy in the 1993 book *Reengineering the Corporation*. Like TQM, BPR engages the customer, control, and culture strategies. Typically, it also brings new information technologies into the redesign process. While TQM involves many modest improvement projects often occurring at the same time, BPR is a "big bang" tool. Reengineering projects usually focus on organizations' most important processes, and each one can take a year or more to complete. Hence BPR is a much more challenging tool, which can be used in far fewer situations. It requires significant political will and leadership, because it usually disrupts organizational life for hundreds of people.

Like TQM, reengineering rarely has leverage to bring changes at the governance and administrative system levels.

Opting Out or Chartering

This metatool allows an existing or new public organization to operate outside the jurisdiction of most government control systems. The best known examples are charter schools in the U.S. and grant-maintained schools in the U.K., which have in effect seceded from their districts. (See chapter 6, pp. 157–160, 169–170, and 175.) Opting out combines the core, control, customer, and consequences strategies. A charter school, for example, is uncoupled from its district; it is free of most rules and regulations; it must attract customers to earn its revenue; and it can grow, shrink, or die, depending upon how well it pleases its customers and fulfills the conditions of its charter. Because charter and opt-out policies engage four strategies and bring fundamental change at the governing and administration system levels, they are very powerful metatools.

Community Governance Bodies

A community governance body is a steering organization that is controlled by a community. An old and familiar example in the U.S. is an elected school board. More recent examples are the progress boards sprouting up in Oregon and other states (described in chapter 4), which set long-term goals for their states or communities. More limited examples include Chicago's local school councils and the U.K.'s school governing bodies. Made up primarily of community members, both elected and appointed, they play the steering role at individual schools.

This metatool can improve steering (core) while empowering communities (control). Because it does not engage the powerful consequences and customer strategies, however, this is one of the weaker metatools.

ALIGNING STRATEGIES AND
ADMINISTRATIVE SYSTEMS

Strategies not only need to be aligned with one another to be effective, they need to be aligned with administrative systems. If you try to reinvent a governing system or organization without changing its administrative systems, you will fail. The budget, personnel, procurement, and auditing systems will constantly undermine your strategies, because they will continue to reward—even demand—bureaucratic behavior.

Administrative systems are like the systems that keep an organism alive: the circulatory, nervous, musculoskeletal, respiratory, and organ systems. They are not the DNA; their form is dictated by the DNA. They carry out the work of the DNA, by shaping and maintaining the organism. Government's administrative systems were grown from bureaucratic DNA, so they shape bureaucratic organizations.

If you want to embed the five C's in your organizations, you *must* reinvent these systems. If you don't, you will have entrepreneurial DNA trying to shape organizations through a bureaucratic nervous system, circulatory system, musculoskeletal system, and organ system. The signals won't get through.

When Minnesota changed public education by introducing choice and competition, it changed the way state funds moved in the system, but otherwise left most of the administrative systems intact. As a result, many of the signals have not reached teachers. Some do feel more accountable to their customers. But still tied down by rigid, centralized budget, personnel, and procurement systems, most have not experienced any increase in control over their schools or consequences for their performance. Hence many have not changed the way they teach.

Something similar happened at first with Margaret Thatcher's Next Steps reforms. When the early executive agencies were created, they negotiated increased flexibility with their departments. But they constantly chafed at the restrictive budget and personnel systems, and the Next Steps Team spent years pushing the Treasury Department to change those systems. Gradually, step by step, Treasury loosened its central controls. But until those reforms reached critical mass, the agencies could not realize the promise of their new flexible performance frameworks. Within the old administrative control systems, the flexibility just wasn't real.

Administrative systems translate the basic instructions or rules of the governing system into countless mandates for organizations. Their power shapes all three levels below them: the organization, its work processes, and its people. You can change your organization, processes, and people without changing your administrative control systems, but you will find those systems pushing back in the other direction. When employees and managers start reinventing, they will constantly bump up against the constraints built into their administrative systems.

Bureaucratic administrative systems conflict most obviously with the control strategy, which is based on trusting employees and organizations to do things right. But they also frustrate the consequences strategy, because they typically attach few rewards or sanctions to performance. You cannot use performance management or enterprise management if your budget and personnel systems don't create incentives for performance. Nor can you use enterprise management or public-versus-private competition if you must rely on traditional budget, finance, and accounting systems, since they don't generate the cost data that allow you to set prices appropriately or compare different providers.

Finally, bureaucratic administrative systems make it harder to change your organizational culture. Unless you change the rules of the game, says Sunnyvale City Manager Tom Lewcock, people won't believe you're serious about reinventing. "It's not what you say you're going to do, it's what you're doing."

It's no surprise, then, that we found reinventors worldwide dismantling the four major administrative control systems they inherited. In New Zealand, the United Kingdom, Australia, and Canada, transforming this level of government has been a cornerstone of reinvention. In 1993, the Clinton administration's National Performance Review also made administrative system reforms its centerpiece, although by 1997 Congress had passed only procurement reform. Across the nation, many cities, counties, and states have also begun to reinvent their administrative systems.

Because these systems are so firmly fixed in the body of government, however, they are difficult to change. If they are like a body's organ systems, then transforming them is akin to doing an organ transplant. In

New Zealand the change process was swift: reinventors swept away entire systems practically overnight, as we described in chapter 4. More often, however, public leaders work piecemeal, gradually rebuilding their systems element by element. Whatever the breadth and speed of the changes, one pattern is universal: the new systems introduce incentives for performance, put the customer in the driver's seat, and shift power to organizations and employees. *Reinventing Government* described how to do some of this with the personnel and budget and finance systems (see pp. 117–130, 155–165, and 236–246.) Our next book will discuss in detail how to reform all your administrative systems.

PUTTING THE PUZZLE TOGETHER

By the early 1990s, the British had so many reinvention strategies and metatools in play that it was causing problems. The emergence of three different initiatives, run by three different teams—the Next Steps Team, the Efficiency Unit, and the Citizen's Charter Unit—confused public managers. Thatcher had created the Efficiency Unit, which had hatched the Next Steps initiative and put together a new team to implement it. John Major, who succeeded Thatcher, did not want to appear to be undoing Thatcher's initiatives, so he left the Efficiency Unit and Next Steps Team alone. But he launched his own initiative—the Citizen's Charter—complete with its own unit. All the while, the powerful Treasury Department continued sending out directives.

By 1992, department and agency managers were getting too many directions from too many places. John Oughton, who ran the Efficiency Unit, described the problem:

> *There was a large element of confusion in the departments about where the central government's priorities were. Treasury would come along and say, "What are your targets for privatization?" And then my predecessor would come along and say, "How are you doing on market testing and contracting?" And departments would sit there and say, "Well, which is really your top priority? Which do you want us to do first?" The answer was, they should be concentrating on all of this.*

Finally, the government brought the three reform units together in a new Office of Public Service and Science, under a cabinet minister. (Responsibility for asset privatization stayed with Treasury and the departments.) But the new office could not speak with one consistent voice to the agencies until it developed an intellectually coherent framework that explained how the strategies and initiatives fit together.

This problem is common. Reinventors usually develop strategies in response to opportunities or urgent necessities, such as economic or fiscal crises. But as the British found, they must at some point learn to paint a coherent picture of their reform strategies, even when those strategies do not have a rational, orderly lineage. Unless you can create and communicate a clear, integrated explanation of your reinvention strategies, other politicians, managers, and the public will have great difficulty sorting out all the signals they are receiving.

British and other reinventors have dealt with this problem by developing decision trees—sequences of questions that not only illustrate how their different strategies fit together, but help them decide which strategy to use in which situation. The British version was developed for its prior options reviews, as we explained in chapter 4. Diana Goldsworthy, a former deputy in the Citizen's Charter group, describes the logical sequence of questions it poses:

> *Why do you need to do all this? If you need to do it, does the government have to do it? If the government has to do it, does the government actually have to do it all itself or could it contract for somebody else? If not, can we organize it and structure it better so that we get a better product at a cheaper price?*

This set of basic questions, Goldsworthy adds, gave the British initiatives "a sort of intellectual coherence, which has enabled us to present all these things as if we invented them yesterday as part of the same politics. And the truth is that, in a sense, we did ask those rather basic questions in that kind of order."

In 1995, Vice President Gore's National Performance Review published a similar decision tree, which we include here.

Sample Decision Tree for Analyzing Agency Programs

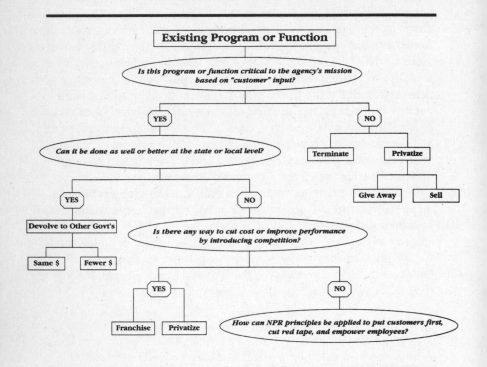

After examining these and other decision trees, we have developed our own, which reflects the strategies and approaches we have found to be most effective. It begins not with the program or function under scrutiny, but with the outcomes—the policy or program goals—desired by elected officials. (See pp. 318–319.)

This decision tree will help you cover all the strategic bases, as you analyze your system or organization and prepare your change strategy. It will help you use and align all five strategies.

Most reinventors, of course, do not have the luxury to proceed this logically. They start not with the first question on the decision tree; they start where they have the most opportunity to make change. When that works, they move on to the next opportunity. In the long run, however, leaders need to think strategically if they are to succeed in making fundamental changes. Someone needs to ask—and answer—these questions. Someone needs to determine how to move from one strategy to the next, how to engage all five strategies, which approaches and tools to use in which situations, and how to align them so they generate the necessary leverage. This is one of the things that effective leaders do.

Ultimately, you cannot reinvent without this kind of leadership. You can manage an organization without leadership, but you cannot reinvent it. Joel Barker explains the difference in his book *Paradigms*.

> *You manage within a paradigm. You lead between paradigms. Give a good manager the system and a manager will optimize it. That is a manager's job. It is called paradigm enhancement. . . . But leaders . . . determine that shifting paradigms is the correct thing to do, and, because they are leaders, instill the courage in others to follow them.*

A Decision Tree for Reinventors

1. *What are the outcomes we desire?*

2. *Should government play a role in producing those outcomes?*
   If not, abandon, sell, or give away the existing asset, or eliminate the existing policy, regulatory, service-delivery, or compliance function.

3. *Should government operate the activity?*
   If not, what arrangement would be best? *Reinventing Government* listed 36 alternatives to public service delivery that policy managers sometimes use to achieve their goals. We have boiled these down to 14 options:

   - Contracting out
   - Regulation of private sector activities
   - Tax incentives or disincentives
   - Franchising
   - Subsidies to producers (grants, loans, equity investments, favorable procurement policies, favorable investment policies)
   - Subsidies to consumers (vouchers, tax credits)
   - Policies allowing use of public property
   - Risk sharing (insurance, loan guarantees)
   - Information for customers
   - Technical assistance
   - Demand management through fees or taxes
   - Persuasion
   - Catalyzing voluntary activity
   - Public-private partnerships

4. *If so, which level of government should operate the activity?*
   - National
   - State/Provincial
   - Regional
   - Local

5. *If government should operate the activity, can the public steering and rowing roles be uncoupled?*
   If so, the options include:

   ■ Flexible performance frameworks
   ■ Competitive contracting systems

6. *How should the organization be given incentives and consequences for performance?*
   The options include:

   ■ Enterprise management
   ■ Managed competition
   ■ Performance management

7. *Should the organization be accountable to its customers?*
   If so, options include:

   ■ Customer choice
   ■ Competitive choice
   ■ Customer quality assurance

8. *Where should control of resources and operations lie?*

   ■ With policy makers and central administrative agencies
   ■ With the organization's top managers
   ■ With work teams within the organization
   ■ With the community
   ■ With some combination of the above

9. *How should we change the organization's culture?*

10. *How do we need to reform our administrative systems to accommodate these changes?*

    ■ The budget and finance system
    ■ The personnel system
    ■ The procurement system
    ■ The auditing system

– 10 –

THE COURAGE TO REINVENT

Never doubt that a small group of thoughtful, committed citizens can change the world; indeed it is the only thing that ever has.
—Margaret Mead

In 1984, Brian Mulroney and the Progressive Conservative Party took power in Canada, after two decades of Liberal Party rule. Mulroney had campaigned in the footsteps of Margaret Thatcher and Ronald Reagan, for smaller government and less bureaucracy. During the campaign he had blustered about handing out "pink slips and running shoes" to bureaucrats.

The day after assuming office, Mulroney appointed his deputy prime minister, Erik Nielsen, to chair a ministerial task force that would review all government programs and recommend which ones to eliminate or consolidate and how to improve performance in the rest.

A year and a half later, the task force published its report. It recommended cutting spending and taxes $7–$8 billion (in Canadian dollars), by reducing business subsidies, eliminating programs, privatizing agencies, contracting functions out, and devolving activities to the provinces. It also recommended massive reforms in the procurement system and an across-the-board "make-or-buy" policy in which the government would systematically study private contracting options, solicit bids, and choose the most cost-effective alternatives, whether public or private.

Three months after publishing the report, Mulroney removed Nielsen from his cabinet, because he had mishandled the resignation of another cabinet member. "After this, the Nielsen task force became an exercise in search of support in government," says Donald Savoie in his book, *Thatcher, Reagan, Mulroney: In Search of a New Bureaucracy*. Although the reports were referred to the appropriate committees in Parliament, they quickly sank from view. The bureaucracy heaved a sigh of relief.

The make-or-buy policy, considered by some business members of the task force its most important recommendation, did go forward. By mid-1988 pilot studies of a dozen functions had shown potential savings of 12–20 percent. In a classic political snafu, however, someone leaked word that the government was going to contract out its mapping service. Caught off guard, cabinet ministers denied the report. The responsible minister claimed he was not aware of the proposal, because it had come not from his department but from the Treasury Board secretariat.

Burned by this controversy, the government decided that departments would henceforth pick their own targets for contracting out, on a voluntary basis. That doomed the initiative. In 1990, the Mulroney government quietly let it die.

Meanwhile Mulroney's effort to sell Canada's public "crown corporations" also foundered on the prime minister's lack of conviction. In 1986 he had set up a secretariat inside the Treasury Board to handle the process. Savoie tells the story of its denouement:

> *Mulroney spoke often about the need to privatize crown corporations, but when the time came to make a firm decision, he backed down. A case in point was Air Canada. His government had agreed, as part of its comprehensive privatization plan, to sell the government-owned airline. However, coming out of a private meeting with a Quebec labor leader and a long-standing acquaintance, Mulroney announced that he had assured his friend that Air Canada was not for sale.*

The government fared little better with its efforts to use the control and consequences strategies. A little over a year after coming to power, Mulroney announced an initiative called Increased Ministerial Authority and Accountability (IMAA). It was a rudimentary flexible performance framework: it called for a gradual reduction in central rules and controls, as well as agreements between the Treasury Board and the departments, to give them more flexibility in return for concrete performance commitments, indicators, and targets.

This led to a few minor improvements, such as departmental power to reclassify nonmanagement positions without permission. A second, later IMAA initiative, obviously patterned after the U.K.'s Next Steps reforms, called for the Treasury Board to negotiate formal three-year memoranda of understanding (MOUs) with the departments, to codify their flexibilities and accountability. Every three years, the board would review their performance.

This too led to modest progress. But as Savoie writes:

> Some six years after IMAA was introduced, only about one-third of government departments had signed the MOU with the Treasury Board that was required to implement the concept fully. Those that have signed are not singing the praise of IMAA, insisting that the paperwork involved and the reporting requirements are not compensated for by the limited freedom they get from central-agency controls. The Treasury Board's pledge, made at the time IMAA was introduced, to review all centrally prescribed rules and regulations so as to remove constraints to good management does not appear to have come to pass.

Why the snail's pace? "A widely respected former secretary to the Treasury Board, now retired, explained that the reason . . . is because the 'work was largely the responsibility of central agencies which had little motivation for change.' "

Reelected in 1988, Mulroney signed off on yet another initiative, this one called "Public Service 2000." PS 2000 set up ten task forces to recommend management reforms in areas such as improving service to the public, resource management, administrative policy, and organizational structure. They were staffed mainly by senior civil servants and chaired by deputy ministers. They came up with 300 recommendations, mostly to decentralize control (delayering, reducing the number of job classifications to 23, reducing central controls, and so forth) and to improve customer service. In June 1991 the government introduced legislation to enact some of those recommendations. It balked at the most important step, however: reducing the power of the Treasury Board, the Public Service Commission, and the other central administrative agencies.

While developing Public Service 2000, the government sent a team over to London to take a closer look at the Next Steps process, then announced that it would create similar agencies, called "special operating agencies" (SOAs). Even this fizzled. By 1994 there were only 15 SOAs, which employed only 3 percent of the civil service. They had gained some flexibility, particularly those organized as enterprise funds (called revolving funds in Canada). But as a 1994 evaluation reported, "The SOA agreement had not significantly changed the way host departments thought of their relationships with SOAs compared with other departmental units."

Why? Savoie laid the blame, again, at the prime minister's feet: "Mulroney did not personally embrace the initiative, as Thatcher did, nor did he appoint a senior government official to oversee its implementation."

Despite initiative after initiative, Mulroney failed in his efforts to transform the Canadian bureaucracy. If anything, his halfhearted efforts left managers more cynical about reform than they had been when he was elected. Canadian officials report that many high-level civil servants were eager to reinvent and envious of their British counterparts. But without real support from the politicians, they couldn't get it done. "Although Mulroney spoke Thatcher's language," Savoie concluded, "he lacked her conviction."

The contrast between Thatcher and Mulroney says volumes about what it takes to reinvent. Thatcher brought in a nationally known business leader to lead her reform effort and gave him her full and visible backing. She weathered two long strikes by public sector unions without backing down. She ignored howls of protest as she privatized one public corporation after another. When her advisors proposed the Financial Management Initiative, she pushed it through. When it proved insufficient and her Efficiency Unit proposed the Next Steps reforms, she backed them to the hilt. And when the education bureaucracy tried to bury her education reforms—particularly her proposal to let schools opt out of their districts—she refused to submit. She demanded the legislation she wanted, then moved it through Parliament. Over 11 years, she stayed the course.

The Labor Party in New Zealand offers an even more dramatic contrast. Roger Douglas and his colleagues had the courage to throw overboard decades of party doctrine and privatize much of the state apparatus they had helped construct. Douglas entered Parliament a habitual advocate of government intervention.

I believed in the ability and rightness of governments to pick winners in business and industry. I saw no problem in their being involved in the market-place in a hands-on way. I thought they could encourage economic growth by directing government money and private funds into selected sectors or industries. . . . In my maiden speech in 1970, I criticised the breweries for raising the price of beer and recommended that the government institute a form of price control.

Douglas radically changed his views, because he could see they weren't working. "I saw the policies weren't helping the poor, the disadvantaged and those on lower incomes. The unwelcome truth was that they actually made the situation worse for the less well-off."

Stan Rodger, who had once led a major public sector union, pushed through 1988 legislation that wiped away virtually all civil service protections. His labor movement colleagues were so angry they took back a medal they had once awarded him. When Richard Prebble was in charge of the department that oversaw the Post Office, he closed half the post offices in his own election district. "There was considerable public outrage at the closures," Prebble recalled a year later. "Many people have still not forgiven me." But like Douglas, neither Rodger nor Prebble flinched.

In the U.K., in New Zealand, in the Air Combat Command, in Indianapolis, in Minnesota, in the Forest Service, and in Hampton, it took significant courage to reinvent government. In chapter 3 we first addressed this fact; we now want to close this book by returning to it. We want to close, as we opened, with a dose of reality. Reinvention pays tremendous dividends, but they do not come easily. It requires fundamental, often difficult changes in the behavior of many key players in the public sector: elected officials, managers, employees, unions, at times even stakeholder groups like business and the media. Let us say it as bluntly as we can: you will not succeed unless you are willing to make those changes. Courage is the reinventor's sixth C.

Brian Mulroney's story is all too common. It is the story of a public leader who wants change but is unwilling to pay the price. Mulroney was unwilling to take the heat from those who would lose out through privatization. He was unwilling to devote his personal attention and political capital to the task of improving government performance. He was unwilling to take real power away from his central control agencies. He was unwilling to invest the time and energy and resources—the blood, sweat, and tears—it takes to reinvent government. And he was unable to stay the course: to keep pushing and pushing until the promise of the Increased Ministerial Authority and Accountability initiative and Public Service 2000 and the special operating agencies had all been realized.

In part 1, we gave you three rules for reinventors, all under the general theme of the book: *be strategic*. We close this book with our final rules for reinventors. There is much, much more to say about the leadership challenges that reinventors face, and we hope to return to the subject in another book. But we would be remiss to leave this book without addressing the challenges reinventors *must* meet if they are to use the five C's successfully. Along with the three already presented, these rules for reinventors spell out the gut issues: what we mean when we talk about the courage to reinvent.

RULES FOR REINVENTORS

1. No New DNA; No Transformation.

2. The Game Has Five Levels; Change as Many as You Can Reach.

3. When You Want People to Let Go, Give Them Something in Return.

As we said in chapter 3, letting go of power and security is difficult. It requires courage; it requires faith in the results; and it often requires a deal, in which those who let go get something back in return. New Zealand's Labor Party leaders gave up their power to tell the Post Office and railroads how many people to employ and where to employ them. The U.S. Congress gave up its power to tell the Eastern Region of the Forest Service exactly where and how to spend each line item of its budget. In return, both Congress and the Labor Party got dramatically better performance for the public.

In Indianapolis, the U.K., and New Zealand, employees gave up their lifetime job security. But in return, many have gained freedom from red tape, richer work lives, more career opportunities and—in Indianapolis—gainsharing bonuses.

4. Take Performance Seriously—And Accept the Consequences.

When Oregon created its Progress Board in 1989, a process we described in chapter 4, the idea was to create long-term outcome goals for the state, called the Oregon Benchmarks. About the same time, the governor's budget office began pushing departments to measure performance and set performance goals. In 1993, Governor Barbara Roberts built her state budget around the Benchmarks. The legislature went along, but most members never bought into the Benchmarks. Similarly, only a few committees took performance measures seriously when they appropriated funds. After Roberts left office in January 1995, neither the new governor nor the legislature paid any attention to the Benchmarks in creating the next biennial budget.

Why? Because most politicians pay little attention to the performance of public institutions. Mayors care about the performance of their police departments, and governors sometimes care about the performance of their public schools. But otherwise, the typical elected official pays almost no attention to performance, until there is a crisis.

Donald Savoie puts it well, writing about the U.K., the U.S., and Canada:

> *Seasoned officials know that, although politicians will speak of empowering employees and serving clients better, what matters most to them is how to diffuse a political crisis (of which there is never a shortage) or how to pilot a new policy or program through the government approval process and then how to package it for public consumption. . . . there are still very few rewards for being known as a good manager.*

This has changed in Sunnyvale, Indianapolis, and other cities. It is changing in the U.K. and New Zealand, though it is still a struggle. The politicians in those two countries now have the tools to focus on performance, but not many have the inclination. Margaret Thatcher, John Major, Roger Douglas, Ruth Richardson, and others cared deeply about performance. In the long run, their successors must share that passion if reinvention is to continue.

The biggest barrier is not resistance, but the pull of other priorities. A senior official who worked closely with Mulroney told Savoie, "I have seen him become consumed by the Canada/U.S. Free Trade Agreement, by national unity, by a looming general election, but never by public service reforms." Successful reinventors become consumed by improving performance.

A second barrier is fear of consequences: What happens if a leader sets performance goals, then fails to reach them? Won't his opponents use that against him at election time? Why should he hand them data that could lead to his defeat? This fear killed the Clinton administration's plans to write performance contracts with each cabinet member. The National Performance Review recommended such contracts, and a handful of secretaries who believed in reinvention quickly volunteered and drafted agreements. But after those were signed, it dawned on members of the Office of Management and Budget that by specifying performance goals in these contracts, they were handing the Republicans a yardstick by which to measure their success or failure. They stopped the initiative in its tracks.

What can overcome this fear? Only courage. The risks are not imaginary. Political opponents will use anything they can to win elections. If elected leaders want to reinvent, they have little choice but to swallow hard and take the risk. They must have faith that they can make it pay off, by improving performance and turning the resulting measures into political assets.

Managers and employees—what we call the institutional sector— face a similar challenge. They too must take the risk of becoming accountable for their performance. Very few people volunteer for this duty. It is normally thrust upon the institutional sector by political leaders and their advisors. When that happens, however, managers and employees have a choice. They can accept the responsibility and make the most of it. They can ignore it. Or they can go along but quietly resist, undermining the initiative. Most managers in Sunnyvale and Indianapolis have taken the first route, though not all.

If we were giving an award for the courage to accept responsibility for performance, we would give it to Steve Fantauzzo, the local union leader in Indianapolis. As we related in chapter 5, AFSCME officials had been saying for some time that their members could outperform any private company if given a level playing field. When Goldsmith offered just that (actually, Indianapolis's playing field is tilted slightly in the employees' favor), Fantauzzo and his members had the courage to play ball. When they convinced management to offer an upside, through gainsharing, it helped tremendously. But they never would have thought to do that had they not taken the challenge seriously and committed themselves to making it work.

The gamble paid off. Indianapolis has not laid off one AFSCME member, and many members are now receiving annual gainsharing bonuses. Fantauzzo and Goldsmith have made competitive bidding work for both the union and the city.

Government's stakeholders also have a role in taking performance seriously. The public and much of the business community already do—though they need to become more strategic about how they demand higher performance. But the media rarely do. And the media are the crucial transmission belts between government and its citizens.

Most mass-media outlets—major newspapers, magazines, and television stations—are in the entertainment business, not the information business. (There are exceptions.) They exist to make a profit, which they do by selling advertisements. To sell more ads at a higher price, they must demonstrate higher market share. And to do that, they must entertain their readers or viewers.

So the media are looking for stories that grab attention and hold it. Hence they focus on conflict, drama, and scandal—not performance.

Duke University professor Robert Behn tells a story that illustrates the point. When Governor Michael Dukakis was touting the success of his welfare reform program, Employment and Training (ET) Choices, the CBS program *60 Minutes* decided to do a story on it.

> *The producer spent several days touring welfare offices and ET training programs, all the time asking: What's the conflict? Who are the bad guys? In the end,* Sixty Minutes *never produced anything on the ET program. We couldn't really determine what the story was, explained the producer; there was no conflict.*

Several years ago Katherine Barrett, then with *Financial World* magazine, visited Oregon to study the Benchmarks. She also talked with members of the Oregon media about the importance of performance measurement and benchmarks. Many of the reporters said they had heard of the Benchmarks, but that they preferred to write about things like state employee layoffs.

Reinventors need to understand these realities and feed the media information in a way that makes it entertaining—as the British have done by publishing performance tables that compare different cities, police forces, fire brigades, schools, and hospitals. But media outlets need to begin taking issues of performance seriously as well. It is useful to publish data comparing the performance of different cities and states, but it would also help if they wrote about what governments were doing right or wrong to produce that performance. If citizens rarely see a newspaper or television story about improving performance in the public sector—if all they see is a steady diet of scandals, conflicts, and abuses—their attitudes will never change, and politicians who invest their energies in improving performance will never get the credit they deserve.

5. Stand Up to the Special Interests.

Whenever government introduces competition or privatizes an asset or eliminates a program, there is an uproar from those whose interests are threatened by the change. This is one of the classic difficulties of any reform process. Machiavelli wrote about it 500 years ago:

> *There is no more delicate matter to take in hand, nor more dangerous to conduct, nor more doubtful in its success, than to set up as a leader in the introduction of changes. For he who innovates will have for enemies all those who are well off under the existing order of things, and only lukewarm supporters in those who might be better off under the new.*

To succeed, political leaders must have the courage to stand up to the interests that block change. Stakeholders such as business and community groups can often help. Managers and employees can occasionally help, but they can seldom lead the charge.

The most effective ways to overcome special interests include the following:

"Damn the torpedoes, full speed ahead." This was Governor Perpich's approach with school choice in Minnesota. When the idea was new and only a third of Minnesotans surveyed favored it, he went full speed ahead, because he had faith that giving parents their choice of public schools was the right thing to do. Rather than worrying about the power of the teachers unions, he confronted them head-on. It took him several years, but the public quickly came to understand that choice was in its interest, and the unions finally backed down.

Margaret Thatcher took the same approach, as did Roger Douglas.

Indeed, Douglas believes in moving as fast as possible, so the interest groups do not have time to regroup.

Do not try to advance a step at a time. Define your objectives clearly and move towards them by quantum leaps. Otherwise the interest groups will have time to mobilize and drag you down.

Structure the debate so it poses the general interest against the special interests. Douglas advocates this approach also. Indeed, this was one reason he and the Labor Party always tried to package their reforms in "large bundles." In 1984, Labor announced its first comprehensive plan for reform: phasing out subsidies in farming, manufacturing, transportation, and other areas; price increases for most government-supplied goods and services; a new 10 percent flat tax (starting in 1986) on all goods and services; and dramatic reductions in income taxes.

"Nothing like that had happened in living memory," says Douglas.

You could hear the jaws dropping open right across the nation as the Budget speech was broadcast, hitting one vested interest after another.

Paradoxically, however, it is harder to complain about damage to your own group, when everyone else is suffering at least as much—and you benefit from their loss, in the medium term.

The major interest groups gathered in the Parliament Buildings the following Monday. Road transport operators complained that road user charges on them had been increased by an appalling 48 percent. They were not supported—they were howled down—by the other groups present. It was seen as selfish and insensitive, with so many hurting at once, for any one group to push its own barrow.

The underlying fact is that, whatever their own losses, each individual group also had a vested interest in the success of the reforms being imposed on all of the other groups in the room.

The Canadian Program Review managed to do the same thing: because everyone sacrificed for the common good, no one protested too loudly. Vice President Gore intended to do this with the National Performance Review recommendations in 1993—packaging the most important ones in one huge bill and forcing Congress to deal with it.

But with national health reform taking precedence, the Clinton administration backed away from the idea. As a result, opponents easily picked off individual proposals as they were introduced in Congress, one by one.

Use opinion surveys to prove you have the general interest on your side. In 1995, Boston's school choice plan came under fire from some white parents who were frustrated because racial balance guidelines had kept their children out of their preferred schools. To counter the attack, the mayor and the Private Industry Council asked a consulting firm to pay for a customer survey of attitudes toward the choice plan. The survey showed that 80 percent of parents were satisfied with the assignment system and almost 90 percent got their first or second choice.

Build constituencies to support your reforms. Minnesota's education reformers consciously built a series of constituencies for school choice. They started with People for Better Schools and the Citizens League. Then they recruited the Minnesota Business Partnership. Next they reached out to minority communities, where parents were particularly eager for public school choice because they could not escape bad schools any other way, since they could not afford private schools. Later they turned the Post-secondary Enrollment Options students and their parents into a potent constituency, as we described in chapter 6.

Mayor Goldsmith turned the inner city and its political representatives into a constituency for reinvention by devoting the savings from his managed competition approach to inner-city infrastructure projects. When Mayor Rendell in Philadelphia used managed competition, he turned to the private sector unions for support. He handed out fact sheets showing city pay and benefits compared with private sector pay and benefits, which demonstrated that the city workers got higher wages and more paid holidays. "Guys would listen to this, and say 'Yeah, bingo, privatize,' " he remembers. He says the private unions became his most important allies.

Those who fail to build constituencies usually fail to reinvent. Massachusetts governor William Weld came into office vowing to reinvent; his inaugural address in 1991 was based on an article David Osborne wrote a year before *Reinventing Government* was published. Weld was perfectly willing to stand up to special interests, but he rarely mobilized any constituencies for change. As a result, he lost repeatedly in the state legislature, and his reinvention drive quickly lost momentum.

6. Protect Your Entrepreneurs: Don't Let Anyone Shoot Your Risk Takers.

The prevailing culture in government is incredibly risk averse, because the politicians, the media, and the auditors are all quick to take potshots at any innovation that fails. Politicians love to snipe at the bureaucracy: Senator William Proxmire for years had his Golden Fleece Awards; Texas Comptroller John Sharp invented a Silver Snout Award to do the same thing. Meanwhile the political parties constantly snipe at each other, and managers who get caught in the cross fire are routine casualties. The media loves the warfare, because it makes good copy. Indeed, they generate a lot of the sniping on their own. The impact on reinvention can be devastating. As Bob Behn says, "One mistake can doom an entire innovation."

This behavior may never change. To combat it, leaders who want to reinvent must have the courage to protect their entrepreneurs. When someone leaked the fact that the Canadian mapping service was going to be contracted out, for example, Mulroney and his cabinet should have stepped in to take the heat. By denying the report, they undermined a promising initiative.

This happens all the time in politics. Elected officials jettison innovators who have become controversial, to dissociate themselves from the controversy. When Mario Cuomo was governor of New York, he made his mark as an innovator in housing for the poor and homeless. The man who made it possible was Bill Eimicke, his housing "czar" from 1983 through 1988. After several years, Cuomo began to trumpet his success. His budget office decided to announce, in a state of the state address, how many low-income housing units the Cuomo administration had assisted since taking office. Eimicke objected, knowing that if they put in a number, the legislature or the press would probably force them to prove it. And without a computerized operation, Eimicke knew that would take an immense amount of work.

Eimicke lost that battle, and sure enough, when the governor claimed they had assisted more than a million units, reporters asked for proof. So Eimicke's staff spent a year culling through manual records and putting together a list of every housing unit the state had built, rehabilitated, or otherwise invested in. Eimicke tells what happened when they released it:

All the press took the list and began visiting the sites. About the eighth unit on the list was something like 32 W. 42nd Street and it was wrong; it was a typo. It was supposed to be something like 42 W. 32nd Street. So the Daily News *went to it and found a vacant lot. If you'd gone to the other address, everything we said was there was there. But they didn't. They put a picture of the vacant lot in the paper, and it was all over. All the other papers picked it up.*

The accusations snowballed, and pretty soon the newspapers were accusing Eimicke of lying about the one million units. Cuomo said nothing, and his aides began telling Eimicke he was through. Knowing he had become a liability, Eimicke resigned. Three years later, after computerizing the records, the administration released figures showing Eimicke's numbers had actually been on the low side.

When a leader lets one of his most creative aides take the fall in this kind of situation—for no reason other than a media feeding frenzy—it sends a chill throughout his organization. No one else is going to stick his or her neck out to make changes after watching something like this. The Cuomo administration launched no new housing programs.

Sometimes the attack comes from auditors rather than reporters. In the mid-1980s, when he was deputy assistant secretary of defense for installations, Bob Stone threw out hundreds of regulations governing military base construction, taking them down from 380 pages to 4. The inspector general (IG), whose staff was there to enforce the regulations, didn't like what he had done. When Stone took the new regulations to the Directives Branch to get them printed, the woman in charge would not print them, because the inspector general had objected. Stone knew he had the authority, so he did what entrepreneurs do: he went around her.

We were having a conference, and I wanted to be able to hand [the new regulations] out, so I said to the guy running it for me, "Look, here's a check for $200, go to a printer, and see how many you can get for $200." Well, the people on my staff were outraged that I was going to buy the whole bundle, and they started kicking in. I think I finally got about $160 refunded. This was personal money; there's no budget for this. We raised $300, had 1,900 of these printed, and mailed them all over the world—to all the generals, all the base engineers.

The IG didn't like that; he had been outflanked. I also sent a copy to [Stone's boss, William Howard] Taft [IV], and Taft loved it.

The IG wrote to Taft and said that I had exceeded my authority and probably violated the law. I think it's one of the last refuges of scoundrels that when you do something they don't like, they act like you violated the law.

There's a law, they said, that limits printing of the DOD seal. Only the Defense Department or authorized people can print it. You can go anywhere in Washington—you want a glass with the seal etched in it, an ashtray, there's lots of places you can get it. But the IG said I had violated the law.

When the IG told Taft I had exceeded my authority, Taft should have called me in and given me a medal. Instead he referred the complaint to the general counsel, and I just survived by the skin of my teeth.

(If we were giving awards for courage, our second one would go to Bob Stone, who has done more reinventing against greater odds than anyone we know.)

Politicians may never accept blunders that cost them politically. But someone has to protect public entrepreneurs who defy silly rules, as Stone did, or make well-intentioned mistakes, or simply run afoul of the media, the press, or the opposition party. Someone has to stand up and take the heat for his employees. If you want to lead a reinvention effort, you have no choice. If you won't protect those who follow you, you won't have anyone following for long.

When Mitch Roob bid out the first competitive contract in Indianapolis and the city's street-repair crews won it, he came under intense pressure to void the bid, as we reported in chapter 5. Mayor Steve Goldsmith had campaigned for privatization, and some of his political advisors desperately wanted the first contract to go to a private firm. But Roob stood his ground, and Goldsmith backed him. Had the mayor reversed the decision, Indianapolis would not be the success story it is today.

In 1974, Community School District 4 in East Harlem—a district that pioneered public school choice—launched its first alternative elementary school, Central Park East. Soon a group of parents complained to the district superintendent about how its principal was running the school. The superintendent immediately sent Sy Fliegel, who ran the district's new Office for Alternative Schools, to work on the problem.

Fliegel first visited the principal, Deborah Meier. "I could tell from the way she looked at me that she didn't trust me," he recalls. "To her I was just another annoying bureaucrat from the district office meddling in her affairs." Then he met with parents three times.

The truth is, after all my investigating, I determined that Debbie Meier was running a superior school. She regarded kids as individuals, an approach that my own teaching experience had convinced me was essential. She cared about youngsters, about learning, and had assembled a staff excited about education. There aren't enough people like that in the world, so when you find the Debbie Meiers, the people who really try to do something, you have to stand by them. They will make some mistakes, and they will always draw fire. But ultimately, people like Debbie and schools like CPE are always worth protecting. . . .

So I went to the parents. I told them in the nicest possible way that even though some of their complaints were true, they were far outweighed by the fact that CPE was a really good place for kids. Meier was staying, I told them, but I would do everything I could to see that their children were placed elsewhere if they chose. In the end fifteen families decided to leave CPE. . . . The crisis was over, the credibility of the new Office of Alternative Schools was enhanced, and a lasting friendship [with Meier] began.

I had learned an important lesson, too. When push comes to shove you have to protect your good people.

Leaders can also protect their entrepreneurs by inoculating them against attack, with honors and awards. Vice President Gore does this very effectively with his Reinvention Labs and Hammer Awards. "There's nothing like the magic of the VP's name," says Joe Thompson, director of the New York City Regional Veterans Administration Office, an early reinvention lab and Hammer Award winner. "He's really said and done some nice things for us, and that just helps in the bureaucracy. Having the VP support your efforts—a lot of times where people might not be inclined to help, they do."

Stakeholders can help inoculate innovators as well. A number of stakeholder organizations, including the Ford Foundation, the Fund for the City of New York, and the Boston Management Consortium (a consortium of 150 Boston area businesses) give awards to public sector individuals or organizations that have demonstrated outstanding or innovative performance.

7. Build Trust, One Transaction at a Time.

Most public institutions swim in a sea of politics, and trust is rare in politics. Managers don't trust politicians, for example. A former British civil servant once spoke for many when he described politicians as "self-advertising, irresponsible nincompoops. . . . They embody everything that my training has taught me to eschew—ambition, prejudice, dishonesty, self-seeking, light-hearted irresponsibility, black-hearted mendacity."

Politicians often feel just as strongly about public employees, and they use just as colorful language. (Many an American politician has echoed George Wallace's favorite description: "pointy-headed bureaucrats.") Many politicians view civil servants as lazy, self-serving bureaucrats who routinely stonewall what the people and their legislators want and get away with it, because they cannot be fired.

Meanwhile employees distrust managers, and managers distrust employees. Unions distrust management, and management distrusts unions. And stakeholders—citizens, businesspeople, private sector unions, community groups, and the media—distrust the whole lot.

Yet if you want to reinvent, you cannot do it in an environment of distrust—unless you have enormous power to give orders and ensure that they are followed. That may have been the case, at least to some degree, in the U.K. and New Zealand, but it is almost never the case in the United States. And even in the U.K. and New Zealand, distrust undermined the reinvention process. When trust between Prime Minister David Lange and Finance Minister Roger Douglas broke down in the late 1980s, it hurt the Labor Party badly. It produced a series of nasty public squabbles, slowed the momentum of reform, and led to Douglas's resignation, followed six months later by Lange's. It was a factor in Labor's electoral defeat in 1990.

In the U.K., Thatcher never trusted the bureaucracy, and its members returned the favor. Nor did the national media ever develop much trust in the Conservative government. Both of these factors hurt John Major when he unveiled his Citizen's Charter. The media immediately dismissed it as an election-year gimmick, and many civil servants did the same.

Building trust is so important because reinvention requires faith. To embrace change, people must have faith that it will work. If they distrust those who are proposing and leading the change—or those with whom they will have to work to make it happen—they will not make that leap of faith. Reinventors must build mutual trust if they want to overcome this obstacle.

How do you build trust? You do it by proving, one transaction at a time, that you can be trusted. When Mayor Goldsmith decided to use competition in Indianapolis, the public workers union, AFSCME, was dead set against him. Gradually he and his managers won their trust. Mitch Roob did it first, when he offered union workers a chance to bid to keep their work. He did it again when he acknowledged the bloated management in his Transportation Department and fired 18 supervisors, most of them active Republicans, to give his workers a chance to compete. Roob and AFSCME's Fantauzzo began to look for common ground—"a way," says the union leader, "to maintain our principles but get out of warfare." Roob built a little more trust when he refused to void the workers' winning bid, despite intense pressure from his own party.

"Mitch brokered our relationship with the mayor," Fantauzzo says.

The mayor committed himself to personal and regular meetings with our leadership. They discovered that he wasn't as big and bad as they thought. He discovered they were not as stupid and lazy as he thought they were.

When Goldsmith, Roob, and other administration leaders began to make sure no union members were laid off as a result of competition, that made a big difference to the union. "It demonstrated a changing philosophy," says Fantauzzo. It started to become clear, he says, that Roob and Goldsmith understood "what's important to the union and how to take that and play it to their own advantage."

The union responded by playing ball. "The position we took was not the normal 'We're going to oppose privatization,'" Fantauzzo says. "We said, 'If it's going to happen, let's properly frame it.'" Union members made honest attempts to bring their costs down. When they proposed good ideas, management responded. When they proposed gainsharing, Goldsmith and his managers agreed.

Along the way there were rough spots. But by 1995, the city's AFSCME employees were ready to endorse their mayor for reelection.

(They remained neutral, as we explained in chapter 5, because the teachers opposed him.)

The most important element of trust building is honesty. Real honesty can have a remarkable impact on people, particularly within a political setting. Peter Hutchinson, the Public Strategies Group consultant who has spent three years as acting Minneapolis school superintendent, talks often about the power of "speaking the truth in love"— speaking the truth out of love for those one is dealing with. He remembers a stakeholder group that formed to discuss the district's problems. It included teachers, principals, parents, students, school board members, union representatives, and community members. At a retreat, the group began talking about why some schools persistently failed to do well. Some people blamed bad teachers. The group agreed that the district did not deal with teachers who performed poorly. It decided—with great trepidation, Hutchinson says—to raise the issue with the executive board of the teachers union. Hutchinson worried that the meeting would simply put the union on the defensive.

It didn't, because people spoke the truth in love. People simply started telling stories about their own experiences with bad teachers in the schools. School board members, parents, even a union person— everybody had a story. "It went on and on," Hutchinson remembers.

All of a sudden, the people speaking started to include members of the executive board. They had stories, too. . . . It was a breakthrough: outside and inside the union we really were observing the same reality.

After the retreat, Hutchinson and the union were able to agree on new contract provisions to swiftly address problems with poor teachers.

To build trust, you also have to make yourself vulnerable. Goldsmith and Roob did this; they had to pay a political price within their own party. And the whole effort could easily have backfired: the union could have sandbagged them. It happens often enough in politics. In Minneapolis, the teachers union leaders had to let themselves become vulnerable. Management could easily have sandbagged them.

In a political world, it is very difficult to maintain a position of honesty and vulnerability. When you do, you will sometimes get burned. If at that point you withdraw, you will probably fail. One of the toughest things a reinventor has to do is maintain his or her honesty and vulnerability after a scorching.

Babak Armajani, CEO of the Public Strategies Group, remembers getting burned when he was deputy commissioner of the Revenue Department in Minnesota. In their efforts to reengineer the department's basic processes, he and his colleagues wanted to invest heavily in information technologies. To come up with $1 million for new investments, they developed a list of proposed cuts elsewhere in the department. When they took their proposed new budget to their appropriations committee, it had the typical reaction: It liked the cuts, but not the new investments. It simply took back the $1 million.

"This was the bleeding edge of change," says Armajani. "We were just crucified by our managers for this. How could we be so stupid?" But Armajani didn't give up. He proposed a two-day retreat with the committee to talk things over. Luckily, the committee agreed. "We fought a lot, but we worked it out," he says. "It led to a great relationship with the committee; they've since been very supportive and proud of the department. By now the committee tells other agencies they ought to be like the Revenue Department—and we had been in the doghouse until then."

Another key to building trust is what we call "the power of confession." If you are willing to acknowledge your mistakes, apologize, and take the hit, you will be amazed by the effect. Confession can be intensely cathartic. And frankly, there is often no hit to take. People are so amazed and grateful to hear an honest apology that they will forgive the transgression.

We have been discussing trust within government, but all of this applies to relations with the public as well. Most citizens have pretty good crap detectors, to use Hemingway's phrase. They can tell when a public official is being honest with them and when he is not. When they see consistent honesty, they develop a bond of trust with that official.

If you want to reinvent, Roger Douglas advises, "never fall into the trap of selling the public short." He decries politicians who, faced with the need for reinvention, "confide privately: '*I* know it's needed, but people out there don't!' Politics is the art of the possible!"

Nobody stops to think that what people may really want is politicians with the vision and the guts to help them to create a better country for their children in the year 2000 and beyond it.

Successful structural reform does not become possible until you trust, respect and inform the electors. You have to put them in a position to make sound judgments about what is going on.

Tell the public, and never stop telling them, right up front:

- *What the problem is and how it arose.*
- *What damage it is doing to their own personal interests.*
- *What your own objectives are in tackling it.*
- *What the costs and the benefits of that action will be.*
- *Why your approach will work better than the other options.*

Ordinary people may not understand the situation in all its technical detail, but they have a lifetime of experience at work and at home to help them sift the wheat from the chaff. They know when key questions are being evaded. They can sense when they are being patronised or conned, and do not like it. They respect people who front up honestly to their questions.

8. Invest in Change.

Reinvention is not free. It costs money, it costs time, it costs political capital. If you're not willing to make the investment, don't bother starting down the path. When we talk to leaders of organizations that have made the greatest strides—the Air Combat Command, Sunnyvale, Phoenix, Hampton, the U.K. Employment Service—they have all been willing to invest heavily in the process of change. At the ACC, Creech set up a "university" at every TAC base. He also created week-long courses for those in line to take on greater responsibility, and he taught most of the courses himself. Mike Loh created a Quality Schoolhouse and trained full-time TQM coordinators for every TAC base. He devoted millions of dollars and hundreds of full-time positions to this effort, in the midst of downsizing and without any extra appropriations. He didn't ask for permission or money; he simply found ways to save money elsewhere and redirected it to quality training.

You should anticipate investing 5 percent of your annual operating budget (excluding pass-through money, such as grants, welfare payments, and the like) in the change process. You won't be able to do this right away, because it takes time to find the savings you will need to generate these funds. But after several years, you should

be spending at least 5 percent of your operating budget for things
such as:

- Training
- Strategic Planning
- Culture Change
- Experimental Programs
- Market Research
- Internal Survey Research
- Rewards and Recognition
- Internal and External Communication

9. Manage the Transition Humanely: Reinvent with a Human Face.

With the exception of New Zealand and the United Kingdom, which
left thousands unemployed because they corporatized or privatized at
such a lightning pace, most of the other governments that are reinvention leaders have laid off few employees. They have used their natural
attrition rates to keep positions open, then moved employees whose
jobs have disappeared into those positions. When that has not been
enough, they have required private contractors to hire the employees,
or set up outplacement efforts and helped them find other jobs.

Indianapolis has done all of this, and in four years laid off only an
estimated 4–5 percent of its employees. National and local governments in the U.K. have used virtually every option we recommended in
chapter 5 for easing the transition (see pp. 132–135). The U.K. down-
sized its national civil service by one third over 18 years—with few
layoffs. Phoenix has required private contractors to hire employees and
provide equivalent benefits, while also setting up a job bank for those
who prefer to stay with the city. Philadelphia has done likewise.
"That's how you win this battle," says Mayor Rendell, "by showing
your humanity."

10. Stay the Course.

As we said in chapter 3, reinvention is a long, hard slog. It takes five
to ten years to transform an organization, at a minimum. Phoenix,
Sunnyvale, and Hampton have been at it for roughly 20, 16, and 12
years—and they're still improving, still using new strategies and tools.

In larger systems, it takes even longer. Leaders in the U.K. and New Zealand have been at it for 18 and 12 years, respectively. The most rapid reinvention we have ever seen was in the Tactical Air Command, where Bill Creech doubled the command's effectiveness and increased productivity by 80 percent in five years. But even there, his successors have continued the process for a dozen years, still finding new challenges and new tools with which to meet them.

To succeed over these long time spans, leaders need what quality management pioneer W. Edwards Deming called "constancy of purpose." They must push very hard, for a very long time, in the same direction. Deming was not sure that politicians could maintain such constancy—and neither is anyone else. Usually we think of politicians holding their fingers in the air, trying to find out which way the wind is blowing. Reinventors, by contrast, must create the wind that sweeps away the remnants of bureaucratic government.

To do that, they need to persevere and to persist. Reinvention is not for the fainthearted or the short of wind. Reinventors must pound on the door, again and again and again. If they can't get it open, they've got to climb in the window.

"The key element is that you have to have courage," says Don Forbes, one of Oregon's most successful reinventors when he ran the Department of Transportation.

And courage means that you stick with it for a long time. I think what happens in organizations is people will start out with the best of intentions—"Here's the new initiative"—and somewhere about one to one-and-a-half years in they run into organizational resistance and back away. And in backing away they set up a suspicious, cynical culture, which learns to always resist, because it works. You've got to be prepared to take a lot of flak, which usually comes a year or two down the road.

Forbes might be describing the Mulroney government, which launched one initiative after another, only to back away each time it met resistance. Whether you are a politician, a manager, an employee, or a stakeholder, you cannot succeed if you cannot fight through the resistance. When Steve Goldsmith tried to bid out management of his wastewater treatment plants, a year into his administration, he hit massive resistance. The plants were already award winners, managers told him. Why rock the boat? Environmentalists opposed the move. The union was so angry it finally sued. And when Goldsmith's hand-picked consulting firm, Ernst & Young, studied the possibility of competitive bidding, it predicted savings of only 5 percent.

But Goldsmith believed in the power of competition. He had constancy of purpose. He pushed ahead, and the final contract saved the city 29.5 percent—more than $65 million over five years.

Even stakeholders must stay the course when they get involved in reinvention. Consider the education reformers in Minnesota we described in chapter 6. Nancy C. Roberts and Paula J. King wrote a book about them, called *Transforming Public Policy: Dynamics of Policy Entrepreneurship and Innovation.* After the authors finished their research, they asked each of the six central reformers about the keys to success. Several cited the necessity of staying the course, one with particular eloquence:

> *A fourth policy entrepreneur, reflecting on his experience with public school choice, insisted that "nothing beats having a strategy. Hoping for the best isn't good enough." The strategy must be plausible and "once committed to it, you have to stick with it, no matter what distractions come your way." He observed that many people "get caught up in tactical warfare and get off the strategic track." You must stay "stubbornly focused on what you have set off to do, and don't let anybody drive you from it." "Unless you get exceptionally lucky, this sort of thing requires extraordinary patience and persistence from the moment of the first public statement on the issue." He noted that it took the group nearly three years to get into a position where a major politician would risk taking on the idea. It took another three years to have the idea firmly embedded in law. "There were many opportunities to settle for less, but you just can't do it."*

The activist might have added that after the six years it took to get legislation on choice, he and others have spent an additional eight years adding a charter-school bill, strengthening that bill, making sure the new programs were evaluated honestly and effectively, communicating the results, and defending their reforms against counterattack. Once the reform legislation passed, their job had only begun.

Ten Rules for Reinventors

1. No new DNA, no transformation.
2. The game has five levels; change as many as you can reach.
3. When you want people to let go, give them something in return.
4. Take performance seriously—and accept the consequences.
5. Stand up to the special interests.
6. Protect your entrepreneurs: Don't let anyone shoot your risk takers.
7. Build trust, one transaction at a time.
8. Invest in change.
9. Manage the transition humanely: Reinvent with a human face.
10. Stay the course.

NOWHERE TO HIDE

No party holds power forever. Sooner or later we all find ourselves out of office. That is the reality of life in a democracy. We may as well use the time we have to do something worthwhile.

—Roger Douglas

This may all seem like too much to expect. Honesty? Trust? Investment? Perseverance? Courage? In *politics*?

Perhaps it is. If so, we are doomed to watch government grow ever more ineffective—which means that many of our most severe problems will grow ever worse.

Most governments in the information age democracies are still in a deep hole. Few citizens believe that they do much of a job. When John Kennedy was president, 76 percent of Americans said they trusted the federal government to do the right thing most of the time. By the 1990s, only 20 percent did. In a 1995 poll, 72 percent of those responding agreed that "the federal government creates more problems than it solves." Some 49 percent said "better management" should be its top priority—more than any other category. (Only 9 percent chose "cutting programs.") In September 1993, when President Clinton released his reinventing government report and his health care plan, 51 percent of those polled said the former should be his top priority, only 43 percent the latter.

In part because it was so fed up with government, the American public began the 1990s by throwing status quo politicians out of office in three elections running. In 1990, the governors felt the voters' wrath. In 1992, the president felt it. And in 1994, Congress felt it. We have experienced a massive upheaval in our electoral landscape. Canada and New Zealand have experienced much the same thing.

There is nowhere left to hide. Elected officials can blame someone else for the problem: the other party, petty bureaucrats, the welfare state. And if they survive the next election, they can continue to govern as they always have. Managers and employees can do much the same thing. But this solution won't last. Bureaucratic government simply does not work in the information age. Sooner or later the public will give up on leaders who do not understand this and do something about it—because people want better results.

Our leaders *must* have the courage to reinvent. Even if they have to break with old political partners, as Rudy Perpich did with the Minnesota teachers unions. Even if they have to give up old, cherished ideas, as Roger Douglas and his Labor colleagues did in New Zealand. Even if they have to learn to trust labor unions and civil servants, as Steve Goldsmith did in Indianapolis.

To make the job easier, we have offered a road map of the five strategies that work. We understand how long the road is, how large the challenges, how difficult the work. In our view, however, this is no reason to be discouraged. It is instead a reason to begin the journey today.

President Kennedy once told a story about a French military commander who ordered his gardener to plant a tree. "Oh, this tree grows slowly," the gardener replied. "It won't mature for a hundred years."

"Then there's no time to lose," the general said. "Plant it this afternoon."

Appendix A:
The Principles of
Reinventing Government

Catalytic Government:
Steering Rather than Rowing

Catalytic governments separate "steering" (policy and regulatory) functions from "rowing" (service-delivery and compliance functions). They then use many different methods (contracts, vouchers, grants, tax incentives, etc.) in addition to public organizations to accomplish their goals, choosing the method that best meets their needs for efficiency, effectiveness, equity, accountability, and flexibility.

Community-Owned Government:
Empowering Rather than Serving

Community-owned governments push control of services out of the bureaucracy, into the community. By funding and empowering communities to solve their own problems, they generate more commitment, better care, and often more creative problem solving. They also reduce dependency.

Competitive Government:
Injecting Competition into Service Delivery

Competitive governments require service deliverers to compete for their business, based on their performance and price. They understand that competition is the fundamental force that gives public organizations no choice but to improve. (This does not apply to regulatory or policy functions.)

Mission-Driven Government:
Transforming Rule-Driven Organizations

Mission-driven governments deregulate internally, eliminating many of their internal rules and radically simplifying their administrative systems, such as budget, personnel, and procurement. They require each agency to get clear on its mission, then free managers to find the best way to accomplish that mission, within legal bounds.

Results-Oriented Government:
Funding Outcomes, Not Inputs

Results-oriented governments shift accountability from inputs ("Did you follow the rules and spend according to the appropriated line items?") to outcomes, or results. They measure the performance of public agencies, set targets, reward agencies that hit or exceed their targets, and use budgets to spell out the level of performance legislators expect for the price they are willing to pay.

Customer-Driven Government: Meeting the
Needs of the Customer, Not the Bureaucracy

Customer-driven governments treat those they serve—the parents whose children they teach, the people who line up to renew driver's licenses, or the general public—as their customers. They use surveys and focus groups to listen to their customers; they set customer service standards and offer guarantees; and whenever possible they give their customers a choice of service providers. With this input and these incentives, they redesign their organizations to deliver maximum value to the customers.

Enterprising Government: Earning Rather than Spending

Enterprising governments focus their energies not only on spending money, but on earning it. They charge user fees and impact fees; they demand a return on their investments; and they use incentives such as enterprise funds, shared earnings, and innovation funds to encourage managers to pay as much attention to earning money as they do to spending it.

Anticipatory Government: Prevention Rather than Cure

Anticipatory governments seek to prevent problems rather than delivering services to correct them. They use strategic planning, future visioning, and other tools to give themselves better foresight. To lengthen decision makers' time horizons, they redesign budget systems, accounting systems, and reward systems to shift the incentives operating on them.

Decentralized Government: From Hierarchy to Participation and Teamwork

Decentralized governments push authority down through the organization or system, encouraging those who deal directly with customers to make more of their own decisions. They restructure organizations to shift control from functional silos, such as procurement offices and maintenance units, to frontline employees. They empower employees by flattening organizational hierarchies, using teams, and creating labor-management partnerships.

Market-Oriented Government: Leveraging Change Through the Market

Market-oriented governments often restructure private markets to solve problems rather than using administrative mechanisms such as service delivery or command-and-control regulation. They create financial incentives—such as effluent fees, green taxes, and tax incentives—that drive private organizations and individuals to behave in ways that solve societal problems.

For more on these principles, see *Reinventing Government*.

APPENDIX B:
RESOURCES FOR
REINVENTORS

The Reinventor's Handbook

As we mentioned earlier, we will soon publish another book that details how to use each of the more than 90 tools and metatools listed in Part II. Using the five strategies as a framework, it will illustrate the use of these tools, as well as how-to's, lessons learned, do's and don't's, pitfalls, and other practical knowledge for reinventors.

The book will contain chapters on each of the 15 approaches outlined in *Banishing Bureaucracy*, plus chapters on performance measurement, total quality management, and business process reengineering. It will also address at length how to transform government's administrative control systems: the budget and finance, personnel, procurement, and auditing systems that are the hallmark of bureaucratic government. Finally, it will describe six new management systems appropriate for 21st century governance: for steering, market testing, performance management, customer relations, labor-management cooperation, and organizational learning.

The Reinventing Government Workbook

To be published in 1997 by Jossey-Bass Publishers, this workbook is designed to introduce frontline employees to the basic ideas of reinventing government. Authored by David Osborne and Victor Colon, it includes segments on each of the ten principles outlined in *Reinventing Government,* by David Osborne and Ted Gaebler. To order, contact Jossey-Bass Publishers.

Address: 350 Sansome St.
           San Francisco, CA 94104
 Phone: 800 956 7739
   Fax: 800 605 2665

The Reinventing Government Video

David Osborne and Ted Gaebler have produced a one-hour video designed to introduce people to the basic ideas of reinventing government and help them grasp its potential. Done in documentary fashion, it intersperses insights from Osborne and Gaebler with four stories of fundamental reinvention: the Air Combat Command, competitive contracting in Indianapolis, public school choice in Minnesota, and tenant management at the Cabrini Green public housing development in Chicago. The video is available from Video Publishing House.

Address: 930 North National Pkwy., Suite 505
           Schaumburg, IL 60173-9921
 Phone: 800 824 8889
           847 517 8744
   Fax: 847 517 8752

The Public Strategies Group

David Osborne is a managing partner of the Public Strategies Group, one of the nation's foremost consulting firms specializing in reinvention. Made up of experienced public sector practitioners, it is led by CEO Babak Armajani, coauthor of *Breaking Through Bureaucracy*. PSG has worked with clients throughout the nation and world. Since 1993 it has also provided leadership services to the Minneapolis public schools, acting as superintendent of the district. In addition to hands-on consulting, the firm offers speakers, seminars, and workshops on a variety of topics related to reinvention, and it produces workbooks and other products for use by practitioners. PSG also operates a network of other consulting firms with expertise in various aspects of reinvention, called the Reinventing Government Network.

Address: 275 E. 4th St., Suite 710
St. Paul, MN 55101
Phone: 612 223 8371
Fax: 612 292 1482
E-mail: reinvent@psgrp.com
Web site: http://www.psgrp.com

For more information, see page 401.

On Purpose Associates

Peter Plastrik is cofounder of On Purpose Associates, a nonprofit firm that assists change-minded government agencies, education organizations, nonprofit organizations, and foundations. With Plastrik are John Cleveland and Joann Neuroth, experienced innovators in public sector steering and management. Since 1991, On Purpose has worked with local, state, and federal government agencies, school districts, community colleges, and national foundations, offering consulting, presentations, and workshops. In addition to reinvention, On Purpose's expertise includes economic development, education reform, and the development of sustainable communities.

Address: 1716 E. Michigan Ave.
Lansing, MI 48912
Phone: 517 371 2517
Fax: 517 371 2601

The Alliance for Redesigning Government

Cofounded in 1993 by David Osborne, the Alliance is a nonprofit learning network that brings change agents together to share ideas, concerns, and practices. It publishes a newsletter (see below), has an on-line database on reinvention (see below), sponsors design labs to build new tools for reinvention, and sponsors conferences and workshops. The Alliance is a program of the National Academy of Public Administration.

Address: 1120 G St., NW, Suite 850
Washington, D.C. 20005
Phone: 202 INNOVTR (466 6887)
Fax: 202 347 3252
E-mail: ARGNET@aol.com.

For more information, see p. 399.

The Public Innovator

A biweekly newsletter published by the Alliance for Redesigning Government, *The Public Innovator* brings you information you can use to improve your organization's performance. Its brief, lively articles, full of pointers and lessons from successful practitioners, come complete with names, phone numbers, fax numbers, and e-mail addresses you can contact for more information. The address and phone number are those given for the Alliance for Redesigning Government above. To request a free trial, see page 399.

The Public Innovator Learning Network

Full of thousands of brief case studies, the Learning Network web site is the place to start your search for information you need to help you reinvent. Whether you want to know how to measure performance or how to listen to your customers, you will find brief essays, case studies, bibliographies, and paths to more information, all available free of charge. You can also jump with the click of a mouse into other databases full of useful information related to reinvention, such as those of the National Performance Review, *Governing* magazine, and *Government Executive* magazine.

Web site: http://www.clearlake.ibm.com/Alliance/

RECOMMENDED READING ON REINVENTION

General

Michael Barzelay and Babak Armajani. *Breaking Through Bureaucracy: A New Vision for Managing in Government.* Berkeley: University of California Press, 1992.

Bill Creech. *The Five Pillars of TQM: How to Make Total Quality Management Work for You.* New York: Truman Talley Books/Dutton, 1994.

Al Gore. The National Performance Review Annual Reports: *From Red Tape to Results: Creating a Government that Works Better and Costs Less; Creating a Government that Works Better and Costs Less: Status Report; Common Sense Government: Works Better and Costs Less;* and *The Best Kept Secrets in Government.* Washington, D.C.: National Performance Review, 1993, 1994, 1995, 1996.

Reaching Public Goals: Managing Government for Results: Resource Guide. Washington, D.C.: National Performance Review, Oct. 1996.

Michael Hammer and James Champy. *Reengineering the Corporation: A Manifesto for Business Revolution.* New York: HarperCollins, 1993.

Tom Peters. *Thriving on Chaos: Handbook for a Management Revolution.* New York: Knopf, 1988.

The Five C's

The Core Strategy
Diana Goldsworthy. *Setting Up Next Steps.* London: Her Majesty's Stationery Office, 1991.

E. S. Savas. *Privatization: The Key to Better Government.* Chatham, N. J.: Chatham House, 1987.

The Consequences Strategy
Audit Commission. *Realising the Benefits of Competition: The Client Role for Contracted Services.* Local Government Report no. 4. London: HMSO, 1993.

Howard Davies. *Fighting Leviathan: Building Social Markets that Work.* London: The Social Market Foundation, 1992.

John D. Donohue. *The Privatization Decision.* New York: Basic Books, 1990.

Ron Jensen. *Managed Competition: A Tool for Achieving Excellence in Government.* Entry in Alliance for Redesigning Government's Public

Innovator Learning Network, an on-line database available on the World Wide Web at http://www.clearlake.ibm.com/Alliance/

Donald F. Kettl. *Sharing Power: Public Governance and Private Markets.* Washington, D.C.: Brookings Institution, 1993.

The Customer Strategy
Seymour Fliegel. *Miracle in East Harlem: The Fight for Choice in Public Education.* New York: Times Books, 1993.

Joe Nathan, ed. *Public Schools by Choice.* St. Paul, Minn.: Institute for Learning and Teaching, 1989.

Joe Nathan. *Charter Schools: Creating Hope and Opportunity for American Education.* San Francisco: Jossey-Bass, 1996.

The Citizen's Charter: The Facts and Figures. Cm. 2970. London: HMSO, 1995.

The Control Strategy
Peter Block. *Stewardship: Choosing Service over Self-Interest.* San Francisco: Berrett-Koehler, 1993.

Gifford and Elizabeth Pinchot. *The End of Bureaucracy and the Rise of the Intelligent Organization.* San Francisco: Berrett-Koehler, 1993.

The Culture Strategy
Joel A. Barker. *Paradigms: The Business of Discovering the Future.* New York: HarperBusiness, 1992.

William Bridges. *Transitions: Making Sense of Life's Changes.* Reading, Mass.: Addison-Wesley, 1980.

William Bridges. *Managing Transitions: Making the Most of Change.* Reading, Mass.: Addison-Wesley, 1991.

Robert W. Jacobs. *Real Time Strategic Change: How to Involve an Entire Organization in Fast and Far-Reaching Change.* San Francisco: Berrett-Koehler, 1994.

James M. Kouzes and Barry Z. Posner. *The Leadership Challenge: How to Keep Getting Extraordinary Things Done in Organizations.* San Francisco: Jossey-Bass, 1995.

Kathleen D. Ryan and Daniel K. Oestreich. *Driving Fear Out of the Workplace: How to Overcome the Invisible Barriers to Quality, Productivity, and Innovation.* San Francisco: Jossey-Bass, 1991.

Peter M. Senge, Charlotte Roberts, Richard B. Ross, Bryan J. Smith, and Art Kleiner. *The Fifth Discipline Fieldbook: Strategies and Tools for Building a Learning Organization.* New York: Doubleday, 1994.

James Q. Wilson. *Bureaucracy: What Government Agencies Do and Why They Do It.* New York: Basic Books, 1989. See chapter 6, "Culture."

International

General
Carl Bertelsmann Prize 1993: Democracy and Efficiency in Local Government. Volume 2. Gütersloh, Germany: Bertelsmann Foundation Publishers, 1994.

Donald Savoie. *Thatcher, Reagan, Mulroney: In Search of a New Bureaucracy.* Pittsburgh and London: University of Pittsburgh Press, 1994.

U.S. General Accounting Office. *Managing for Results: Experiences Abroad Suggest Insights for Federal Management Reforms.* Washington, D.C.: U.S. General Accounting Office, 1995.

Australia
Task Force on Management Improvement. *The Australian Public Service Reformed: An Evaluation of a Decade of Management Reform.* Canberra: Australian Government Publishing Service, 1992.

Patrick Weller and Glyn Davis, eds. *New Ideas, Better Government.* St. Leonards, Australia: Allen & Unwin, 1996.

New Zealand
Jonathan Boston, John Martin, June Pallot, and Pat Walsh. *Public Management: The New Zealand Model.* Auckland, New Zealand: Oxford University Press, 1996.

Roger Douglas. *Unfinished Business.* Auckland, New Zealand: Random House, 1993.

Office of the Auditor General of Canada. *Toward Better Governance: Public Service Reform in New Zealand (1984–94) and Its Relevance to Canada.* Ottawa: Minister of Supply and Services, 1995.

Graham Scott. *Government Reform in New Zealand.* Forthcoming.

United Kingdom
The Civil Service: Continuity and Change. Cm. 2627. London: HMSO, 1994.

Next Steps Agencies in Government: Review 1995. Cm. 3164. London: HMSO, 1996.

NOTES

All quotations that are not attributed in the text or in these endnotes are from interviews with the authors or their associates. Only in cases where there might be some confusion about the source of a quotation have we indicated in a note that it came from an interview.

Introduction: Uphill Battle, USA

pp. 6–7:   Data on Indianapolis, Hampton, Minnesota, U.S. Forest Service, Australia, and New Zealand: See later chapters.

p. 7:   "In Great Britain, Prime Minister Margaret Thatcher sold £20 billion . . . of public activities—with more than 600,000 employees . . .": The figure of £20 billion is from Donald Savoie, *Thatcher, Reagan, Mulroney: In Search of a New Bureaucracy* (Pittsburgh and London: University of Pittsburgh Press, 1994), p. 160. The figure of "more than 600,000" is from Margaret Thatcher, *The Downing Street Years 1979–1990* (New York: HarperPerennial, 1995), p. 687. Savoie, p. 248, uses the figure of 800,000, but we have used Thatcher's more conservative figure.

p. 7:   "While trimming its staff by a third . . .": When Thatcher took office, there were 732,000 civil servants, according to Savoie, *Thatcher, Reagan, Mulroney*. By September 1996 there were 491,757, according to the British Government's Office of Public Service.

p. 8:   Alice Rivlin quote: "Statement by the Chair of the Ministerial Symposium on the Future of Public Services," Organization for Economic Cooperation and Development, Paris, March 6, 1996.

p. 9:   "By 1995, for example, . . .": *Performance Measurement of Municipal Services: How Are America's Cities Measuring Up?* (Philadelphia: Pennsylvania Economy League, Eastern Division, Sept. 1995).

p. 9:   "By mid-decade, 39 states . . .": *Workforce Policies: State Activities and Innovations* (Washington, D.C.: National Association of State Budget Officers, 1995).

p. 14:   "It creates organizations that show up in ratings . . .": "Social Security Administration Tops in Customer Service," Dalbar Financial Services, Inc., Boston, Mass., press release, May 3, 1995. Reported in Vice President Al Gore, *Common Sense Government: Works Better and Costs Less* (Washington, D.C.: National Performance Review, 1995), p. 49.

p. 15:   "It creates inner-city public schools . . .": Seymour Fliegel, *Miracle in East Harlem: The Fight for Choice in Public Education* (New York: Times Books, 1993), p. 229.

p. 15:   "And it creates organizations the private sector uses as benchmarks . . .": Gore, *Common Sense Government*, p. 83.

p. 16:   Sturgess essay: Gary L. Sturgess, "The Decline and Fall of the Industrial State," in *New Ideas, Better Government*, Patrick Weller and Glyn Davis, eds. (St. Leonards, Australia: Allen & Unwin, 1996), pp. 26–37.

p. 16:   Max Weber quotations: Max Weber, "Bureaucracy," in *From Max Weber*, H. H. Gerth and C. Wright Mills, eds., Galaxy Book edition (New York: Oxford University Press, 1958), pp. 196–244.

p. 17:   Canadian survey: Frank Graves, Benoit Gauthier, and Derek Jansen, *Rethinking Government '94: An Overview and Synthesis* (Ottawa: Ekos Research Associates, Inc., 1995). Ekos interviewed 2,400 Canadians with 200 questions, then did a second survey of 1,600 of the original 2,400 with 150 questions.

p. 18:   Phoenix Department of Public Works: See David Osborne and Ted Gaebler, *Reinventing Government: How the Entrepreneurial Spirit Is Transforming the Public Sector* (Reading, Mass.: Addison-Wesley, 1992), pp. 76–79.

Chapter 1: The Five C's:
Changing Government's DNA

p. 21:   Economic statistics on British GDP, inflation, public spending, etc.: Thatcher, *The Downing Street Years*, pp. 7, 8, 36, 38, 676.

p. 21:   "By comparison, government in the U.S. consumed about 35 percent of GDP at the time": *Statistical Abstract of the United States: 1995*, 115th edition (Washington, D.C.: U.S. Bureau of the Census, 1995), Tables 474 and 699.

p. 21:   "At her first cabinet meeting . . .": Savoie, *Thatcher, Reagan, Mulroney*, p. 92, and Thatcher, *The Downing Street Years*, pp. 32, 46.

p. 22:   "They led to the elimination of 12,000 positions . . .": Savoie, *Thatcher, Reagan, Mulroney*, p. 140.

p. 22:   "Thatcher also took on the public sector unions . . .": Thatcher, *The Downing Street Years*, pp. 40, 272–274, 284.

p. 22:   "In her 11 years, the government sold more than 40 major state-owned enterprises . . .": Citizen's Charter Unit, *Raising the Standard: Britain's*

Citizen's Charter and Public Service Reforms (London: Foreign & Commonwealth Office, 1992), p. 10. On public housing: Joan Spice, *Management Reform in Four Countries* (Ottawa: MAB-MIAC Task Force on Management Improvement, Nov. 1992), chapter 2, p. 4.

p. 22: "By 1987 these sales . . . £5 billion a year": Savoie, *Thatcher, Reagan, Mulroney*, p. 160; "helping Thatcher balance her last four budgets . . .": Thatcher, *The Downing Street Years*, p. 841.

p. 22: "By 1994, the cumulative total was $75 billion . . .": *Privatization 1994* (Los Angeles: Reason Foundation, 1994), p. 43.

p. 22: Thatcher quote: Thatcher, *The Downing Street Years*, p. 687.

p. 23: "During Thatcher's reign . . .": Ibid., pp. 45, 676.

p. 23: "They threw around slogans . . .": Savoie, *Thatcher, Reagan, Mulroney*, p. 92.

p. 23: "In fact, Thatcher triggered a revolt . . .": Thatcher, *The Downing Street Years*, p. 417.

p. 24: "But not one had asked the bureaucrats . . .": Kate Jenkins, "Next Steps: Institutional Impact and Beyond," address to the Australian Fulbright Symposium, Brisbane, June 1994. A former member of the Efficiency Unit, Jenkins was part of the team that conducted the study.

p. 24: Rayner quote: Savoie, *Thatcher, Reagan, Mulroney*, p. 174. Savoie was quoting an essay by Lord Rayner entitled "The Unfinished Agenda."

p. 25: "In addition, the Efficiency Unit pointed out, . . .": Kate Jenkins, Karen Caines, and Andrew Jackson, *Improving Management in Government: The Next Steps*, Report to the Prime Minister by the Efficiency Unit (London: HMSO, 1988), pp. 3–5.

p. 25: On the Next Steps report and its implementation, see Diana Goldsworthy, *Setting Up Next Steps* (London: HMSO, May 1991); Patricia Greer, *Transforming Central Government: The Next Steps Initiative* (Buckingham, Philadelphia: Open University Press, 1994); Savoie, *Thatcher, Reagan, Mulroney*, pp. 205–213; and Spice, *Management Reform in Four Countries*.

p. 27: Numbers of Next Steps agencies: 1988–1989, 1991, 1992: Savoie, *Thatcher, Reagan, Mulroney*, pp. 211–212; 1996: personal communication from Jeremy Cowper, head of the Next Steps Team, Sept. 6, 1996.
        "Nearly 75 percent of the civil service . . .": Personal communication from Jeremy Cowper, Sept. 6, 1996.

p. 29: Agencies hitting 75 and 83 percent of performance targets: *Next Steps Review: 1995*, Cm. 3164 (London: HMSO, 1996), p. v.

p. 29: Vehicle Inspectorate data: *Improving Management in Government: The Next Steps Agencies: Review 1991*, Cm. 1760 (London: HMSO, 1991), p. 67; and *The Next Steps Agencies: Review 1992*, Cm. 2111 (London: HMSO, 1992), p. 92.

p. 29: Social Security Information Technology Services Agency information and data: *Improving Management in Government: The Next Steps Agencies: Review 1991*, p. 59; *The Next Steps Agencies: Review 1992*, p. 83; *Next Steps Review: 1993*, Cm. 2430 (London: HMSO, 1993), pp. 111–112; *Next Steps Review: 1994*, Cm. 2750 (London: HMSO, 1994), pp. 105–106; and *Next Steps Review: 1995*, pp. 272–273.

p. 29: "Later it pushed the comparisons down . . .": *The Citizen's Charter: The Facts and Figures* (London: HMSO, 1995), p. 19.

p. 30: "The surveys show general improvement . . ." See *Notes: News of the Employment Service*, June 1993, August 1993, and June 1994, published by the Employment Service; and *Improving Management in Government: The Next Steps Agencies: Review 1991*, pp. 24–25; *The Next Steps Agencies: Review 1992*, pp. 35–36; *Next Steps Review: 1993*, pp. 50–51; *Next Steps Review: 1994*, pp. 31–32; *Next Steps Review: 1995*, pp. 50–55. Also personal communication from Jeremy Cowper, Sept. 19, 1996.

p. 30: "In 1994–1995, the 80-plus agencies . . .": Personal communication from Jeremy Cowper, Sept. 19, 1996.

p. 30: 15 percent reduction in the size of the civil service: Personal communication from Eugenie Turton, director of the Citizen's Charter Unit, Sept. 12, 1996.

p. 30: Treasury and Civil Service Committee quotation: *Next Steps: Briefing Note*, published by the Next Steps Team in the Office of Public Service, February 26, 1996, p. 6.

p. 30: ". . . the Labor Party announced . . .": Savoie, *Thatcher, Reagan, Mulroney*, p. 212.

p. 31: "Competing for Quality" white paper: *Competing for Quality: Buying Better Public Services*, Cm. 1730 (London: HMSO, Nov. 1991).

p. 31: "It did, however, promise . . .": Ibid., p. 11.

p. 31: "Within the first five years, . . .": Personal communication from Jeremy Cowper, Sept. 6, 1996.

p. 31: "In September 1995, the government reported . . .": *The Citizen's Charter: The Facts and Figures*, p. 41.

p. 31: "Where public and private providers have competed . . .": Interview with John Oughton, then head of the Efficiency Unit and Market Testing Program, June 1994.

p. 32: "Regardless of who wins, savings are averaging 21 percent . . .": *Next Steps Review: 1995*, p. v.

p. 32: "As one aide put it, . . .": Quotation is from John Oughton, then head of the Efficiency Unit and Market Testing Program, June 1994.

p. 34: "There were 40 national charters . . .": *The Citizen's Charter: The Facts and Figures*. See, for example, pp. 1, 2, 5, 8, 11, 14, 15, 23, 29, 43, 55, and 62.

p. 34: National Health Service improvements: *The Citizen's Charter: The Facts and Figures*, p. 7.

p. 34:   British Rail statistics: Ibid., p. 14.

p. 34:   Passport Office statistics: Memorandum from Citizen's Charter Unit, Feb. 6, 1996.

p. 34:   "By early 1996, the London Underground . . .": *The Citizen's Charter: The Facts and Figures*, p. 15.

p. 34:   "More than 400 public organizations . . .": Personal communication from Eugenie Turton, director of the Citizen's Charter Unit.

p. 35:   "Excerpts from the Patient's Charter": *The Patient's Charter & You* (London: Department of Health, Jan. 1995).

p. 35:   "Excerpts from the Passenger's Charter": *The British Rail Passenger's Charter* (London: British Railways Board).

p. 35:   "As the railways are privatized . . .": *The Citizen's Charter: The Facts and Figures*, p. 15.

p. 37:   Kolderie quotation: Ted Kolderie, ed., *An Equitable and Competitive Public Sector* (Minneapolis: Hubert H. Humphrey Institute of Public Affairs, University of Minnesota, 1984), p. 77.

p. 37:   Beer, Eisenstat, and Spector quote: Michael Beer, Russell A. Eisenstat, and Bert Spector, "Why Change Programs Don't Produce Change," *Harvard Business Review*, Nov.–Dec. 1990, pp. 159–166.

Chapter 2: Levels of the Game:
Targeting the Strategies

p. 54:   Statistics on Operation Desert Storm: Bill Creech, *The Five Pillars of TQM: How to Make Total Quality Management Work for You* (New York: Dutton, 1994), pp. 120, 136.

p. 54:   "In the late 1970s, . . .": Osborne and Gaebler, *Reinventing Government*, pp. 255–256. These statistics originated with the Tactical Air Command. They were presented by General W. L. Creech in an address at the Armed Services Leadership and Management Symposium, in Oct. 1983, called "Leadership and Management—the Present and the Future." We have checked these statistics, as well as those from Creech's book, against statistics for other years provided us by TAC and its successor, the Air Combat Command—for example, those TAC submitted in 1989 for the U.S. Senate Productivity Award, which it won—and found them to be consistent.

p. 54:   Creech quotation: "Each squadron . . .": Creech, *The Five Pillars of TQM*, pp. 129–130.

p. 55:   "He broke up the centralized supply operation, . . .": Jay Finegan, "Four-Star Management," *Inc.*, Jan. 1987, pp. 42–51.

p. 55:   "He moved aircraft parts . . . *fix it right*' ": Creech, *The Five Pillars of TQM*, pp. 133–135.

p. 55:   "Creech asked frontline teams . . .": Ibid., p. 314.

p. 55:   Creech quotation: "Their 'new cost-awareness . . .' ": Ibid., p. 447.

p. 55:   ". . . titanium 'turkey feathers' . . .": Ibid., p. 448.

p. 55:   Creech quotation: "Accountability for poor performance . . .": Ibid., pp. 130–132.

p. 56:   "He also tried the culture strategy . . . uniforms became commonplace": Ibid. pp. 52–53, 171–173.

p. 56:   "By 1983, TAC's productivity had increased 80 percent": Ibid., p. 35.

p. 56:   Crash rate statistics: Ibid., pp. 316–317.

p. 56:   Aircraft repair statistics and sortie rates: Ibid., p. 136.

p. 56:   "TAC did this without significant infusions of money or people": Creech, "Leadership and Management—the Present and the Future." The statistics we are referring to here cover the period 1978–1983. The Reagan defense buildup began with the fiscal year 1982 budget, which was passed in 1981. But because defense expenditures take a long time to wind their way down to military bases, the new money did not begin to be felt, according to General Creech, until at least 1983. Hence it had little impact on this period of improvement.

p. 56:   "And according to a 1984 analysis . . .": Creech, *The Five Pillars of TQM*, p. 137.

p. 57:   "By the late 1980s, . . .": Tactical Air Command presentation to the examiners for the 1989 U.S. Senate Productivity Award, provided by Air Combat Command, Langley Air Force Base.

p. 59:   Statistics on ACC teams in Utah and Tacoma, and improvements in travel and pharmacies: John M. Loh, "Quality: The Leadership Dimension," presentation to the Aerospace Defense Quality Symposium, San Diego, California, Apr. 7, 1992; pp. 6–7.

p. 59:   "When Walmart wanted to benchmark . . .": Gore, *Common Sense Government*, p. 83.

p. 60:   "The results showed significant improvement . . .": ACC survey and trend data, provided by Air Combat Command, Langley Air Force Base; and "ACC Quality," a presentation given by General Loh to the U.S. Senate Productivity Awards Examiners in 1993.

p. 61:   Creech quotation: "You can be a principal catalyst . . .": Creech, *The Five Pillars of TQM*, pp. 453–454.

p. 61:   "Stone and Farbrother credit those visits . . .": Personal communications with Bob Stone and Doug Farbrother.

p. 62:   Creech quotation: "At an impromptu get-together . . .": Creech, *The Five Pillars of TQM*, p. 454.

p. 62:   "When Vice President Gore held town meetings . . .": From personal experience; David Osborne served as a senior advisor to Vice President Gore in 1993.

p. 62:   Petronius quote: Quoted in Rt. Hon Ian Lang, MP, Secretary of State for

Scotland, "The Government's View," *Eglinton Management Review*, Spring 1994, pp. 6–12.

p. 63:   "The result: their performance didn't change much": See *Special Operating Agencies: Taking Stock* (Ottawa: Auditor General of Canada, May 1994).

p. 63:   "One civil servant told . . .": Savoie, *Thatcher, Reagan, Mulroney*, p. 241.

p. 63:   Drucker quotation: Quoted in Creech, *The Five Pillars of TQM*, p. 226, from Peter Drucker, *The Frontiers of Management*.

p. 65:   Creech quotation: "Employees soon write 'TQM' . . . off . . .": Creech, *The Five Pillars of TQM*, p. 235.

p. 65:   Creech quotation: ". . . new incentives . . . availed us little": Ibid., pp. 203–204.

Chapter 3: Gut Check: What It Takes to Use the Strategies

p. 67:   William Bridges quotation: William Bridges, *Managing Transitions: Making the Most of Change* (Reading, Mass: Addison-Wesley, 1993), p. 4.

Chapter 4: The Core Strategy: Creating Clarity of Purpose

p. 75:   "The sales generated . . .": R. C. Mascarnehas, "State-Owned Enterprises," in *Reshaping the State: New Zealand's Bureaucratic Revolution*, ed. Jonathan Boston, John Martin, Jule Pallot, and Pat Walsh (Auckland: Oxford University Press, 1991).

p. 76:   "In 1950, New Zealanders enjoyed . . .": Graham C. Scott, *Government Reform in New Zealand*, forthcoming.

p. 76:   "Since then, this island nation . . .": Roger Douglas, *Unfinished Business* (Auckland: Random House, New Zealand Ltd., 1993), p. 14.

p. 76:   Unemployment figures: Interview with Jonathan Boston, associate professor of public policy, Victoria University of Wellington.

p. 76:   "By 1984, New Zealand . . .": Scott, *Government Reform in New Zealand*.

p. 76:   "They had tried to restrain . . .": Ibid.

p. 76:   "By 1984, the national budget exceeded . . .": Douglas, *Unfinished Business*, p. 22.

p. 76:   Inflation figures: Ibid.

p. 76:   Interest payments on the debt: Roger Douglas, "The Politics of Successful Structural Reform," unpublished manuscript.

p. 77:   Douglas quotation: Douglas, *Unfinished Business*, p. 22.

p. 77: "By 1988, they had cut...": Douglas, "The Politics of Successful Structural Reform."

p. 77: "In addition,.. ": *Toward Better Governance: Public Service Reform in New Zealand (1984–94) and Its Relevance to Canada* (Ottawa: Office of the Auditor General of Canada, 1995), pp. 14–16. For more on New Zealand's early reforms, see Boston et al., *Reshaping the State*; Douglas, *Unfinished Business*, pp. 19–36; and Scott, *Government Reform in New Zealand*.

p. 78: "By 1984, New Zealand's government owned...": Douglas, "The Politics of Successful Structural Reform," p. 20.

p. 78: Douglas quotation: Douglas, *Unfinished Business*, p. 176.

p. 78: "But it also regulated coal mining,...": Douglas, "The Politics of Successful Structural Reform."

p. 78: "Overall, government-run businesses...": Auditor General of Canada, *Toward Better Governance*, p. 13.

p. 79: "In the previous two decades,...": Roger Douglas, "National Policy-Makers' Experience—New Zealand," address to the World Bank Conference on Privatization, Washington, D.C., June 11–13, 1990, p. 9.

p. 79: Douglas quotation: Ibid.

p. 80: "The change affected some 60,000 government employees...": Mascarnehas, "State-Owned Enterprises," in *Reshaping the State*, p. 35. Total national government employment was about 250,000, but nearly half of this was in education and health care, not part of the "core" government bureaucracy.

p. 80: SOE personnel reductions: Forest SOE, from Scott, *Government Reform in New Zealand*; railroad SOE, from Douglas, "National Policy-Makers' Experience," p. 13; telecommunications SOE, from Douglas, *Unfinished Business*, p. 180.

p. 80: Douglas quotation: "The Post Office,...": Douglas, "National Policy-Makers' Experience," p. 13.

p. 80: "Within five years,...": Auditor General of Canada, *Toward Better Governance*, p. 23.

p. 80: "Telecommunications increased its productivity... $41 million profit": Scott, *Government Reform in New Zealand*.

p. 80: "The Forest Corporation turned a $70 million loss...": Douglas, *Unfinished Business*, p. 44.

p. 80: "The postal system... by a third": Scott, *Government Reform in New Zealand*.

p. 80: "As a whole, the SOEs increased...": Auditor General of Canada, *Toward Better Governance*, p. 23.

p. 80: "By 1992, they were paying...": Scott, *Government Reform in New Zealand*.

p. 81:   Douglas quotation: "We were getting increased efficiencies . . .": Douglas, "National Policy-Makers' Experience," p. 16.

p. 81:   "Echoing an argument . . .": Mascarnehas, "State-Owned Enterprises," in *Reshaping the State*, pp. 30–31.

p. 81:   "Several times the sales process was reopened . . .": Ibid.

p. 81:   "And a public controversy erupted . . .": Ibid.

p. 81:   "By 1991, the government had sold . . .": Scott, *Government Reform in New Zealand*.

p. 82:   "By 1995, it had sold more than 20 . . .": Jonathan Boston, John Martin, June Pallot, and Pat Walsh, *Public Management: The New Zealand Model* (Auckland: Oxford University Press, 1996), p. 67.

p. 82:   Scott quotation: Scott, *Government Reform in New Zealand*.

p. 83:   Palmer quotation: Palmer quoted in State Services Commission, *Public Sector Reform 1993* (Wellington, New Zealand: State Services Commission, 1993), p. 3.

p. 83:   Rodger quotation: "What is good . . .": quoted in Pat Walsh, "The State Sector Act of 1988," in *Reshaping the State*, p. 73.

p. 85:   "Roger Douglas and Prime Minister David Lange . . .": Douglas, *Unfinished Business*, pp. 37–52.

p. 85:   "At the same time, Labor's privatization program . . .": Interview with Jonathan Boston, associate professor of public policy, Victoria University of Wellington.

p. 85:   "Labor had made . . . it lost fiscal control": Scott, *Government Reform in New Zealand*.

p. 86:   Logan committee quotations: Steering Group, *Review of State Sector Reforms* (Wellington: Cabinet State Sector Committee, Nov. 29, 1991), p. 1.

p. 87:   For more on how New Zealand's National Party designed a strategic management system, see Jonathan Boston and June Pallot, "Linking Strategy and Performance: Developments in the New Zealand Public Sector," in *Journal of Policy Analysis and Management* (forthcoming).

p. 88:   "Under the new system, . . . majority in Parliament": Boston et al., *Public Management*, p. 48.

p. 89:   ". . . privatizing about two-thirds of the government's commercial assets": Ibid., p. 67.

p. 89:   "It cut total employment . . .": Ibid., p. 78.

p. 89:   "And it caused 'a radical refashioning' ": Ibid.

p. 89:   "Since 1984, . . . more than 3,000": Ibid.

p. 89:   "Unemployment dropped . . .": Scott, *Government Reform in New Zealand*.

p. 89:   "New investment was growing rapidly, as were exports": *The Next Three Years* (Wellington: The National Party, 1994).

p. 89: "In 1993 the World Competitiveness Report...": *New Zealand's Reformed State Sector* (Wellington: State Services Commission, 1994).

p. 89: "Rapid economic growth ... 35 percent of GDP": Graham C. Scott, "Improving Fiscal Responsibility," *Agenda: A Journal of Policy Analysis and Reform*, vol. 2, no. 1 (1995), p. 8.

p. 89: "Government-owned businesses, ... government was cutting taxes": Scott, *Government Reform in New Zealand*.

p. 90: "Agency executives say ...": Boston et al., *Public Management*, p. 87.

p. 91: 1986 ministerial task force in Canada: Savoie, *Thatcher, Reagan, Mulroney*, pp. 127–131.

p. 92: For more on Canada's Program Review process, see Paul Martin, *The Budget Plan* (Ottawa: Canada Department of Finance, Feb. 1994); Martin, *The Budget Speech* on Feb. 22, 1994 (Ottawa: Canada Department of Finance); and Martin, *The Budget Speech* on Feb. 27, 1995 (Ottawa: Canada Department of Finance).

p. 93: Material on Clinton administration's performance review: From personal experience. David Osborne served as a senior advisor to Vice President Gore and was chief author of the National Performance Review report in 1993, *From Red Tape to Results: Creating a Government That Works Better and Costs Less*.

p. 93: British "prior options review" process: See *Next Steps Review 1994*, p. iv.; and Office of Public Service, *Guidance on Agency Reviews* (London: Cabinet Office, Dec. 1995).

p. 94: "As the first 126 executive agencies ... £2.6 billion worth of services": See notes to p. 31.

p. 96: "Uncoupling steering and rowing ...": See Osborne and Gaebler, *Reinventing Government*, chapter 1.

p. 96: "It is virtually identical ...": Peter F. Drucker, *Management: Tasks, Responsibilities, Practices* (New York: Harper & Row, 1974), pp. 572–585.

p. 96: Logan quotation: Quoted in Auditor General of Canada, *Toward Better Governance*, p. 39.

p. 97: "*Reinventing Government* listed 36 alternatives ...": Osborne and Gaebler, *Reinventing Government*, pp. 332–348.

p. 97: "Ministers in New Zealand ... audited for accuracy": Scott, *Government Reform in New Zealand*.

p. 98: "As the Treasury explained ...": New Zealand Department of Treasury, *Government Management* (Wellington: Government Printer, 1987), pp. 49–64.

p. 98: "They help elected officials ...": Roger Douglas, 1988 budget, quoted in Auditor General of Canada, *Toward Better Governance*, p. 60.

p. 98: "And they avoid ...": New Zealand Department of Treasury, *Government Management*, pp. 49–64.

p. 98:   "As the State Services Commission explains, . . .": Boston et al., *Public Management*, p. 73.

p. 98:   "By breaking up large, conglomerate departments, . . .": Scott, *Government Reform in New Zealand*.

p. 100: "Canada has created . . .": For more on Canadian special operating agencies, see *Special Operating Agencies: Taking Stock* (Ottawa: Auditor General of Canada, May 1994).

p. 103: Sunnyvale document quoted: City of Sunnyvale, "Outcome Management: Overview," pp. 1–2.

p. 103: Lewcock quotation: Personal communication with authors.

p. 104: Sample Oregon Benchmarks are from *Oregon Benchmarks: Standards for Measuring Statewide Progress and Institutional Performance: Report to the 1995 Legislature* (Salem: Oregon Progress Board, Dec. 1994).

p. 105: Scott quotation: "This is intended . . .": Scott, "Improving Fiscal Responsibility," p. 3.

p. 105: Scott quotation: "The long-term forecasts . . .": Ibid., p. 11.

p. 105: Scott quotations: "that the financial implications . . .": Ibid., p. 6.

p. 111: "30 Swiss towns and villages . . .": E. S. Savas, *Privatization: The Key to Better Government* (Chatham, N.J.: Chatham House, 1987), p. 183.

p. 112: "During the Gulf War . . . subsidiary of a British company": Sturgess, "The Decline and Fall of the Industrial State," in *New Ideas, Better Government*, p. 36.

p. 112: "They report that the uncoupled model, 'while retained in statute . . .' ": Boston et al., *Public Management*, p. 92.

p. 112: Drucker quotation: Drucker, *Management*, p. 579.

p. 113: "In fact New Zealand's Labor Party pushed through legislation . . .": Boston et al., *Public Management*, pp. 183–202; Rita C. Kidd, "A Lesson from New Zealand," *Government Technology* (April 1996), p. 36.

Chapter 5: The Consequences Strategy:
Creating Consequences for Performance

p. 116: "Without any warning, Roob . . .": Stephen Goldsmith, "Moving Municipal Services into the Marketplace," Briefing No. 14 (New York: Carnegie Council Privatization Project, 1992).

p. 116: Goldsmith quotation: Ibid., p. 4.

p. 117: ". . . from a high of $450,000 . . .": Howard Husock, *Organizing Competition in Indianapolis: Mayor Stephen Goldsmith and the Quest for Lower Costs*, Kennedy School of Government Case Study, parts A, B, and sequel (Cambridge, Mass.: Harvard University, 1995).

p. 118: "The private water utility . . . $2 million a year": Goldsmith, "Moving

Municipal Services into the Marketplace"; interviews with Deputy Mayor Skip Stitt.

p. 119: Fantauzzo quotation: quoted in William D. Eggers and John O'Leary, *Revolution at the Roots* (New York: Free Press, 1996), p. 111.

p. 119: "Overall the city was to save $14.8 million . . .": Figures from presentation by Michael Carter, assistant administrator for finance in Indianapolis's Solid Waste Division, at "Reinvention Works" seminar sponsored by the National Academy of Public Administration's Alliance for Redesigning Government, Washington, D.C., March 27, 1996.

p. 120: "Motivated both by this target and the competition, . . . throughout city government": R. Joseph Gelarden, "Trash Haulers Get Cash for Saving Money for City," *Indianapolis Star*, March 18, 1995.

p. 122: "A 29.5 percent reduction . . .": In a November 11, 1993 letter from Michael Stayton, director of public works, to Mayor Goldsmith, on behalf of the Advanced Wastewater Treatment Contract Management Review Committee, the city estimated the five-year city government operating and capital investment budget for AWT at $221.8 million. The WREP proposal for that period cost $156.9 million, a reduction of $64.9 million.

p. 123: "In its first year of operation . . . by 70 percent," and ". . . union grievances also fell . . .": Details of first-year operations are contained in White River Environmental Partnership report to the Indianapolis City/County Council, *Indianapolis Advanced Wastewater Treatment Facilities: One Year Summary*, March 20, 1995.

p. 123: "The state Department of Environmental Management . . .": See Welton W. Harris II, "Environmental Board Member Defends City in Fish Kills," *The Indianapolis News*, June 22, 1995; and a letter to the editor from William Beranek Jr., president of the Indiana Environmental Institute: "Phase Out the Overflows," *Indianapolis Business Journal*, Oct. 17–23, 1994, p. 7A. "The cause of the kill is inherent in the design of our storm and sanitary sewer systems," Beranek wrote. "It was not the fault of anyone."

p. 124: "By 1996, the city had held 64 public-private competitions . . . did not bid": Indianapolis does not keep separate records of public-versus-private competitions. However, the mayor's office maintains a spreadsheet of innovative projects and the savings they will generate over seven years, known as "Enterprise Group Activity." It includes competitive bidding, as well as outsourcing, consolidations, asset sales, and reengineering projects. Typically, published accounts of savings achieved in Indianapolis reflect the total of all these activities. Our data on public-versus-private competitions were developed by identifying such projects on the Oct. 5, 1995, spreadsheet, from interviews, and from an Oct. 5, 1995, memorandum to Peter Plastrik from Deputy Mayor Skip Stitt.

p. 125: "By 1996, the mayor had eliminated . . . because of competitive bidding": Job elimination data is from an Oct. 4, 1995, memorandum from Deputy Mayor Skip Stitt to Peter Plastrik. Indianapolis does not keep records of employment changes resulting solely from public-versus-private competitions. However, in the Oct. 4, 1995, memo Stitt estimated that since Dec. 31, 1991, as many as 1,365 city employee positions had been subject to either public-private competitive bidding or to outsourcing.

p. 128: "Following the success of . . .": In a May 11, 1995, memorandum to the Indianapolis Airport Authority, board members Gordon St. Angelo and Michael W. Wells reported that from 1984 to 1994 the airport had experienced a 38 percent increase in costs charged to airlines.

p. 128: "The authority's May 11 press release . . .": Indianapolis Airport Authority, "Private Management of Airport Could Save More than $100 Million, Improve Service," press release, May 11, 1995.

p. 129: "By 1992, when the Conservatives . . .": Audit Commission, *Realising the Benefits of Competition: The Client Role for Contracted Services* (London: HMSO, 1993), p. 1.

p. 130: Flanagan and Perkins quotation: Jim Flanagan and Susan Perkins, "Public/Private Competition in the City of Phoenix, Arizona," *Government Finance Review*, June 1995, p. 7.

p. 133: "In Philadelphia, when a private contractor . . .": Steven Cohen and William Eimicke, "Reinventing Government: A Critical Analysis from Three Cities." Paper prepared for presentation to the Trinity Symposium on Public Management, San Antonio, Tex., July 23, 1995.

p. 134: "In Philadelphia, Phoenix, and the U.K. . . .": Re: Philadelphia and Phoenix, ibid. Re: the U.K., see the following note.

p. 134: "In the U.K., European Community . . .": Audit Commission, *Realising the Benefits of Competition: The Client Role for Contracted Services* (London: HMSO, 1993), p. 22.

p. 134: "In Philadelphia, when Mayor Ed Rendell . . .": Mayor Edward Rendell, address to top appointees of the Guiliani administration, Gracie Mansion, New York City, Mar. 5, 1994.

p. 136: "While reducing prices, . . .": Task Force on Management Improvement, *The Australian Public Service Reformed: An Evaluation of a Decade of Management Reform* (Canberra: Australian Government Publishing Service, 1992), pp. 319–322.

p. 137: "Australia broke 60 percent . . . the Australian government": Ibid., p. 283.

p. 139: Kettl quotation: "a murky in-between world": Donald F. Kettl, "Restructuring the Federal Government: Downsizing, Dumbsizing, or Smartsizing," statement to the U.S. Senate Committee on Governmental Affairs, May 18, 1995, p. 6.

p. 143:   Davies quotation: Howard Davies, *Fighting Leviathan: Building Social Markets that Work* (London: The Social Market Foundation, 1992), p. 24.

p. 143:   "By 1991, the national government. . . . 'cease trading' ": *Competing for Quality: Buying Better Public Services*, Cm. 1730 (London: HMSO, Nov. 1991), p. 25.

p. 143:   Jensen quotation: Ron Jensen, *Managed Competition: A Tool for Achieving Excellence in Government.* Entry in Alliance for Redesigning Government's "Public Innovator Learning Network," an on-line database available on the World Wide Web at http://www.clear lake.ibm.com/Alliance/.

p. 145:   "In 1995, the bonus was $250": Information provided by Tharon Greene, Hampton's director of human resources. In the 1995 citizen survey, 89 percent of citizens were satisfied or very satisfied. The city spent a total of $329,000 on bonuses for citizen satisfaction.

p. 147:   James quotation: William James, *Letters* (Boston: Atlantic Monthly Press, 1920), p. 33.

p. 147:   "The Seven Motivating Factors": Frederick Herzberg, *Work and the Nature of Man* (New York: World Publishing, 1966).

p. 147:   "In Australia, when researchers . . .": *The Australian Public Service Reformed*, pp. 154–55.

p. 150:   "For instance, the first-year appraisals . . .": Parliament of the Commonwealth of Australia, Senate Standing Committee on Finance and Public Administration, *Performance Pay Report*, Dec. 1993.

p. 150:   "This happened in the first year . . .": This and other results of the Australian performance pay program are presented in a memorandum issued jointly by the Public Service Commission, Department of Industrial Relations, and Department of Finance: "Memorandum to Agencies on Performance Appraisal and Performance Based Pay," Apr. 27, 1994.

p. 150:   "It was also the norm . . .": Savoie, *Thatcher, Reagan, Mulroney*, pp. 296–297.

p. 150:   Behn quotation: Robert D. Behn, "Measuring Performance Against the 80–30 Syndrome," *Governing*, June 1993, p. 70.

p. 154:   Data on Naval Air Warfare Center deal: City of Indianapolis, "Goldsmith Declares Victory in NAWC Privatization," press release from Office of the Mayor, May 14, 1996.

Chapter 6: The Customer Strategy: Putting the Customer in the Driver's Seat

p. 158:   For a more complete definition of charter schools, see Joe Nathan, *Charter Schools: Creating Hope and Opportunity for American Education* (San Francisco: Jossey-Bass, 1996), pp. 1–4.

p. 160: Ted Kolderie quotation: quoted in R. Craig Sautter, "Charter Schools: A New Breed of Public Schools," *Policy Briefs*, report 2 (1993), North Central Regional Educational Laboratory, Oak Brook, Ill., p. 3.

p. 162: "Within two years, 5,700 students were participating . . ": Jessie Montano, "Choice Comes to Minnesota," in *Public Schools by Choice*, ed. Joe Nathan (St. Paul, Minn.: Institute for Learning and Teaching, 1989), pp. 176–177.

p. 162: ". . . 60 percent were B, C, and D students": Ibid., p. 174.

p. 162: "At the University of Minnesota, 50 percent were from the inner city": Memorandum from Darryl Sedio, director, Advanced High School Student Services, University of Minnesota, to Minnesota house and senate members, Apr. 17, 1995.

p. 163: "They quickly doubled . . .": *Postsecondary Enrollment Options Program* (St. Paul: Program Evaluation Division, Office of the Legislative Auditor, State of Minnesota, Mar. 1996).

p. 163: Statistics on Post-Secondary Enrollment Options program: Ibid.

p. 163: "Overall, the percentage of Minnesota juniors . . .": Ibid., p. 16.

p. 164: "By the end, there were 61 participants . . .": Nancy C. Roberts and Paula J. King, *Transforming Public Policy: Dynamics of Policy Entrepreneurship and Innovation* (San Francisco: Jossey-Bass, 1996), p. 53; personal communication from Ted Kolderie.

p. 164: "Perpich had set a deadline . . . measure performance": Roberts and King, *Transforming Public Policy*, p. 59.

p. 165: "The reformers also managed . . . of public schools": Interview with Dan Loritz, Sept. 24, 1996.

p. 165: "They succeeded beyond their adversaries' wildest dreams: . . .": Roberts and King, *Transforming Public Policy*, p. 62.

p. 165: "Though Perpich chose . . . open their borders": Ibid., p. 65, and interview with Dan Loritz, Sept. 24, 1996.

p. 166: Tenbusch and Garet survey: James P. Tenbusch and Michael S. Garet, "Organizational Change at the Local School Level under Minnesota's Open Enrollment Program," paper prepared for presentation at the American Education Research Association Annual Meeting in Atlanta, Apr. 1993.

p. 166: Tenbusch and Garet quotation: "Open enrollment . . .": Ibid., p. 34.

p. 166: "Not surprisingly, . . .": Ibid., pp. 22–23.

p. 166: Tenbusch and Garet quotation: Rural school administrators . . . "have been forced . . .": Ibid., p. 21.

p. 168: "By 1996 there were more than 140 . . .": Cheryl M. Lange and Camilla A. Lehr, *At-Risk Students in Second Chance Programs: Reasons for Transfer and Continued Attendance*, Research Report 21 (Minneapolis: University of Minnesota, Enrollment Options for Students with Disabilities Project, 1996).

p. 168: "Indeed, in 1994–1995 alone, . . .": Statistics from Minnesota Association of Alternative Programs.

p. 168: "An early survey . . .": Joe Nathan and James Ysseldyke, "What Minnesota Has Learned About School Choice," *Phi Delta Kappan*, May 1994, p. 685.

p. 169: Cheryl Lange quotation: "Half of the students surveyed . . .": Cheryl Lange, "Open Enrollment Project: Review," unpublished, p. 7.

p. 169: "The New Country School in LeSueur, Minnesota, . . .": Nancy Miller, "Innovation in the Land of the Green Giant," *Charter School Strategies Inc. Newsletter*, vol. 1, no. 3 (July 1995), Minneapolis; and personal communication from Ted Kolderie.

p. 170: "By the 1995–1996 school year, 19 percent . . .": Personal communication from Joe Nathan, updating Mike Malone, Joe Nathan, and Darryl Sedio, *Facts, Figures and Faces: A Look at Minnesota's School Choice Programs* (Minneapolis: Center for School Change, Hubert H. Humphrey Institute of Public Affairs, November 1993).

p. 170: Nathan quotation: "Most of the studies . . .": quoted in George Cantor, "Public School Choice: A Catalyst for Change or a Waste of Time?" *Detroit News*, June 30, 1996, p. 5B.

p. 171: Lange quotation: "Administrators and school board members . . .": Cheryl P. Lange, "Open Enrollment and Its Impact on Selected School Districts," (Ph.D. diss., University of Minnesota, 1995), p. 104.

p. 171: Lange quotation: "Districts whose superintendents . . .": Ibid., p. 70.

p. 171: Quotation from superintendent: "We have just gone through . . .": Ibid., p. 56.

p. 171: Quotation from rural superintendent: "Open enrollment has a lot of impact . . .": Ibid., p. 67.

p. 172: Lange quotation: "Open enrollment impacts . . .": Ibid., p. 108.

p. 172: "In all three charter schools . . .": Interview with Joe Nathan, Sept. 24, 1996.

p. 173: "By 1994, 86 percent . . .": Gordon S. Black and John C. Geraci, "Minnesota Public Opinion Survey: Report of Findings and Questionnaire," prepared for the Center of the American Experiment by the Gordon S. Black Corporation, Feb. 8, 1994.

p. 173: "As early as 1989, . . .": Rebecca Woosley, "School Choice Benefits Students, Teachers," *Wingspread Journal* (fall/winter 1990): pp. 1–5; and interview with Joe Nathan, Sept. 24, 1996.

p. 174: New Zealand school reforms: Scott, *Government Reform in New Zealand*.

p. 174: British education reform: Much of this information is from the Department for Education. See, for example, Department for Education, *Choice and Diversity: A New Framework for Schools*, Cm. 2029 (London: HMSO, July 1992); Department for Education, *Our Children's Education: The Updated Parent's Charter* (London: HMSO,

1994); Department for Education and Employment, *Self-Government for Schools*, Cm. 3315 (London: HMSO, June 1996); *The City Technology Colleges: A New Choice of School* (London: Department of Education and Science, Oct. 1986); and *The City Technology Colleges Trust: Who We Are, What We Do, Where We Are* (London: City Technology Colleges Trust).

p. 175: "Several years ago the Boston School Committee . . .": Joe Nathan, *Charter Schools*, p. 85.

p. 175: "But forced to compete, . . .": James A. Peyser, "Changing the Monopoly Structure of Public Education," *Dialogue*, Pioneer Institute for Public Policy Research, no. 12 (March 1966).

p. 182: Cohen and Brand quote: Steven Cohen and Ronald Brand, *Total Quality Management in Government* (San Francisco: Jossey-Bass, 1993), p. 39.

p. 182: President Clinton's executive order: "Executive Order 12862, Setting Customer Service Standards," in President Bill Clinton and Vice President Al Gore, *Putting Customers First: Standards for Serving the American People* (Washington, D.C.: National Performance Review, Sept. 1994), p. 63.

p. 186: Michael Alves quotation: "We have found that there is no independent effect . . .": Quoted in Edith Rasell and Richard Rothstein, eds., *School Choice: Examining the Evidence* (Washington, D.C.: Economic Policy Institute, 1993), p. 137.

p. 186: Lange quotation: "It was as if they were outside . . .": Lange, "Open Enrollment and Its Impact on Selected School Districts," p. 69.

p. 187: Pryde quotation: "Freeing parents to choose . . .": Quoted in Rasell and Rothstein, eds., *School Choice*, p. 138.

p. 191: Michael Alves quotation: "After implementing . . .": Quoted in Rasell and Rothstein, eds., *School Choice*, p. 137.

p. 192: "The National Health Service . . . and passenger information": See *The Citizen's Charter: The Facts and Figures*.

p. 193: Citizen's Charter report quotation: "This makes them more accountable . . .": Ibid., p. 34.

p. 193: Citizen's Charter principles: Ibid., p. vi.

p. 194: "Several major services . . .": See *The Citizen's Charter: The Facts and Figures*, Appendix 1.

p. 194: Health Information Service: Ibid., pp. 9, 92.

p. 194: "The Charter also asked . . .": Ibid., Appendix 1.

p. 194: "It promised '. . . general public' ": *Raising the Standard*, p. 13.

p. 194: The Charter Mark: *The Citizen's Charter Mark Scheme 1994, Guide for Applicants* (London: HMSO, 1994), pp. 29–31.

p. 195: Royal Mail Statistics: *The Citizen's Charter: The Facts and Figures*, p. 27.

p. 195: "The Driving Standards Agency . . .": Ibid., p. 17.

p. 195:   "The Driver and Vehicle Licensing Agency . . .": Ibid.

p. 195:   "Customer satisfaction with local government . . .": "Citizen's Charter: Not All Bad News," *The Economist*, Aug. 19–25, 1995.

p. 195:   "The Citizen's Charter has inspired imitations . . .": *The Citizen's Charter: The Facts and Figures*, p. 1; and *Quality and Affordable Service for Canadians: Establishing Service Standards in the Federal Government* (Ottawa: Planning and Communications Directorate, Treasury Board of Canada Secretariat, 1995). See p. 2 in particular.

p. 195:   President Clinton's executive order: Executive Order 12862: "Setting Customer Service Standards," Sept. 11, 1993.

p. 196:   "By 1995, 214 federal agencies . . .": President Bill Clinton and Vice President Al Gore, *Putting Customers First '95: Standards for Serving the American People* (Washington, D.C.: National Performance Review, Oct. 1995), p. 3.

p. 202:   U.S. Postal Service data: President Bill Clinton and Vice President Al Gore, *Putting Customers First '95: Standards for Serving the American People* (Washington, D.C.: U.S. Government Printing Office, 1995), p. 6. May 1996 figures are from U.S. Postal Service's External First-Class Measurement System. Local overnight mail delivery is measured by Price Waterhouse, under a contract with the Postal Service.

Chapter 7: The Control Strategy:
Shifting Control Away from the Top and Center

p. 203:   "By the mid-1980s . . . Louisiana combined": Pamela Varley, *"What if We Could Start Over?" The U.S. Forest Service Champions "Bottom-Up" Management*, draft of John F. Kennedy School of Government Case Study A (Cambridge, Mass.: Harvard University), p. 2.

p. 203:   "And it took a few . . . and policies": The story of Robertson's stack has been told throughout Region 9 and in newspapers. See, for instance, Erik Gunn, "Pruning Bureaucracy's Thick Forest," *The Milwaukee Journal*, Sept. 26, 1993, and Karl H. Mettke, *A Catalyst for Change in the Eastern Region of the Forest Service* (Milwaukee: U.S. Forest Service Region 9), p. 3.

p. 204:   "When a consulting firm . . .": Mettke, *A Catalyst for Change*, p. 3.

p. 205:   "The Mark Twain National Forest . . .": Data about the national forest is from Mark Twain National Forest, *Welcome to the Mark Twain!*, a promotional brochure.

p. 208:   "At Mark Twain . . .": Eastern Region of the U.S. Forest Service, *Shaping a New Culture*, brochure obtained from regional office in Milwaukee.

p. 208:   "The staff did more and more . . .": Communications to authors from Karl Mettke, Eastern Region headquarters, concerning budget, personnel, and forest accomplishments and trends from 1986 to 1993.

p. 208:   SEC, Inc. quotations: *Mark Twain National Forest Land and Resource Management Plan Five Year Implementation Review* (Sedona, Ariz.: SEC, Inc., Apr. 3, 1991).

p. 210:   "When Marita asked employees . . . it saved $500,000 a year": From Eastern Region, *Shaping a New Culture*; Mettke, *A Catalyst for Change*; and interviews with Region 9 personnel.

p. 210:   "But in 1993, the region . . . Bucket disappeared": Varley, *"What If We Could Start Over?"* Case Study A, pp. 7–13, and Case Study C, pp. 1–4.

p. 211:   "By 1995, the regional . . . than in 1989": *The Regional Office's Changing Culture*, internal document obtained from Eastern Region of the U.S. Forest Service in Milwaukee.

p. 211:   "It ate up only 7 percent . . .": From "R.O.A.s % of Region, FY 1993 Final," chart provided by Karl Mettke, Eastern Region of Forest Service.

p. 212:   Robertson quotation: F. Dale Robertson, *Chartering a Management Philosophy for the Forest Service*, internal Forest Service document, Dec. 19, 1989.

p. 212:   "Roger Douglas remembers . . . was preposterous' ": Douglas, "National Policy-Makers' Experience," pp. 11–12.

p. 213:   "In 1986, David Packard's Commission . . . or connivance": President's Blue Ribbon Commission on Defense Management, *A Quest for Excellence: Final Report to the President* (Washington, D.C.: U.S. Department of Defense, June 1986), pp. xxiii–xxiv.

p. 213:   Creech quotation: Creech, *The Five Pillars of TQM*, p. 388.

p. 214:   Handy quotation: Charles Handy, *The Age of Reason* (Boston: Harvard Business School Press, 1990), p. 259.

p. 214:   Levin and Sanger quotation: Martin A. Levin and Mary Bryna Sanger, *Making Government Work: How Entrepreneurial Executives Turn Bright Ideas into Real Results* (San Francisco: Jossey-Bass, 1994), p. 259.

p. 215:   Creech quotation: Creech, *The Five Pillars of TQM*, pp. 259–260.

p. 216:   Creech quotation: Ibid., p. 387.

p. 216:   Phoenix quotation: From City of Phoenix, "An Overview of Organizational Change," published by the city auditor, p. 12.

p. 216:   Scott quotation: Scott, *Government Reform in New Zealand*.

p. 218:   "Studies dating back to 1976 . . .": See Task Force on Management Improvement, *Australian Public Service Reformed*, chapter 2.

p. 219:   U.S. General Accounting Office quotations: *Managing for Results: Experiences Abroad Suggest Insights for Federal Management Reforms* (Washington, D.C.: U.S. General Accounting Office, 1995), pp. 5–6.

p. 223:   Creech quotation: Creech, *The Five Pillars of TQM*, p. 127.

p. 225:   Codd quotation: Michael Codd, "Better Government through Redrawing of Boundaries and Functions," in Weller and Davis, eds., *New Ideas, Better Government*.

p. 228:   Creech quotation: Creech, *The Five Pillars of TQM*, p. 281.

p. 231:   "In Denver, Savannah, . . .": William R. Potapchuk, "New Approaches to Citizen Participation: Building Consent," *National Civic Review*, spring 1991, p. 166.

p. 235:   Creech quotation: Creech, *The Five Pillars of TQM*, p. 317.

p. 236:   National Performance Review quotation: Al Gore, *Common Sense Government*, pp. 25–26.

p. 239:   "Singapore has introduced . . .": Scott, *Government Reform in New Zealand*.

p. 239:   "Malaysia has initiated . . . and the U.K. have": Ibid.

p. 239:   "Costa Rica is developing . . .": Ibid.

Chapter 8: The Culture Strategy:
Creating an Entrepreneurial Culture

p. 242:   "In fact, participation . . .": According to Tharon Greene, the city's human resources director, the number of employee-involvement groups grew from 71 in 1990 to 115 in 1994.

p. 244:   "Its population was . . . cuts were imminent": James Eason, "Presentation to City of Wilson, North Carolina," talking points for Jan. 25, 1994, speech.

p. 249:   Daniel quotation: memorandum from Thomas H. Daniel to City Manager Robert J. O'Neill Jr., Nov. 23, 1988.

p. 253:   Virginia Municipal League quotation: "President's Award: Entrepreneurial Government. Changing the Business of Government," *Virginia Town & City*, Oct. 1993, pp. 24–25.

p. 255:   Broderick quotation: From Otto Broderick, "A Second Look at the Well-Performing Government Organization," in *The Well-Performing Government Organization*, ed. James C. McDavid and D. Brian Marson (Ottawa: Institute of Public Administration of Canada, 1991), p. 22.

p. 256:   "When Tom Glynn . . . the equipment": Levin and Sanger, *Making Government Work*, pp. 174–175.

p. 257:   Godfrey quotation: Bill Godfrey, "Can Large Government Learn? The Challenge of Strategic Change at the Australian Taxation Office," in Peter M. Senge et al., *The Fifth Discipline Fieldbook: Strategies and Tools for Building a Learning Organization* (New York: Doubleday, 1994), p. 495.

p. 258:   Behn quotation: Robert Behn, "Innovation and Public Values: Mistakes, Flexibility, Purpose, Equity, Cost Control, and Trust," paper prepared for Conference on the Fundamental Questions of Innovation, Duke University, May 3–4, 1991, p. 1.

p. 259:   Kotter quotation: John P. Kotter, "Why Transformation Efforts Fail," *Harvard Business Review*, Mar.–Apr. 1995, p. 67.

p. 260:   Sedgwick quotation: Steven Sedgwick, "State of the Service," presentation to Institute of Public Administration, Canberra, Australia, Oct. 28, 1993.

p. 264: Kuhn quotation: "something like a paradigm . . .": Thomas S. Kuhn, *The Structure of Scientific Revolutions*, 2d ed. (Chicago: University of Chicago Press, 1970), p. 113.

p. 264: Kuhn quotation: "For the normal cards . . .": Ibid., p. 63.

p. 264: Barker quotation: Joel A. Barker, *Paradigms: The Business of Discovering the Future* (New York: HarperBusiness, 1992), pp. 100–101.

p. 267: Kuhn quotation: Quoted in Barker, *Paradigms*, p. 73.

p. 267: Bridges quotations: William Bridges, *Managing Transitions*, pp. 5–6.

p. 268: ". . . defines a touchstone": *The American Heritage Dictionary of the English Language*, 2d ed., s.v. "touchstone."

p. 269: "A habit is defined . . .": Ibid., 3d ed., s.v. "habit."

p. 271: Covey quotation: Stephen R. Covey, *The 7 Habits of Highly Effective People: Powerful Lessons in Personal Change* (New York: Simon & Schuster, 1989), pp. 46–47.

p. 274: For Senge's discussion of "governing ideas," see Peter M. Senge, *The Fifth Discipline: The Art & Practice of the Learning Organization* (New York: Doubleday, 1990), pp. 223–225.

p. 275: *Fifth Discipline Fieldbook* quotation: Senge et al., *The Fifth Discipline Fieldbook*, p. 235.

p. 279: Fliegel quotation: Fliegel, *Miracle in East Harlem*, p. 167.

p. 281: "When President Clinton met . . .": from Federal Quality Institute, *Federal Quality News*, Oct. 1993.

p. 283: Couper and Lobitz quotation: David C. Couper and Sabine H. Lobitz, *Quality Policing: The Madison Experience* (Washington, D.C.: Police Executive Research Forum, 1991), p. 57.

p. 284: Doubelle quotation: Evan S. Doubelle, Inaugural Address, City College of San Francisco, Nov. 5, 1990.

p. 285: Couper quotation: Couper and Lobitz, *Quality Policing*, p. 62.

p. 286: Couper quotation: Ibid., p. 63.

p. 288: Kitfield quotation: James Kitfield, *Prodigal Soldiers: How the Generation of Officers Born of Vietnam Revolutionized the American Style of War* (New York: Simon & Schuster, 1995), pp. 179–180.

p. 290: Bridges quotations: *Managing Transitions*, pp. 27–28.

p. 292: Hammer and Champy quotation: Michael Hammer and James Champy, *Reengineering the Corporation: A Manifesto for Business Revolution* (New York: HarperCollins, 1993), p. 75.

p. 296: "Bill Creech's first . . . plane or pilot": Creech, *The Five Pillars of TQM*, pp. 78–83.

p. 297: Kitfield quotation: Kitfield, *Prodigal Soldiers*, p. 181.

p. 297: Kitfield quotation: "How did we . . .": Ibid., pp. 414–415.

p. 298: Kitfield quotation: "John, I was flying . . .": Ibid., p. 426.

Chapter 9: Aligning the Strategies

p. 301:   Thatcher quotation: Quoted in Savoie, *Thatcher, Reagan, Mulroney*, p. 210.

p. 301:   "As it created executive agencies, the Next Steps Team made it clear . . .": Interview with Diana Goldsworthy, then deputy director of the Citizen's Charter Unit, June 1994.

p. 301:   "This new initiative wreaked havoc . . . for several years": Sylvie Trosa, *Next Steps: Moving On* (London: Office of Public Service and Science, Feb. 1994), pp. 12–13; and interviews with Sonia Phippard, then director of the Next Steps Team, and Diana Goldsworthy, then deputy director of the Citizen's Charter Unit, June 1994.

p. 302:   Canadian Auditor General's Office quotation: *Toward Better Governance*, p. 80.

p. 303:   Scott quotation: Scott, *Government Reform in New Zealand*.

p. 307:   "For several decades, Arizona has competitively bid out . . .": See David Osborne, *Laboratories of Democracy* (Boston: Harvard Business School Press, 1988), pp. 122–128.

p. 316:   National Performance Review decision tree: *Reinvention Roundtable*, National Performance Review, Apr. 1995, p. 7.

p. 317:   Joel Barker quotation: Barker, *Paradigms*, p. 164.

Chapter 10: The Courage to Reinvent

p. 320:   Margaret Mead quotation: Quoted in Roberts and King, *Transforming Public Policy*, p. 92.

p. 320:   "During the campaign he had blustered . . .": Savoie, *Thatcher, Reagan, Mulroney*, p. 105.

p. 320:   Nielsen ministerial task force: Ibid., pp. 127–131.

p. 321:   Make-or-buy policy: Ibid., pp. 155–157.

p. 321:   Savoie quotation: "Mulroney spoke often about the need . . .": Ibid., p. 167.

p. 321:   "Increased Ministerial Authority and Accountability": Ibid., pp. 180–181.

p. 322:   Savoie quotation: "Some six years after IMAA . . .": Ibid., pp. 269–270.

p. 322:   Savoie quotation: "A widely respected former secretary . . .": Ibid., p. 270.

p. 322:   Public Service 2000: Ibid., pp. 228–231.

p. 323:   Special operating agencies: Ibid., pp. 231–234.

p. 323:   Quotation from 1994 evaluation: Auditor General of Canada, *Special Operating Agencies*, p. 25.

p. 323:   Savoie quotation: "Mulroney did not personally embrace . . .": Savoie, *Thatcher, Reagan, Mulroney*, p. 231.

p. 323: Savoie quotation: "Although Mulroney spoke . . .": Ibid., p. 271.

p. 324: Douglas quotations: Douglas, *Unfinished Business*, pp. 9–10.

p. 324: Prebble quotation: Richard Prebble, "How to Privatise Postal Services: Lessons from New Zealand," lecture delivered at the Canada Post Privatization Conference, Toronto, June 1989.

p. 326: Savoie quotation: "Seasoned officials know that, . . .": Savoie, *Thatcher, Reagan, Mulroney*, p. 295.

p. 326: Quotation from senior official: "I have seen him . . .": Ibid., p. 272.

p. 327: "This fear killed . . . in its tracks": Interviews with participants in National Performance Review.

p. 328: Behn quotation: Behn, "Innovation and Public Values," pp. 20–21.

p. 328: "Several years ago Katherine Barrett, . . .": Duncan Wyse and Michael Marsh, "The State of Oregon: Setting Measurable Standards for Progress," presentations at the Managing for Results: Performance Measures in Government Conference in Austin, Tex., Oct. 27–29, 1993, p. 56.

p. 329: Machiavelli quotation: Niccolo Machiavelli, *The Prince* (New York: Dover Publications, 1992), p. 13.

p. 330: Douglas quotation: "Do not try to advance . . .": Douglas, "The Politics of Successful Structural Reform," p. 14.

p. 330: Douglas quotation: "Nothing like that had happened . . .": Ibid., p. 15.

p. 331: "In 1995, Boston's school choice plan . . . second choice": Karen Avenoso, "Most Parents Back School Choice Plan, Says Boston Survey," *Boston Globe*, Dec. 14, 1995, p. 40.

p. 331: "Minnesota's education reformers consciously built . . .": See Roberts and King, *Transforming Public Policy*.

p. 331: Rendell quotation: Mayor Edward Rendell, address to top appointees of the Guiliani administration, Gracie Mansion, New York City, Mar. 5, 1994.

p. 332: Behn quotation: Behn, "Innovation and Public Values," p. 22.

p. 332: "When Mario Cuomo was governor . . .": See Osborne, *Laboratories of Democracy*, pp. 211–246.

p. 334: Fliegel quotation: Fliegel, *Miracle in East Harlem*, pp. 33–40.

p. 336: Quotation from former British civil servant: Quoted in Savoie, *Thatcher, Reagan, Mulroney*, p. 112. Savoie cites David Dilks, *The Cadogan Diaries* (London: Cassell, 1971), p. 22, for this quotation.

p. 339: Douglas quotation: Douglas, "The Politics of Successful Structural Reform," p. 27.

p. 340: "At the ACC, Creech set up . . . courses himself": Creech, *The Five Pillars of TQM*, pp. 364, 375.

p. 341: Rendell quotation: Rendell, address to top appointees of the Guiliani administration, Gracie Mansion, New York City, Mar. 5, 1994.

p. 343: Roberts and King quotation: Roberts and King, *Transforming Public Policy*, p. 219.

p. 344: Douglas quotation: Roger Douglas, "The Politics of Successful Struc-
         tural Reform," *Wall Street Journal*, Jan. 17, 1990.

p. 344: "When John Kennedy was president, . . .": Gore, *From Red Tape To
         Results*, p. 1.

p. 344: "In a 1995 poll, . . . 'cutting programs')": Apr. 12, 1995 memorandum
         from Peter D. Hart and Robert M. Teeter to the Council for Excellence
         in Government, containing the results of a national survey of a cross
         section of 1,003 American adults conducted between Mar. 16 and 18,
         1995, "to determine Americans' attitudes toward the role of govern-
         ment in society."

p. 344: "In September 1993, when President Clinton . . .": USA Today/CNN/
         Gallup poll, reported in Richard Benedetto, "Poll: People Want Gov-
         ernment to Work, Period," *USA Today*, Sept. 16, 1993.

INDEX

Accountability
  basic approaches to, 183–187
  competitive choice and, 184, 189–192
  consequences and, 304
  control strategy and, 215, 216, 234
  customer choice approach and, 184, 187–189
  customer quality assurance and, 184–185, 192–198
  customer strategy and, 40–42, 68, 173–179, 183–187
  customer voice and, 185
  dual, 178–179, 201
  enterprise management and, 138
Accounting systems, 105–106
Accrual accounting, 105–106
ACC. See Air Combat Command
Adaptive capacity, 14
Administrative entities (Arizona), 307
Administrative systems
  aligning with strategies, 312–314
  cultural transitions and, 292
  described, 50
Advanced placement (AP) courses, 163
Advantage plan check process (Sunnyvale, California), 177
AFSCME. See American Federation of State, County, and Municipal Employees
Air Combat Command (ACC), 15, 58–60, 62, 65, 66, 131, 147, 180–181, 217, 226, 288–289, 294–295
Airman Leadership School, 59
Air New Zealand, 75, 81
Alliance for Redesigning Government, 352

Alves, Michael, 185–186, 191
American Federation of State, County, and Municipal Employees (AFSCME), 115, 116, 118–119, 120, 121, 122, 123, 327–328, 337–338
American Sign Language, 169
Anticipatory government, 349
Area Learning Centers and Alternative Programs Act (1987), 167
Argentina, 238, 239
Arizona, 307. See also Phoenix
Armajani, Babak, 13, 271, 339, 351
Asset privatization, 22–23, 95, 239
At-risk students, 165, 167–170
Attitudes, employee, 2–4, 60, 253
Attrition, 133
Auditing systems
  competitive bidding and, 143
  innovation and, 62
  organizational controls and, 240
  quality assurance and, 194
Austin, Texas, 272, 279
Australia
  civil service reform in, 7, 9
  consequences strategy and, 136–137, 140, 147, 150
  control strategy and, 218–219, 220, 224–225
  culture strategy and, 260, 283
Australian Public Service (APS), 260
Authoritarian controls, 217, 228

BAA, 128
Banyard, Steve, 281
Barker, Joel, 264, 317
Barnett, Camille, 272

Barrett, Katherine, 328
Base Closure and Realignments
  Commission (U.S.), 155
Beer, Michael, 37
Behn, Robert, 150, 258, 328, 332
Benchmarks, 104–105, 131, 142, 276,
  326, 328
Berra, Yogi, 39
Bertelsmann Foundation, 114
Beta sites, 221
Bidding process. *See* Competitive bidding
Big Bang Day (New Zealand), 78–81
"Big Bucket" budget, 207, 209, 210–211,
  218
Birch, Liz, 154
Blue-ribbon commissions, 91
Bonding events, 273
Bonuses, 146, 150, 251
Boston Management Consortium, 335
Boston, Massachusetts, 175
Brandl, John, 172
Brazil, 238, 239
Bridges, William, 67, 266–267, 278, 290
Bright Flag program, 60
British Airports Authority (BAA), 128
British Airways, 23
British Rail, 33, 34, 35, 192, 194, 195, 197
Broderick, Otto, 255
Budgets
  culture change and, 293–294
  long-term, 106, 138
  lump-sum, 207, 209, 210–211, 218
  performance, 104–105, 106, 146
  running costs, 218–219
Bunting, Mary, 241–242, 249, 252, 253,
  269
Bureaucracies. *See also* Public
  organizations
  administrative systems and, 312–314
  community empowerment and, 235
  control systems and, 212–214
  culture of, 235, 257–259, 292
  invention of, 15–17
  as monopolies, 17, 185, 258–259
  obsolescence of, 17–18
  replacing language of, 276
Business
  compared to government, 12–13
  government as owner of, 81
Business Myth, 13

Business process reengineering (BPR), 11,
  44, 51, 64, 225, 310–311

Cairns, John, 164
California Contract Cities Association,
  100
California. *See* Los Angeles; San
  Francisco; Sunnyvale; Visalia
Callahan, Joni, 157
Canada
  civil service reform in, 63, 91–92, 100,
    101, 320–323, 330
  control strategy and, 219, 220
  Mulroney government in, 91–92, 320–
    323, 324–325, 326–327, 342
  public survey on government in, 17
Capital charge, 85
Carlson, Larry, 159
Carter, Jimmy, 141
Carter, Michael, 127
Carver, Julianne, 159
Catalytic government, 96, 347
Celebrating success, 253–254, 273
Center for School Change, 167
Centralization, 224, 228–229
Central Park East school, 334–335
Chamber of Commerce, 231
Champy, James, 11, 292, 310
Chartering, 158, 160, 169–170, 192, 220,
  221, 311
Charter Mark, 33, 36, 194–195, 286
Charter schools, 158, 160, 169–170, 192,
  220
Chicago, Illinois, 231
Chiles, Lawton, 223, 261
Choice. *See also* School choice
  accountability and, 184–186
  competitive, 184, 189–192
Choice plans, 185–186
Christchurch, New Zealand, 114
Citizen-satisfaction bonus, 251
Citizen's Charter, 32–36, 41, 176, 185,
  192–196, 197–198, 239, 314, 336
Citizens League (Minnesota), 162, 164,
  331
City governments. *See* Local governments
City Inc., 167–168
Civic entrepreneurs, 12
Civil service system
  Australia's reform of, 7, 9

Canada's reform of, 63, 91–92, 100,
    101, 320–323, 330
New Zealand's reform of, 83–87, 89,
    97, 101, 102, 107–108, 112–113,
    323–324, 329–330
United Kingdom's reform of, 21–36,
    67, 70, 97, 101, 108
Clarke, Michael, 23
Clearing the decks approach, 91–95
Cleveland, John, 352
Clinton, Bill, 9, 93, 155, 182, 195, 272,
    281, 344
Coal mining industry, 78, 80
Codd, Mike, 225
Cold War, 57
Collaboration
    competition and, 153–154
    culture strategy and, 247–248
    planning and, 233
Colon, Victor, 350
Commitment
    culture change and, 295–298
    to reinvention process, 341–343
Communications
    common excuses for lack of, 290
    importance of, 290–291
Communities
    empowerment of, 42–43, 69–70, 218,
        229–235
    planning process and, 229–230
Community-based regulation and
    compliance, 233
Community Boards, 111
Community governance bodies, 233, 311–
    312
Community-government partnerships,
    233
Community investment funds, 233
Community managed organizations, 233
Community-owned government, 347
Comparative data, 199
Competition
    collaboration and, 153–154
    consequences strategy and, 129–135
    enterprise management and, 131, 136–
        141
    incentives and, 40
    managed competition and, 131, 141–
        144, 151–152, 154–156
    monopolies and, 17, 129–130

performance management and, 131–
    132, 144–150
privatization and, 118, 120–128
in public services delivery, 31–
    32
school choice and, 170–173
Competitive benchmarking, 131, 142,
    151
Competitive bidding, 100, 118, 120–126,
    130, 141–144, 307–308
Competitive choice approach, 184, 189–
    192
Competitive government, 347–348
Competitive public choice systems, 192,
    309
Compliance functions, 25, 40, 95–102,
    111–112, 151, 182–183, 189, 233
Compliance organizations, 45–47, 199–
    200, 236–237, 293
Compliers, 182–183
Compulsory competitive tendering, 22,
    129, 143
Confession, 339
Congressional systems, 94
Consequences strategy, 115–156
    approaches of, 130–132
    case example of, 115–128
    common questions about, 152–154
    community empowerment and, 234
    competition and, 129–130
    compliance organizations and, 47
    control strategy and, 216, 234, 303
    described, 40
    enterprise management and, 131, 136–
        141, 151
    implementing, 68–69
    managed competition and, 131, 141–
        144, 151–152
    metatools created with, 305
    new approaches to, 154–156
    no-layoff policies and, 132–135
    performance management and, 131–
        132, 144–150, 152, 304
Conservative Myth, 13
Conservative Party (U.K.), 21, 32, 70, 129
Constancy of purpose, 342
Constituents
    building, 331
    customers as, 198–199
Contestability, 96

Contests, 270
Contracting process
  competitive bidding and, 100, 118,
    120–126, 130, 141–144
Control strategy, 203–240
  accountability and, 215, 216
  administrative systems and, 313–314
  approaches to, 217–218
  bureaucratic systems and, 211–214
  case examples of, 54–55, 59–60, 203–
    211
  common questions about, 235–238
  community empowerment and, 218,
    229–235
  compliance organizations and, 47, 236–
    237
  consequences strategy and, 216, 303
  customer strategy and, 186–187
  described, 42–43
  developing nations and, 238–240
  employee empowerment and, 217–218,
    224–229, 260, 304–305
  five steps in, 215
  implementing, 69–70
  metatools created with, 305
  organizational empowerment and, 217,
    218–224
  policy organizations and, 237–238
  regulatory organizations and, 237–238
  total quality management and, 310
  trust and, 212–214
Corbitt, Lynn, 224
Core benchmarks, 104
Core strategy, 75–114
  case example of, 75–90
  clarity of purpose and, 91–95, 110
  common questions about, 110–114
  described, 39–40
  directional clarity and, 102–108
  implementing, 67–68, 109–110
  integrating approaches in, 108–109
  local government and, 113–114
  metatools created with, 305
  optimizing implementation of, 302–303
  performance management and, 304
  role clarity and, 95–102
  three basic approaches of, 90–91
Corlett, Clive, 237, 289, 291
Corporatization, 79, 82, 137, 239, 308
Corruption, 144, 238, 239, 240

Costa Rica, 239
Council-manager governments, 45
Couper, David, 213, 228, 281, 283, 285–
  286, 292
Courage, 324, 342
Covenants, 271–272
Covey, Steven R., 271
"Creaming," 191
Credle, Walt, 247, 274, 275
Creech, General W. L. "Bill," 54–57, 61–
  62, 63, 66, 113, 213, 215–216, 217,
  220, 223–224, 225, 228, 235, 285,
  288, 295, 296–298, 340, 342
Crook, Barry, 279
Crookston College, 281–283
Cross-functional teams, 54
Cross-walking/cross-talking, 270
Cultural change
  commitment and, 295–298
  cultural paradigms and, 265–268
  downsizing and, 293–294
  effects of, 250–255
  government organizations and, 234–
    235, 259–262
  lessons for leading, 278–293
  leverage and, 52, 295
  reinvention process and, 5
Cultural touchstones, 268
Culture strategy, 241–298
  approaches of, 268–269, 277, 278
  case examples of, 56, 60, 241–255
  changing habits and, 269–271
  common questions about, 293–295
  described, 43
  employee empowerment and, 304–305
  implementing, 70
  leadership lessons and, 278–293
  metatools created with, 305
  mission statement and, 248–250
  need for, 259–262
  organizational culture and, 255–257
  paradigm shifts and, 265–268
  persistence and commitment with, 295–
    298
  public bureaucracies and, 257–259
  total quality management and, 310
  touching hearts and, 271–273
  winning minds and, 274–277
Cuomo, Mario, 332–333
Customer choice approach, 184, 187–189

Customer complaint systems, 196
Customer-driven government, 10, 348
Customer empowerment, 178, 198
Customer information systems and
    brokers, 189
Customer quality assurance approach,
    184–185, 192–198
Customer redress, 196
Customer revolution, 286
Customers
    compliers vs., 182–183
    as constituents, 198–199
    defining, 179–183
    meeting, 270
Customer service, 33, 192–198, 253
Customer service standards, 196
Customer strategy, 157–202
    accountability and, 173–179
    approaches to, 183–187
    case example of, 157–173
    common questions about, 198–201
    competitive choice and, 184, 189–
        192
    control strategy and, 186–187
    customer choice approach and, 184,
        187–189
    customer quality assurance and, 184–
        185, 192–198
    customer voice and, 185
    defining the customer in, 179–183
    described, 40–42
    implementing, 68
    metatools created with, 305
    power of, 201–202
    school choice and, 157–178
    total quality management and, 310
Customer voice, 185

Daniels, Mitch, 130
Daniel, Thomas, 249
Davies, Howard, 143
Decentralization, 36, 113, 215–216, 221,
    226
Decentralized government, 349
Decision trees, 315–319
"Decline and Fall of the Industrial State,
    The" (Sturgess), 16
Delayering process, 226
Deming, W. Edwards, 11, 342
Democracy, 227–228

Democratic-Farmer-Labor (DFL) Party,
    160, 162
Department of Administrative Services
    (DAS/Australia), 137
Department of Defense (U.S.), 94, 213,
    223, 295
Department of Labor (U.S.), 256
Deregulation, 221, 225–227
Developing nations, 238–240
Devolution, 95
Directional clarity, 102–108
Disadvantaged students, 167–170
Discipline, progressive, 148–149
Dissonance, 266, 269, 278
DNA, organizational, 38–43, 48, 63
Doubelle, Evan, 284
Douglas, Roger, 77, 78, 79, 81, 85, 212,
    323–324, 329–330, 336, 339–340,
    344, 345
Downsizing, 11, 60, 132–133, 293, 341
Drucker, Peter, 11, 63, 96, 112–113
Dual accountability, 178–179, 201
Dukakis, Michael, 328

Eason, James, 6, 244–245, 248, 253, 259,
    263
East Harlem, New York, 15, 279, 334
Edmonton, Alberta, 220
Education
    charter schools and, 158, 160, 169–170
    disadvantaged students and, 167–170
    employee, 149, 340
    open enrollment and, 162, 165–167,
        171, 172
    school choice and, 6–7, 44, 66, 157–
        173, 186–187, 303
Effectiveness
    Citizen's Charter and, 32–36
    efficiency vs., 11, 32
    employee empowerment and, 227–228
Efficiency, 11, 32
Efficiency dividends, 30, 146, 224
Efficiency scrutinies, 22
Efficiency Unit (U.K.), 22, 23, 24, 25–27,
    301, 314, 323
Eimicke, Bill, 332–333
Eisenstat, Russell, 37
Elected officials, 4, 27, 41, 42, 107, 179,
    198–199, 220, 222–223, 257–258,
    327, 336, 345

Emotional commitments, 272
Emotionally disturbed students, 168
Employee Myth, 13
Employees
    annual survey of, 60
    bureaucratic controls and, 213
    changing habits of, 269–271
    culture change and, 250–252, 260,
        280–281
    empowerment of, 127, 207, 209, 214–
        218, 224–229, 260, 304–305
    mission statement and, 248–250
    morale of, 2–4, 253, 301
    as stakeholders, 201
    suggestion programs for, 226
    training for, 149, 340
Employment
    ideal of full, 76
    no-layoff policies and, 132–135
Employment and Training Administration,
    256
Employment and Training (ET) Choices,
    328
Empowerment
    community, 42–43, 69–70, 218, 229–235
    customer, 178, 198
    employee, 127, 207, 209, 214–216,
        217–218, 224–229, 260, 304–305
    individual, 59–60, 64
    organizational, 217, 218–224, 246, 303
Enabling councils, 101
England, 134, 192–193, 286. See also
    United Kingdom
Enterprise Florida, 231
Enterprise funds, 137, 308
Enterprise management, 47, 131, 136–
    141, 151, 190, 220
Enterprising government, 348–349
Entrepreneurial government, 14, 15, 252,
    253, 293, 304–305, 343
Environmentalists, 122, 343
Environmental Protection Agency, 187, 199
Ernst & Young, 343
Essex, Massachusetts, 176
European Economic Community, 76, 134
Externships, 270

Failure, honoring, 273
Fantauzzo, Steve, 115–116, 119, 121, 123,
    126–128, 142, 327–328, 337

Farbrother, Doug, 61, 295–296
Farnham, Rick, 123
Favoritism, 3–4
Fear, 287
Federal decentralization, 96
Federal Quality Institute, 52
Fence sitters, 279
Fiander, Alan, 68
Fifth Discipline, The (Senge), 274, 275
Financial Management Initiative, 23–24,
    323
Financial penalties, 148
Financial World, 328
First hiring preference clause, 134
Fiscal Responsibility Act (New Zealand),
    105
Five C's strategies. See also names of
    individual strategies
    aligning with administrative systems,
        312–314
    decision trees and, 315–319
    leverage and, 43–44, 49–53
    metatools created from, 305–312
    optimizing implementation of, 301–305
    overview of, 39–43
    recommended reading on, 354–356
Five Pillars of TQM, The (Creech), 61
Flanagan, Jim, 130, 141
Flexible performance frameworks, 99–
    100, 216–217, 303, 306–307, 321
Fliegel, Sy, 279, 334–335
Florida, 223, 231
Fogden, Michael, 29–30
Forbes, Don, 222, 342
Ford Foundation, 335
Foreign language programs, 167
Forest Lake, Minnesota, 157–159, 185
Forestry industry, 79, 80
Functional silos, 54, 226
Fund for the City of New York, 335

Gaebler, Ted, 52, 91, 280–281, 350, 351
Gainsharing, 126, 127, 130, 146, 328
Gallagher, Kevin, 241, 242–243, 249, 251,
    253, 279
Garet, Michael, 166
General Accounting Office (GAO), 219
Generally accepted accounting practice
    (GAAP), 105
Genetic code, organizational, 38–43

Germany, 114
Gilchrist, Mark, 157
Gill, Derek, 89
Glynn, Tom, 256
Goals
    long-term, 87–88, 107
    outcome, 87–88, 102, 103–104, 106,
        108
    output, 87, 102, 103
Godfrey, Bill, 257
Goldschmidt, Neil, 103–104
Goldsmith, Steve, 6, 115–128, 129–130,
    131, 132, 154–156, 197, 327–328,
    331, 334, 337–338, 342–343, 345
Goldsworthy, Diana, 32, 36, 195, 197–
    198, 315
Gore, Al, 9, 61, 62, 100, 219, 289, 315,
    330, 335
Governing ideas, 274–277
Governing magazine, 353
Governing systems, 49, 50, 51
Government. *See also* Bureaucracies;
    Public organizations
    business compared to, 12–13
    community partnerships with, 233
    competitive choice systems and, 191
    entrepreneurial, 14, 15, 252, 253, 293,
        304–305, 343
    five myths of reforming, 13
    functions best suited for, 111–112, 151
    market structuring by, 188–189
    as owner of businesses, 81
    principles of reinventing, 347–349
    steering functions and, 111–112
Government Executive magazine, 353
Grant maintained schools, 175
Great Britain. *See* United Kingdom
Greene, Tharon, 149, 243, 250, 251, 254,
    255
Gross domestic product (GDP), 76, 89
Gulf War, 54, 57, 112, 297
Gurley, Donald, 241, 242, 244, 247, 252,
    253

Habits, changing, 269–271, 277
Hammer Awards, 289, 335
Hammer, Michael, 11, 292, 310
Hampton, Virginia, 6, 52, 145, 147, 229–
    230, 235, 241–255, 259, 274, 292, 305
Hands-on organizational experiences, 270

Handy, Charles, 214
Harvard Business Review, 37
Health care, 190
Hearts, touching, 271–273
Herman Miller, 52
Herzberg, Frederick, 147
Heseltine, Michael, 23
Hierarchy
    determining organizational need for,
        228
    employee empowerment and, 217–218,
        224–227
    in government agencies, 204–205, 207,
        258
    of human needs, 147
    of leverage, 49–53
High School Graduation Incentives Act,
    167
Holewa, Bob, 174
Holt, Craig, 222, 295
Honesty, 338
Honoring failure, 273
Horner, Chuck, 297–298
Hughes Technical Services, 155
Humphrey Institute, 167
Hundredth monkey story, 279
Hunt, Michelle, 52
Hutchinson, Peter, 256, 271–272, 282,
    284–285, 295, 338

Ibbs, Sir Robin, 24, 25–26
Ideas, governing, 274–277
Incentives
    competitive choice and, 191
    consequences as, 40, 85
    culture change and, 280, 286
    designing, 145, 147–150
    performance, 216
Increased Ministerial Authorship and
    Accountability (IMAA), 321–322,
    325
Indianapolis, Indiana, 6, 115–128, 133,
    141, 147, 153, 154–156, 307, 327,
    334, 337–338, 341
Inflation, 21, 76
Information brokers, 189
In-house schoolhouses, 276
Inland Revenue agency, 199, 200, 237,
    281, 289, 291, 293
Innovation, 40, 62, 152, 251, 332–336

In Search of Excellence (Peters and
    Waterman), 213, 215
Inspectors general (IGs), 62, 143, 333–
    334
Institutional sponsors, 270
Integration, racial, 179, 191–192
Intergovernmental deregulation, 221
Internal enterprise management, 137,
    308–309
Internships, 270
Investments
    in reinvention process, 340–341
    tools for touching hearts as, 273

James, Ed, 286, 289
James, William, 147
Jensen, Ron, 129, 141, 143
Job banks, 133
Job dislocation, 133–134
Job rotation, 270
Job training, 149, 340
Johnson, Curtis, 164
Johnson, Verne, 164
Jordan, James, 209, 210, 288, 293

Keillor, Garrison, 150
Kemp, Peter, 26–27
Kennedy, Joan, 229–230, 232, 235, 254
Kennedy, John, 344, 345
Kettl, Donald F., 139, 140
King, Paula J., 343
Kirk, David, 87
Kitfield, James, 288, 297, 297–298
Kitzhaber, John, 104
Kolderie, Ted, 37, 160, 163, 164
Kotter, John, 259
Kuhn, Thomas, 263–264, 265, 266, 267

Labor-management partnerships, 226
Labor Party (New Zealand), 75, 77, 83,
    85–86, 107, 113, 140, 323, 330, 336
Labor Party (U.K.), 34
Labor unions
    privatization and, 115–124, 125, 127–128
    public school choice and, 163–165
Lake Wobegon syndrome, 150
Lakewood Plan, 100
Lange, Cheryl, 168–169, 170–171, 186
Lange, David, 85, 336
Langley Air Force Base, 61, 285

Language changes, 276
Latin America, 239
Leadership
    commitment needed for, 295–298
    of cultural transitions, 278–293
Leadership succession, 56–57
Learning culture, 295
Learning groups, 276
LeSueur, Minnesota, 169
Levels of government, 49–53
    administrative systems, 49, 50–51
    governing systems, 49–50
    organizations, 49, 51
    people, 49, 52
    work processes, 49, 51
Leverage
    accountability as, 184
    consequences as, 130, 187
    cultural change and, 52, 295
    customer choice as, 187
    five C's strategies and, 39–43, 49–53
    hierarchy of, 49–53
    increasing, 43–44
Levi, Connie, 162
Levin, Martin, 214, 280
Lewcock, Tom, 103, 176–177, 260, 313
Liberal Myth, 13
Liberal Party (Canada), 92, 320
Lobitz, Sabine, 283
Local authority trading enterprises
    (LATEs), 113–114
Local governments
    council-manager form of, 45
    privatization in, 115–128
    reinventing, 91, 113–114, 244–248
Locus of control, 215
Logan, Basil, 86–87, 96
Loh, John Michael, 57–60, 61, 62, 66, 180–
    181, 217, 228, 285, 288–289, 340
London, England, 101, 134, 192–193, 286
London Underground, 34, 192–193, 194,
    197
Long-term budgets, 106, 138
Long-term commitments, 293
Long-term goals, 87–88, 102, 103–104,
    106, 107
Loose-tight system, 215
Loritz, Dan, 37, 160, 161, 178
Los Angeles, California, 100, 152
Lump-sum budgets, 207, 209, 210

MacDill Air Force Base, 15, 59
Machiavelli, Niccolò, 329
Madison, James, 211
Madison, Wisconsin, 213, 228, 281, 285, 293
Major, John, 7, 31, 32, 33, 49, 176, 185, 192, 197, 198, 301, 314, 336
Making Government Work (Levin and Sanger), 214, 280
Malaysia, 239
Managed competition, 131, 141–144, 151–152, 154–156, 240
Management. *See also* Total quality management
  in civil service, 24–25
  core strategy and, 109–110
  enterprise, 47, 131, 136–141, 151, 190, 220
  organizational level reinvention of, 53–60
  outcome, 103
  performance, 131–132
  responsibilities of, 82
  visibility and, 283–284
Management delayering, 226
Management information systems, 240
Managing Transitions: Making the Most of Change (Bridges), 67, 266, 290
Manhattan Center for Science and Math, 15
Marblehead, Massachusetts, 175
Marita, Floyd "Butch," 204, 205, 208–211, 213, 214, 223, 225, 227, 235–236, 278, 284, 292, 293
Market forces
  government structure and, 188–189
  political forces vs., 139–141
Marketing practices, 191, 289
Market-oriented government, 349
Market testing, 31, 110
Marks & Spencer, 21
Mark Twain National Forest, 205–208, 218, 224
Martin, Donald "Pepper," 207
Masch, Jim, 148, 260
Maslow, Abraham, 145, 147
Massachusetts, 175–176
Massachusetts Bay Transit Authority, 256
Masterson, Michael, 213, 214
Mead, Margaret, 320

Media, 328–329, 332
Medicaid/Medicare, 190
Meeting the customers, 270
Meier, Deborah, 334–335
Memoranda of understanding (MOU), 322
Mental models, 274–277
Merit pay increases, 150
Metatools, 44, 305–312
  business process reengineering, 11, 44, 51, 64, 225, 310–311
  community governance bodies, 233, 311–312
  competitive bidding, 100, 118, 120–126, 130, 141–144, 307–308
  competitive public choice systems, 192, 309
  corporatization, 79, 82, 137, 239, 308
  enterprise funds, 137, 308
  flexible performance frameworks, 99–100, 216–217, 303, 306–307
  internal enterprise management, 137, 309
  opting out or chartering, 158, 160, 169–170, 192, 220, 221, 311
  performance budgeting, 104–105, 106, 146, 306
  total quality management, 11, 44, 51, 57, 64, 182, 201, 225, 281, 294, 309–310
  vouchers and reimbursement programs, 192, 309
Metro Deaf School, 169–170
Mettke, Karl, 211
Micromanagement, 101, 213, 229, 246
Military bases
  organizational reinvention on, 15, 59, 61, 285
  privatization of, 154–156
Milwaukee, Wisconsin, 205, 208
Minds, winning, 274–277
Minneapolis, Minnesota, 256–257, 271, 284
Minnesota. *See also* Forest Lake; LeSueur; Minneapolis
  education system in, 256–257, 271, 284
  enterprise management in, 137, 220
  Revenue Department reforms in, 293, 339
  school choice in, 6–7, 157–163, 178, 186, 192, 199, 303, 309, 331

Minnesota Business Partnership, 164, 331
Mission-driven government, 348
Mission statement
  culture strategy and, 276
  of Hampton, Virginia, 248–250
  of Tactical Air Command, 58
Missouri, 205, 206, 207
Mistakes, 235–236, 258, 261
Modeling behavior, 281–283
Model Installations Program, 61
Monopolies
  problems with, 129–130
  public bureaucracies as, 17, 185, 258–259
  regulation of, 136
Monteith, Michael, 230, 246, 247, 248, 249, 250, 255
Montessori schools, 157–159, 185
Montreal, Quebec, 231
Morale, employee, 2–4, 253, 301
Morse, Eric, 205–208, 210
Motivation, 147
Muldoon, Robert, 75
Mulroney, Brian, 91–92, 320–323, 324–325, 326–327, 342
Municipal governments. *See* Local governments
Musgrave, Terrence, 101, 134

Nathan, Joe, 162, 164, 167, 170, 172, 303
National Academy of Public Administration, 352
National Audit Office (U.K.), 68
National Forest Service (U.S.), 7, 203–211, 220, 278, 284, 292, 293
National Health Service (U.K.), 34, 49, 192, 194
National Party (New Zealand), 75, 76, 86, 88, 90
National Performance Review, 9, 93, 195, 202, 219, 220, 226, 236, 289, 295, 313, 315, 327, 330, 353
Nation at Risk, A, 161
Native American charter schools, 192
Navy, U.S., 154–156
Neighborhood College, 234, 241, 242
Neighborhood Services Department, 252
Neuroth, Joann, 352
Neutral zone, 267–268
New Country School, 169
New covenants, 271–272

New symbols/stories, 273
New York City, 15, 51, 52, 132, 279, 290, 332–333, 334–335
New Zealand
  bureaucratic controls in, 212, 313–314
  civil service reform in, 7–8, 83–87, 89, 97, 101, 102, 107–108, 112–113, 323–324, 329–330
  consequences strategy and, 136, 137, 140, 152
  control strategy and, 219, 220, 231, 234
  customer strategy and, 174
  Fiscal Responsibility Act of, 105
  flexible performance framework in, 216–217, 307
  local government in, 113–114
  long-term goals for, 87–88
  performance budgeting in, 306
  privatization in, 75–83, 89, 303
  school choice in, 174
Next Steps initiative, 9, 26–27, 28, 29, 30, 40, 42, 44, 49–50, 63, 68, 96, 97, 176, 220, 226, 301, 312–313, 314, 322–323
Nielson, Erik, 91, 320
"Noah Principle," 245
No-layoff policies, 132–135, 337, 341
Norbin, Jane, 158–129, 173
Nuclear Regulatory Agency, 236
Nurrungar, Australia, 112

Occupational Safety and Health Administration (OSHA), 236
Office of Management and Budget, 8, 204
O'Leary, Bob, 261
Ombudsman, 143, 194, 196
O'Neill, Bob, 6, 145, 241, 245–255, 259, 263, 274, 279, 281, 292, 305
O'Neill, Terry, 235
On Purpose Associates, 352
Open enrollment, 162, 165–167, 171, 172
Operating costs, 29
Operation Desert Storm, 54, 57
Opting out, 221, 311
Oregon, 102, 103–105, 107–108, 220, 222, 237, 295, 326, 328, 342
Oregon Shines project, 103–104
Organism metaphor, 38
Organizational culture
  administrative systems and, 313

changing, 259–262
described, 255–257
emotional commitments and, 272
factors shaping, 262–265
habits and, 269–271
lessons for leading change in, 278–293
paradigm shifts in, 265–268
public bureaucracies and, 257–259
Organizational decentralization, 226
Organizational deregulation, 221, 225
Organizational development, 294
Organizational empowerment, 217, 218–224, 246, 303
Organizational structure, 63–64, 228–229
Organization for Economic Cooperation and Development, 8
Organization level changes, 50, 51, 53–60
Organizations. *See* Public organizations
Orientation process, 276
Osborne, David, 331, 350, 351, 352
Oughton, John, 301, 314
Outcome goals, 87–88, 102, 103–104, 106, 108, 318
Outcome management, 103
Output goals, 87, 102, 103
Outsourcing, 126
Oversight board, 143

Packard Commission on Defense Management, 213
Palk, Nigel, 192, 261
Palmer, Geoffrey, 79, 83
Panzer, Ed, 241–242, 243, 246
Paradigms
explained, 263–265
shifting, 265–268, 317
Paradigms (Barker), 264, 317
Parliamentary systems, 45, 88, 91, 94
Passenger's Charter, 35
Passi, Marcia, 169–170
Passport Office (U.K.), 34, 195
Path to 2030 (Kirk), 87
Patient's Charter, 35
Paton, Richard, 92
Patronage, 238, 239, 240
Payne, Larry, 204, 209, 293
Peer pressure, 149
Pennsylvania, 133, 134, 331
People for Better Schools, 162

People level changes, 50, 52
People Myth, 13
Perfect, Mark, 28–29
Performance appraisals, 149–150
Performance awards, 146
Performance-based organizations (PBOs), 100
Performance benchmarks, 276
Performance budgeting, 104–105, 106, 146, 306
Performance contracts and agreements, 146, 246
Performance data, 222–223
Performance management, 131–132, 144–150, 152, 187, 240, 246, 304
Performance pay, 146
Performance reviews, 92–94, 95
Perkins, Susan, 130
Perpich, Rudy, 160–167, 198, 329, 345
Peterson, Max, 205
Peters, Tom, 11
Petronius, 62
Philadelphia, Pennsylvania, 133, 134, 331
Phippard, Sonia, 110
Phoenix, Arizona, 18, 52, 114, 129, 133, 134, 141–142, 294, 341
Pillow, George, 126
Pilot schools, 175
Pinchot, Gifford, 203, 204
Pinewoods Recreational Facility, 207
Pioneers, 278, 285–286
Planning
collaborative, 233
community empowerment and, 229–230
strategic, 106–107, 110, 270
Plastrik, Peter, 352
Police departments, 152, 213, 228, 236, 286, 293
Policrats, 109
Policy-making functions, 99
Policy organizations, 45–47, 200, 237–238
Political correctness, 289
Political forces vs. market forces, 139–141
Politicians. *See* Elected officials
Poplar Bluff, Missouri, 207

Postal service
  New Zealand, 78–79, 80
  United States, 202
Postsecondary Options program, 162–163,
  165, 199, 283, 331
Power. *See also* Empowerment
  control strategy and, 42–43
  hoarding, 228
  passing to employees, 225–227
Powers, Bill, 177
Prebble, Richard, 79, 324
President's Award for Entrepreneurial
  Government, 253
Primary customers, 181–183
Prior options reviews, 31, 95
Private goods, 190
Private Industry Council, 331
Privatization
  in Argentina, 239
  competition and, 118, 120–128
  functions suitable for, 110–112
  in Indianapolis, 115–128, 337
  of military bases, 154–156
  in New Zealand, 75–83, 89
  reinvention and, 11
  in United Kingdom, 22–23, 301
Problem-solving groups, 247
Prodigal Soldiers (Kitfield), 297
Producer capture, 98, 99
Productivity
  gainsharing and, 127
  performance management and, 145–
  150
Program reviews, 91, 92, 95
Progressive Conservative Party (Canada),
  320
Progressive discipline, 148–149
"Proud Look," 56
Proxmire, William, 332
Pryde, Paul, 187
Psychic pay, 146
Psychological incentives, 145, 147
Public choice systems, 189
Public Finance Act of 1989 (New
  Zealand), 83, 105
Public Innovator Learning Network, 353
Public Innovator, The (newsletter), 353
Public organizations. *See also*
  Bureaucracies
  changing the culture of, 234–235

community managed, 233
culture of, 234, 257–259, 292
customer strategy and, 201–202
empowerment of, 217, 218–224
enterprise management and, 131, 136–
  141, 151
four types of, 45–47
functions best suited for, 111–112, 151
managed competition and, 131, 141–
  144, 152
performance management and, 131–
  132, 144–150, 152
size of, 294–295
Public schools. *See* Education; School
  choice
Public sector bureaucratic culture, 257
Public Service 2000 initiative, 322, 325
Public Strategies Group (PSG), 13, 256,
  271, 281, 339, 351
Public systems
  alternatives to, 96–97
  functions best suited for, 111–112, 151
  leverage and, 49–53
  rewriting genetic code of, 38–43
Purchase agreements, 306
Purchaser/provider split, 110
Purpose
  clarity of, 91–95, 110
  organizational, 39–40

Quality assurance, 184–185, 192–198
Quality guarantees, 196
Quality inspectors, 196
Quality management. *See* Total quality
  management
Quality performance measures (QPMs),
  217
Quality Policing (Couper and Lobitz), 283
Quality School, 59, 340
Quasi-privatization methods, 95
Quie, Al, 164

Racial integration, 179, 191–192
Randall, Ruth, 163
Rating inflation, 150
Rayner, Sir Derek, 21–22, 23, 24
Reagan, Ronald, 36, 320
Redesigning work, 270, 273
Reengineering the Corporation (Hammer
  and Champy), 292, 310–311

Regulation, 136, 233
Regulatory organizations, 45–47, 200, 237–238
Reichgott, Ember, 165
Reichlin, Douglas B., 124
Reimbursement programs, 192, 309
Reinventing Government: How the Entrepreneurial Spirit Is Transforming the Public Sector (Osborne and Gaebler), 2, 6, 9–10, 11, 14, 15, 17, 53, 91, 96, 97, 98, 105, 129, 160, 183, 184, 185, 189, 231, 244, 314, 318, 331
Reinventing Government Network, 13, 351
Reinventing Government video (Osborne and Gaebler), 351
Reinventing Government Workbook, The (Osborne and Colon), 350
Reinvention
　commitment to, 341–343
　decision trees for, 315–319
　defining, 10–14
　implementing strategies for, 300–305
　laboratories for, 221, 289, 335
　principles of, 347–349
　recommended reading on, 353–357
　resources for, 350–353
　rules for, 325–343, 344
Reinventor's Handbook, The (Osborne and Plastrik), 350
Rendell, Ed, 134, 331, 341
Reorganization, 63–64
Reprogramming authority, 204
Republican Party, 116, 118
Resisters, 279, 287–288
Resources for reinventors, 350–357
Restructuring, 60–61
Results-oriented government, 348
Rewarding success, 289
Richardson, Ruth, 86
Right Start training program, 59
Risk taking, 261, 287, 332–336
Rituals, 273
Rivlin, Alice, 8
Roberts, Barbara, 104, 107, 326
Roberts, Nancy C., 343
Robertson, F. Dale, 203, 205–206, 209, 210, 212
Rodger, Stan, 83, 324

Role clarity, 95–102
Rolla, Missouri, 205, 206
Roob, Mitch, 116–117, 334, 337
Roosevelt, Teddy, 203
Ross, Doug, 224, 232, 256, 275
Rowing functions, 25, 40, 82, 84, 95–102, 110, 112–113
Rule sunsets, 221
Running costs budget, 218–219
Rural school districts, 166

Saboteurs, 287
St. Louis, Missouri, 205
San Francisco, California, 111, 284
Sanger, Mary Bryna, 214, 280
Sargeant, Don, 281–283
Savoie, Donald, 63, 321, 322, 323, 326
Say, J. B., 15
School choice, 157–178
　accountability and, 173–179
　charter schools and, 158, 160, 169–170, 220
　control strategy and, 186–187, 303
　disadvantaged students and, 167–170
　open enrollment and, 162, 165–167, 171, 172
　results of, 6–7, 170–173
Scott, Graham, 77, 79, 82, 83, 86, 88, 89, 90, 98, 105, 216, 303
SEC, Inc., 208
Secondary customers, 181–183
Second chance program, 167–168, 172–173
Sedgwick, Steven, 260
Sedio, Darryl, 162, 163
Segregation, 191
Self-managed work teams, 226
Self-renewing system, 14
SELTIC. *See* Service, Efficiency, and Lower Taxes for Indianapolis Commission
Senge, Peter, 274
Service-delivery functions, 25, 40, 95–102, 189–190, 200–201
Service, Efficiency, and Lower Taxes for Indianapolis Commission (SELTIC), 119, 130, 197
Service organizations, 45–47
Shared savings, 146

Shared vision, 276
Sharp, John, 92–93, 332
Singapore, 239
Site-based management, 221
Site visits, 276
60 Minutes (TV show), 328
Smokey the Bear, 203
Snead, Chris, 244, 254
Social market, 190
Social Security Administration, 14
Special interests, 329–331
Special operating agencies (SOAs), 63, 323
Spector, Bert, 37
Spence, Jeanie, 60
Sponsors, institutional, 270
Stakeholders, 181–182, 231, 335, 336, 342
Standardized tests, 172–173
State-owned enterprises (SOEs), 7–8, 79, 80–83, 114, 140
State Sector Act of 1988 (New Zealand), 83
Stayton, Michael, 120, 121, 122, 124, 128
Steering functions, 25, 39–40, 67, 82, 84, 87–88, 90, 95–102, 107, 110, 112–113
Steering organizations, 107
Stitt, Charles "Skip," 118, 121, 125, 126, 128, 129, 134
Stokes, Robbie, 286
Stone, Bob, 61, 333–334
Stories, cultural, 273
Strategic Air Command (SAC), 58
Strategic planning, 106, 110, 270
Strategy. See also Five C's strategies
  decision trees for determining, 315–319
  defining, 27–28
  development of, 106
  organizational structure and, 63–64
  tool selection and, 64–65
Structure, organizational, 63–64, 228–229
Structure of Scientific Revolutions, The (Kuhn), 263
Sturgess, Gary, 16
Success, selling, 288–289
Sunnyvale, California, 102, 103, 104, 106, 108, 145, 148, 154, 176–178, 260–261, 286, 289, 304–305, 313

Sunset reviews, 94, 95
Surfacing the givens exercise, 76
Surveys
  customer, 185, 199, 331
  employee, 60
Sweden, 100
Switzerland, 111
Symbols, cultural, 273

Tacoma, Washington, 59
Tactical Air Command (TAC), 18, 53–62, 66, 223–224, 285, 288, 297–298, 342
Taft, William Howard, IV, 61, 333–334
Taxation
  compliance and, 199–200, 237, 293
  New Zealand's reform of, 77
Tax revolt, 8
Teachers union, 163–165
Team listening, 291
Teamwork, 153–154
Technology schools, 175
Telecommunications industry, 80
Tenbusch, James, 166
Ten Commandments of Government, 258
Tenure, 31
Texas, 92–93, 272, 279
Thatcher, Margaret
  interest groups and, 329
  Next Steps initiative of, 9, 25–30, 40, 301, 312–313, 314
  reinvention of government by, 7, 21–24, 31, 36, 40, 42, 49, 81, 323
Thatcher, Reagan, Mulroney: In Search of a New Bureaucracy (Savoie), 321
Thomas, Jeffrey, 125
Thompson, Joe, 51, 290, 296, 335
Thunderbirds, 296–297
Tools, reinvention, 64–65. See also Metatools
  for changing habits, 270
  for clearing the decks, 95
  for community empowerment, 233
  for competitive choice, 192
  for customer choice, 189
  for customer quality assurance, 196
  for employee empowerment, 226
  for enterprise management, 137
  for improving your aim, 106
  for managed competition, 142

for organizational empowerment, 221
for performance management, 146
for touching hearts, 273
for uncoupling steering and rowing, 100
for winning minds, 276
Total Quality Management in Government (Cohen and Brand), 182
Total quality management (TQM), 11, 44, 51, 57, 64, 182, 201, 225, 281, 294, 309–310
Touchstones, 268
Training, employee, 149, 340
Transforming Public Policy: Dynamics of Policy Entrepreneurship and Innovation (Roberts and King), 343
Transitions, managing, 341
Trust
building, 336–340
bureaucratic controls and, 212–214
paradigm shifts and, 267

Uncoupling process, 95–102, 112–113
Unemployment, 76, 89, 132–133, 341
Unions. *See* Labor unions
United Kingdom. *See also* Citizen's Charter; Next Steps initiative
civil service reform in, 7, 9, 21–36, 67, 70, 97, 101, 102, 108
consequences strategy and, 129, 134, 141, 145
control strategy and, 219, 220, 224, 231, 234
culture strategy and, 259–260, 286, 287, 289, 291, 293
customer strategy and, 174–175, 176, 188, 192–196
school choice in, 174–175
United States. *See also* National Performance Review
customer quality assurance in, 195–196
school choice in, 175
University of Minnesota, 66, 162, 167, 281–283
Urgent benchmarks, 104
User fees, 137
Utah, 59

Valentines, 273
Values statement, 251
Venture teams, 251
Virginia. *See* Hampton, Virginia
Visalia, California, 280–281
Visibility, 283–284
Vision, shared, 248–250, 276
Voice, customer, 185
Volker, Derek, 219, 283
Voting power, 42, 198
Voucher programs, 192, 309
Vulnerability, 338–339

Waiters, Gail, 261
Waiver policies, 221
Waldegrave, William, 259–260
Walking in the customer's shoes, 270
Wallace, George, 336
Waste Management Company, 141
Wastewater treatment, 120–124
Watts, Ben G., 218
Weber, Max, 16
Web sites, 353
Weld, William, 331
White River Environmental Partnership (WREP), 121–124
"Why Change Programs Don't Produce Change" (Beer, Eisenstadt, and Spector), 37
Winning compliance approach, 199
Wirtz, Art, 206–207
Wisconsin, 205, 208, 213, 228, 281, 285, 293
WorkOuts, 270
Workplace changes, 273
Work processes, 50, 51–52
Work teams, 226
World Competitiveness Report, 89
Wyse, Duncan, 104

YMCA (Hampton, Virginia), 249–250
Ysseldyke, James, 168

Become an active member in the movement to banish bureaucracy — Join the Alliance for Redesigning Government!

Cofounded by David Osborne in 1993, the Alliance exists to bring change agents together to share ideas, concerns, and practices. Since its inception, the Alliance has developed a number of resources to support you as a change agent fighting to create 21st-century government.

❖ *The Public Innovator* **newsletter** – The latest news on efforts to redesign government – at local, state, and federal levels.

❖ *The Public Innovator* **Learning Network** – Our extensive web site features case studies from all areas of reinvention and links to other sites of interest.

❖ **Design Labs** – In-depth projects that bring together teams of practitioners and experts to create, test, refine, and implement new approaches.

❖ **Conferences** – Our conferences provide you with practical and usable tools for your reinvention efforts, plus the opportunity to network with others in the reinvention arena.

❖ **And much more to come!**

Whether you are on the front lines of government reinvention or a citizen interested in learning how government can become more effective, the Alliance can provide you with the information you need to understand the process; the tools you need to make a difference!

To join this proactive network for government change, simply complete the card below and send it to us.

✔ I need to know more about the Alliance and its activities. Please send the information I have requested below.

❑ General information on the Alliance ❑ Upcoming conferences

❑ *The Public Innovator* Learning Network ❑ Membership

❑ Three FREE issues of *The Public Innovator* ❑ Design Labs

Name_____ Phone(____)____-_____
Organization_____
Address_____
City_____ State_____ Zip_____

LLIANCE FOR REDESIGNING GOVERNMENT
National Academy of Public Administration

See what other innovators have been doing—
Visit the Alliance's web site

Information on Alliance activities, case studies, links to other sites of interest to innovators — you'll find all this and more at:

http://www.clearlake.ibm.com/Alliance

Stop by today or e-mail us at ARGNET@aol.com!

"Results-Driven Governance: Practitioners as Leaders"

This is your chance to see the strategies for reinventing government in action and to talk to others on the front line. Not just a discussion of theory, this conference will show you how the various strategies are being utilized today. You'll leave with practical, *usable* knowledge.

Join us March 25–27, 1997, at Baltimore's beautiful Renaissance Hotel.

For more information or to receive an information packet, call (800) 525-6338.

If the card is missing, call (202) 466-6887 or send your name and address to:
The Alliance for Redesigning Government • 1120 G Street, NW • Suite 850 •
Washington, DC 20005

Place
Postage
Here

Alliance for Redesigning Government
1120 G Street, NW
Suite 850
Washington, DC 20005

Serious About Reinventing?

Are you serious about banishing bureaucracy from your organization but not quite sure where to start? No matter where you are in the process of reinventing your organization, The Public Strategies Group can provide you with tools to further implement the five C's in your organization.

The principals of The Public Strategies Group, who include author David Osborne, have experienced firsthand the challenges of implementing fundamental change in public sector organizations. We have succeeded enough to know it can be done and failed enough to have learned a great deal about it.

The Public Strategies Group (PSG) is an enterprise comprised of some of this country's most advanced thinkers and practitioners of postbureaucratic government. Together with its consortium of innovative public sector consultants called the Reinventing Government Network, PSG helps public agencies transform themselves into customer-focused, results-driven enterprises. We work primarily with public sector organizations. Our vision is a public sector that delights its customers with outstanding service at a reasonable price.

Please contact us:
The Public Strategies Group, Inc.
http://www.psgrp.com
612-227-9774
reinvent@psgrp.com

☐ YES, I'M INTERESTED!

We would like to offer you the opportunity to deepen your understanding of the strategies in *Banishing Bureaucracy*.

O I would like to talk with a Public Strategies Group or Reinventing Government Network expert who has experience in applying these principles in government organizations.

O I am particularly interested in the following strategies:

☐ Core   ☐ Consequences   ☐ Customer
         ☐ Control   ☐ Culture

O I am particularly interested in the following tools:

_____
_____
_____
_____

To best meet your needs, please tell us a little about yourself and your interests:

☐ Economics/Trade   ☐ Education
☐ Human Resources   ☐ Environment
☐ Information Technology ☐ Finance
☐ Procurement   ☐ Other
☐ Health and Human Services

Name:_____
Title:_____
Organization:_____
Address:_____
         _____
         _____
Phone:_____
Fax:_____
Email:_____

BUSINESS REPLY MAIL

FIRST CLASS MAIL PERMIT #4588   ST. PAUL, MN

Postage will be paid by addressee

THE PUBLIC STRATEGIES GROUP
275 4TH ST E STE 710
SAINT PAUL MN 55101-9728